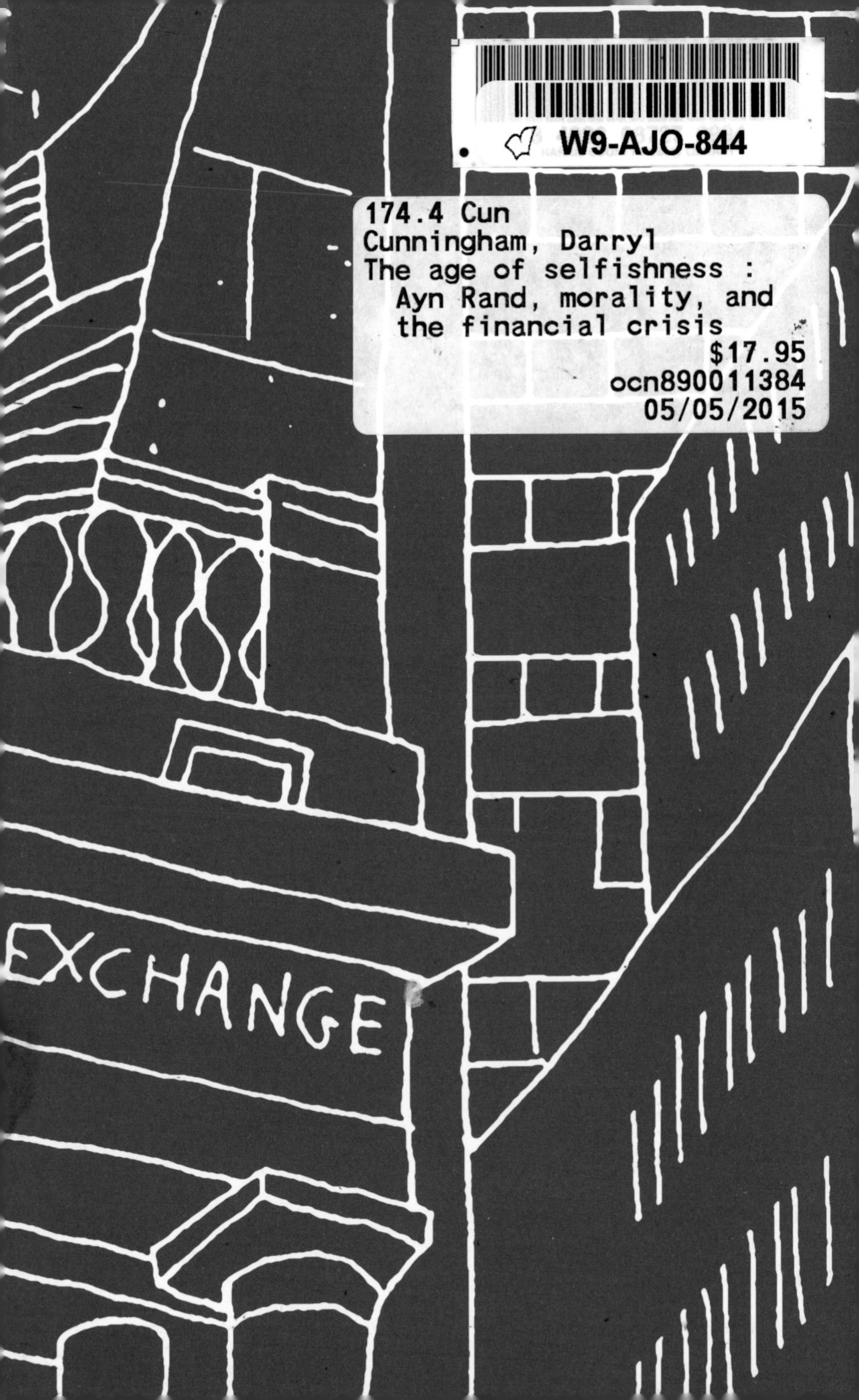
EXCHANGE

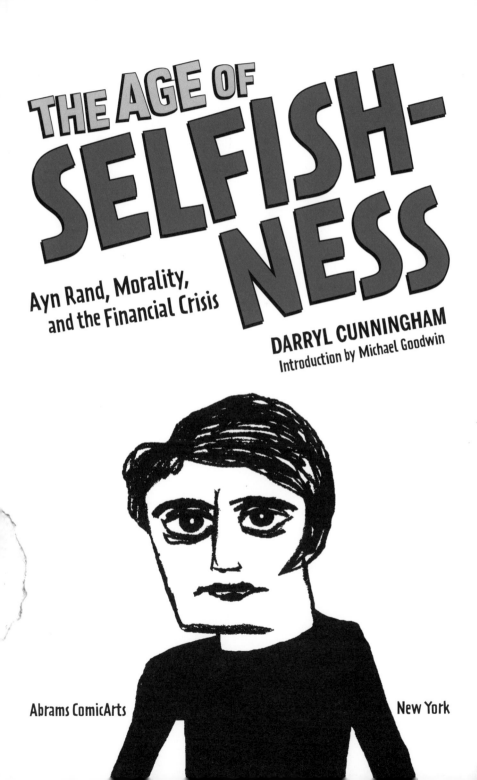

THE AGE OF SELFISH-NESS

Ayn Rand, Morality, and the Financial Crisis

DARRYL CUNNINGHAM

Introduction by Michael Goodwin

Abrams ComicArts   New York

ALSO BY DARRYL CUNNINGHAM

How to Fake a Moon Landing

Editor: Nicole Sclama
Project Manager: Charles Kochman
Designer: Pamela Notarantonio
Managing Editor: Jen Graham
Production Manager: Kathy Lovisolo

Library of Congress Cataloging-in-Publication Data
Cunningham, Darryl.
 The age of selfishness : Ayn Rand, morality, and the financial crisis / Darryl Cunningham ; introduction by Michael Goodwin.
  pages cm
 ISBN 978-1-4197-1598-3 (hardcover) — ISBN 978-1-61312-767-4 (ebook)
 1. Economics—Moral and ethical aspects. 2. Selfishness. 3. Rand, Ayn. 4. Objectivism (Philosophy) 5. Global Financial Crisis,
2008–2009. I. Title.
 HB72.C79 2015
 174'.4—dc23
2014029589

Printed and bound in China
10 9 8 7 6 5 4 3 2 1

Abrams ComicArts books are available at special discounts when purchased in quantity for premiums and promotions as well as fundraising or educational use. Special editions can also be created to specification. For details, contact specialsales@abramsbooks.com or the address below.

THE ART OF BOOKS SINCE 1949

115 West 18th Street
New York, NY 10011
www.abramsbooks.com

CONTENTS

INTRODUCTION

When I was a kid, I read Captain Marvel and Superman comics. I didn't read them because I was a big, strong guy like Cap or Supe; I read them because I was a skinny kid. I loved reading about Superman *because* I didn't resemble him at all.

That, I think, helps explain Ayn Rand's lasting appeal. Rand's fans are rarely the sort of intrepid, self-reliant, go-it-alone entrepreneurial heroes she writes about. Rather, they've typically spent their lives in the comfortable embrace of large institutions, going from school to university to corporation, or from think tank to government and back again. If Paul Ryan—a government bureaucrat if ever there was one—loves reading about John Galt and Hank Rearden, it's *because* he doesn't resemble them at all.

Not that we should dismiss Rand. It's easy to call her writing "badly executed on every level of language, plot, and characterization," as Thomas Mallon wrote in the *New Yorker* in 2009, or to mock her ideas as "stuff that seems very deep when you're nineteen years old," as Bill Maher put it in 2013. But judging her books as literature or as serious social science misses the point. Her books, like Superman comics, are fantasies. And fantasies are powerful.

The fact that Rand's novels, despite their numbing length, are fundamentally simplistic—even, well, cartoonish—makes the fantasy more compelling, not less.

But while Rand's novels are cartoonish, Darryl Cunningham's cartoons are not. In *The Age of Selfishness*, Cunningham's pithy prose and funky art tell a complex, important tale. Cunningham connects the dots from Ayn Rand to Alan Greenspan to the mess we're in today, tackling tangled subjects with clarity and zing.

It's an involved story, one that requires the full power of comics to pull off. By the end of the book, readers have learned how collateralized debt obligations and credit default swaps work; seen behind the scenes at the Commodity Futures Trading Commission and Countrywide Financial; looked into the psychology behind liberalism and conservatism; and understood the complexities of Obamacare and of the forces opposed to it.

Cunningham leaves room for the contradictions in Rand's character, like how her books celebrated individualists while she surrounded herself with—in fact, could only bear the company of—sycophants who repeated her opinions back to her. This absolutist cast of mind permeated Rand's life and her ideas; in a way, she escaped the Soviets only to bring their worst mental habits with her. As Cunningham shows, she would purge colleagues who showed too much independence of thought. The fact that she never purged Alan Greenspan tells us more about Greenspan than the 288 pages of Bob Woodward's fawning biography.

In all this, Cunningham never gives in to the temptation to be simplistic. His Rand is (accurately) portrayed as sad and needy, but she's no cartoon villain. Alan Greenspan's role in creating our current mess is clearly explained—and here Cunningham does a great service, providing an essential corrective to the rote accolades Greenspan still receives from the press—but there's nothing of the cackling mastermind in him. The Wall Streeters Greenspan loosed on our economy seem no more to blame than piglets are to blame for gorging at feeding time.

In fact, when I finished *The Age of Selfishness*, Rand's own words from *Atlas Shrugged* came to my mind:

> He felt as if, after a journey of years through a landscape of devastation, past the ruins of great factories, the wrecks of powerful engines, the bodies of invincible men, he had come upon the despoiler, expecting to find a giant—and had found a rat eager to scurry for cover at the first sound of a human step. If this is what has beaten us, he thought, the guilt is ours.

Ayn Rand's acolytes have changed our world, and changed it for the worse, but not because they're fiendish or even particularly brilliant. They've succeeded because they've mistaken myth for reality, and because they've operated largely in the world of finance—a world most of us find hopelessly murky. In *The Age of Selfishness*, Cunningham has turned on the lights. He has shown us the forces that we're up against and, in the end, how unimpressive they are. If we let them beat us, the guilt is ours.

MICHAEL GOODWIN
New York, NY

MICHAEL GOODWIN, a writer and editor with a degree in Chinese studies, is the author of the *New York Times* bestseller *Economix: How Our Economy Works (and Doesn't Work), in Words and Pictures*. Goodwin has lived in China and India and now lives in New York City.

PREFACE

This book is inspired by a writer and novelist largely unknown in Europe. Even in the United States, where she is most famous, she is surely a fringe thinker. Why, with all that there is to say about politics and finance in the modern world, did I start with Ayn Rand?

I first read about Rand when I was in my twenties. Her upside-down moral philosophy of objectivism—selfishness is a virtue and altruism a moral failing—was so opposed to everything I believed that I was drawn to her with a mixture of horror and fascination. It was, and still is, shocking to me that anyone could be so nakedly self-serving.

Rand hits a nerve with people. We either reject her beliefs totally or embrace them wholeheartedly. There is no middle ground. We can't be indifferent to her philosophy. If we are to the left, we'll take her writings as a personal attack. If we are on the right, she will outline many of our innermost beliefs more clearly than we have ever thought about them ourselves.

Rand sells. At least, in America she sells. Two of her novels, *The Fountainhead* (1943) and *Atlas Shrugged* (1957), typically sell more than 300,000 copies a year. Since the 2008 financial crisis, sales of her apocalyptic novel *Atlas Shrugged* have tripled. A total of 600,000 copies of the book were sold in 2009. In the United States, more than 13 million copies of these two books are in circulation.

I wrote about Ayn Rand for the same reasons that she is so popular with those on the political right: because she is emblematic of so much deeply held right-wing thinking. Her life and writing demonstrate a conservatism boiled down to its purest essence, both good and bad: individualism, self-reliance, and selfishness.

Rand was my gateway into understanding not just the conservative mind, but how this mind-set has brought about the triumph of neoliberal politics over the last thirty years—the encouragement of free trade and open markets, privatization, deregulation, and the extension of the role of the private sector in modern society. These elements all culminated in the catastrophic financial crisis of 2008 and in human costs on a massive scale, affecting everyone from the middle classes to the very poorest across the globe.

This book is split into three sections. The first section is a biography of Ayn Rand. As well as chronicling the main events of the author's life, it outlines her novels and her philosophy of objectivism and demonstrates the huge influence she had, not just on the American political right as a whole, but specifically on Alan Greenspan, who was a key player in the events leading to the financial crisis.

The second section details the economic crisis itself. It explains how trade derivatives (a kind of insurance that can also be used for speculation and gambling) combined with the collapse of the U.S. housing market, sheer greed among those in the banking sector and the mortgage industry, and weak government regulation brought the world's economy to its knees.

The third section is an overview of where we are today, starting with a look at the psychology of conservative and liberal thinking. What are the strengths and weaknesses of these two very different political persuasions? What does science tell us about them?

This last section also considers the vanishing influence of the left, the scapegoating of the poor and minorities as a response to the crisis, and how this scapegoating has contributed to the rise of both the Tea Party movement in the United States and the U.K. Independence Party.

Ayn Rand understood that politics and economics have a moral dimension. It's never the case that business is just business—it's always personal. But the different approaches to morality held by the left and by the right inevitably lead to opposing outcomes. For the last thirty years the political right has been in ascendance in the West, and it has shaped the world with its own vision of morality. In a democratic state where we have the power of the vote, isn't it time we take back control from those who see virtue in the acquisition of money over the virtue of equality for all?

DARRYL CUNNINGHAM
Yorkshire, England

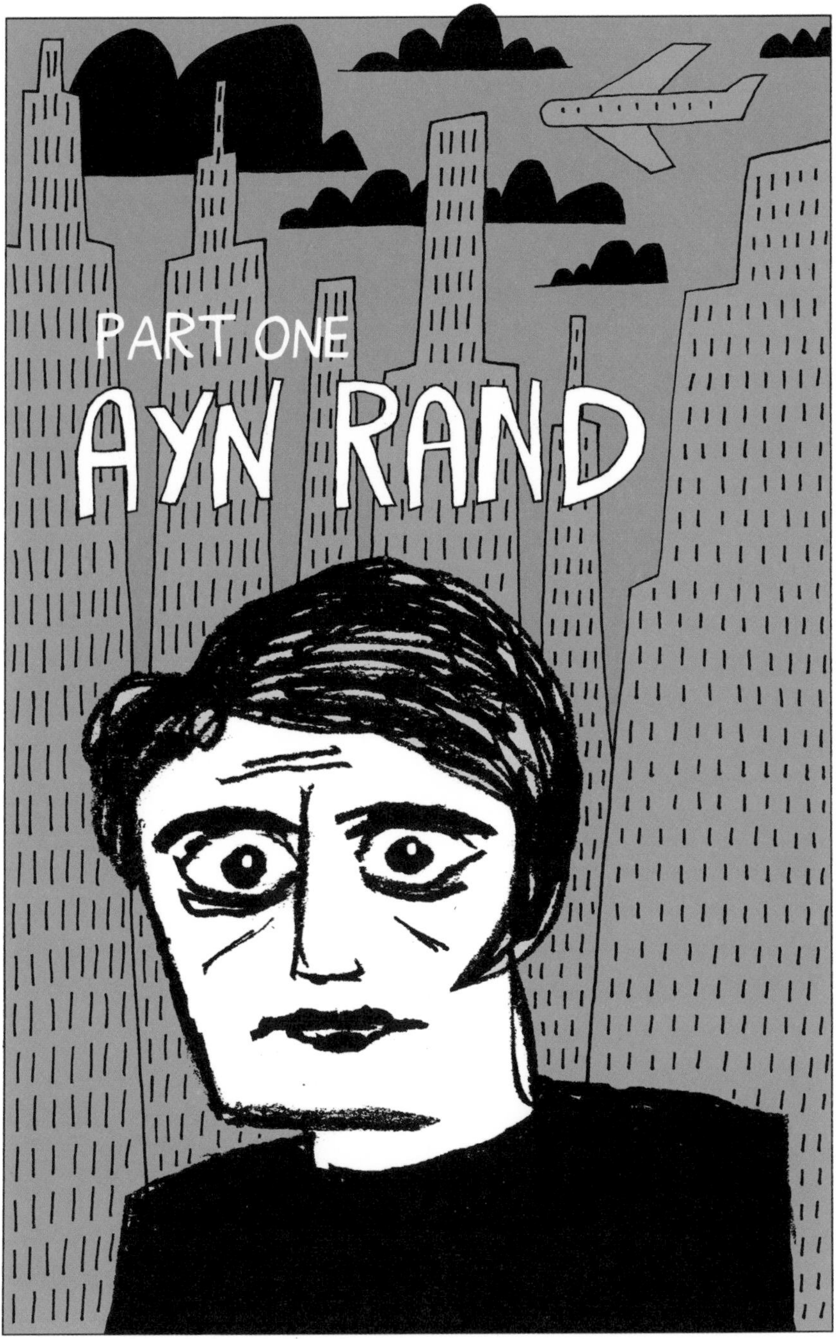
PART ONE
AYN RAND

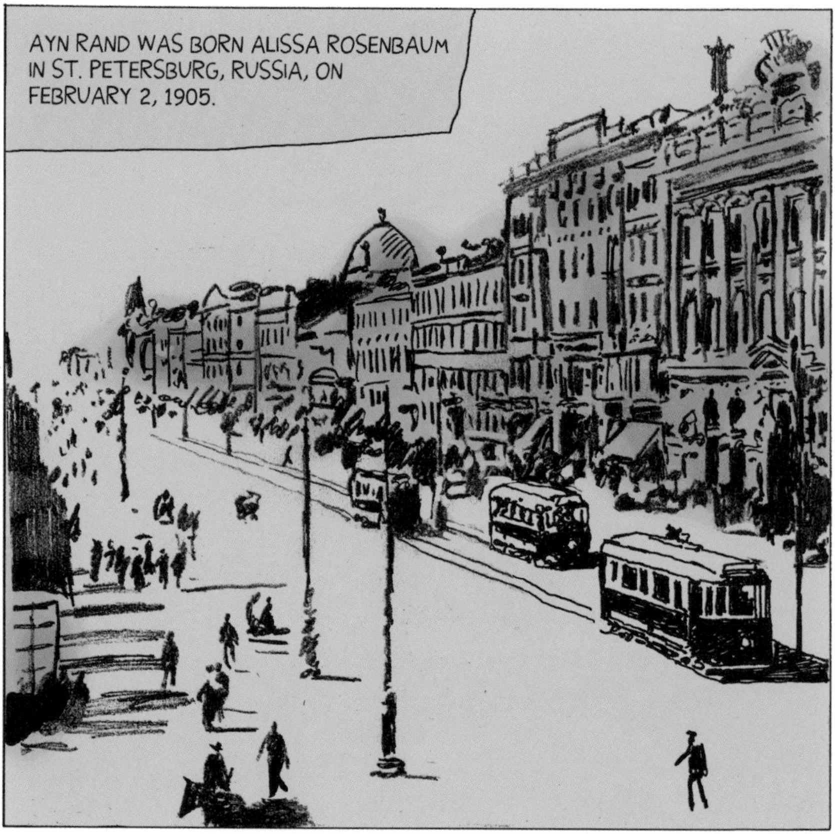
AYN RAND WAS BORN ALISSA ROSENBAUM IN ST. PETERSBURG, RUSSIA, ON FEBRUARY 2, 1905.

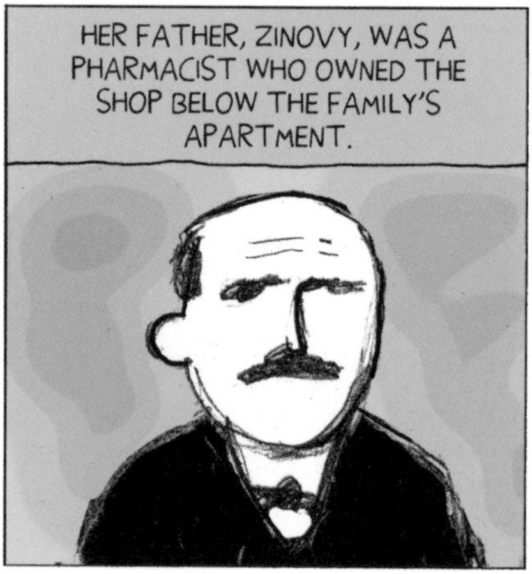
HER FATHER, ZINOVY, WAS A PHARMACIST WHO OWNED THE SHOP BELOW THE FAMILY'S APARTMENT.

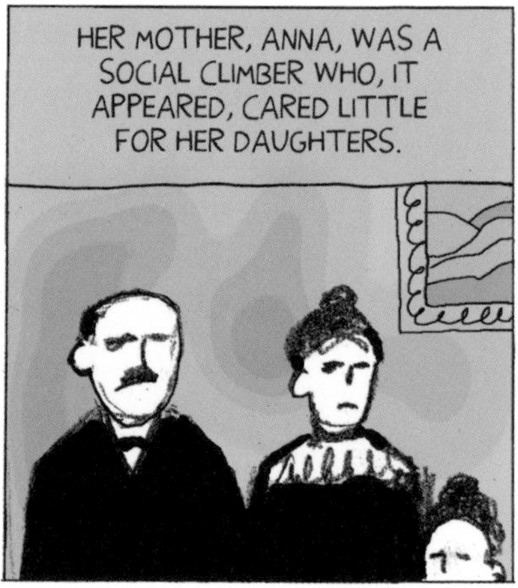
HER MOTHER, ANNA, WAS A SOCIAL CLIMBER WHO, IT APPEARED, CARED LITTLE FOR HER DAUGHTERS.

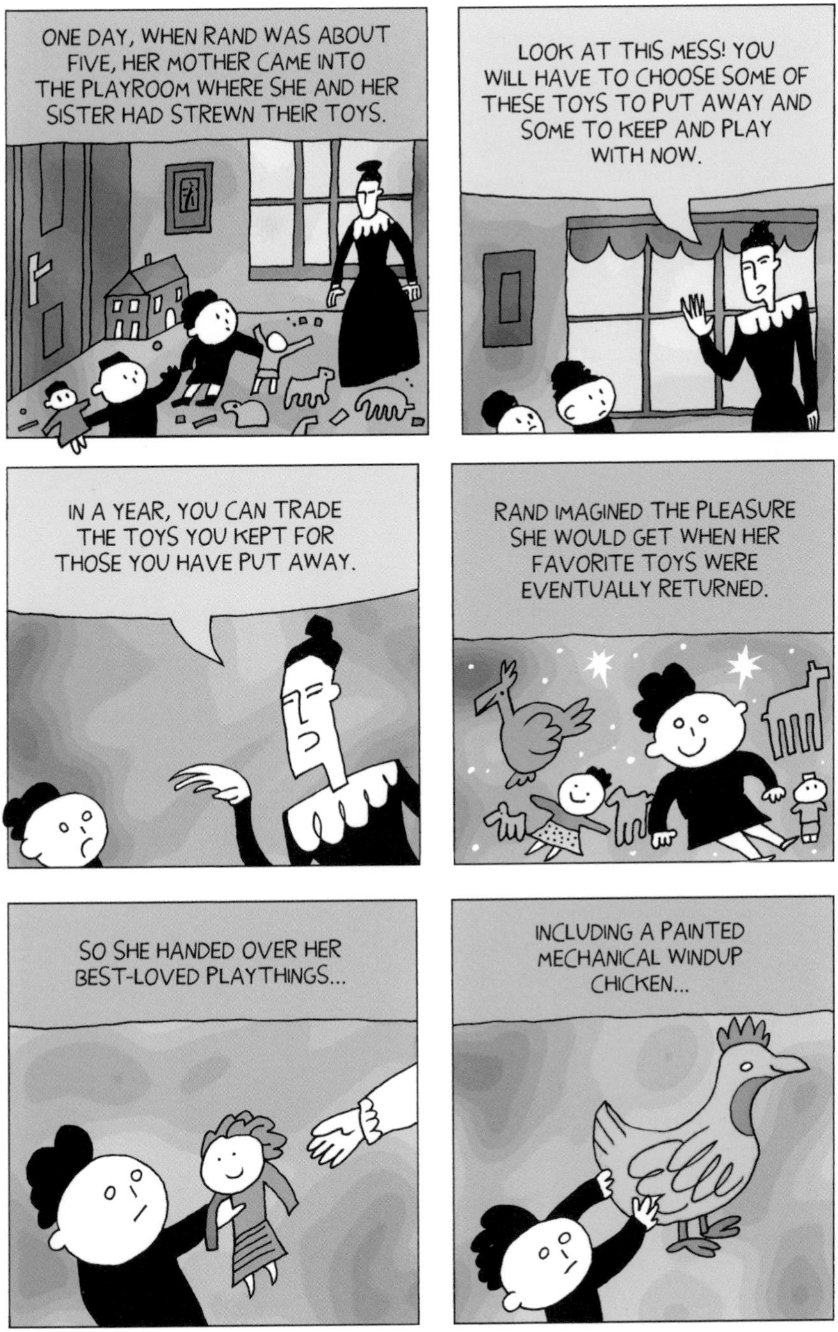
ONE DAY, WHEN RAND WAS ABOUT FIVE, HER MOTHER CAME INTO THE PLAYROOM WHERE SHE AND HER SISTER HAD STREWN THEIR TOYS.
LOOK AT THIS MESS! YOU WILL HAVE TO CHOOSE SOME OF THESE TOYS TO PUT AWAY AND SOME TO KEEP AND PLAY WITH NOW.
IN A YEAR, YOU CAN TRADE THE TOYS YOU KEPT FOR THOSE YOU HAVE PUT AWAY.
RAND IMAGINED THE PLEASURE SHE WOULD GET WHEN HER FAVORITE TOYS WERE EVENTUALLY RETURNED.
SO SHE HANDED OVER HER BEST-LOVED PLAYTHINGS...
INCLUDING A PAINTED MECHANICAL WINDUP CHICKEN...

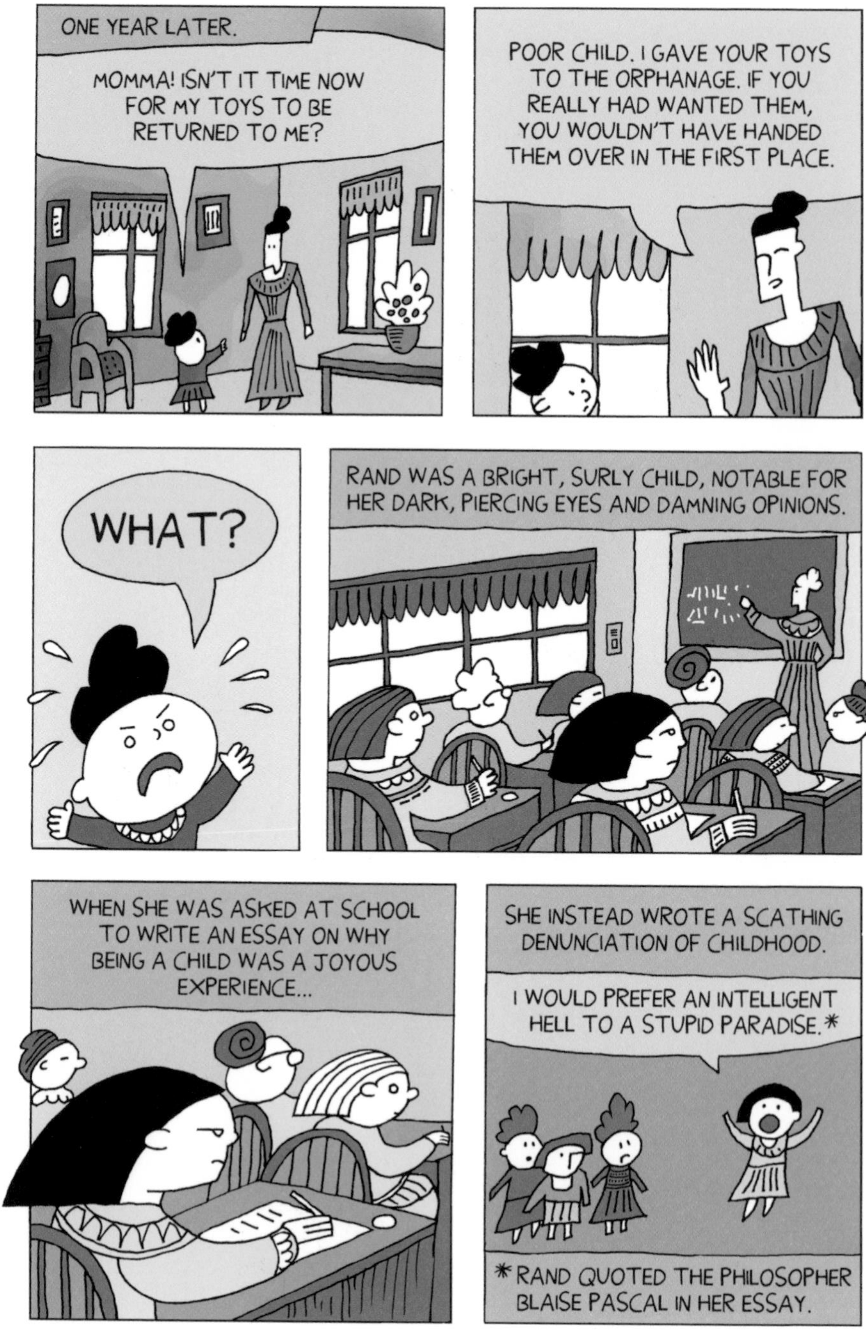
ONE YEAR LATER.
MOMMA! ISN'T IT TIME NOW FOR MY TOYS TO BE RETURNED TO ME?
POOR CHILD. I GAVE YOUR TOYS TO THE ORPHANAGE. IF YOU REALLY HAD WANTED THEM, YOU WOULDN'T HAVE HANDED THEM OVER IN THE FIRST PLACE.
WHAT?
RAND WAS A BRIGHT, SURLY CHILD, NOTABLE FOR HER DARK, PIERCING EYES AND DAMNING OPINIONS.
WHEN SHE WAS ASKED AT SCHOOL TO WRITE AN ESSAY ON WHY BEING A CHILD WAS A JOYOUS EXPERIENCE...
SHE INSTEAD WROTE A SCATHING DENUNCIATION OF CHILDHOOD.
I WOULD PREFER AN INTELLIGENT HELL TO A STUPID PARADISE.*
* RAND QUOTED THE PHILOSOPHER BLAISE PASCAL IN HER ESSAY.

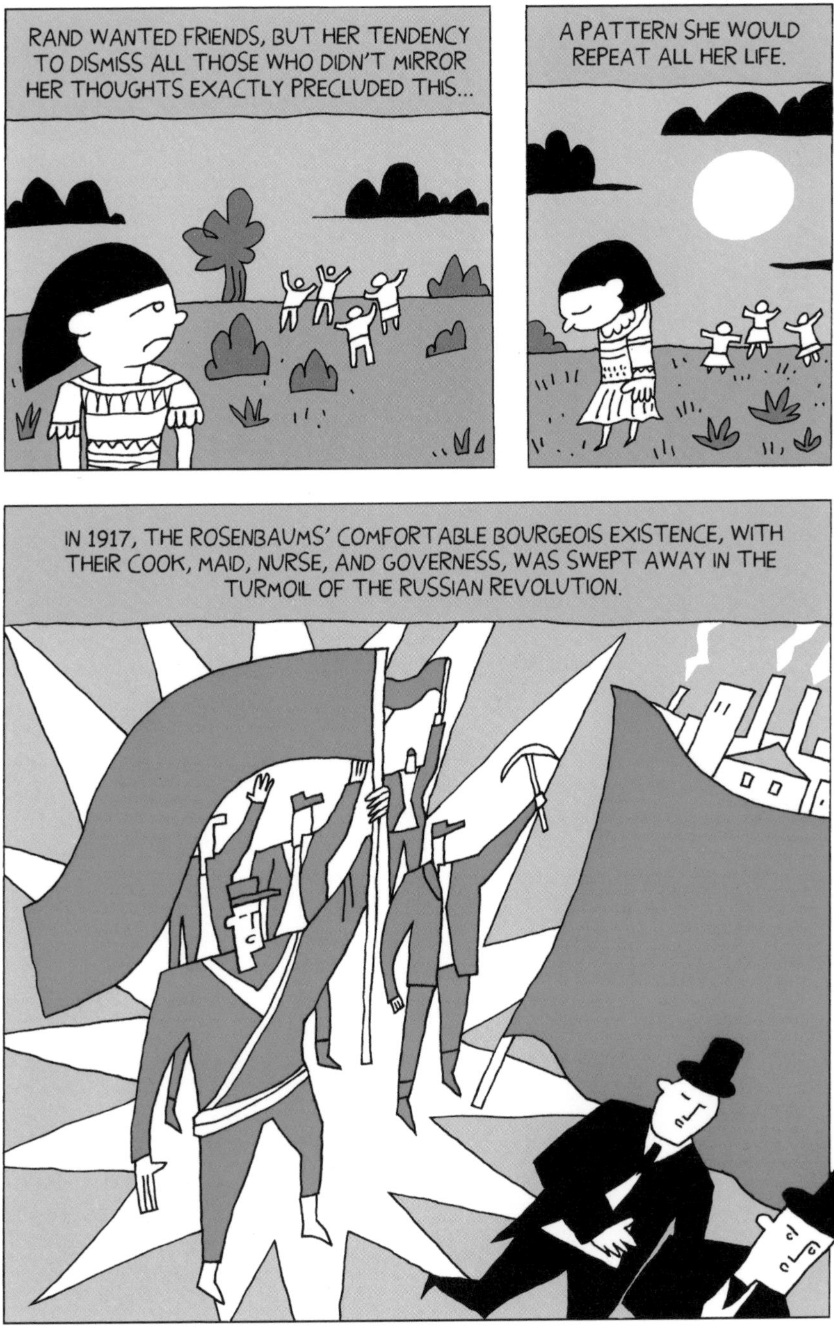
RAND WANTED FRIENDS, BUT HER TENDENCY TO DISMISS ALL THOSE WHO DIDN'T MIRROR HER THOUGHTS EXACTLY PRECLUDED THIS...
A PATTERN SHE WOULD REPEAT ALL HER LIFE.
IN 1917, THE ROSENBAUMS' COMFORTABLE BOURGEOIS EXISTENCE, WITH THEIR COOK, MAID, NURSE, AND GOVERNESS, WAS SWEPT AWAY IN THE TURMOIL OF THE RUSSIAN REVOLUTION.

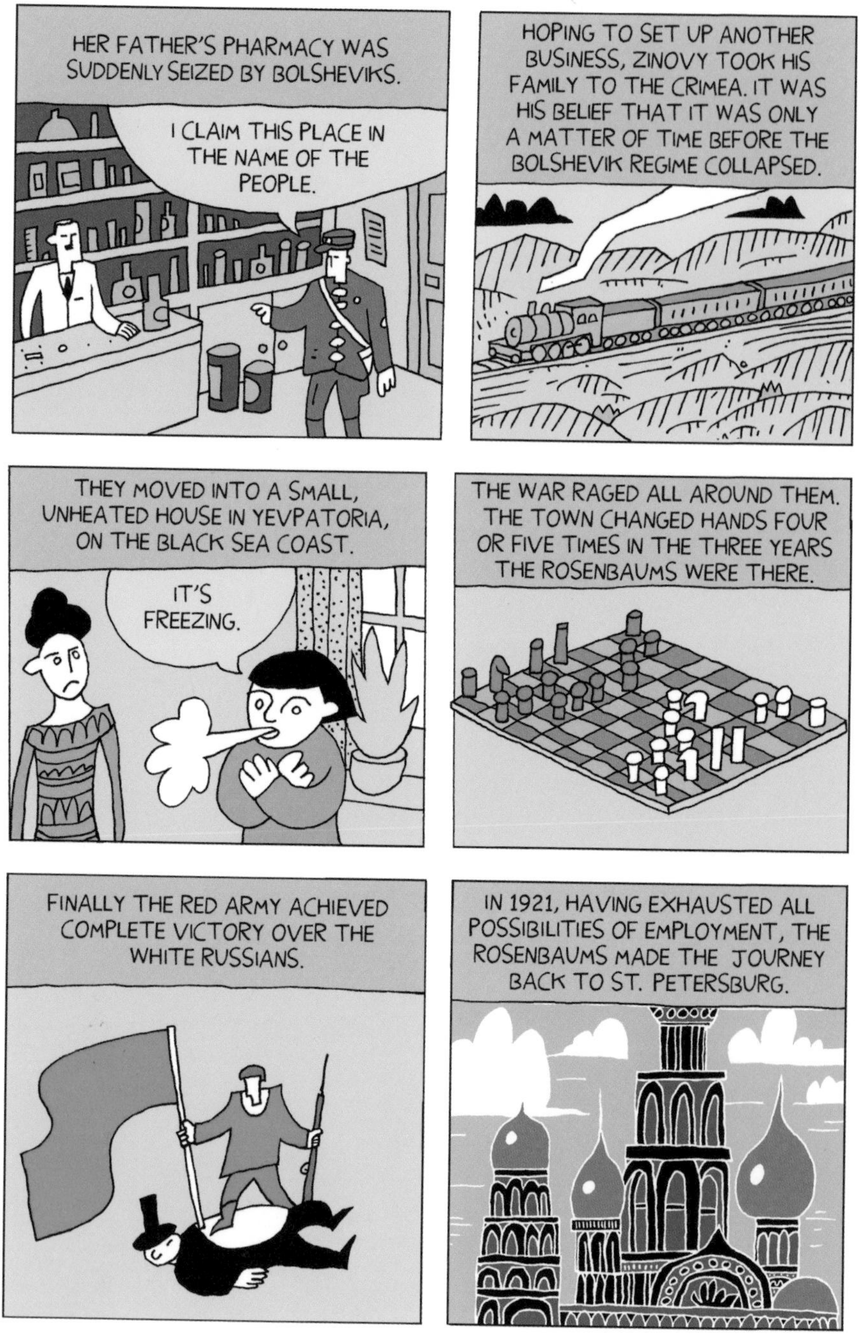
HER FATHER'S PHARMACY WAS SUDDENLY SEIZED BY BOLSHEVIKS.
I CLAIM THIS PLACE IN THE NAME OF THE PEOPLE.
HOPING TO SET UP ANOTHER BUSINESS, ZINOVY TOOK HIS FAMILY TO THE CRIMEA. IT WAS HIS BELIEF THAT IT WAS ONLY A MATTER OF TIME BEFORE THE BOLSHEVIK REGIME COLLAPSED.
THEY MOVED INTO A SMALL, UNHEATED HOUSE IN YEVPATORIA, ON THE BLACK SEA COAST.
IT'S FREEZING.
THE WAR RAGED ALL AROUND THEM. THE TOWN CHANGED HANDS FOUR OR FIVE TIMES IN THE THREE YEARS THE ROSENBAUMS WERE THERE.
FINALLY THE RED ARMY ACHIEVED COMPLETE VICTORY OVER THE WHITE RUSSIANS.
IN 1921, HAVING EXHAUSTED ALL POSSIBILITIES OF EMPLOYMENT, THE ROSENBAUMS MADE THE JOURNEY BACK TO ST. PETERSBURG.

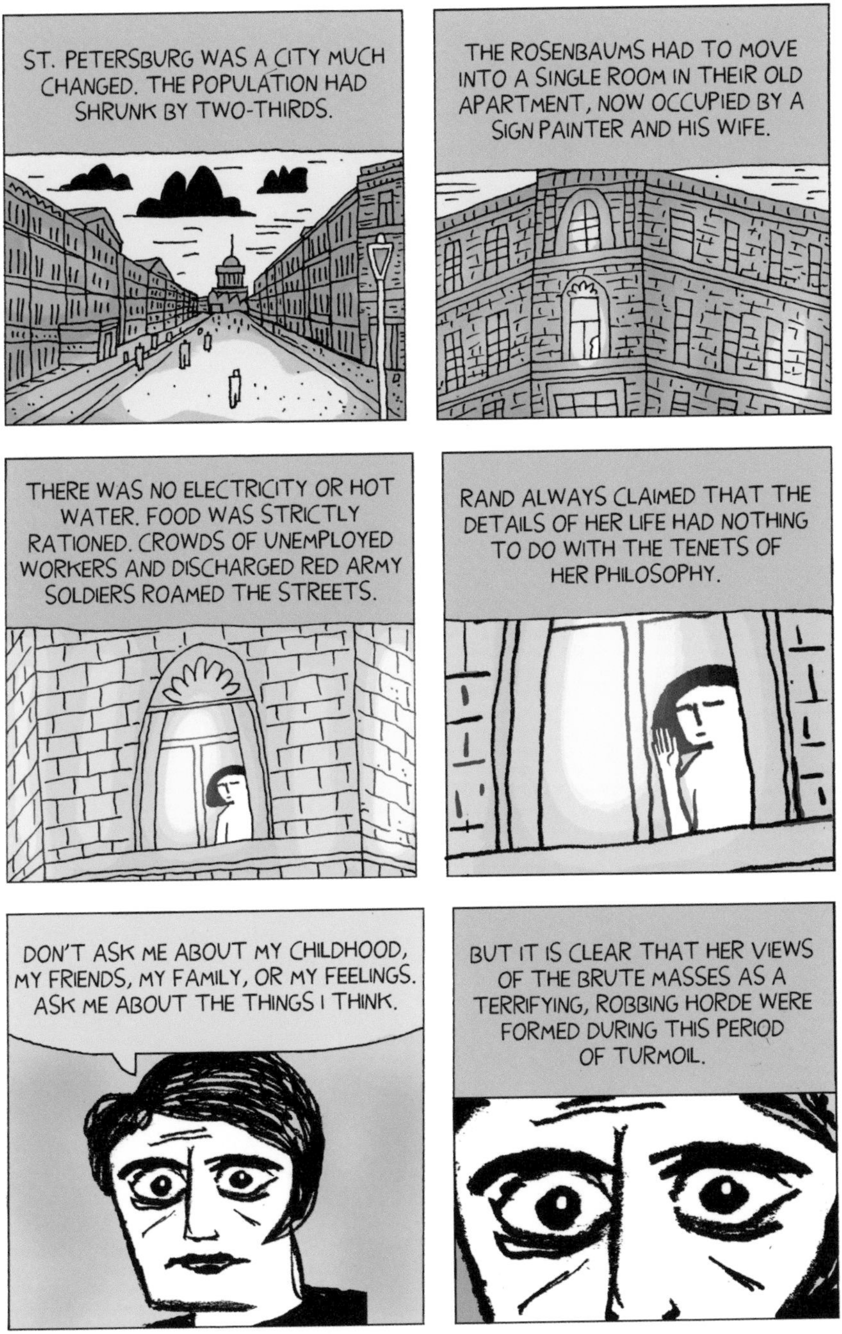
ST. PETERSBURG WAS A CITY MUCH CHANGED. THE POPULATION HAD SHRUNK BY TWO-THIRDS.
THE ROSENBAUMS HAD TO MOVE INTO A SINGLE ROOM IN THEIR OLD APARTMENT, NOW OCCUPIED BY A SIGN PAINTER AND HIS WIFE.
THERE WAS NO ELECTRICITY OR HOT WATER. FOOD WAS STRICTLY RATIONED. CROWDS OF UNEMPLOYED WORKERS AND DISCHARGED RED ARMY SOLDIERS ROAMED THE STREETS.
RAND ALWAYS CLAIMED THAT THE DETAILS OF HER LIFE HAD NOTHING TO DO WITH THE TENETS OF HER PHILOSOPHY.
DON'T ASK ME ABOUT MY CHILDHOOD, MY FRIENDS, MY FAMILY, OR MY FEELINGS. ASK ME ABOUT THE THINGS I THINK.
BUT IT IS CLEAR THAT HER VIEWS OF THE BRUTE MASSES AS A TERRIFYING, ROBBING HORDE WERE FORMED DURING THIS PERIOD OF TURMOIL.

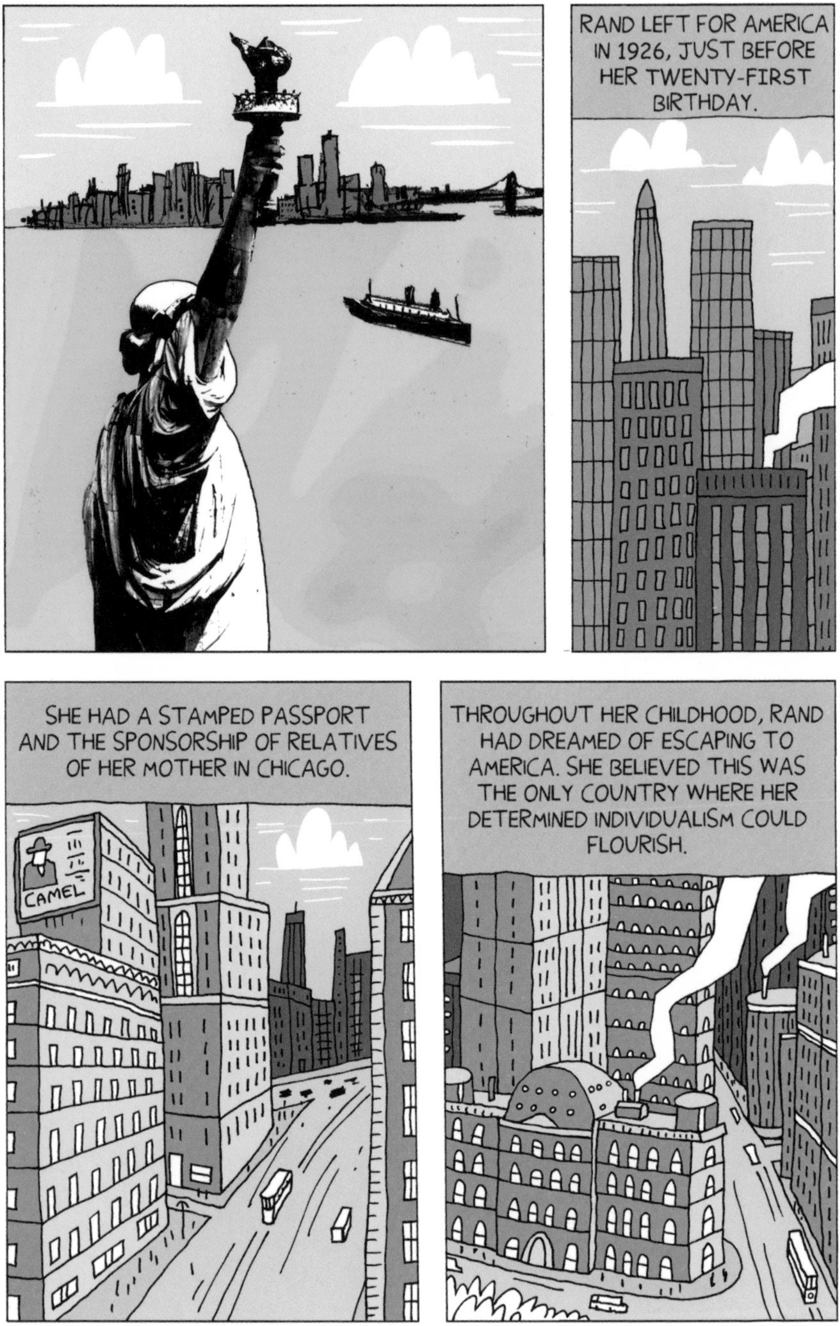
RAND LEFT FOR AMERICA IN 1926, JUST BEFORE HER TWENTY-FIRST BIRTHDAY.
SHE HAD A STAMPED PASSPORT AND THE SPONSORSHIP OF RELATIVES OF HER MOTHER IN CHICAGO.
CAMEL
THROUGHOUT HER CHILDHOOD, RAND HAD DREAMED OF ESCAPING TO AMERICA. SHE BELIEVED THIS WAS THE ONLY COUNTRY WHERE HER DETERMINED INDIVIDUALISM COULD FLOURISH.

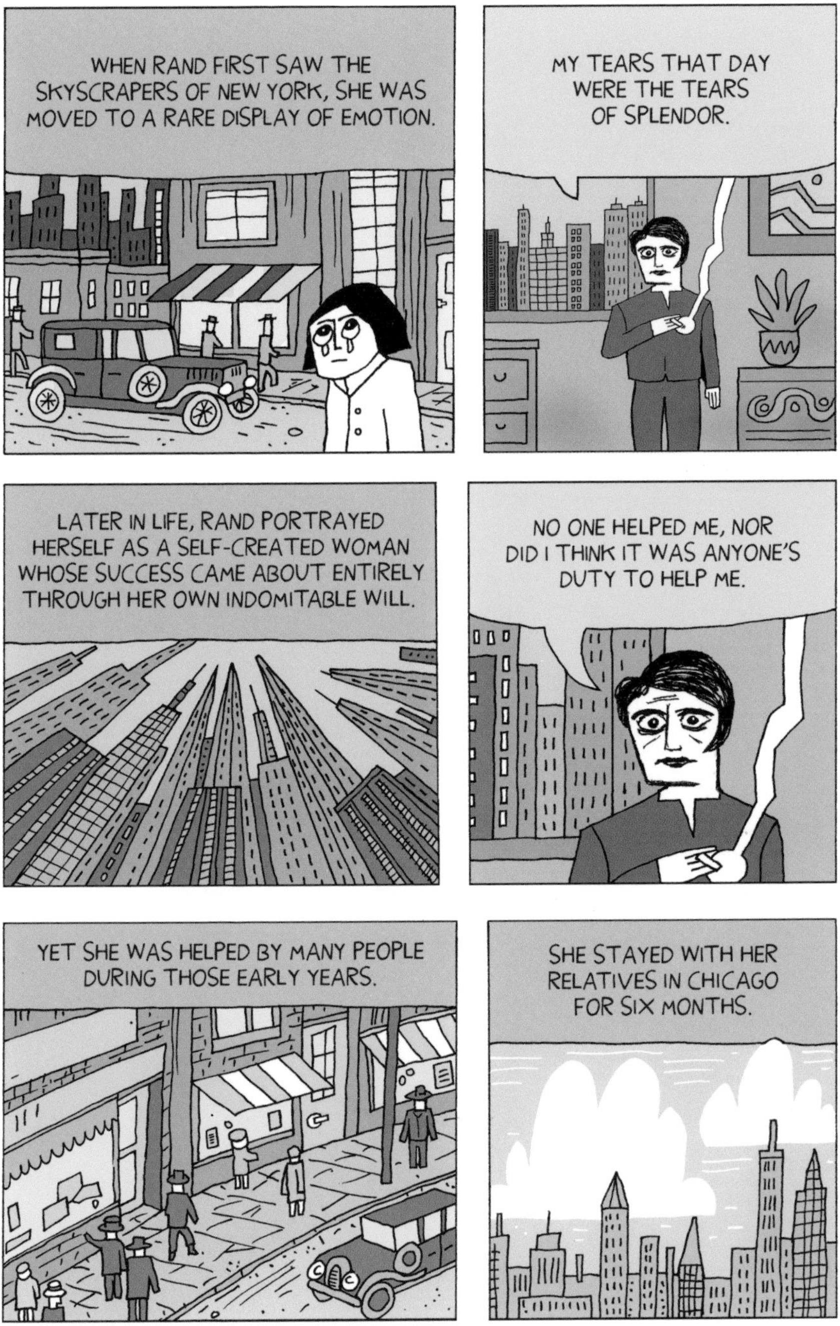
WHEN RAND FIRST SAW THE SKYSCRAPERS OF NEW YORK, SHE WAS MOVED TO A RARE DISPLAY OF EMOTION.
MY TEARS THAT DAY WERE THE TEARS OF SPLENDOR.
LATER IN LIFE, RAND PORTRAYED HERSELF AS A SELF-CREATED WOMAN WHOSE SUCCESS CAME ABOUT ENTIRELY THROUGH HER OWN INDOMITABLE WILL.
NO ONE HELPED ME, NOR DID I THINK IT WAS ANYONE'S DUTY TO HELP ME.
YET SHE WAS HELPED BY MANY PEOPLE DURING THOSE EARLY YEARS.
SHE STAYED WITH HER RELATIVES IN CHICAGO FOR SIX MONTHS.

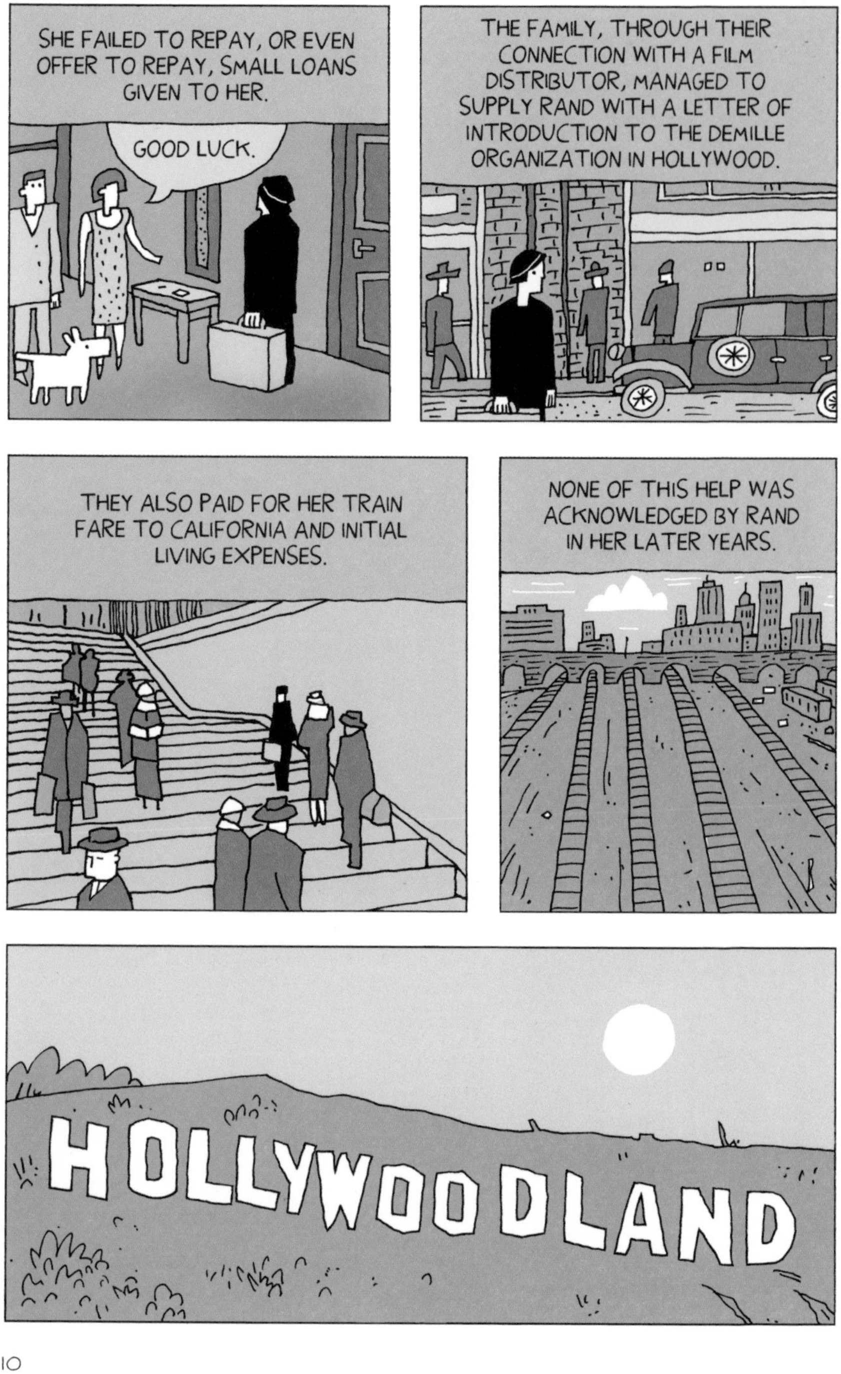
SHE FAILED TO REPAY, OR EVEN OFFER TO REPAY, SMALL LOANS GIVEN TO HER.
GOOD LUCK.
THE FAMILY, THROUGH THEIR CONNECTION WITH A FILM DISTRIBUTOR, MANAGED TO SUPPLY RAND WITH A LETTER OF INTRODUCTION TO THE DEMILLE ORGANIZATION IN HOLLYWOOD.
THEY ALSO PAID FOR HER TRAIN FARE TO CALIFORNIA AND INITIAL LIVING EXPENSES.
NONE OF THIS HELP WAS ACKNOWLEDGED BY RAND IN HER LATER YEARS.
HOLLYWOODLAND

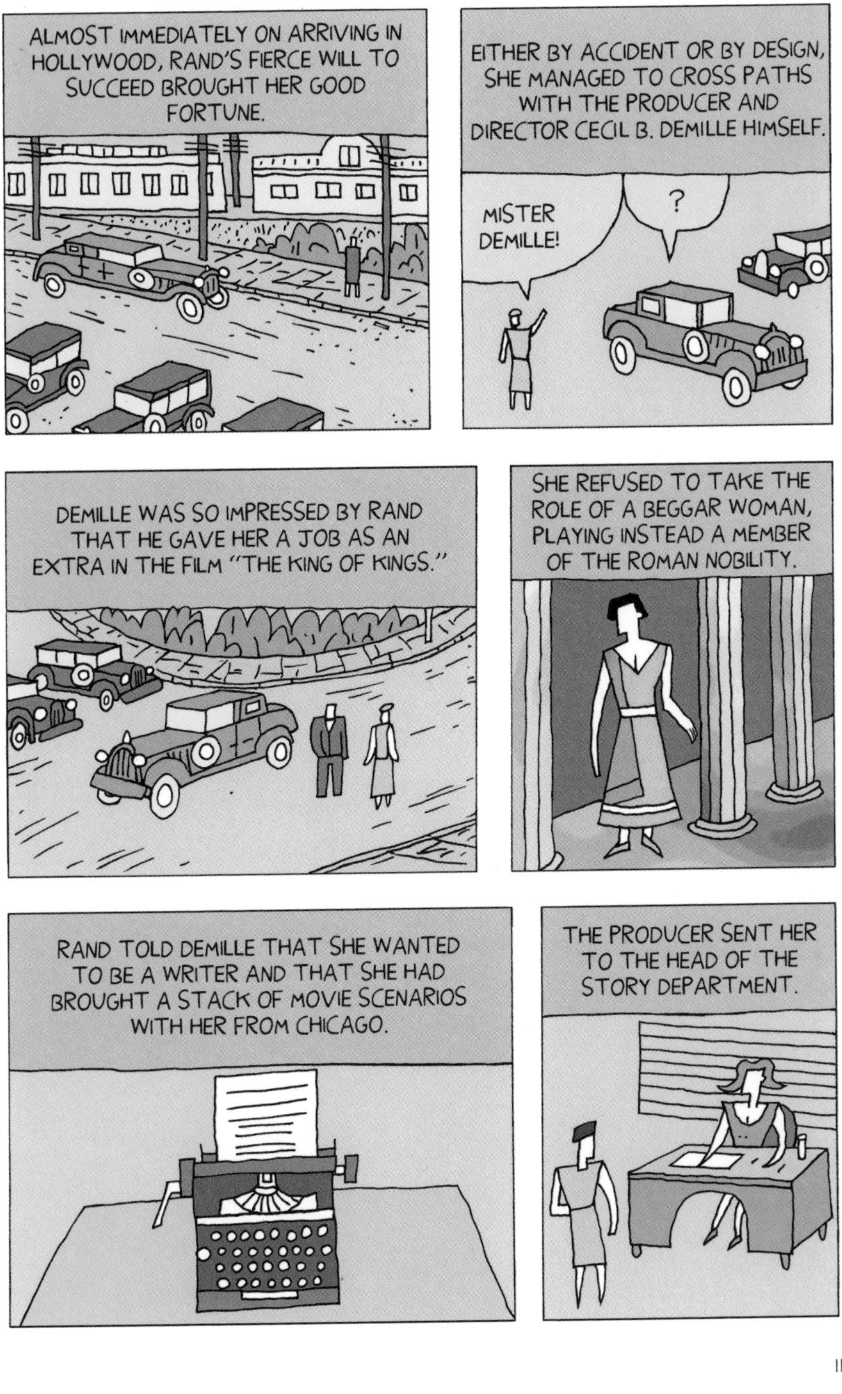
ALMOST IMMEDIATELY ON ARRIVING IN HOLLYWOOD, RAND'S FIERCE WILL TO SUCCEED BROUGHT HER GOOD FORTUNE.
EITHER BY ACCIDENT OR BY DESIGN, SHE MANAGED TO CROSS PATHS WITH THE PRODUCER AND DIRECTOR CECIL B. DEMILLE HIMSELF.
MISTER DEMILLE!
?
DEMILLE WAS SO IMPRESSED BY RAND THAT HE GAVE HER A JOB AS AN EXTRA IN THE FILM "THE KING OF KINGS."
SHE REFUSED TO TAKE THE ROLE OF A BEGGAR WOMAN, PLAYING INSTEAD A MEMBER OF THE ROMAN NOBILITY.
RAND TOLD DEMILLE THAT SHE WANTED TO BE A WRITER AND THAT SHE HAD BROUGHT A STACK OF MOVIE SCENARIOS WITH HER FROM CHICAGO.
THE PRODUCER SENT HER TO THE HEAD OF THE STORY DEPARTMENT.

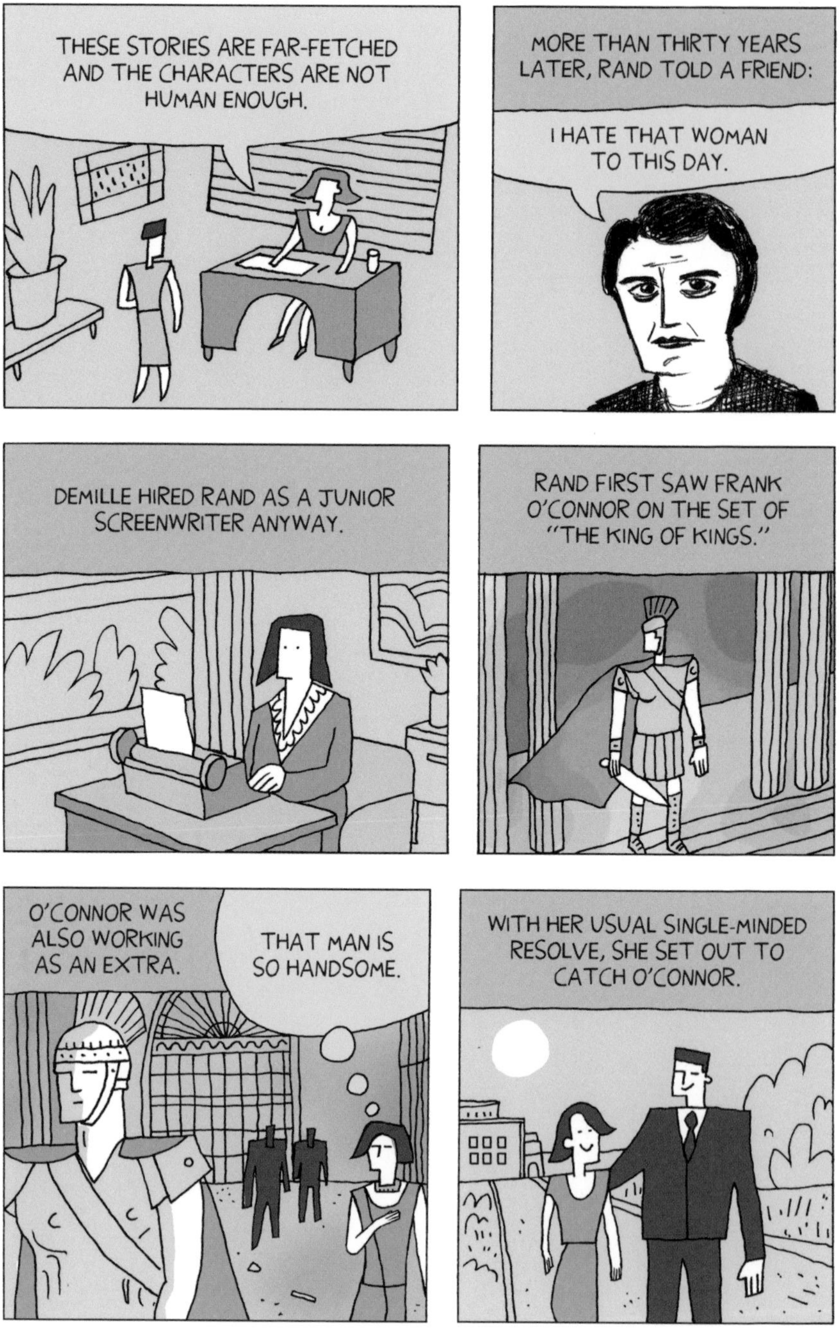
THESE STORIES ARE FAR-FETCHED AND THE CHARACTERS ARE NOT HUMAN ENOUGH.
MORE THAN THIRTY YEARS LATER, RAND TOLD A FRIEND:
I HATE THAT WOMAN TO THIS DAY.
DEMILLE HIRED RAND AS A JUNIOR SCREENWRITER ANYWAY.
RAND FIRST SAW FRANK O'CONNOR ON THE SET OF "THE KING OF KINGS."
O'CONNOR WAS ALSO WORKING AS AN EXTRA.
THAT MAN IS SO HANDSOME.
WITH HER USUAL SINGLE-MINDED RESOLVE, SHE SET OUT TO CATCH O'CONNOR.

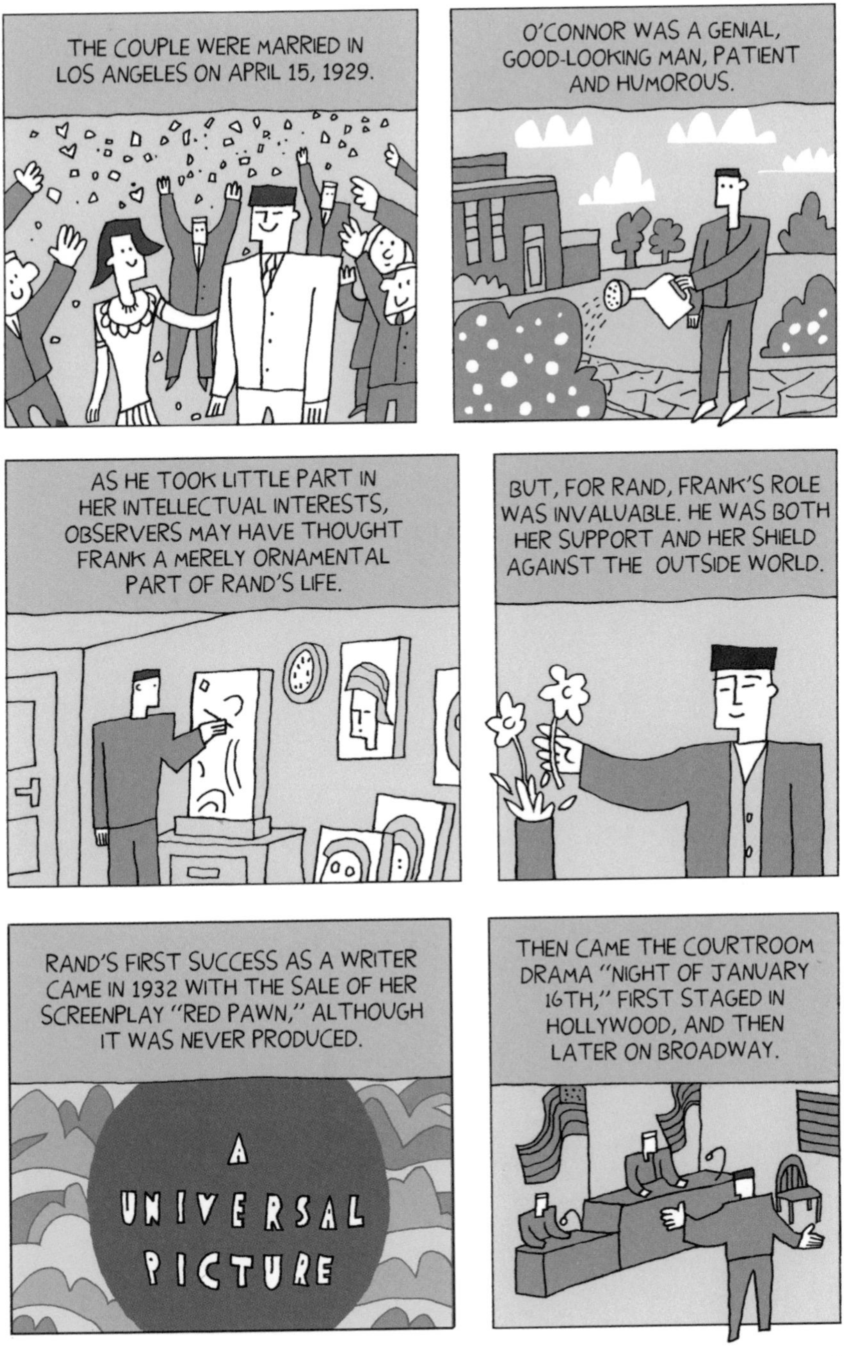
THE COUPLE WERE MARRIED IN LOS ANGELES ON APRIL 15, 1929.
O'CONNOR WAS A GENIAL, GOOD-LOOKING MAN, PATIENT AND HUMOROUS.
AS HE TOOK LITTLE PART IN HER INTELLECTUAL INTERESTS, OBSERVERS MAY HAVE THOUGHT FRANK A MERELY ORNAMENTAL PART OF RAND'S LIFE.
BUT, FOR RAND, FRANK'S ROLE WAS INVALUABLE. HE WAS BOTH HER SUPPORT AND HER SHIELD AGAINST THE OUTSIDE WORLD.
RAND'S FIRST SUCCESS AS A WRITER CAME IN 1932 WITH THE SALE OF HER SCREENPLAY "RED PAWN," ALTHOUGH IT WAS NEVER PRODUCED.
A UNIVERSAL PICTURE
THEN CAME THE COURTROOM DRAMA "NIGHT OF JANUARY 16TH," FIRST STAGED IN HOLLYWOOD, AND THEN LATER ON BROADWAY.

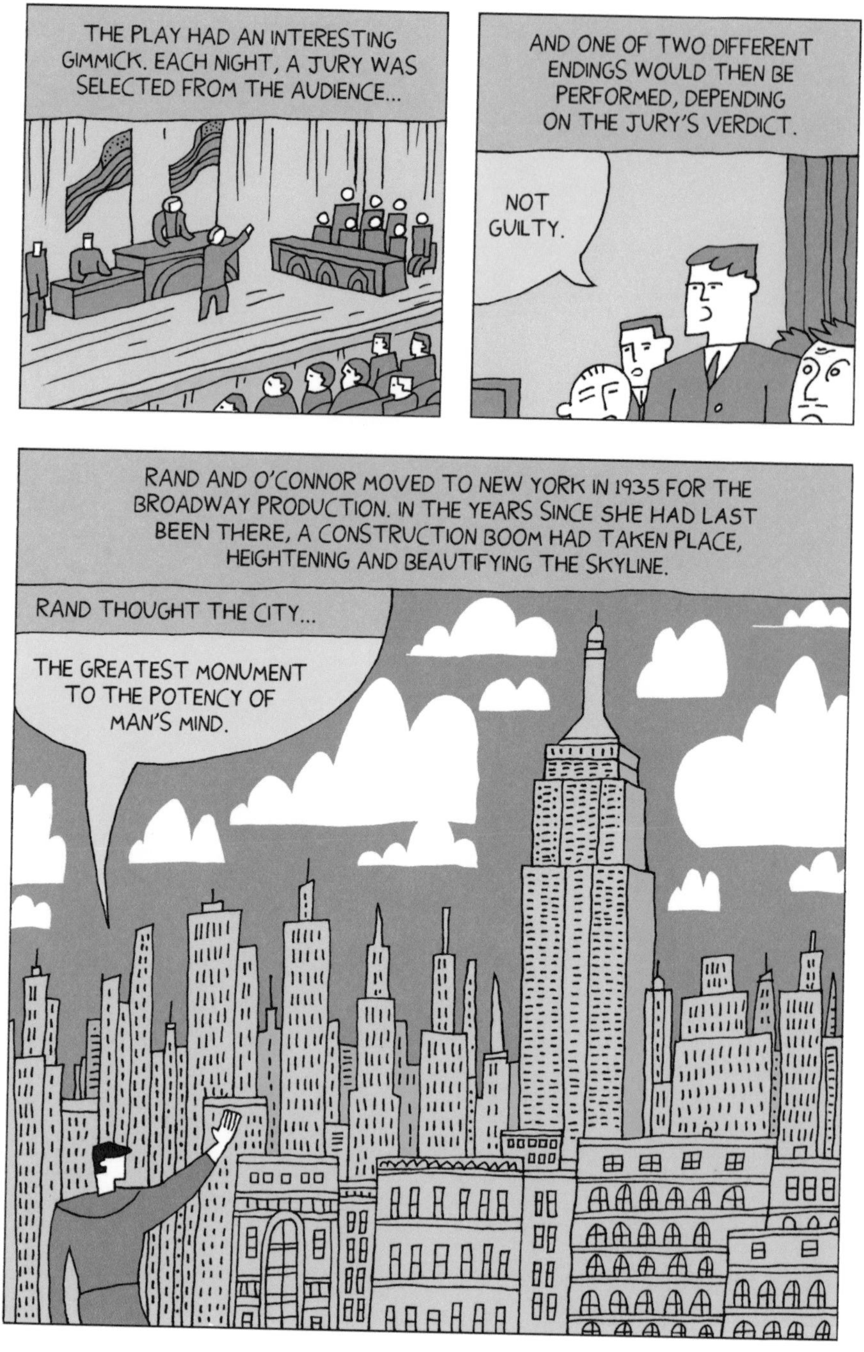
THE PLAY HAD AN INTERESTING GIMMICK. EACH NIGHT, A JURY WAS SELECTED FROM THE AUDIENCE...
AND ONE OF TWO DIFFERENT ENDINGS WOULD THEN BE PERFORMED, DEPENDING ON THE JURY'S VERDICT.
NOT GUILTY.
RAND AND O'CONNOR MOVED TO NEW YORK IN 1935 FOR THE BROADWAY PRODUCTION. IN THE YEARS SINCE SHE HAD LAST BEEN THERE, A CONSTRUCTION BOOM HAD TAKEN PLACE, HEIGHTENING AND BEAUTIFYING THE SKYLINE.
RAND THOUGHT THE CITY...
THE GREATEST MONUMENT TO THE POTENCY OF MAN'S MIND.

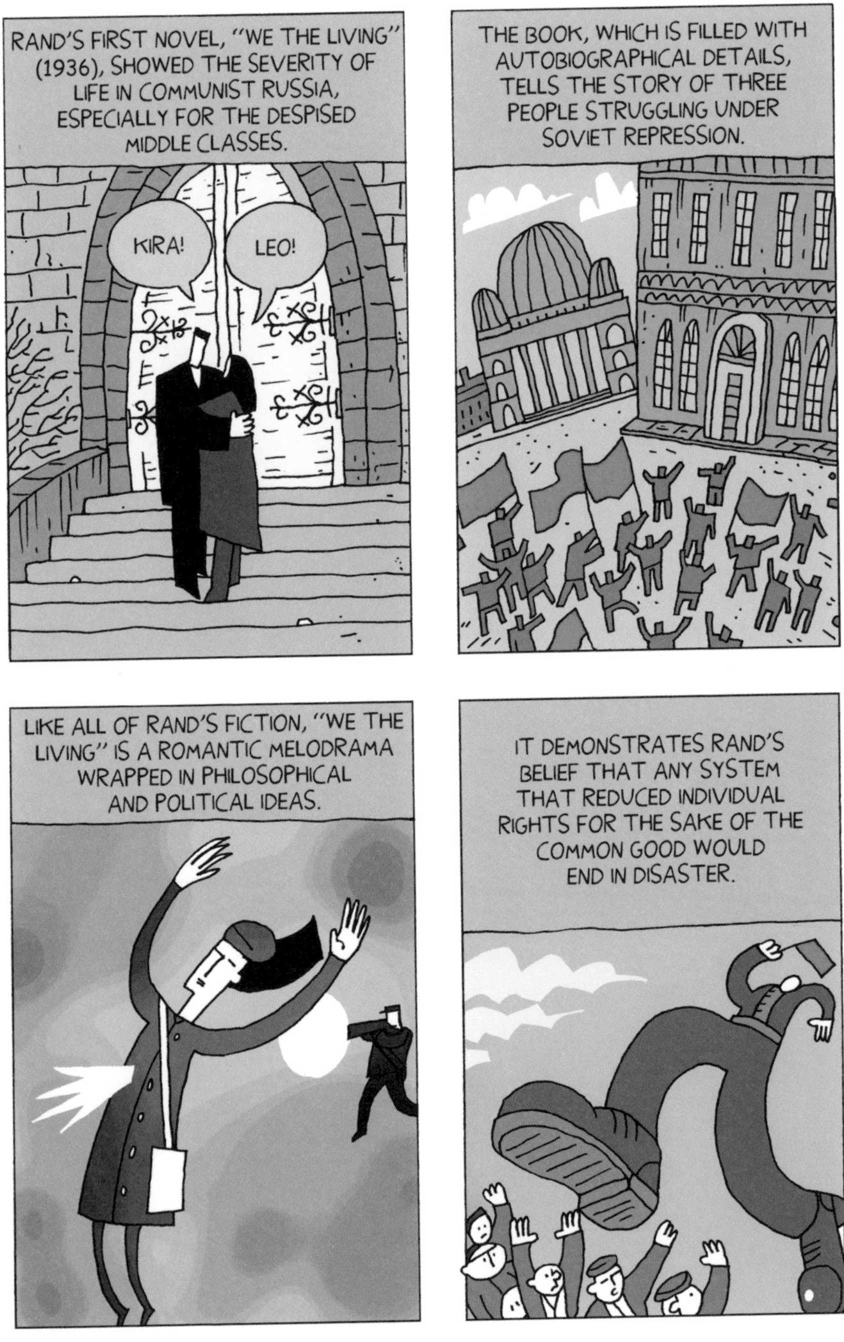
RAND'S FIRST NOVEL, "WE THE LIVING" (1936), SHOWED THE SEVERITY OF LIFE IN COMMUNIST RUSSIA, ESPECIALLY FOR THE DESPISED MIDDLE CLASSES.
KIRA!
LEO!
THE BOOK, WHICH IS FILLED WITH AUTOBIOGRAPHICAL DETAILS, TELLS THE STORY OF THREE PEOPLE STRUGGLING UNDER SOVIET REPRESSION.
LIKE ALL OF RAND'S FICTION, "WE THE LIVING" IS A ROMANTIC MELODRAMA WRAPPED IN PHILOSOPHICAL AND POLITICAL IDEAS.
IT DEMONSTRATES RAND'S BELIEF THAT ANY SYSTEM THAT REDUCED INDIVIDUAL RIGHTS FOR THE SAKE OF THE COMMON GOOD WOULD END IN DISASTER.

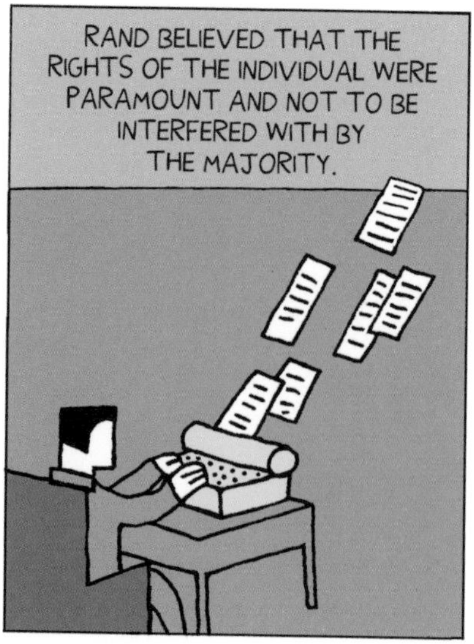
RAND BELIEVED THAT THE RIGHTS OF THE INDIVIDUAL WERE PARAMOUNT AND NOT TO BE INTERFERED WITH BY THE MAJORITY.

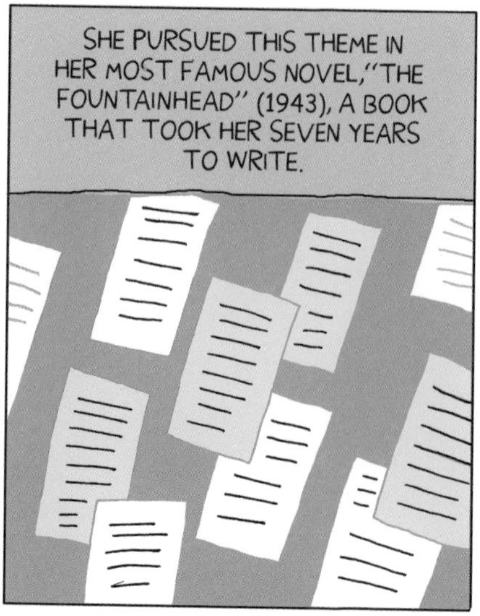
SHE PURSUED THIS THEME IN HER MOST FAMOUS NOVEL, "THE FOUNTAINHEAD" (1943), A BOOK THAT TOOK HER SEVEN YEARS TO WRITE.

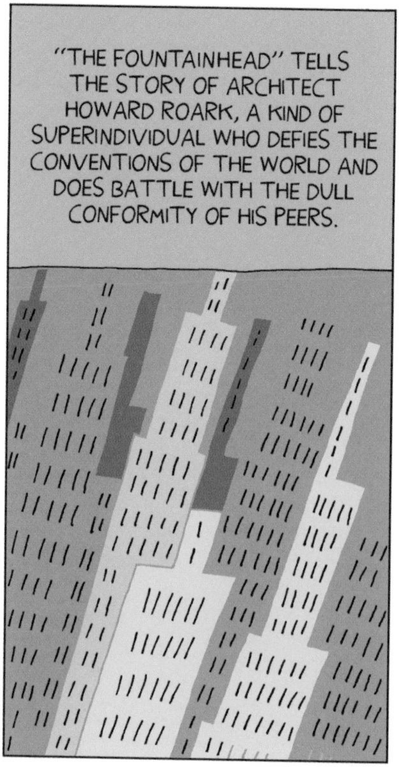
"THE FOUNTAINHEAD" TELLS THE STORY OF ARCHITECT HOWARD ROARK, A KIND OF SUPERINDIVIDUAL WHO DEFIES THE CONVENTIONS OF THE WORLD AND DOES BATTLE WITH THE DULL CONFORMITY OF HIS PEERS.

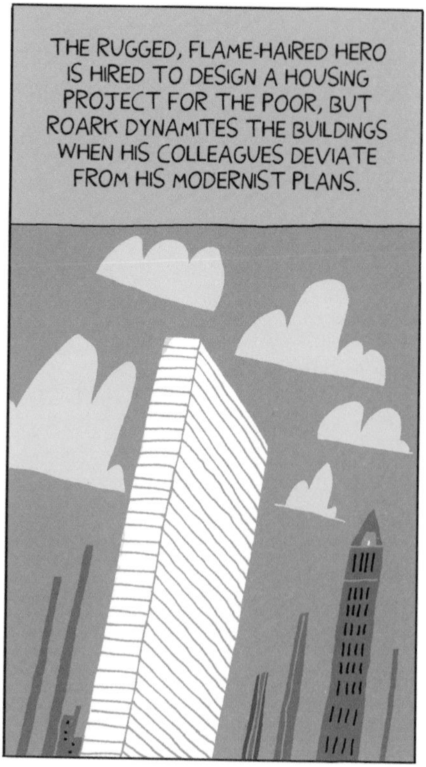
THE RUGGED, FLAME-HAIRED HERO IS HIRED TO DESIGN A HOUSING PROJECT FOR THE POOR, BUT ROARK DYNAMITES THE BUILDINGS WHEN HIS COLLEAGUES DEVIATE FROM HIS MODERNIST PLANS.

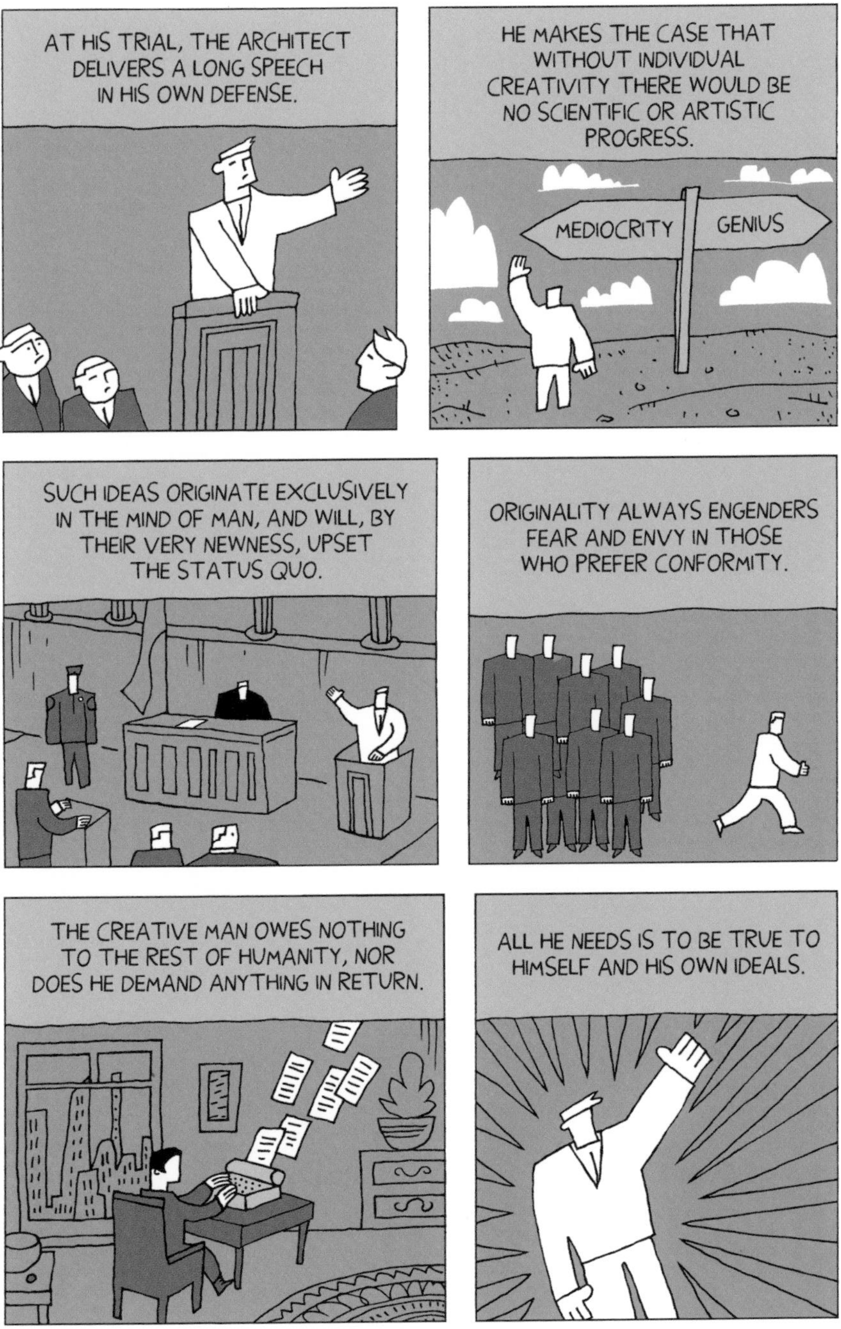
AT HIS TRIAL, THE ARCHITECT DELIVERS A LONG SPEECH IN HIS OWN DEFENSE.
HE MAKES THE CASE THAT WITHOUT INDIVIDUAL CREATIVITY THERE WOULD BE NO SCIENTIFIC OR ARTISTIC PROGRESS.
MEDIOCRITY
GENIUS
SUCH IDEAS ORIGINATE EXCLUSIVELY IN THE MIND OF MAN, AND WILL, BY THEIR VERY NEWNESS, UPSET THE STATUS QUO.
ORIGINALITY ALWAYS ENGENDERS FEAR AND ENVY IN THOSE WHO PREFER CONFORMITY.
THE CREATIVE MAN OWES NOTHING TO THE REST OF HUMANITY, NOR DOES HE DEMAND ANYTHING IN RETURN.
ALL HE NEEDS IS TO BE TRUE TO HIMSELF AND HIS OWN IDEALS.

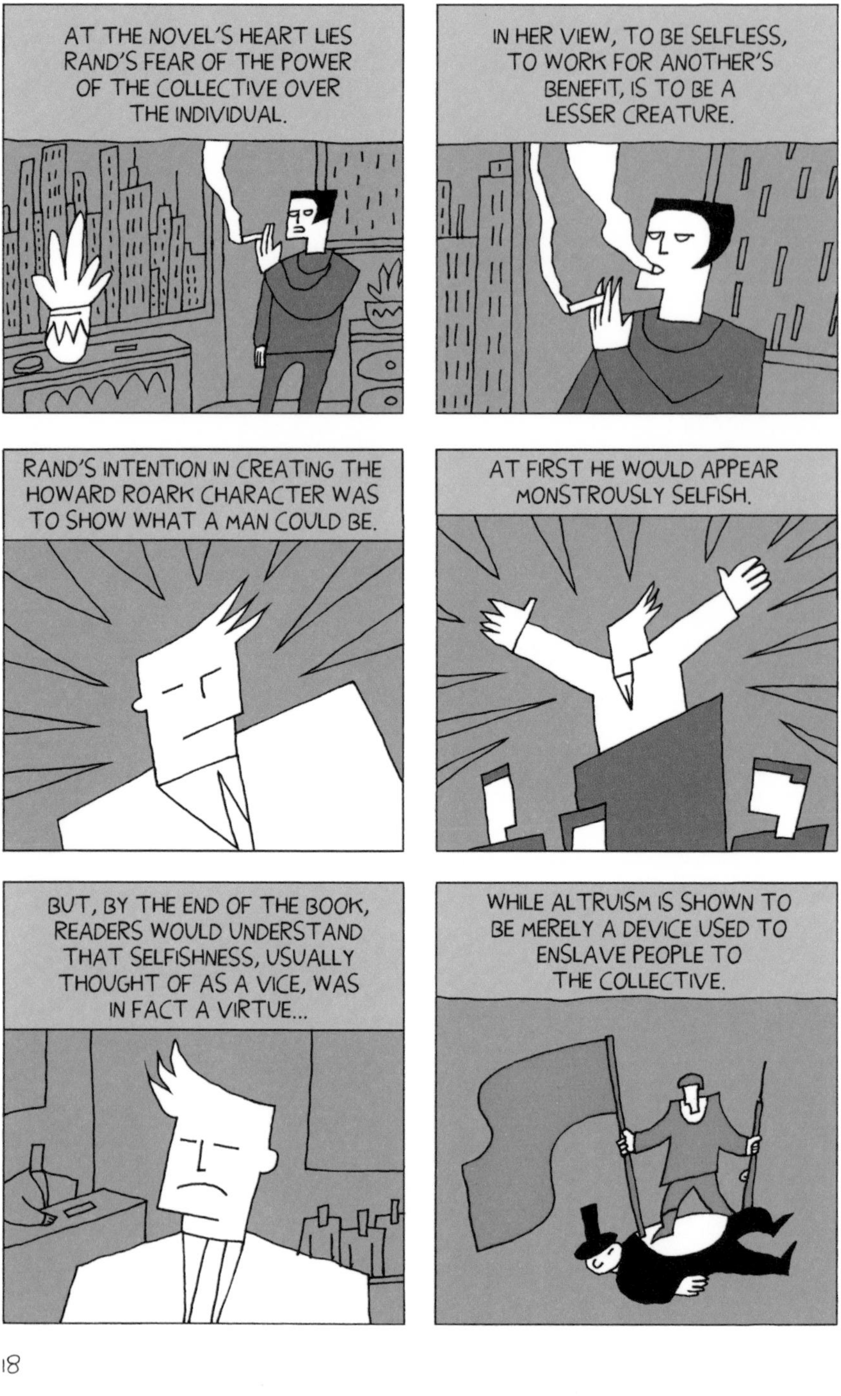
AT THE NOVEL'S HEART LIES RAND'S FEAR OF THE POWER OF THE COLLECTIVE OVER THE INDIVIDUAL.
IN HER VIEW, TO BE SELFLESS, TO WORK FOR ANOTHER'S BENEFIT, IS TO BE A LESSER CREATURE.
RAND'S INTENTION IN CREATING THE HOWARD ROARK CHARACTER WAS TO SHOW WHAT A MAN COULD BE.
AT FIRST HE WOULD APPEAR MONSTROUSLY SELFISH.
BUT, BY THE END OF THE BOOK, READERS WOULD UNDERSTAND THAT SELFISHNESS, USUALLY THOUGHT OF AS A VICE, WAS IN FACT A VIRTUE...
WHILE ALTRUISM IS SHOWN TO BE MERELY A DEVICE USED TO ENSLAVE PEOPLE TO THE COLLECTIVE.

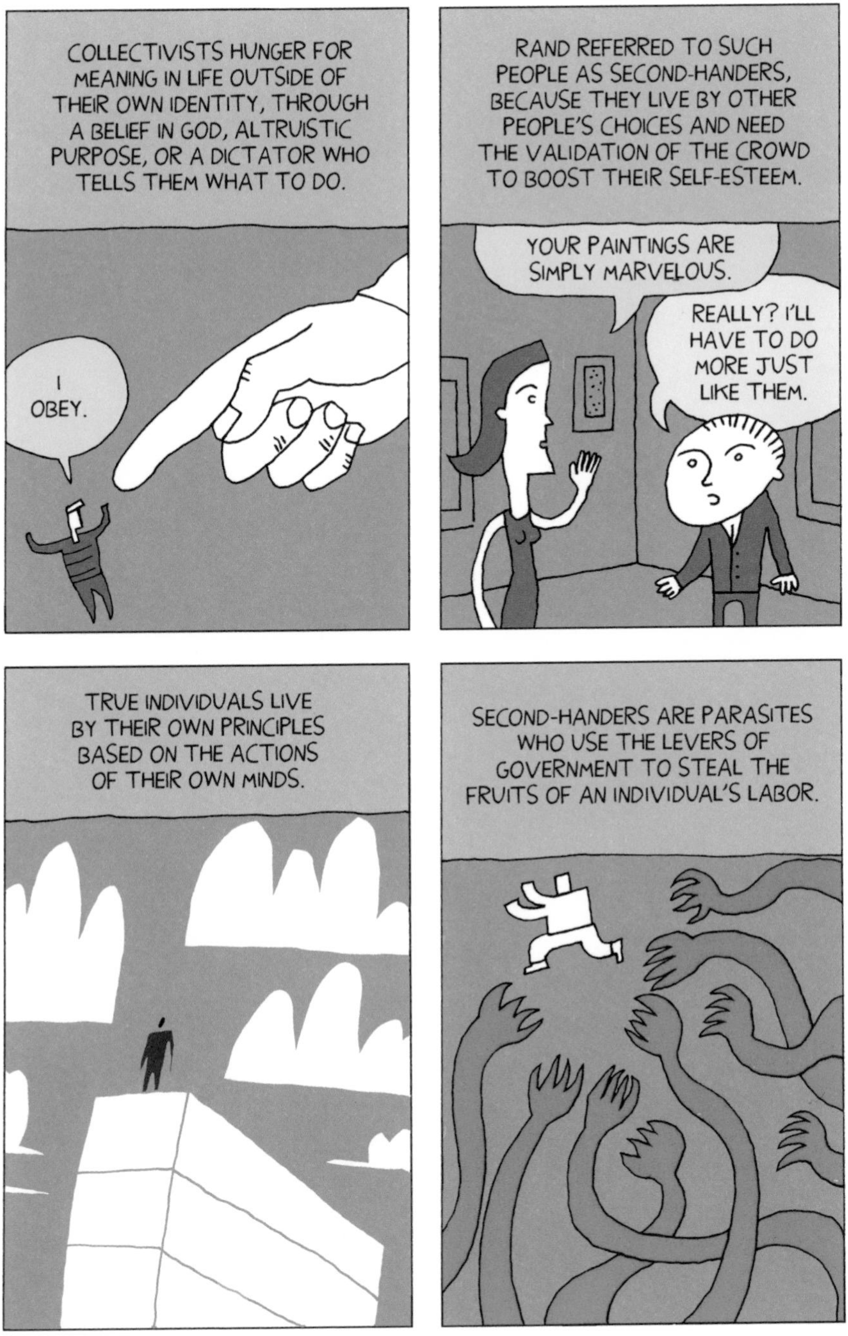
COLLECTIVISTS HUNGER FOR MEANING IN LIFE OUTSIDE OF THEIR OWN IDENTITY, THROUGH A BELIEF IN GOD, ALTRUISTIC PURPOSE, OR A DICTATOR WHO TELLS THEM WHAT TO DO.
I OBEY.
RAND REFERRED TO SUCH PEOPLE AS SECOND-HANDERS, BECAUSE THEY LIVE BY OTHER PEOPLE'S CHOICES AND NEED THE VALIDATION OF THE CROWD TO BOOST THEIR SELF-ESTEEM.
YOUR PAINTINGS ARE SIMPLY MARVELOUS.
REALLY? I'LL HAVE TO DO MORE JUST LIKE THEM.
TRUE INDIVIDUALS LIVE BY THEIR OWN PRINCIPLES BASED ON THE ACTIONS OF THEIR OWN MINDS.
SECOND-HANDERS ARE PARASITES WHO USE THE LEVERS OF GOVERNMENT TO STEAL THE FRUITS OF AN INDIVIDUAL'S LABOR.

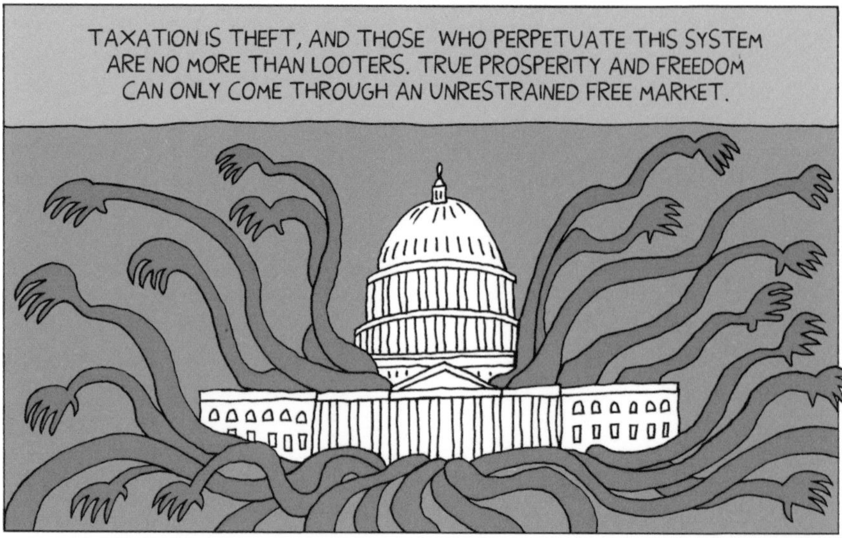
TAXATION IS THEFT, AND THOSE WHO PERPETUATE THIS SYSTEM ARE NO MORE THAN LOOTERS. TRUE PROSPERITY AND FREEDOM CAN ONLY COME THROUGH AN UNRESTRAINED FREE MARKET.

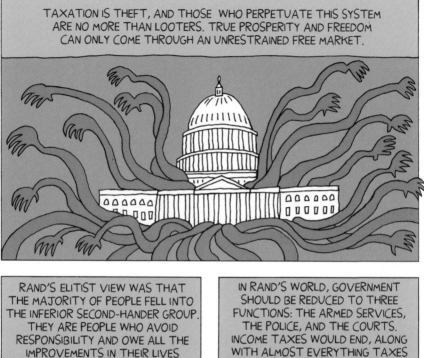

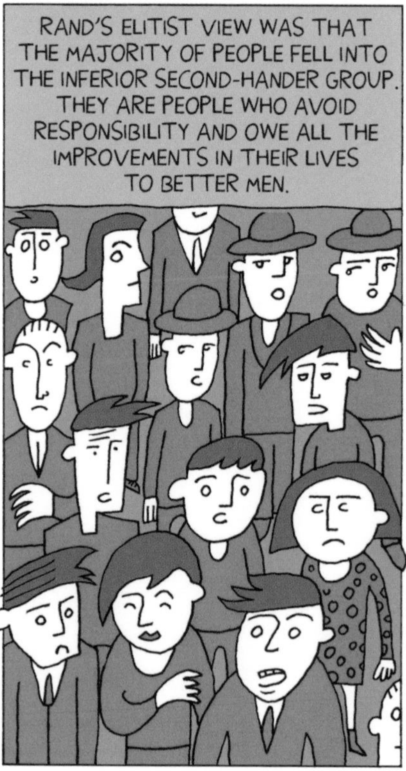
RAND'S ELITIST VIEW WAS THAT THE MAJORITY OF PEOPLE FELL INTO THE INFERIOR SECOND-HANDER GROUP. THEY ARE PEOPLE WHO AVOID RESPONSIBILITY AND OWE ALL THE IMPROVEMENTS IN THEIR LIVES TO BETTER MEN.

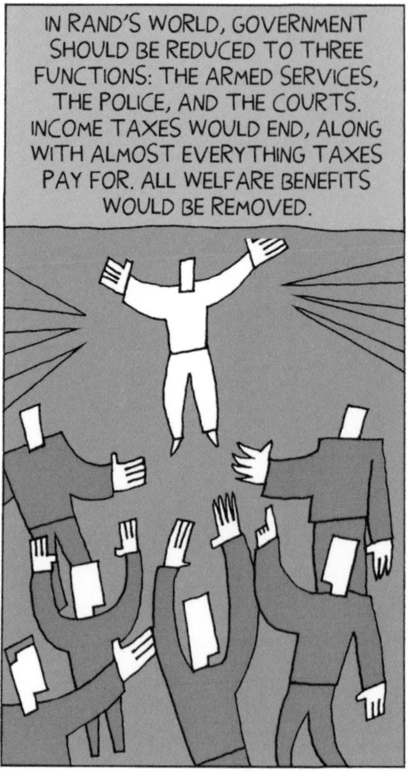
IN RAND'S WORLD, GOVERNMENT SHOULD BE REDUCED TO THREE FUNCTIONS: THE ARMED SERVICES, THE POLICE, AND THE COURTS. INCOME TAXES WOULD END, ALONG WITH ALMOST EVERYTHING TAXES PAY FOR. ALL WELFARE BENEFITS WOULD BE REMOVED.

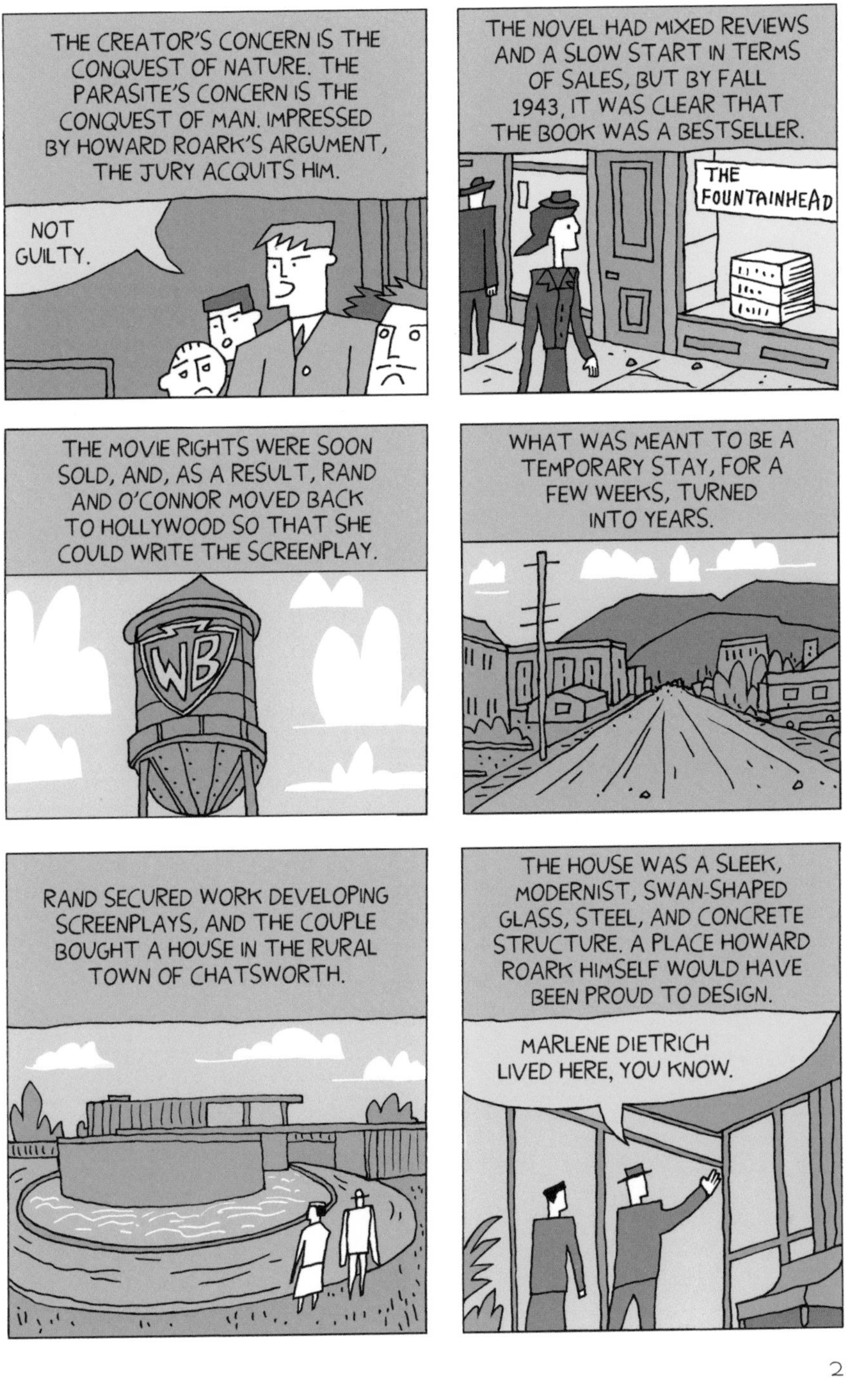
THE CREATOR'S CONCERN IS THE CONQUEST OF NATURE. THE PARASITE'S CONCERN IS THE CONQUEST OF MAN. IMPRESSED BY HOWARD ROARK'S ARGUMENT, THE JURY ACQUITS HIM.
NOT GUILTY.
THE NOVEL HAD MIXED REVIEWS AND A SLOW START IN TERMS OF SALES, BUT BY FALL 1943, IT WAS CLEAR THAT THE BOOK WAS A BESTSELLER.
THE FOUNTAINHEAD
THE MOVIE RIGHTS WERE SOON SOLD, AND, AS A RESULT, RAND AND O'CONNOR MOVED BACK TO HOLLYWOOD SO THAT SHE COULD WRITE THE SCREENPLAY.
WB
WHAT WAS MEANT TO BE A TEMPORARY STAY, FOR A FEW WEEKS, TURNED INTO YEARS.
RAND SECURED WORK DEVELOPING SCREENPLAYS, AND THE COUPLE BOUGHT A HOUSE IN THE RURAL TOWN OF CHATSWORTH.
THE HOUSE WAS A SLEEK, MODERNIST, SWAN-SHAPED GLASS, STEEL, AND CONCRETE STRUCTURE. A PLACE HOWARD ROARK HIMSELF WOULD HAVE BEEN PROUD TO DESIGN.
MARLENE DIETRICH LIVED HERE, YOU KNOW.

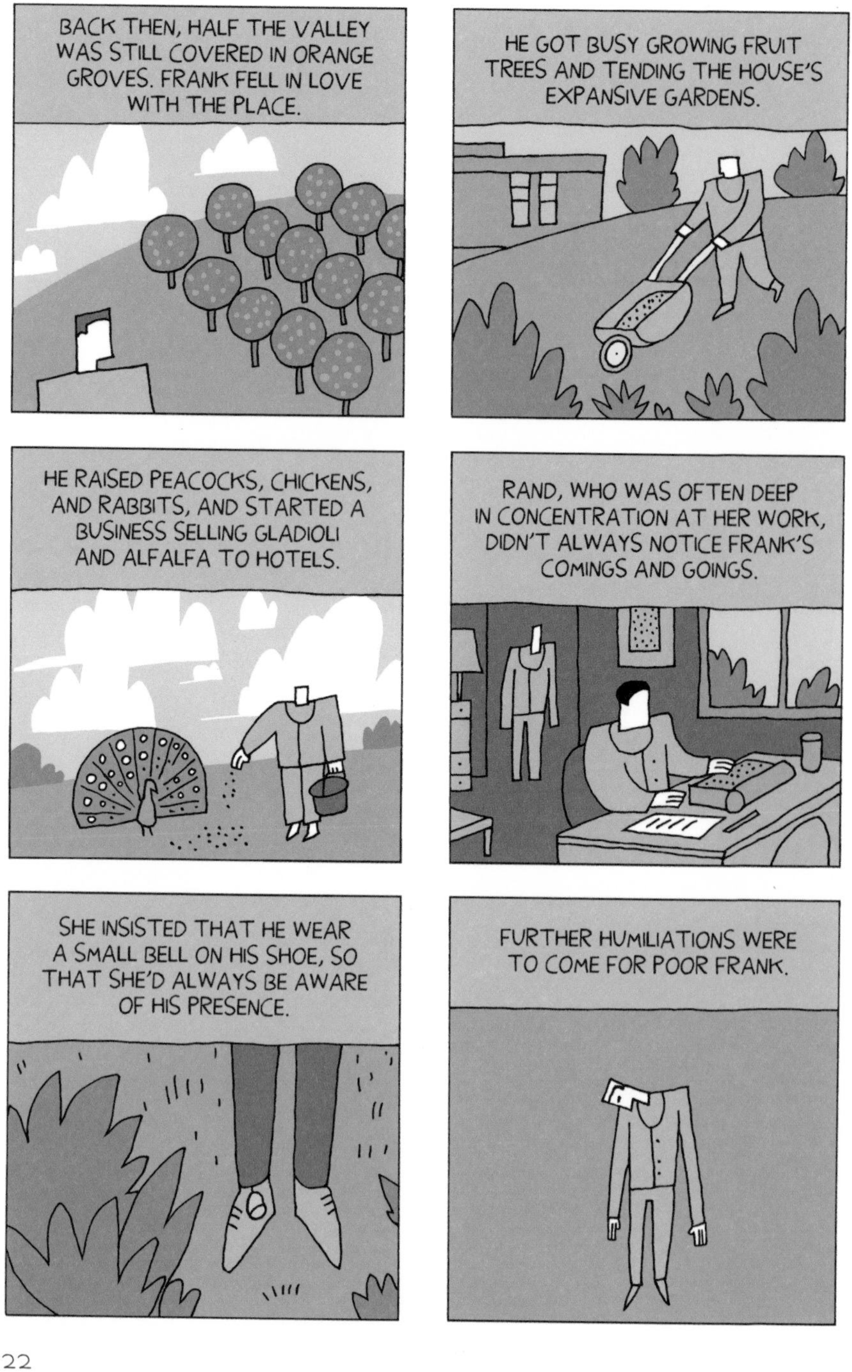
BACK THEN, HALF THE VALLEY WAS STILL COVERED IN ORANGE GROVES. FRANK FELL IN LOVE WITH THE PLACE.
HE GOT BUSY GROWING FRUIT TREES AND TENDING THE HOUSE'S EXPANSIVE GARDENS.
HE RAISED PEACOCKS, CHICKENS, AND RABBITS, AND STARTED A BUSINESS SELLING GLADIOLI AND ALFALFA TO HOTELS.
RAND, WHO WAS OFTEN DEEP IN CONCENTRATION AT HER WORK, DIDN'T ALWAYS NOTICE FRANK'S COMINGS AND GOINGS.
SHE INSISTED THAT HE WEAR A SMALL BELL ON HIS SHOE, SO THAT SHE'D ALWAYS BE AWARE OF HIS PRESENCE.
FURTHER HUMILIATIONS WERE TO COME FOR POOR FRANK.

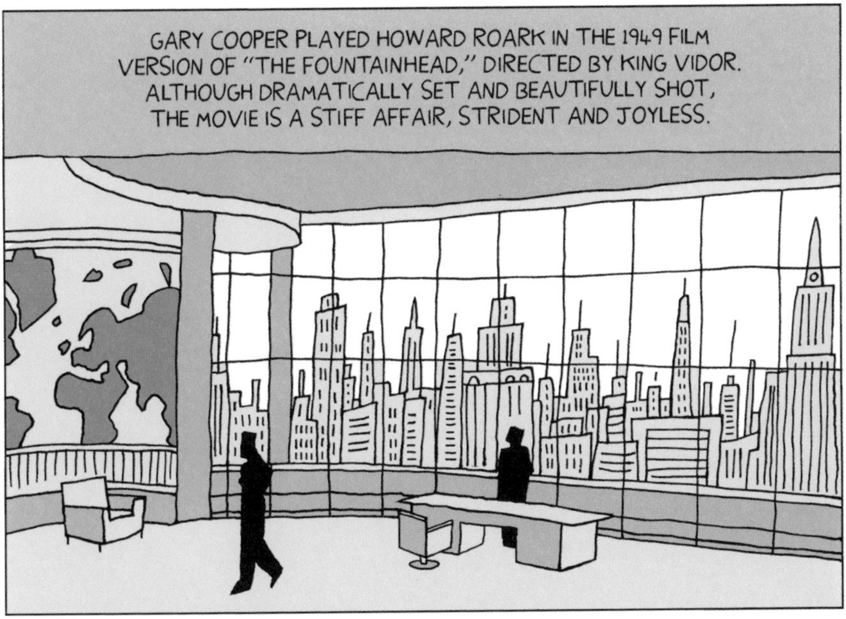
GARY COOPER PLAYED HOWARD ROARK IN THE 1949 FILM VERSION OF "THE FOUNTAINHEAD," DIRECTED BY KING VIDOR. ALTHOUGH DRAMATICALLY SET AND BEAUTIFULLY SHOT, THE MOVIE IS A STIFF AFFAIR, STRIDENT AND JOYLESS.

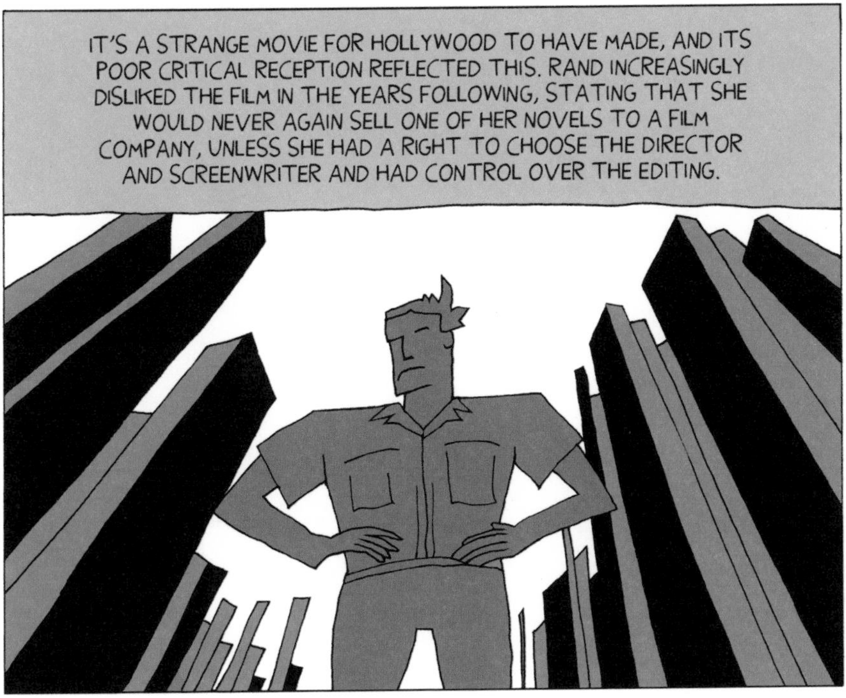
IT'S A STRANGE MOVIE FOR HOLLYWOOD TO HAVE MADE, AND ITS POOR CRITICAL RECEPTION REFLECTED THIS. RAND INCREASINGLY DISLIKED THE FILM IN THE YEARS FOLLOWING, STATING THAT SHE WOULD NEVER AGAIN SELL ONE OF HER NOVELS TO A FILM COMPANY, UNLESS SHE HAD A RIGHT TO CHOOSE THE DIRECTOR AND SCREENWRITER AND HAD CONTROL OVER THE EDITING.

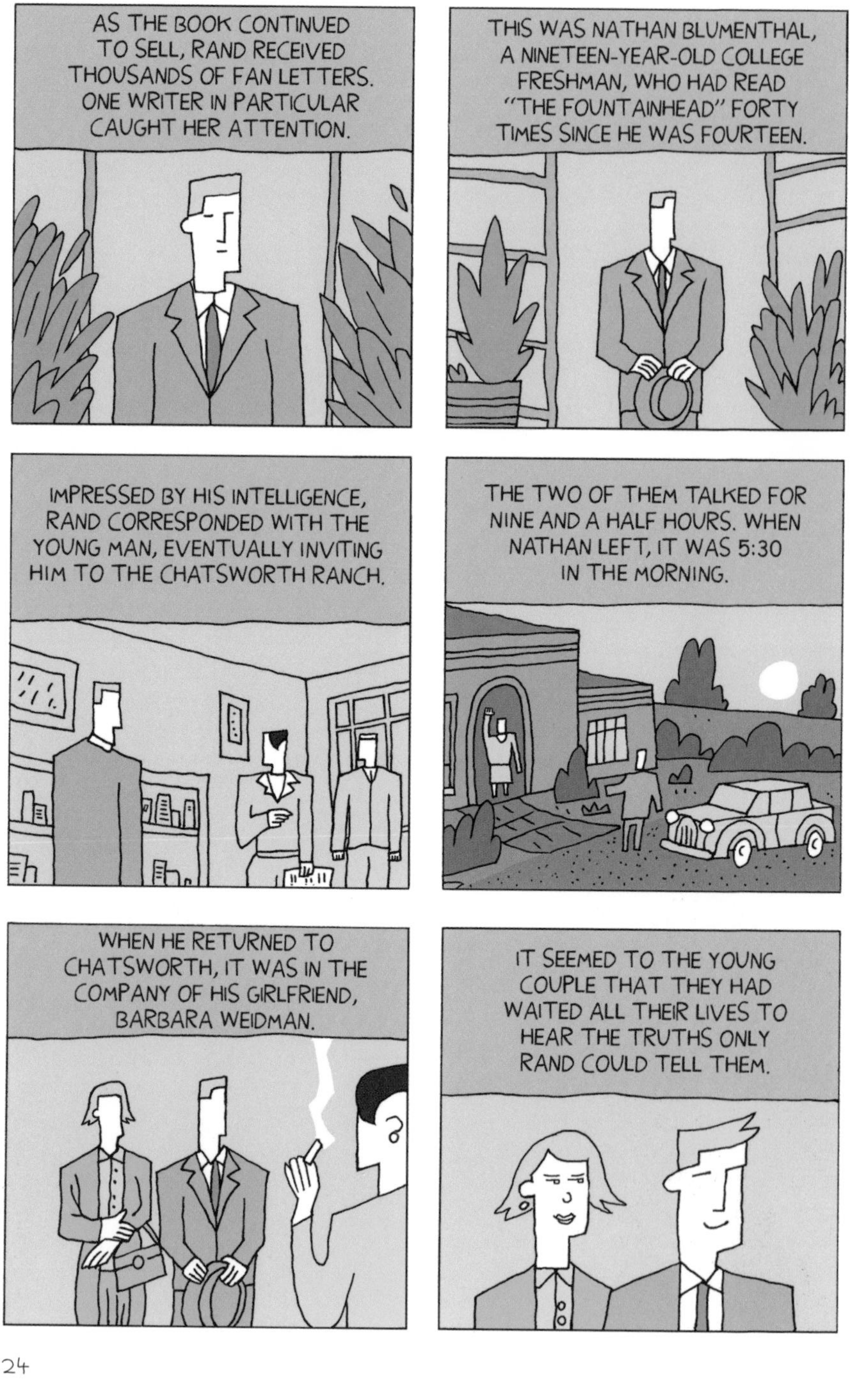
AS THE BOOK CONTINUED TO SELL, RAND RECEIVED THOUSANDS OF FAN LETTERS. ONE WRITER IN PARTICULAR CAUGHT HER ATTENTION.
THIS WAS NATHAN BLUMENTHAL, A NINETEEN-YEAR-OLD COLLEGE FRESHMAN, WHO HAD READ "THE FOUNTAINHEAD" FORTY TIMES SINCE HE WAS FOURTEEN.
IMPRESSED BY HIS INTELLIGENCE, RAND CORRESPONDED WITH THE YOUNG MAN, EVENTUALLY INVITING HIM TO THE CHATSWORTH RANCH.
THE TWO OF THEM TALKED FOR NINE AND A HALF HOURS. WHEN NATHAN LEFT, IT WAS 5:30 IN THE MORNING.
WHEN HE RETURNED TO CHATSWORTH, IT WAS IN THE COMPANY OF HIS GIRLFRIEND, BARBARA WEIDMAN.
IT SEEMED TO THE YOUNG COUPLE THAT THEY HAD WAITED ALL THEIR LIVES TO HEAR THE TRUTHS ONLY RAND COULD TELL THEM.

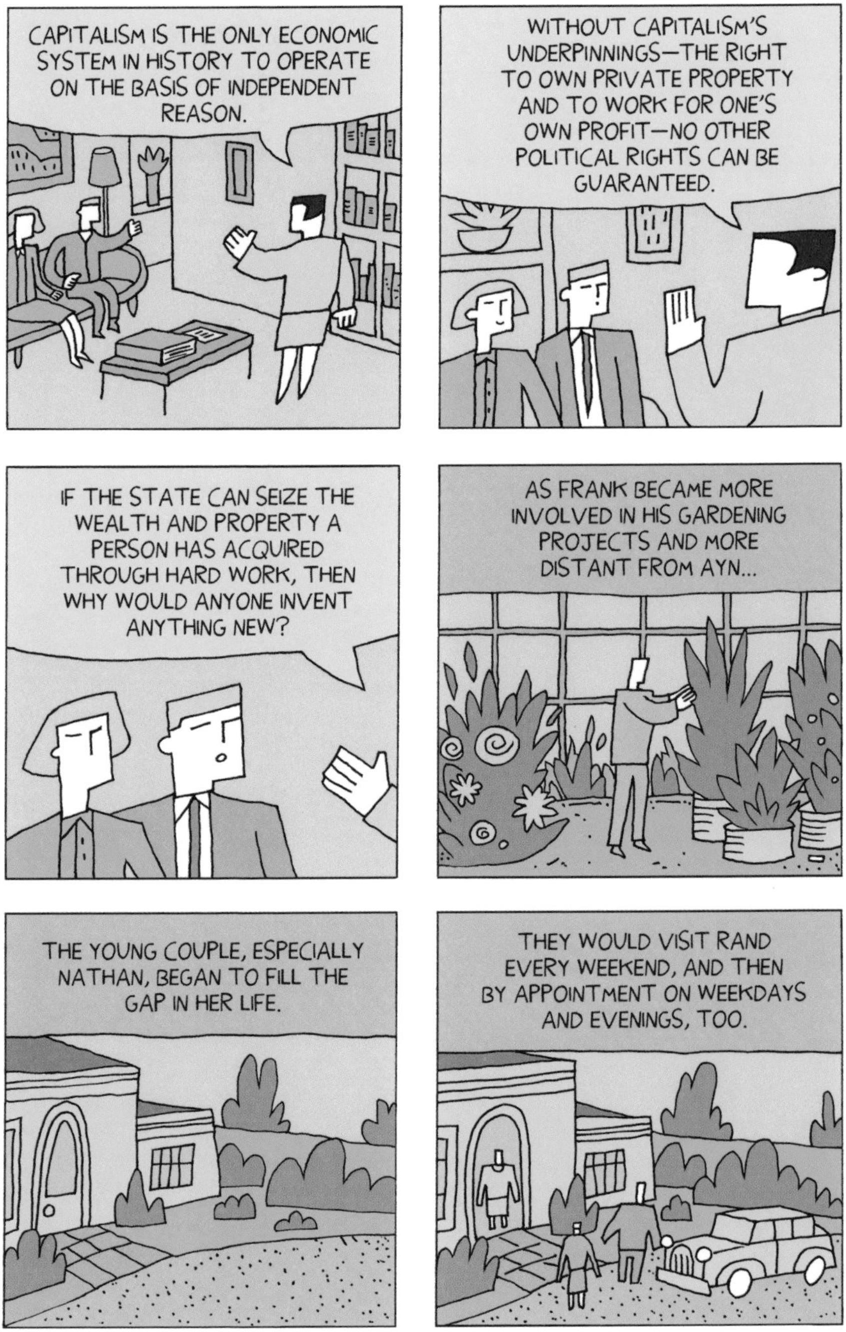
CAPITALISM IS THE ONLY ECONOMIC SYSTEM IN HISTORY TO OPERATE ON THE BASIS OF INDEPENDENT REASON.
WITHOUT CAPITALISM'S UNDERPINNINGS—THE RIGHT TO OWN PRIVATE PROPERTY AND TO WORK FOR ONE'S OWN PROFIT—NO OTHER POLITICAL RIGHTS CAN BE GUARANTEED.
IF THE STATE CAN SEIZE THE WEALTH AND PROPERTY A PERSON HAS ACQUIRED THROUGH HARD WORK, THEN WHY WOULD ANYONE INVENT ANYTHING NEW?
AS FRANK BECAME MORE INVOLVED IN HIS GARDENING PROJECTS AND MORE DISTANT FROM AYN...
THE YOUNG COUPLE, ESPECIALLY NATHAN, BEGAN TO FILL THE GAP IN HER LIFE.
THEY WOULD VISIT RAND EVERY WEEKEND, AND THEN BY APPOINTMENT ON WEEKDAYS AND EVENINGS, TOO.

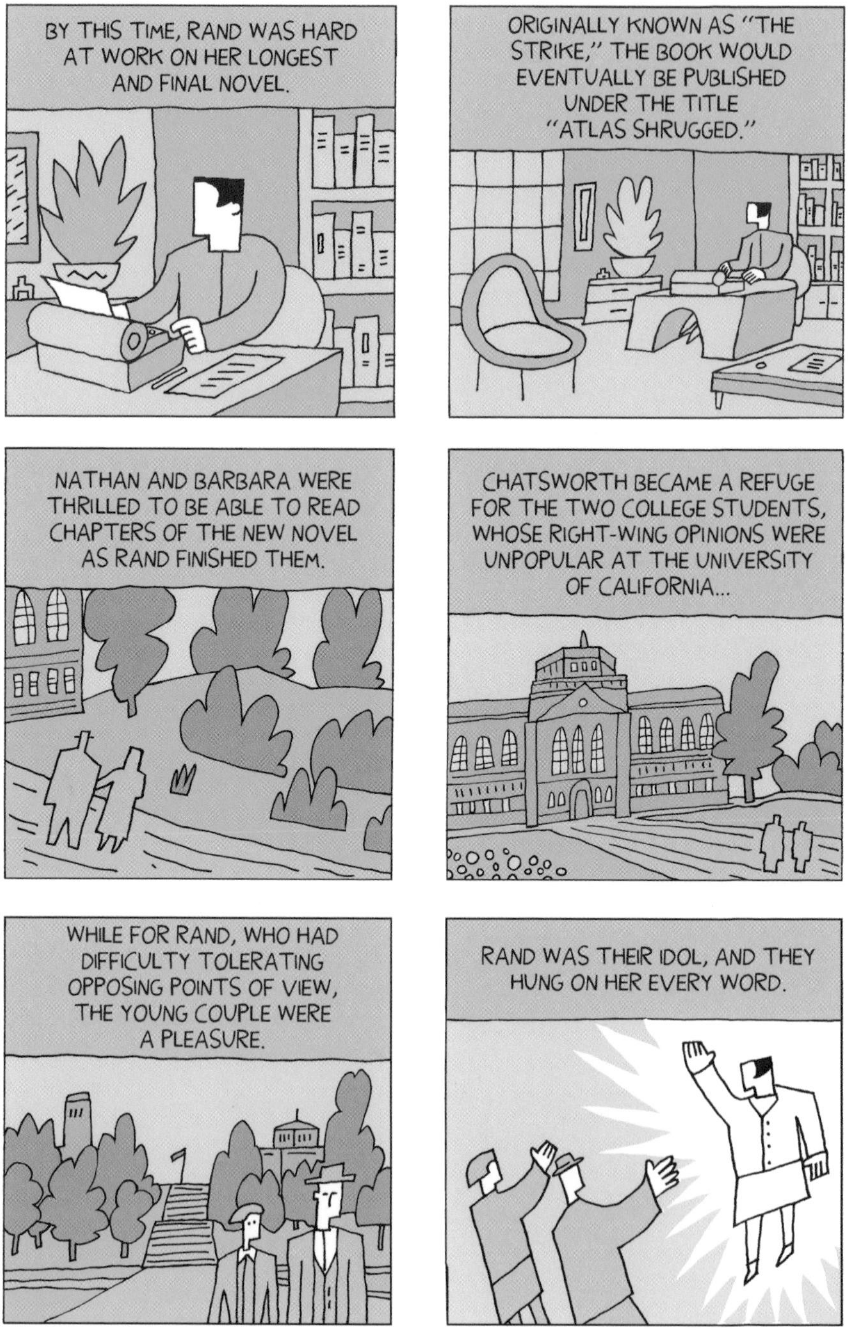
BY THIS TIME, RAND WAS HARD AT WORK ON HER LONGEST AND FINAL NOVEL.
ORIGINALLY KNOWN AS "THE STRIKE," THE BOOK WOULD EVENTUALLY BE PUBLISHED UNDER THE TITLE "ATLAS SHRUGGED."
NATHAN AND BARBARA WERE THRILLED TO BE ABLE TO READ CHAPTERS OF THE NEW NOVEL AS RAND FINISHED THEM.
CHATSWORTH BECAME A REFUGE FOR THE TWO COLLEGE STUDENTS, WHOSE RIGHT-WING OPINIONS WERE UNPOPULAR AT THE UNIVERSITY OF CALIFORNIA...
WHILE FOR RAND, WHO HAD DIFFICULTY TOLERATING OPPOSING POINTS OF VIEW, THE YOUNG COUPLE WERE A PLEASURE.
RAND WAS THEIR IDOL, AND THEY HUNG ON HER EVERY WORD.

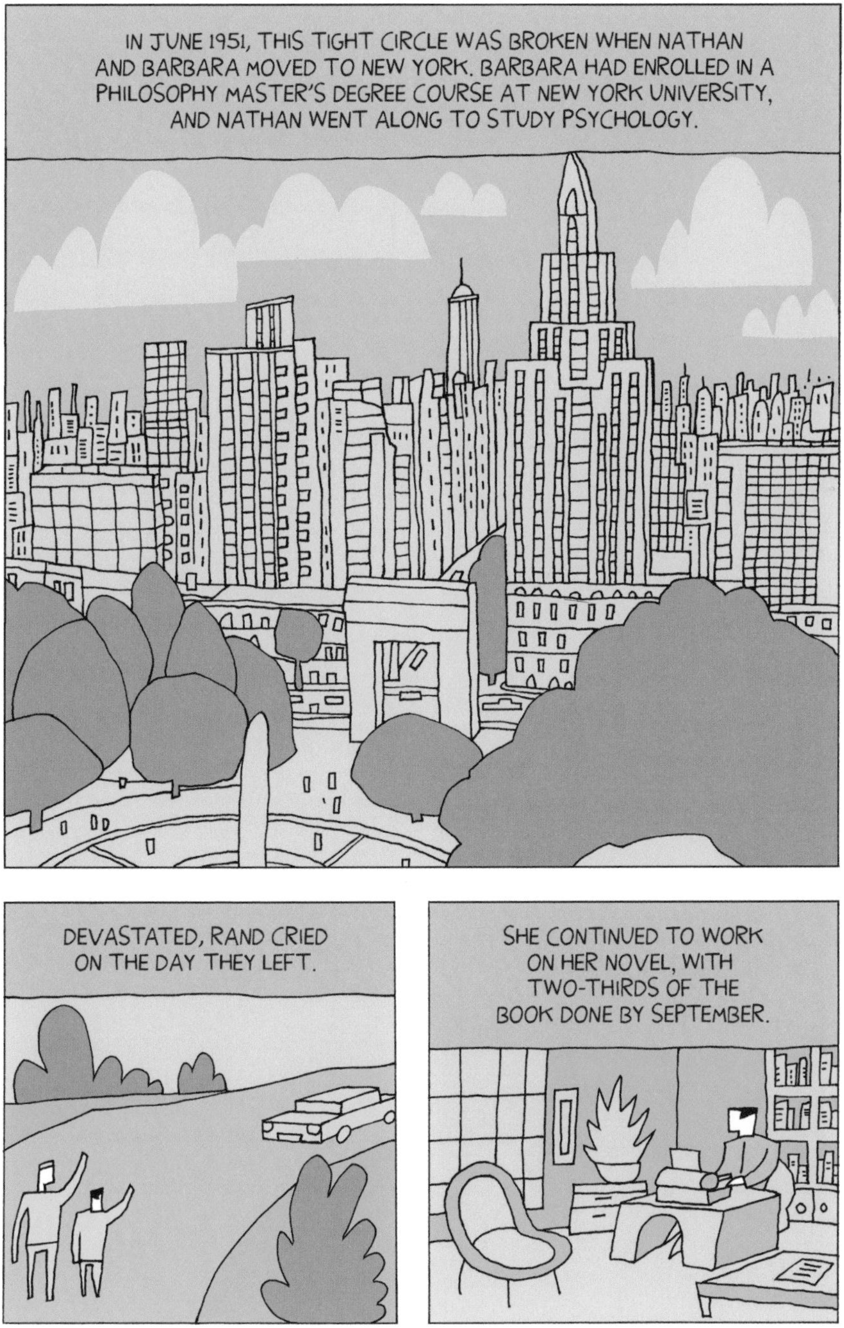
IN JUNE 1951, THIS TIGHT CIRCLE WAS BROKEN WHEN NATHAN AND BARBARA MOVED TO NEW YORK. BARBARA HAD ENROLLED IN A PHILOSOPHY MASTER'S DEGREE COURSE AT NEW YORK UNIVERSITY, AND NATHAN WENT ALONG TO STUDY PSYCHOLOGY.
DEVASTATED, RAND CRIED ON THE DAY THEY LEFT.
SHE CONTINUED TO WORK ON HER NOVEL, WITH TWO-THIRDS OF THE BOOK DONE BY SEPTEMBER.

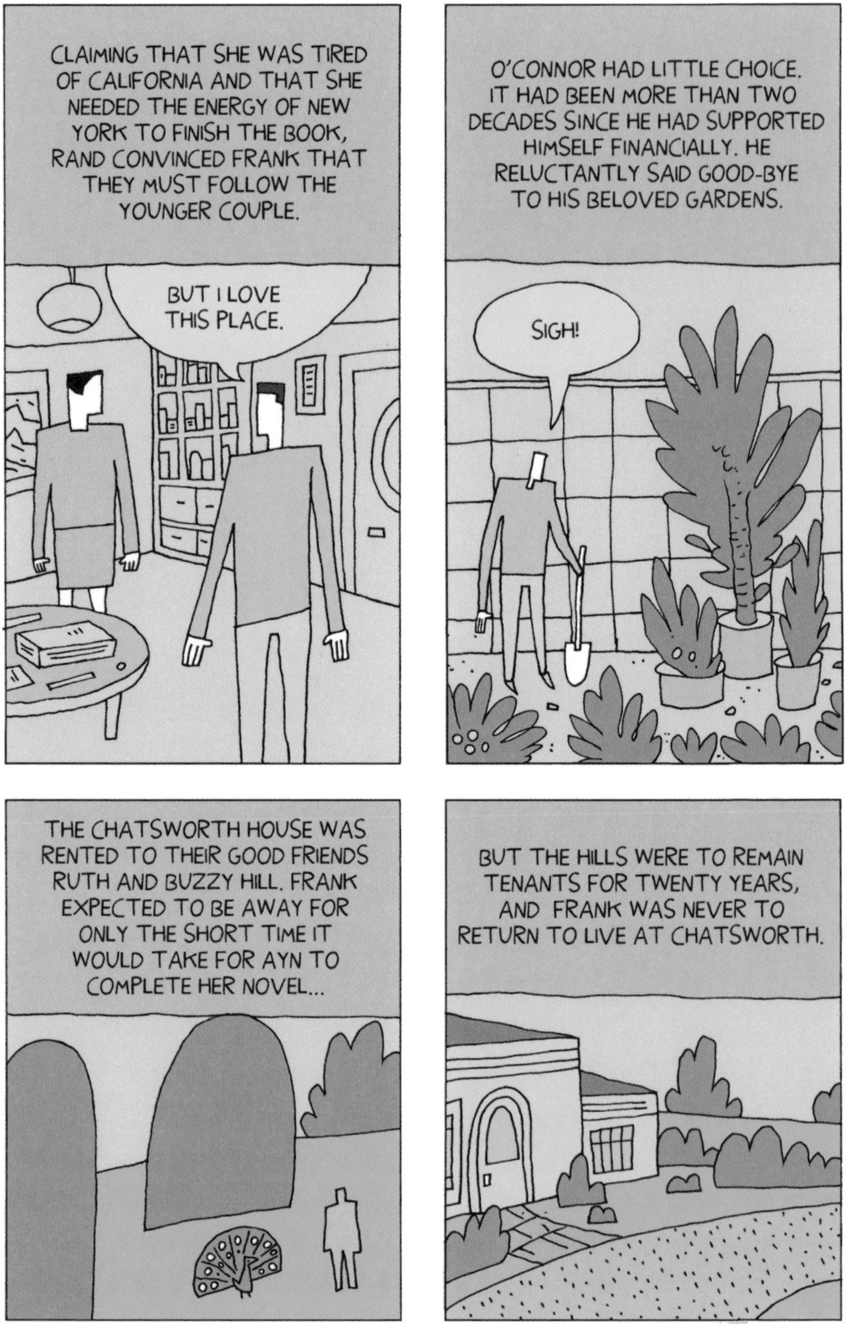
CLAIMING THAT SHE WAS TIRED OF CALIFORNIA AND THAT SHE NEEDED THE ENERGY OF NEW YORK TO FINISH THE BOOK, RAND CONVINCED FRANK THAT THEY MUST FOLLOW THE YOUNGER COUPLE.
BUT I LOVE THIS PLACE.
O'CONNOR HAD LITTLE CHOICE. IT HAD BEEN MORE THAN TWO DECADES SINCE HE HAD SUPPORTED HIMSELF FINANCIALLY. HE RELUCTANTLY SAID GOOD-BYE TO HIS BELOVED GARDENS.
SIGH!
THE CHATSWORTH HOUSE WAS RENTED TO THEIR GOOD FRIENDS RUTH AND BUZZY HILL. FRANK EXPECTED TO BE AWAY FOR ONLY THE SHORT TIME IT WOULD TAKE FOR AYN TO COMPLETE HER NOVEL...
BUT THE HILLS WERE TO REMAIN TENANTS FOR TWENTY YEARS, AND FRANK WAS NEVER TO RETURN TO LIVE AT CHATSWORTH.

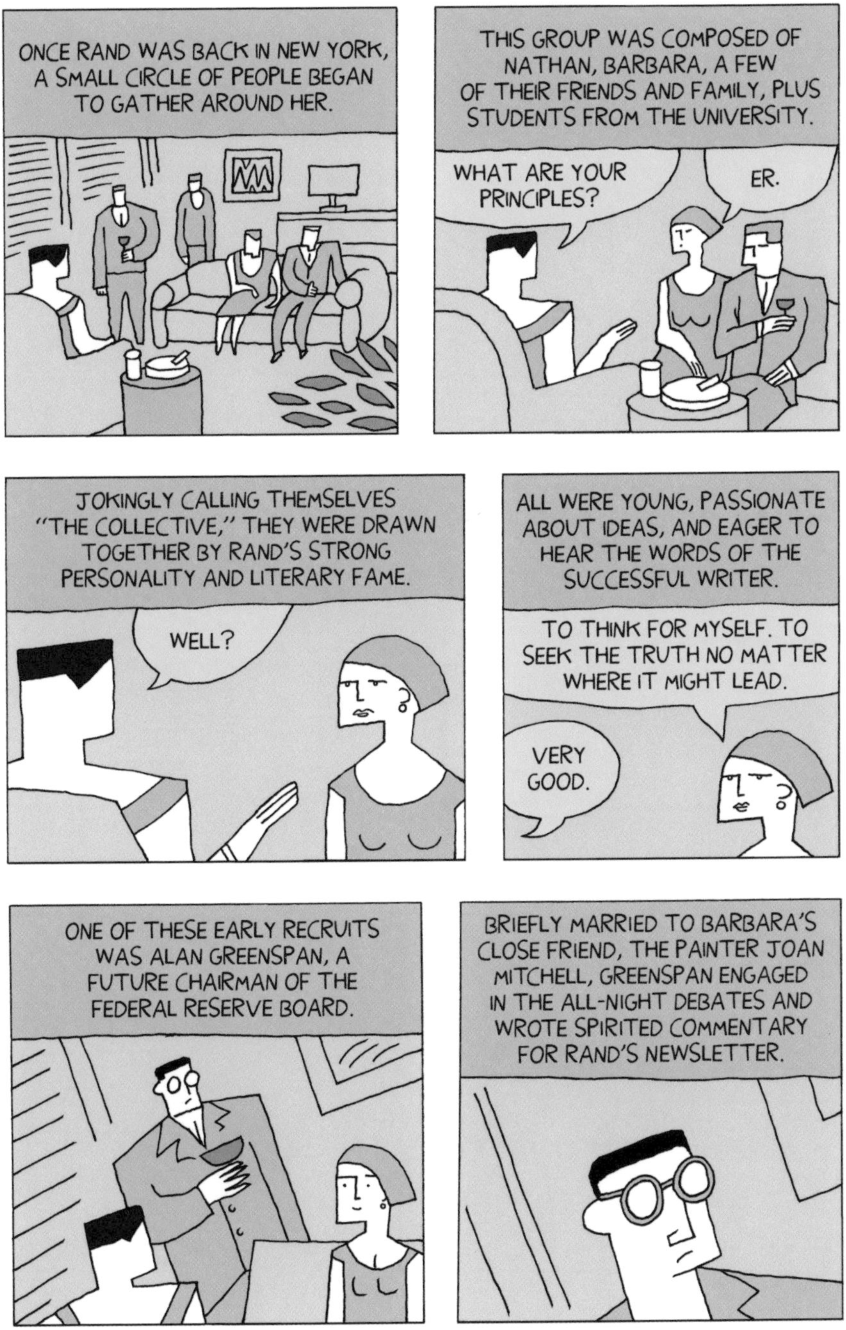
ONCE RAND WAS BACK IN NEW YORK, A SMALL CIRCLE OF PEOPLE BEGAN TO GATHER AROUND HER.
THIS GROUP WAS COMPOSED OF NATHAN, BARBARA, A FEW OF THEIR FRIENDS AND FAMILY, PLUS STUDENTS FROM THE UNIVERSITY.
WHAT ARE YOUR PRINCIPLES?
ER.
JOKINGLY CALLING THEMSELVES "THE COLLECTIVE," THEY WERE DRAWN TOGETHER BY RAND'S STRONG PERSONALITY AND LITERARY FAME.
WELL?
ALL WERE YOUNG, PASSIONATE ABOUT IDEAS, AND EAGER TO HEAR THE WORDS OF THE SUCCESSFUL WRITER.
TO THINK FOR MYSELF. TO SEEK THE TRUTH NO MATTER WHERE IT MIGHT LEAD.
VERY GOOD.
ONE OF THESE EARLY RECRUITS WAS ALAN GREENSPAN, A FUTURE CHAIRMAN OF THE FEDERAL RESERVE BOARD.
BRIEFLY MARRIED TO BARBARA'S CLOSE FRIEND, THE PAINTER JOAN MITCHELL, GREENSPAN ENGAGED IN THE ALL-NIGHT DEBATES AND WROTE SPIRITED COMMENTARY FOR RAND'S NEWSLETTER.

GREENSPAN WAS BORN IN THE WASHINGTON HEIGHTS AREA OF NEW YORK IN 1926.

HIS PARENTS DIVORCED WHEN HE WAS FIVE YEARS OLD. HIS MOTHER TOOK HIM TO LIVE WITH HER OWN PARENTS IN THE BRONX.

AS A CHILD, GREENSPAN SHOWED PRECOCIOUS INTELLIGENCE. HE WAS ABLE TO ADD UP THREE-DIGIT NUMBERS IN HIS HEAD.

DO IT AGAIN, ALAN.

THEY WERE A MUSICAL FAMILY. GREENSPAN TOOK UP THE CLARINET, SHARING A CLASS WITH STAN GETZ AND LATER PLAYING IN WOODY HERMAN'S BAND.

DESCRIBED AS SOLITARY AND A STRAIGHT ARROW, GREENSPAN ASSERTED HIS INDEPENDENCE FROM HIS FAMILY BY REFUSING TO BE BAR MITZVAHED.

I'M A SECULAR JEW.

HE STUDIED ECONOMICS AT NEW YORK UNIVERSITY, EARNING UNDERGRADUATE AND GRADUATE DEGREES IN THE SUBJECT.

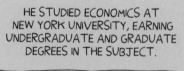

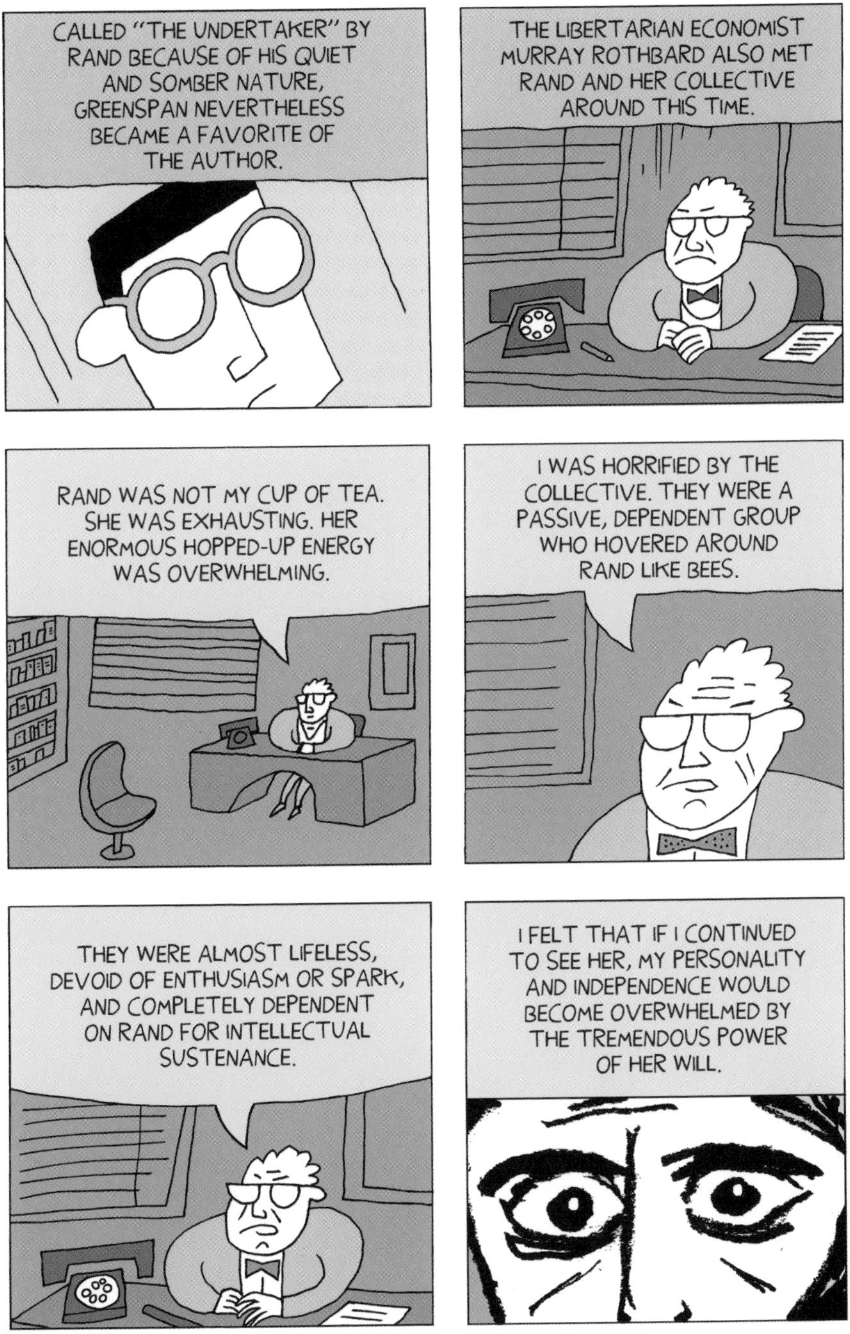
CALLED "THE UNDERTAKER" BY RAND BECAUSE OF HIS QUIET AND SOMBER NATURE, GREENSPAN NEVERTHELESS BECAME A FAVORITE OF THE AUTHOR.
THE LIBERTARIAN ECONOMIST MURRAY ROTHBARD ALSO MET RAND AND HER COLLECTIVE AROUND THIS TIME.
RAND WAS NOT MY CUP OF TEA. SHE WAS EXHAUSTING. HER ENORMOUS HOPPED-UP ENERGY WAS OVERWHELMING.
I WAS HORRIFIED BY THE COLLECTIVE. THEY WERE A PASSIVE, DEPENDENT GROUP WHO HOVERED AROUND RAND LIKE BEES.
THEY WERE ALMOST LIFELESS, DEVOID OF ENTHUSIASM OR SPARK, AND COMPLETELY DEPENDENT ON RAND FOR INTELLECTUAL SUSTENANCE.
I FELT THAT IF I CONTINUED TO SEE HER, MY PERSONALITY AND INDEPENDENCE WOULD BECOME OVERWHELMED BY THE TREMENDOUS POWER OF HER WILL.

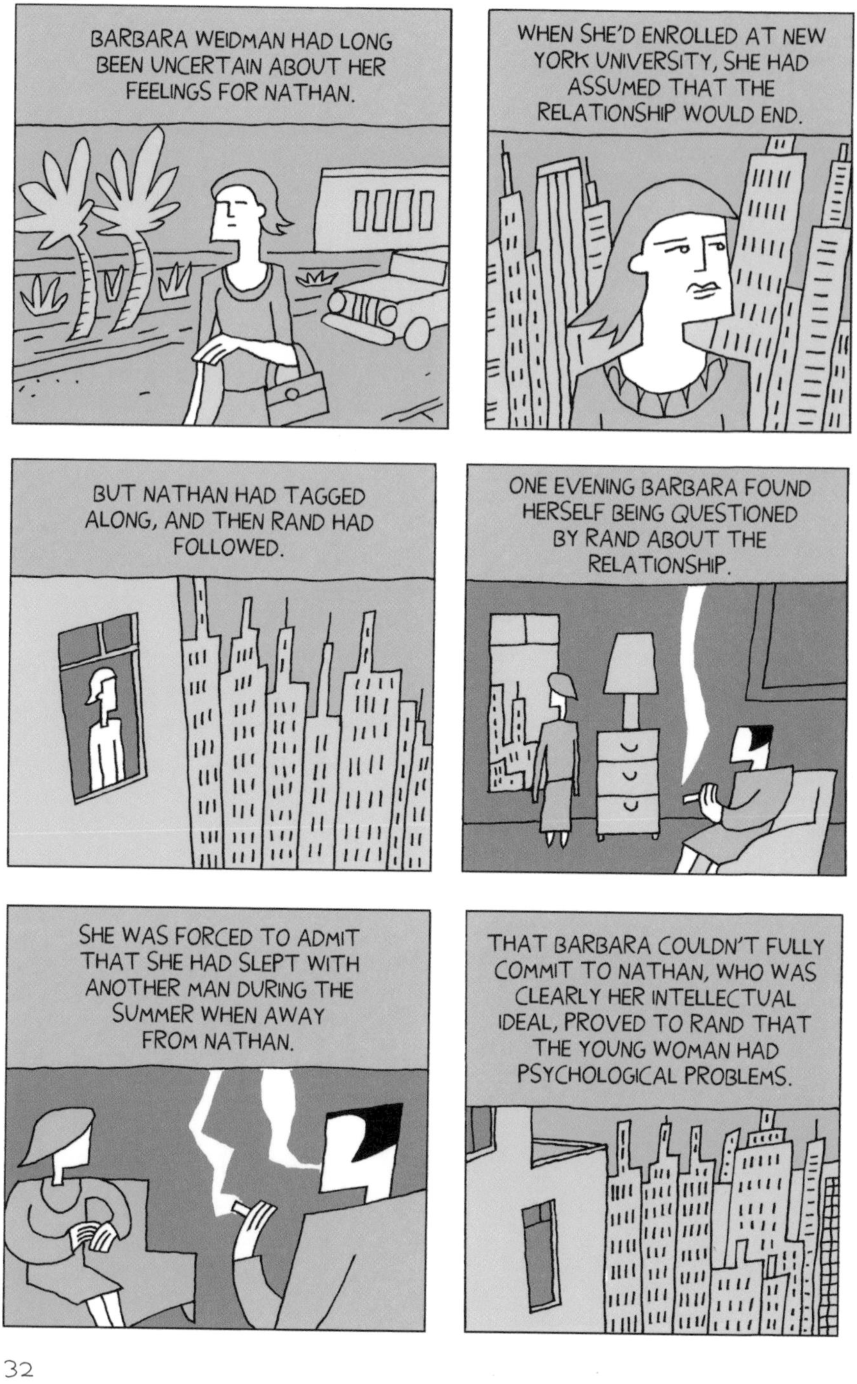
BARBARA WEIDMAN HAD LONG BEEN UNCERTAIN ABOUT HER FEELINGS FOR NATHAN.
WHEN SHE'D ENROLLED AT NEW YORK UNIVERSITY, SHE HAD ASSUMED THAT THE RELATIONSHIP WOULD END.
BUT NATHAN HAD TAGGED ALONG, AND THEN RAND HAD FOLLOWED.
ONE EVENING BARBARA FOUND HERSELF BEING QUESTIONED BY RAND ABOUT THE RELATIONSHIP.
SHE WAS FORCED TO ADMIT THAT SHE HAD SLEPT WITH ANOTHER MAN DURING THE SUMMER WHEN AWAY FROM NATHAN.
THAT BARBARA COULDN'T FULLY COMMIT TO NATHAN, WHO WAS CLEARLY HER INTELLECTUAL IDEAL, PROVED TO RAND THAT THE YOUNG WOMAN HAD PSYCHOLOGICAL PROBLEMS.

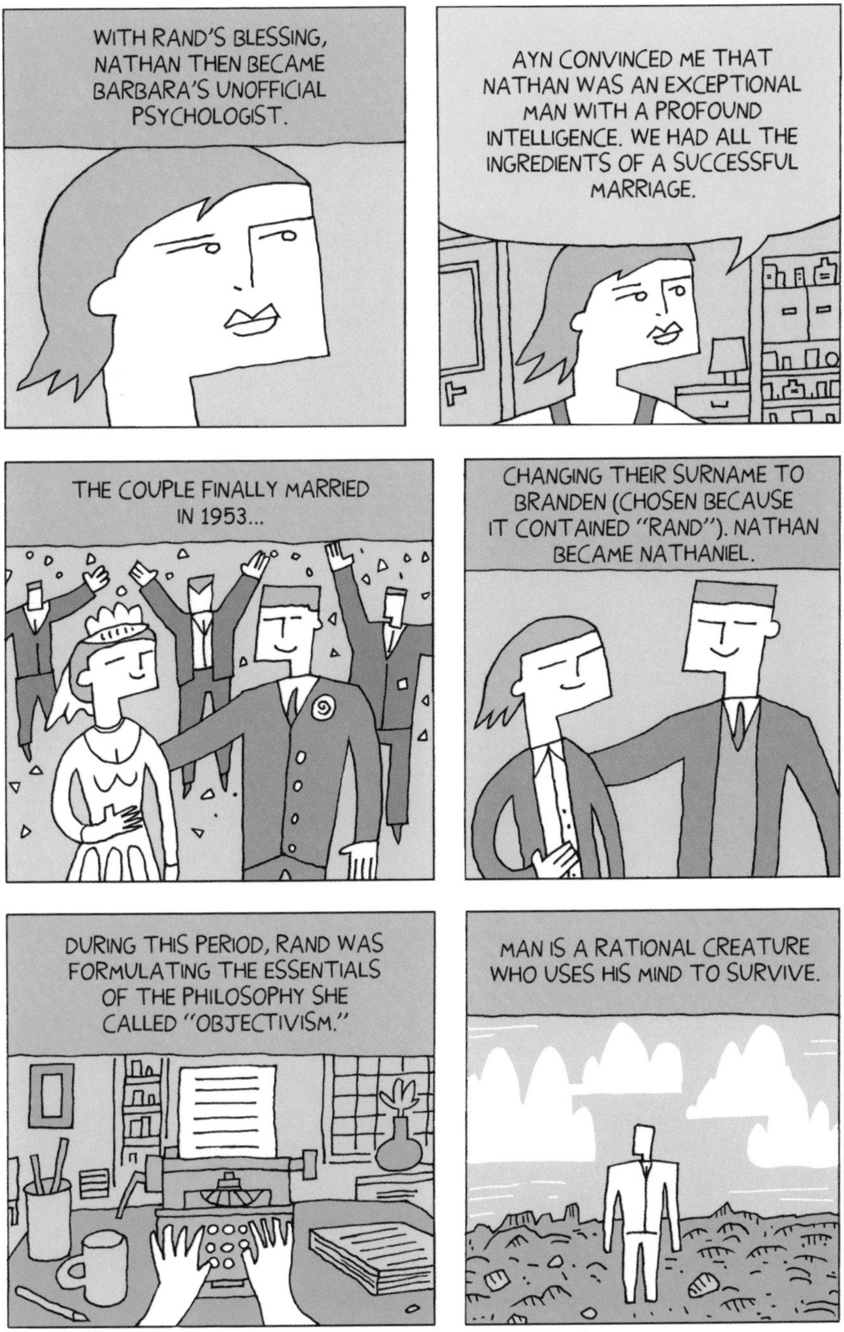
WITH RAND'S BLESSING, NATHAN THEN BECAME BARBARA'S UNOFFICIAL PSYCHOLOGIST.
AYN CONVINCED ME THAT NATHAN WAS AN EXCEPTIONAL MAN WITH A PROFOUND INTELLIGENCE. WE HAD ALL THE INGREDIENTS OF A SUCCESSFUL MARRIAGE.
THE COUPLE FINALLY MARRIED IN 1953...
CHANGING THEIR SURNAME TO BRANDEN (CHOSEN BECAUSE IT CONTAINED "RAND"). NATHAN BECAME NATHANIEL.
DURING THIS PERIOD, RAND WAS FORMULATING THE ESSENTIALS OF THE PHILOSOPHY SHE CALLED "OBJECTIVISM."
MAN IS A RATIONAL CREATURE WHO USES HIS MIND TO SURVIVE.

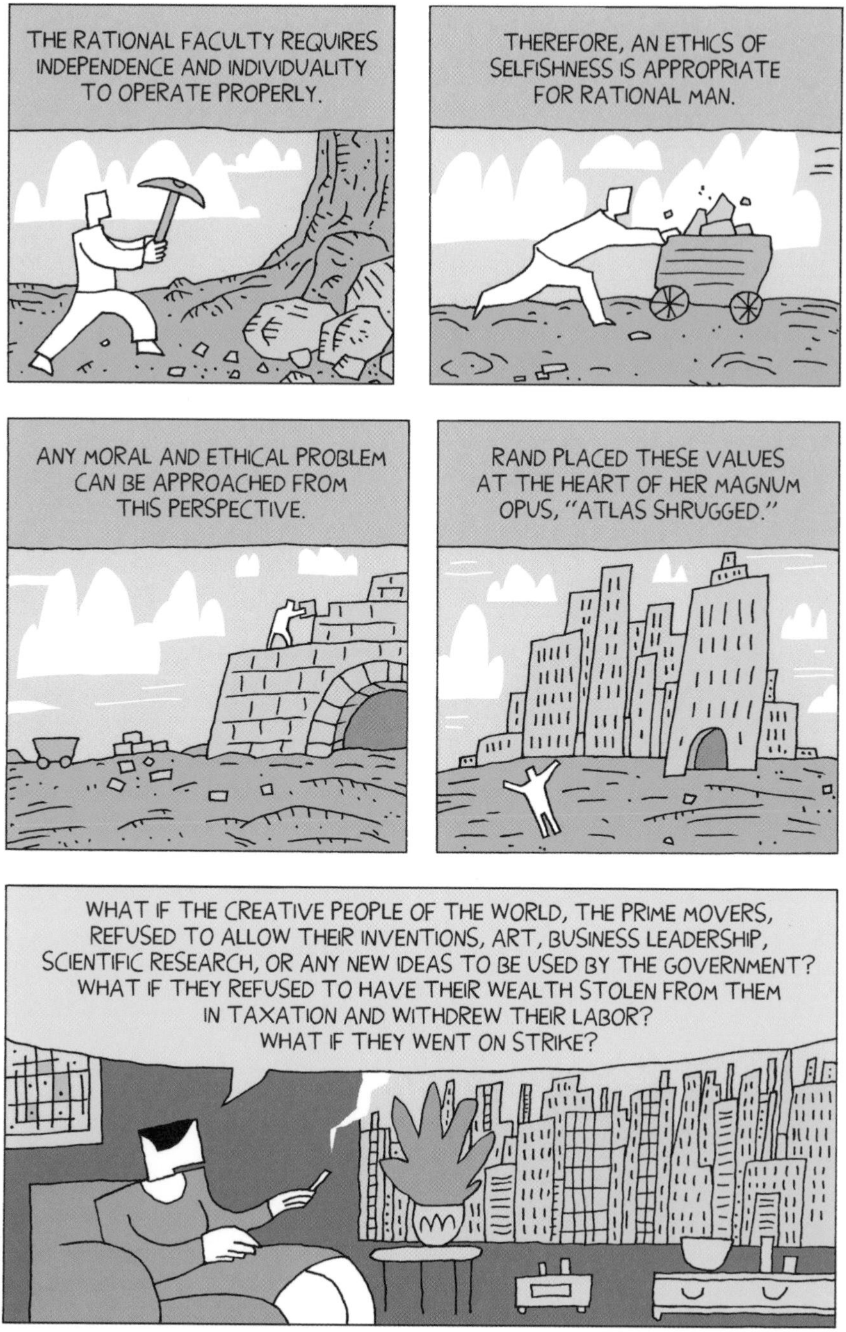
THE RATIONAL FACULTY REQUIRES INDEPENDENCE AND INDIVIDUALITY TO OPERATE PROPERLY.
THEREFORE, AN ETHICS OF SELFISHNESS IS APPROPRIATE FOR RATIONAL MAN.
ANY MORAL AND ETHICAL PROBLEM CAN BE APPROACHED FROM THIS PERSPECTIVE.
RAND PLACED THESE VALUES AT THE HEART OF HER MAGNUM OPUS, "ATLAS SHRUGGED."
WHAT IF THE CREATIVE PEOPLE OF THE WORLD, THE PRIME MOVERS, REFUSED TO ALLOW THEIR INVENTIONS, ART, BUSINESS LEADERSHIP, SCIENTIFIC RESEARCH, OR ANY NEW IDEAS TO BE USED BY THE GOVERNMENT? WHAT IF THEY REFUSED TO HAVE THEIR WEALTH STOLEN FROM THEM IN TAXATION AND WITHDREW THEIR LABOR? WHAT IF THEY WENT ON STRIKE?

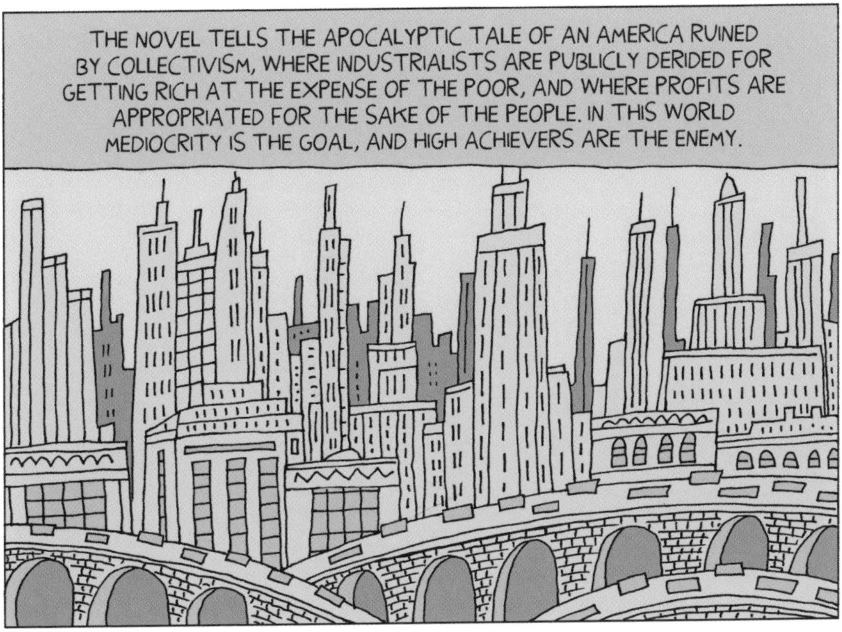
THE NOVEL TELLS THE APOCALYPTIC TALE OF AN AMERICA RUINED BY COLLECTIVISM, WHERE INDUSTRIALISTS ARE PUBLICLY DERIDED FOR GETTING RICH AT THE EXPENSE OF THE POOR, AND WHERE PROFITS ARE APPROPRIATED FOR THE SAKE OF THE PEOPLE. IN THIS WORLD MEDIOCRITY IS THE GOAL, AND HIGH ACHIEVERS ARE THE ENEMY.

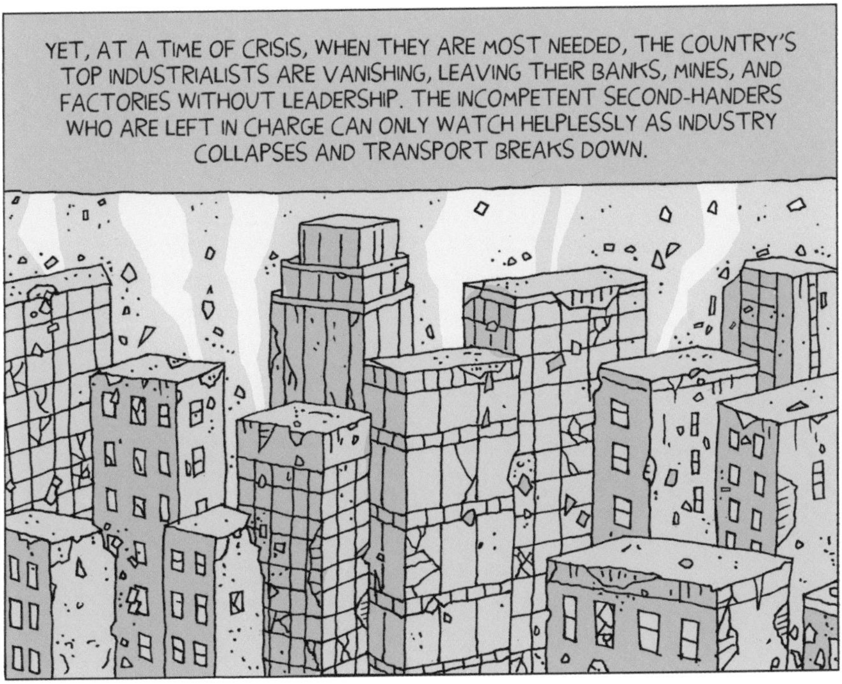
YET, AT A TIME OF CRISIS, WHEN THEY ARE MOST NEEDED, THE COUNTRY'S TOP INDUSTRIALISTS ARE VANISHING, LEAVING THEIR BANKS, MINES, AND FACTORIES WITHOUT LEADERSHIP. THE INCOMPETENT SECOND-HANDERS WHO ARE LEFT IN CHARGE CAN ONLY WATCH HELPLESSLY AS INDUSTRY COLLAPSES AND TRANSPORT BREAKS DOWN.

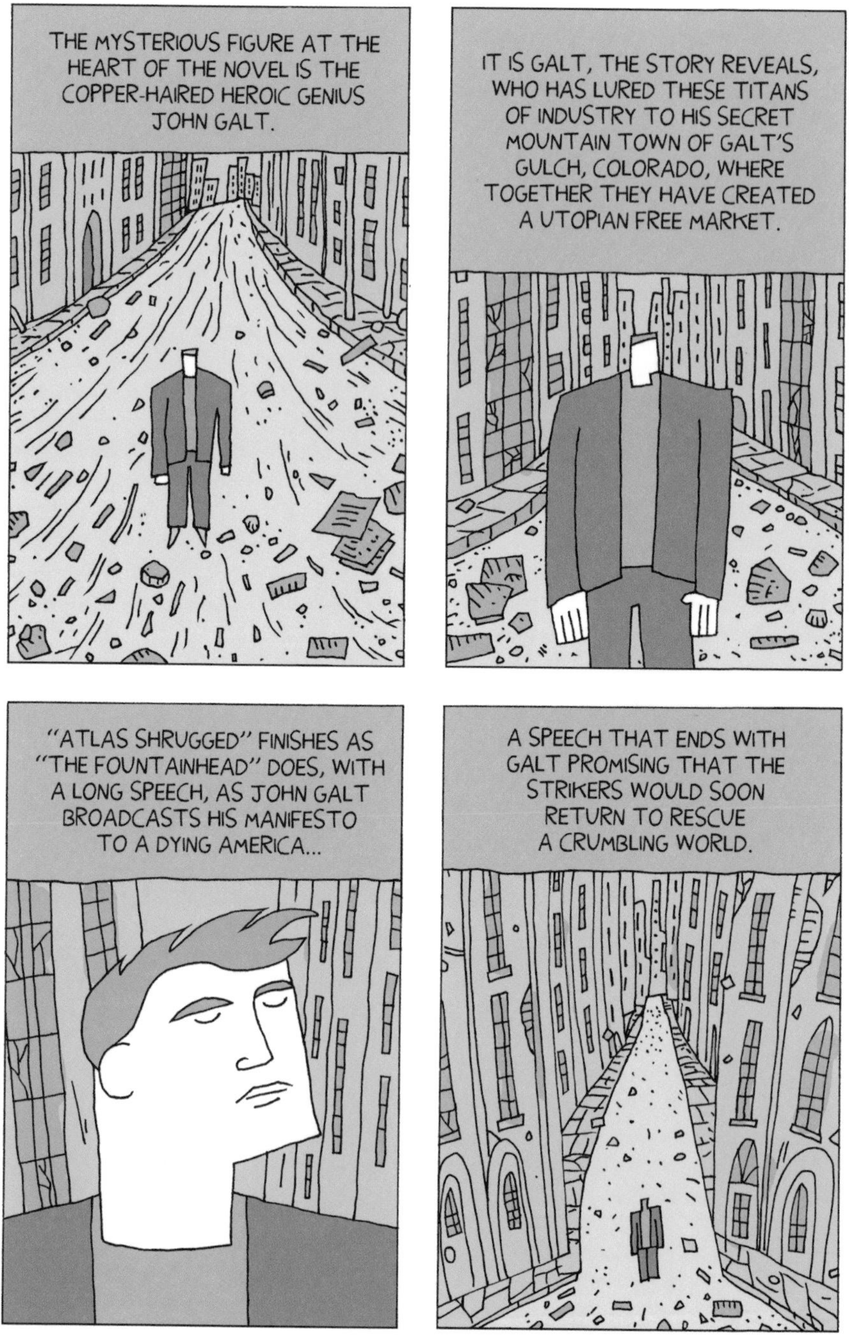
THE MYSTERIOUS FIGURE AT THE HEART OF THE NOVEL IS THE COPPER-HAIRED HEROIC GENIUS JOHN GALT.
IT IS GALT, THE STORY REVEALS, WHO HAS LURED THESE TITANS OF INDUSTRY TO HIS SECRET MOUNTAIN TOWN OF GALT'S GULCH, COLORADO, WHERE TOGETHER THEY HAVE CREATED A UTOPIAN FREE MARKET.
"ATLAS SHRUGGED" FINISHES AS "THE FOUNTAINHEAD" DOES, WITH A LONG SPEECH, AS JOHN GALT BROADCASTS HIS MANIFESTO TO A DYING AMERICA...
A SPEECH THAT ENDS WITH GALT PROMISING THAT THE STRIKERS WOULD SOON RETURN TO RESCUE A CRUMBLING WORLD.

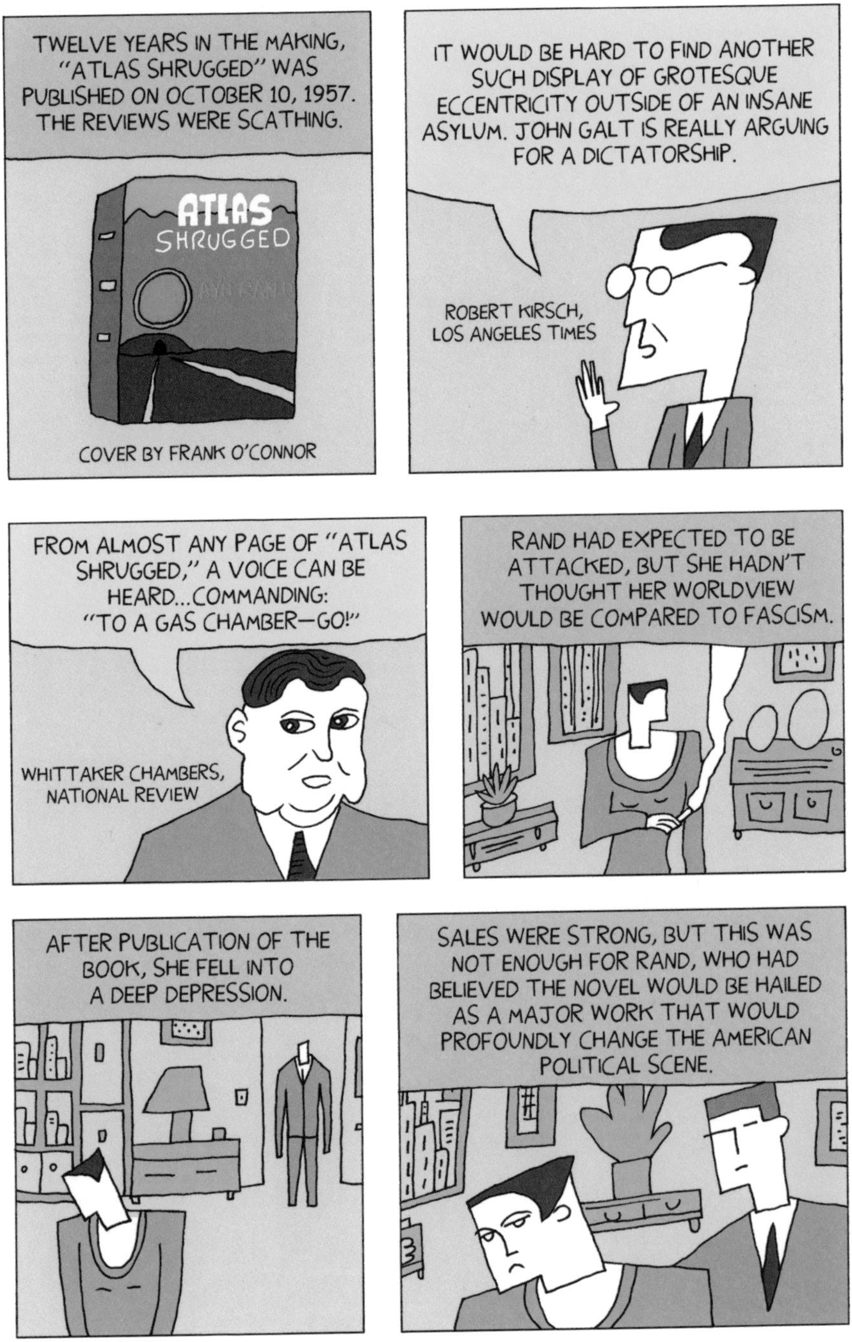
TWELVE YEARS IN THE MAKING, "ATLAS SHRUGGED" WAS PUBLISHED ON OCTOBER 10, 1957. THE REVIEWS WERE SCATHING.
ATLAS
SHRUGGED
COVER BY FRANK O'CONNOR
IT WOULD BE HARD TO FIND ANOTHER SUCH DISPLAY OF GROTESQUE ECCENTRICITY OUTSIDE OF AN INSANE ASYLUM. JOHN GALT IS REALLY ARGUING FOR A DICTATORSHIP.
ROBERT KIRSCH, LOS ANGELES TIMES
FROM ALMOST ANY PAGE OF "ATLAS SHRUGGED," A VOICE CAN BE HEARD...COMMANDING: "TO A GAS CHAMBER—GO!"
WHITTAKER CHAMBERS, NATIONAL REVIEW
RAND HAD EXPECTED TO BE ATTACKED, BUT SHE HADN'T THOUGHT HER WORLDVIEW WOULD BE COMPARED TO FASCISM.
AFTER PUBLICATION OF THE BOOK, SHE FELL INTO A DEEP DEPRESSION.
SALES WERE STRONG, BUT THIS WAS NOT ENOUGH FOR RAND, WHO HAD BELIEVED THE NOVEL WOULD BE HAILED AS A MAJOR WORK THAT WOULD PROFOUNDLY CHANGE THE AMERICAN POLITICAL SCENE.

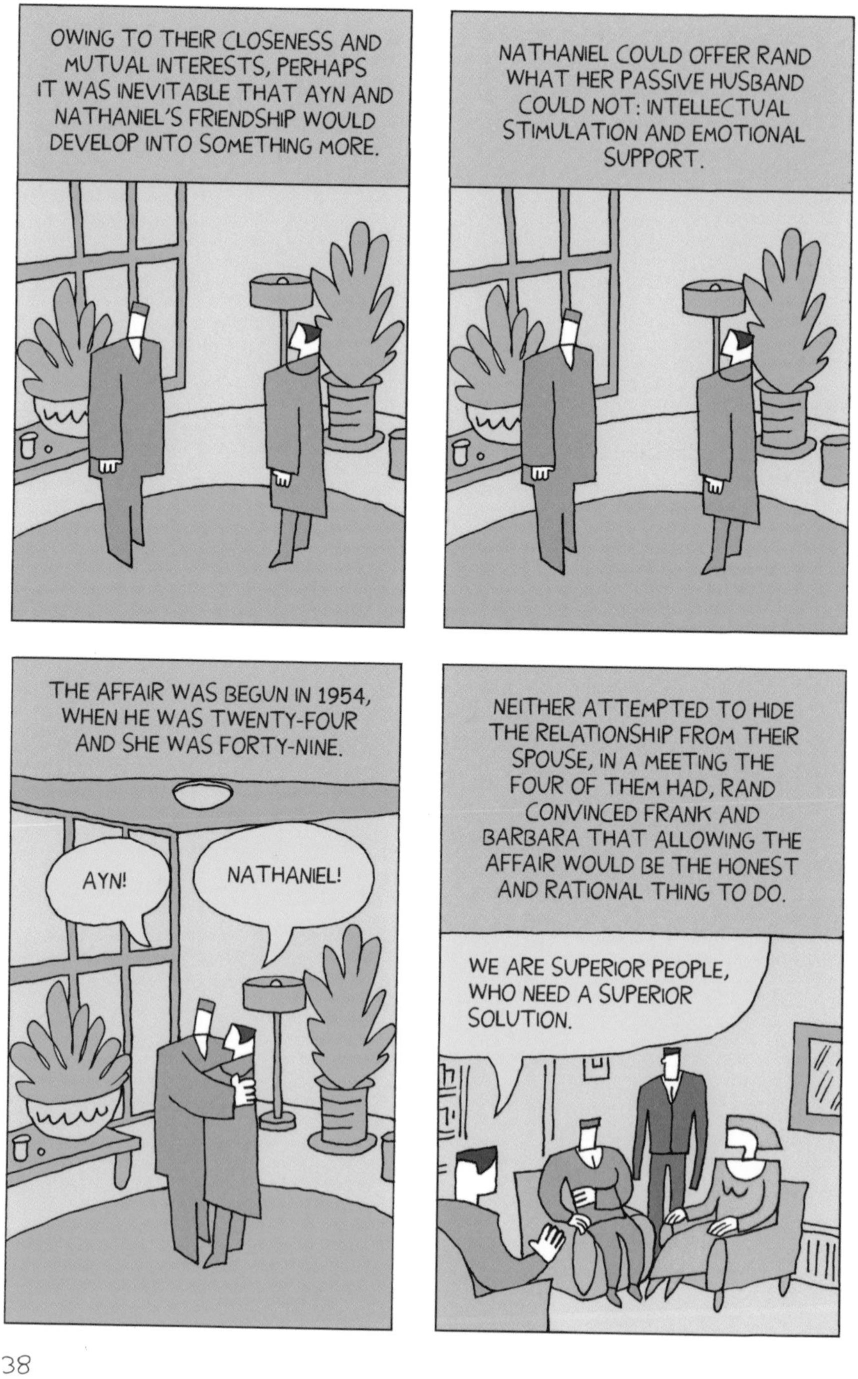
OWING TO THEIR CLOSENESS AND MUTUAL INTERESTS, PERHAPS IT WAS INEVITABLE THAT AYN AND NATHANIEL'S FRIENDSHIP WOULD DEVELOP INTO SOMETHING MORE.
NATHANIEL COULD OFFER RAND WHAT HER PASSIVE HUSBAND COULD NOT: INTELLECTUAL STIMULATION AND EMOTIONAL SUPPORT.
THE AFFAIR WAS BEGUN IN 1954, WHEN HE WAS TWENTY-FOUR AND SHE WAS FORTY-NINE.
AYN!
NATHANIEL!
NEITHER ATTEMPTED TO HIDE THE RELATIONSHIP FROM THEIR SPOUSE, IN A MEETING THE FOUR OF THEM HAD, RAND CONVINCED FRANK AND BARBARA THAT ALLOWING THE AFFAIR WOULD BE THE HONEST AND RATIONAL THING TO DO.
WE ARE SUPERIOR PEOPLE, WHO NEED A SUPERIOR SOLUTION.

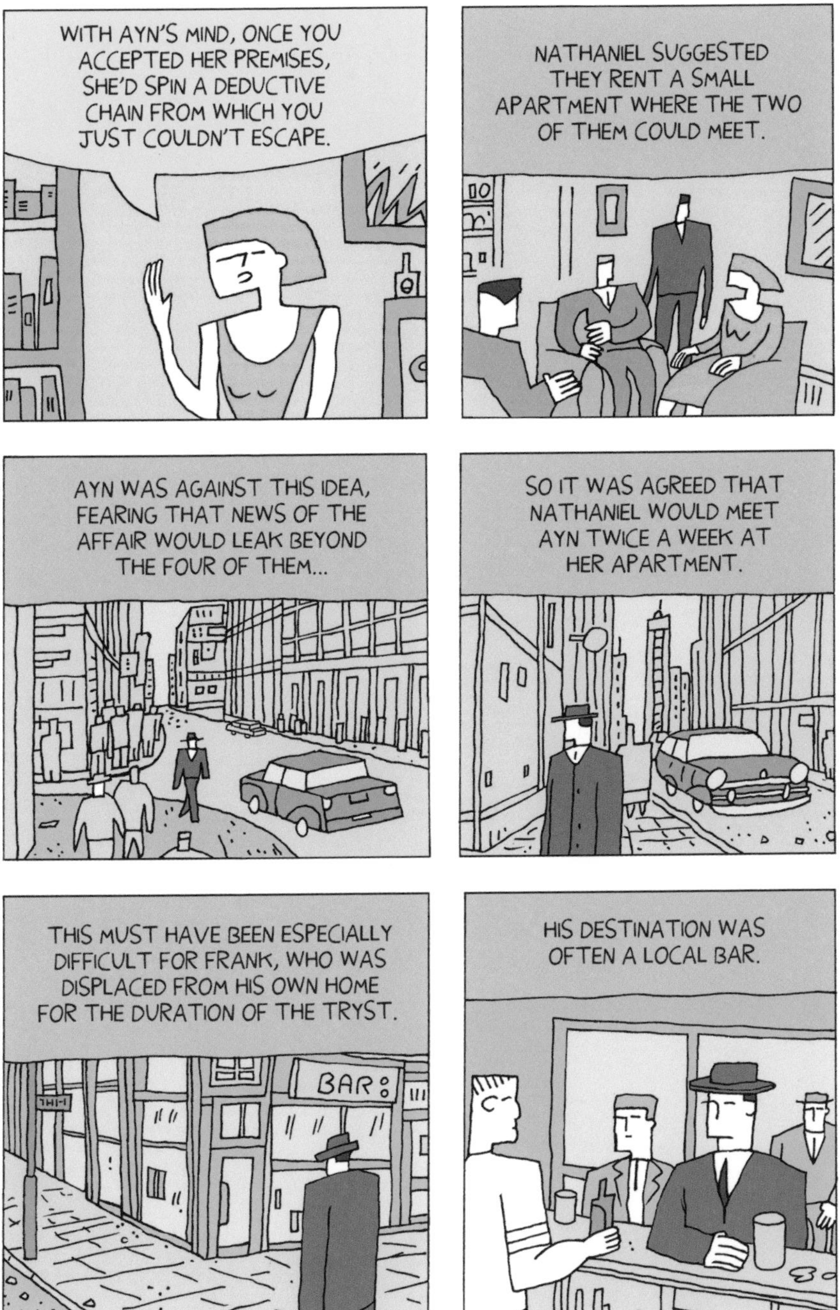
WITH AYN'S MIND, ONCE YOU ACCEPTED HER PREMISES, SHE'D SPIN A DEDUCTIVE CHAIN FROM WHICH YOU JUST COULDN'T ESCAPE.
NATHANIEL SUGGESTED THEY RENT A SMALL APARTMENT WHERE THE TWO OF THEM COULD MEET.
AYN WAS AGAINST THIS IDEA, FEARING THAT NEWS OF THE AFFAIR WOULD LEAK BEYOND THE FOUR OF THEM...
SO IT WAS AGREED THAT NATHANIEL WOULD MEET AYN TWICE A WEEK AT HER APARTMENT.
THIS MUST HAVE BEEN ESPECIALLY DIFFICULT FOR FRANK, WHO WAS DISPLACED FROM HIS OWN HOME FOR THE DURATION OF THE TRYST.
BAR
HIS DESTINATION WAS OFTEN A LOCAL BAR.

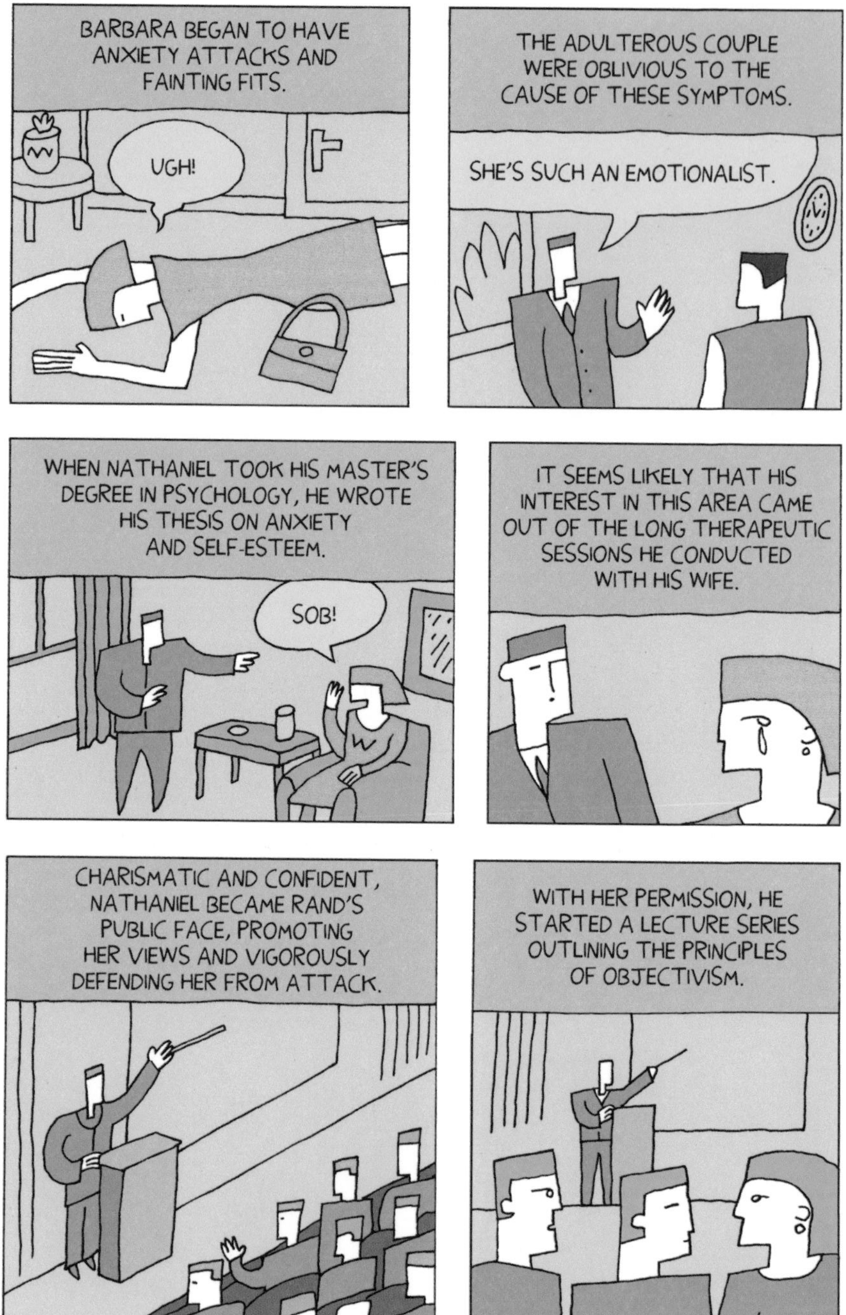
BARBARA BEGAN TO HAVE ANXIETY ATTACKS AND FAINTING FITS.
UGH!
THE ADULTEROUS COUPLE WERE OBLIVIOUS TO THE CAUSE OF THESE SYMPTOMS.
SHE'S SUCH AN EMOTIONALIST.
WHEN NATHANIEL TOOK HIS MASTER'S DEGREE IN PSYCHOLOGY, HE WROTE HIS THESIS ON ANXIETY AND SELF-ESTEEM.
SOB!
IT SEEMS LIKELY THAT HIS INTEREST IN THIS AREA CAME OUT OF THE LONG THERAPEUTIC SESSIONS HE CONDUCTED WITH HIS WIFE.
CHARISMATIC AND CONFIDENT, NATHANIEL BECAME RAND'S PUBLIC FACE, PROMOTING HER VIEWS AND VIGOROUSLY DEFENDING HER FROM ATTACK.
WITH HER PERMISSION, HE STARTED A LECTURE SERIES OUTLINING THE PRINCIPLES OF OBJECTIVISM.

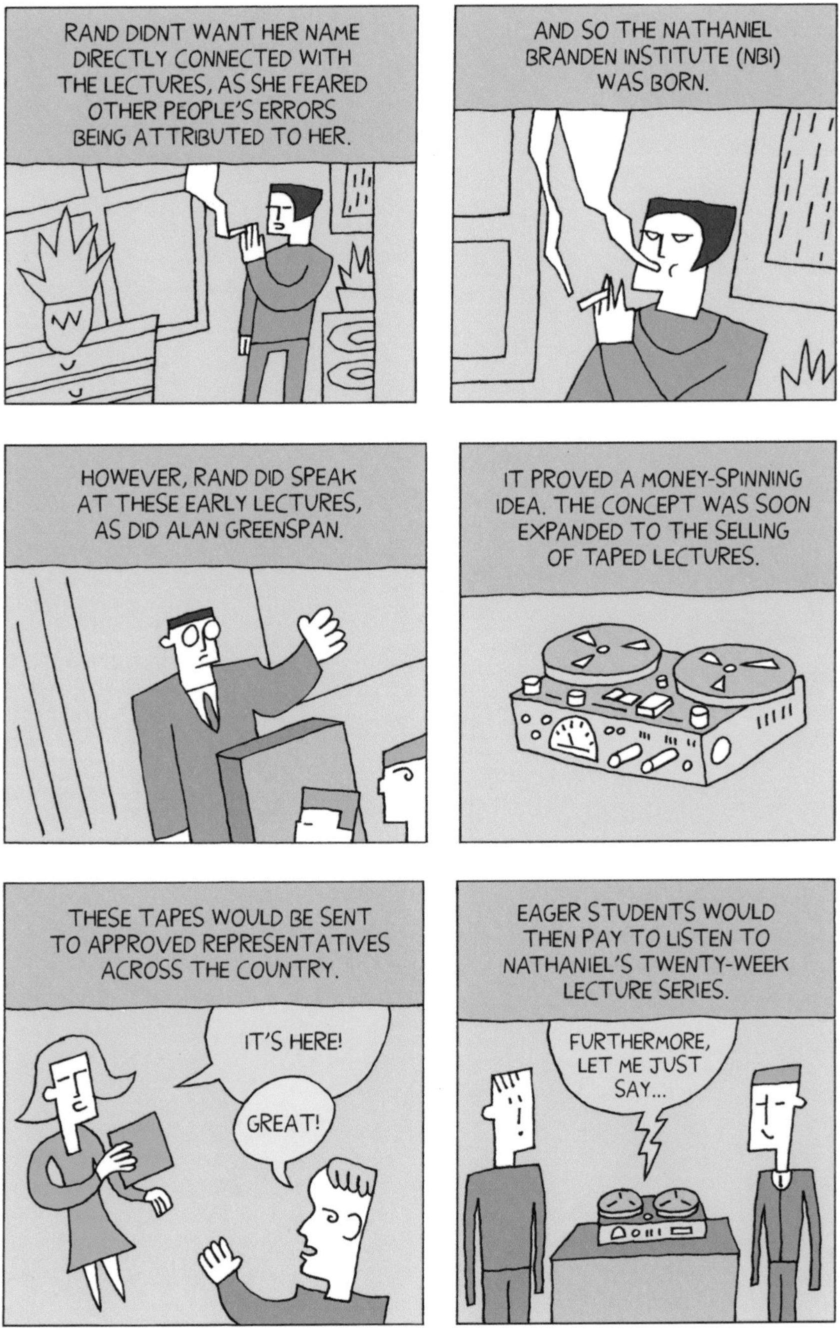
RAND DIDN'T WANT HER NAME DIRECTLY CONNECTED WITH THE LECTURES, AS SHE FEARED OTHER PEOPLE'S ERRORS BEING ATTRIBUTED TO HER.
AND SO THE NATHANIEL BRANDEN INSTITUTE (NBI) WAS BORN.
HOWEVER, RAND DID SPEAK AT THESE EARLY LECTURES, AS DID ALAN GREENSPAN.
IT PROVED A MONEY-SPINNING IDEA. THE CONCEPT WAS SOON EXPANDED TO THE SELLING OF TAPED LECTURES.
THESE TAPES WOULD BE SENT TO APPROVED REPRESENTATIVES ACROSS THE COUNTRY.
IT'S HERE!
GREAT!
EAGER STUDENTS WOULD THEN PAY TO LISTEN TO NATHANIEL'S TWENTY-WEEK LECTURE SERIES.
FURTHERMORE, LET ME JUST SAY...

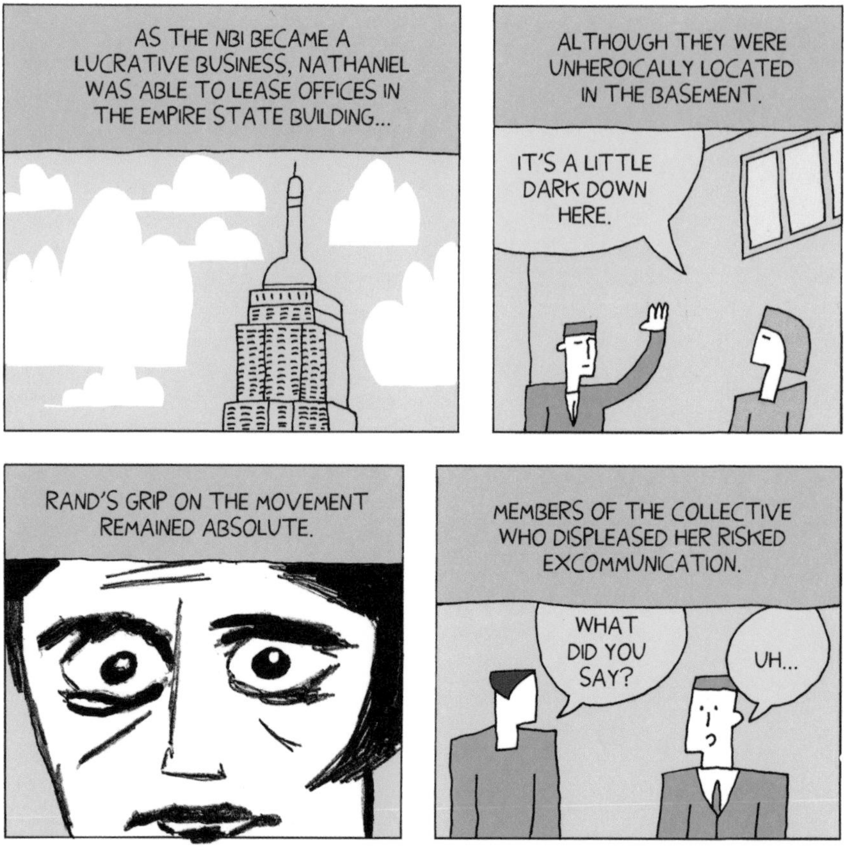
AS THE NBI BECAME A LUCRATIVE BUSINESS, NATHANIEL WAS ABLE TO LEASE OFFICES IN THE EMPIRE STATE BUILDING...
ALTHOUGH THEY WERE UNHEROICALLY LOCATED IN THE BASEMENT.
IT'S A LITTLE DARK DOWN HERE.
RAND'S GRIP ON THE MOVEMENT REMAINED ABSOLUTE.
MEMBERS OF THE COLLECTIVE WHO DISPLEASED HER RISKED EXCOMMUNICATION.
WHAT DID YOU SAY?
UH...
PERCEIVED DEVIATION FROM THE OBJECTIVIST LINE WOULD ENGENDER EXCRUCIATING PERSONAL INTERROGATION AT ONE OF RAND'S APARTMENT GATHERINGS, EVENTS THAT WERE BASICALLY TRIALS.

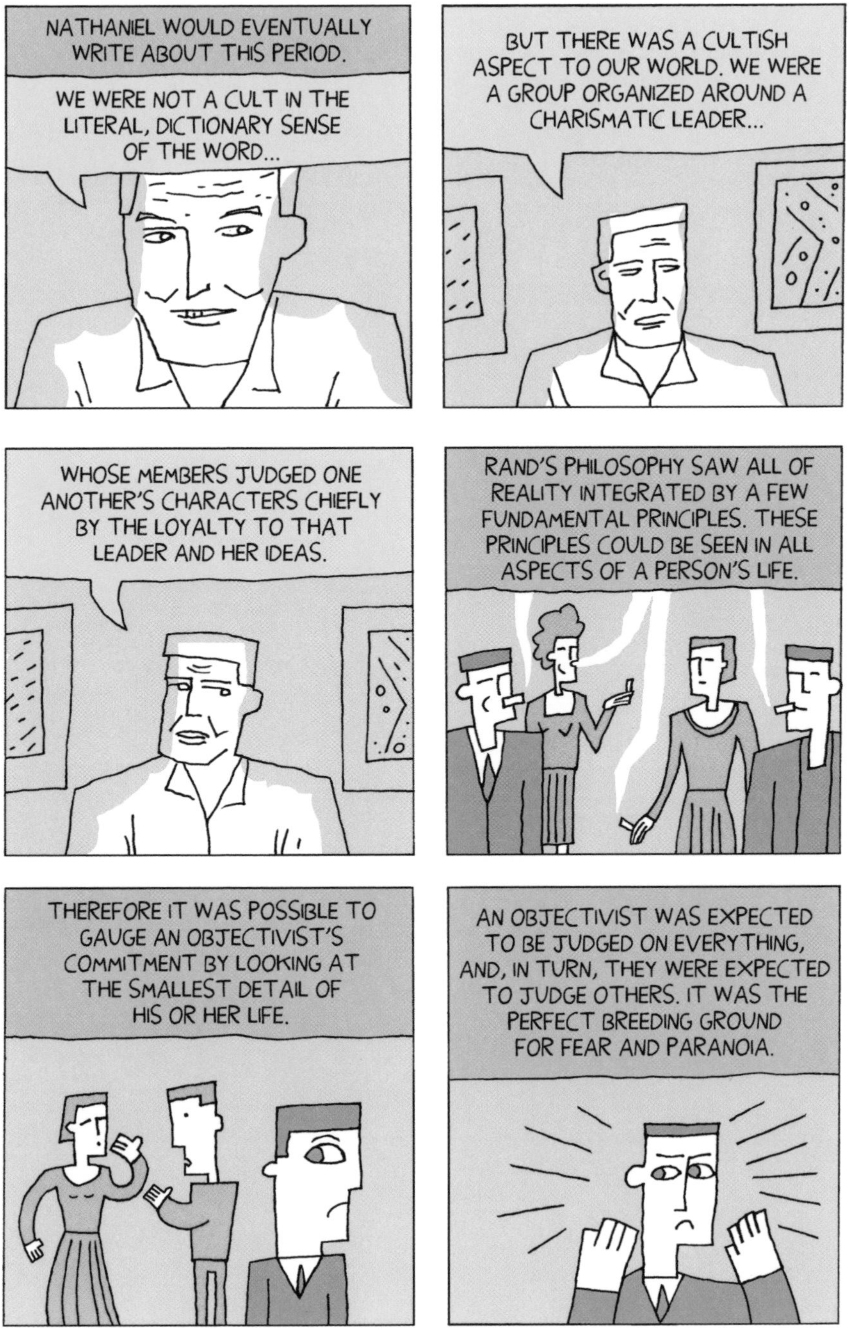
NATHANIEL WOULD EVENTUALLY WRITE ABOUT THIS PERIOD.
WE WERE NOT A CULT IN THE LITERAL, DICTIONARY SENSE OF THE WORD...
BUT THERE WAS A CULTISH ASPECT TO OUR WORLD. WE WERE A GROUP ORGANIZED AROUND A CHARISMATIC LEADER...
WHOSE MEMBERS JUDGED ONE ANOTHER'S CHARACTERS CHIEFLY BY THE LOYALTY TO THAT LEADER AND HER IDEAS.
RAND'S PHILOSOPHY SAW ALL OF REALITY INTEGRATED BY A FEW FUNDAMENTAL PRINCIPLES. THESE PRINCIPLES COULD BE SEEN IN ALL ASPECTS OF A PERSON'S LIFE.
THEREFORE IT WAS POSSIBLE TO GAUGE AN OBJECTIVIST'S COMMITMENT BY LOOKING AT THE SMALLEST DETAIL OF HIS OR HER LIFE.
AN OBJECTIVIST WAS EXPECTED TO BE JUDGED ON EVERYTHING, AND, IN TURN, THEY WERE EXPECTED TO JUDGE OTHERS. IT WAS THE PERFECT BREEDING GROUND FOR FEAR AND PARANOIA.

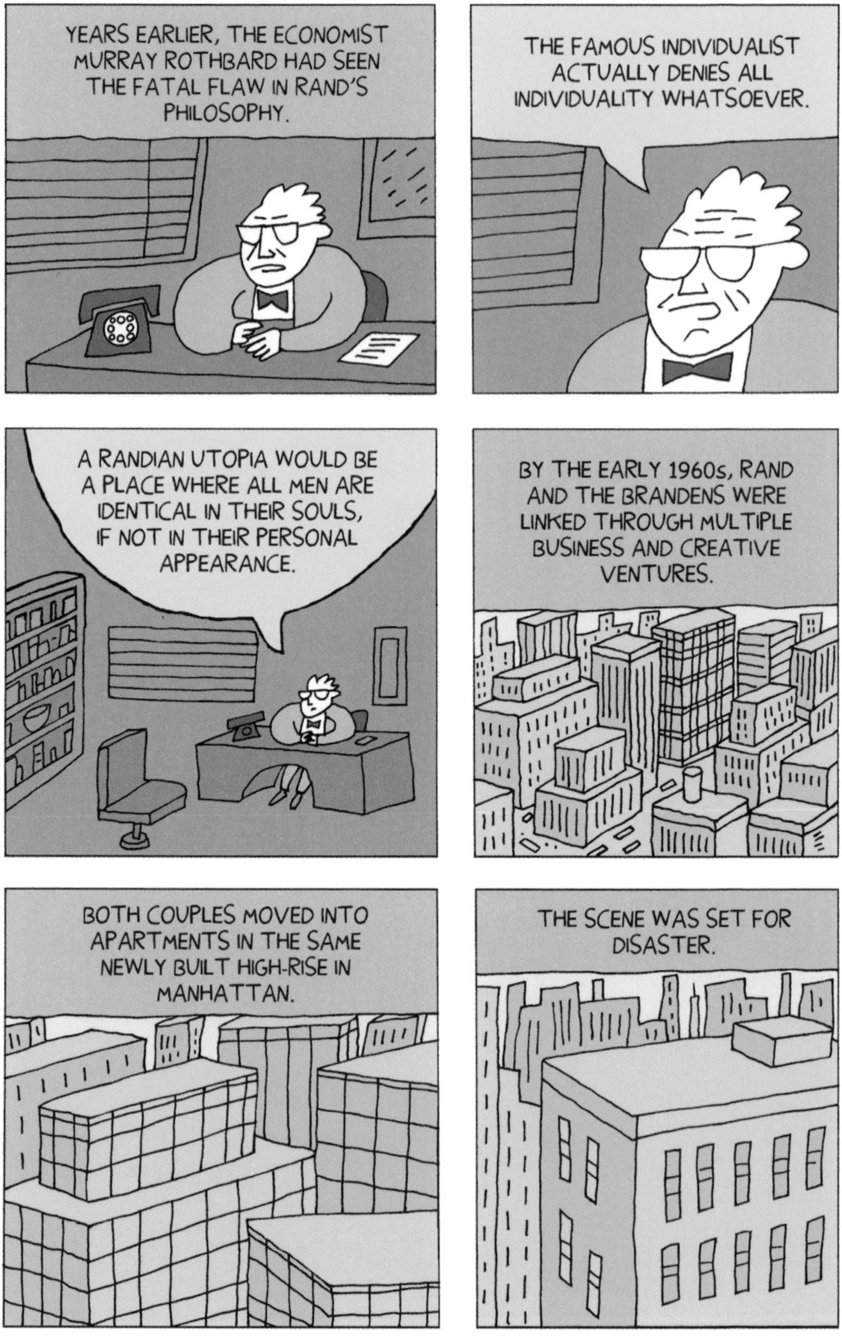
YEARS EARLIER, THE ECONOMIST MURRAY ROTHBARD HAD SEEN THE FATAL FLAW IN RAND'S PHILOSOPHY.
THE FAMOUS INDIVIDUALIST ACTUALLY DENIES ALL INDIVIDUALITY WHATSOEVER.
A RANDIAN UTOPIA WOULD BE A PLACE WHERE ALL MEN ARE IDENTICAL IN THEIR SOULS, IF NOT IN THEIR PERSONAL APPEARANCE.
BY THE EARLY 1960s, RAND AND THE BRANDENS WERE LINKED THROUGH MULTIPLE BUSINESS AND CREATIVE VENTURES.
BOTH COUPLES MOVED INTO APARTMENTS IN THE SAME NEWLY BUILT HIGH-RISE IN MANHATTAN.
THE SCENE WAS SET FOR DISASTER.

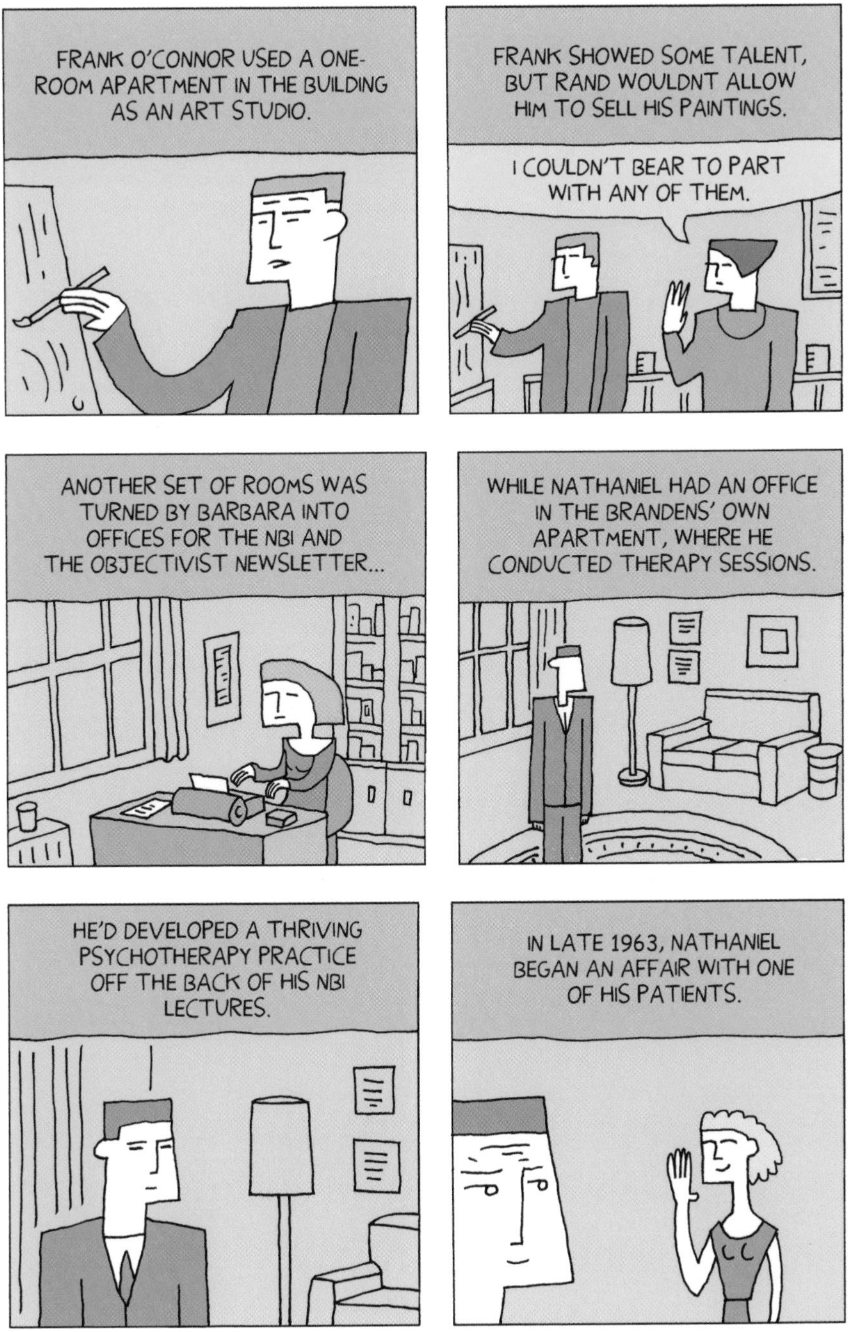
FRANK O'CONNOR USED A ONE-ROOM APARTMENT IN THE BUILDING AS AN ART STUDIO.
FRANK SHOWED SOME TALENT, BUT RAND WOULDNT ALLOW HIM TO SELL HIS PAINTINGS.
I COULDN'T BEAR TO PART WITH ANY OF THEM.
ANOTHER SET OF ROOMS WAS TURNED BY BARBARA INTO OFFICES FOR THE NBI AND THE OBJECTIVIST NEWSLETTER...
WHILE NATHANIEL HAD AN OFFICE IN THE BRANDENS' OWN APARTMENT, WHERE HE CONDUCTED THERAPY SESSIONS.
HE'D DEVELOPED A THRIVING PSYCHOTHERAPY PRACTICE OFF THE BACK OF HIS NBI LECTURES.
IN LATE 1963, NATHANIEL BEGAN AN AFFAIR WITH ONE OF HIS PATIENTS.

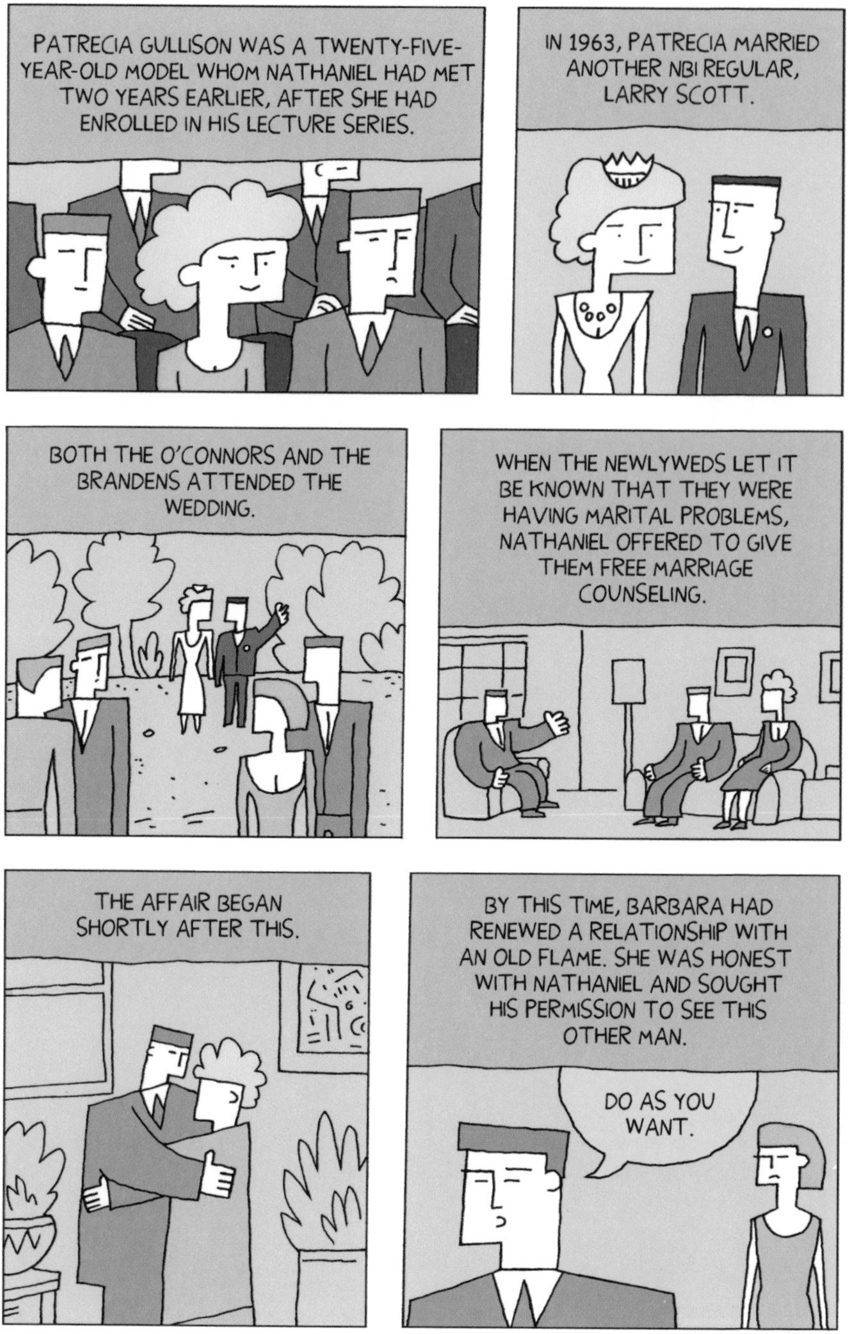
PATRECIA GULLISON WAS A TWENTY-FIVE-YEAR-OLD MODEL WHOM NATHANIEL HAD MET TWO YEARS EARLIER, AFTER SHE HAD ENROLLED IN HIS LECTURE SERIES.
IN 1963, PATRECIA MARRIED ANOTHER NBI REGULAR, LARRY SCOTT.
BOTH THE O'CONNORS AND THE BRANDENS ATTENDED THE WEDDING.
WHEN THE NEWLYWEDS LET IT BE KNOWN THAT THEY WERE HAVING MARITAL PROBLEMS, NATHANIEL OFFERED TO GIVE THEM FREE MARRIAGE COUNSELING.
THE AFFAIR BEGAN SHORTLY AFTER THIS.
BY THIS TIME, BARBARA HAD RENEWED A RELATIONSHIP WITH AN OLD FLAME. SHE WAS HONEST WITH NATHANIEL AND SOUGHT HIS PERMISSION TO SEE THIS OTHER MAN.
DO AS YOU WANT.

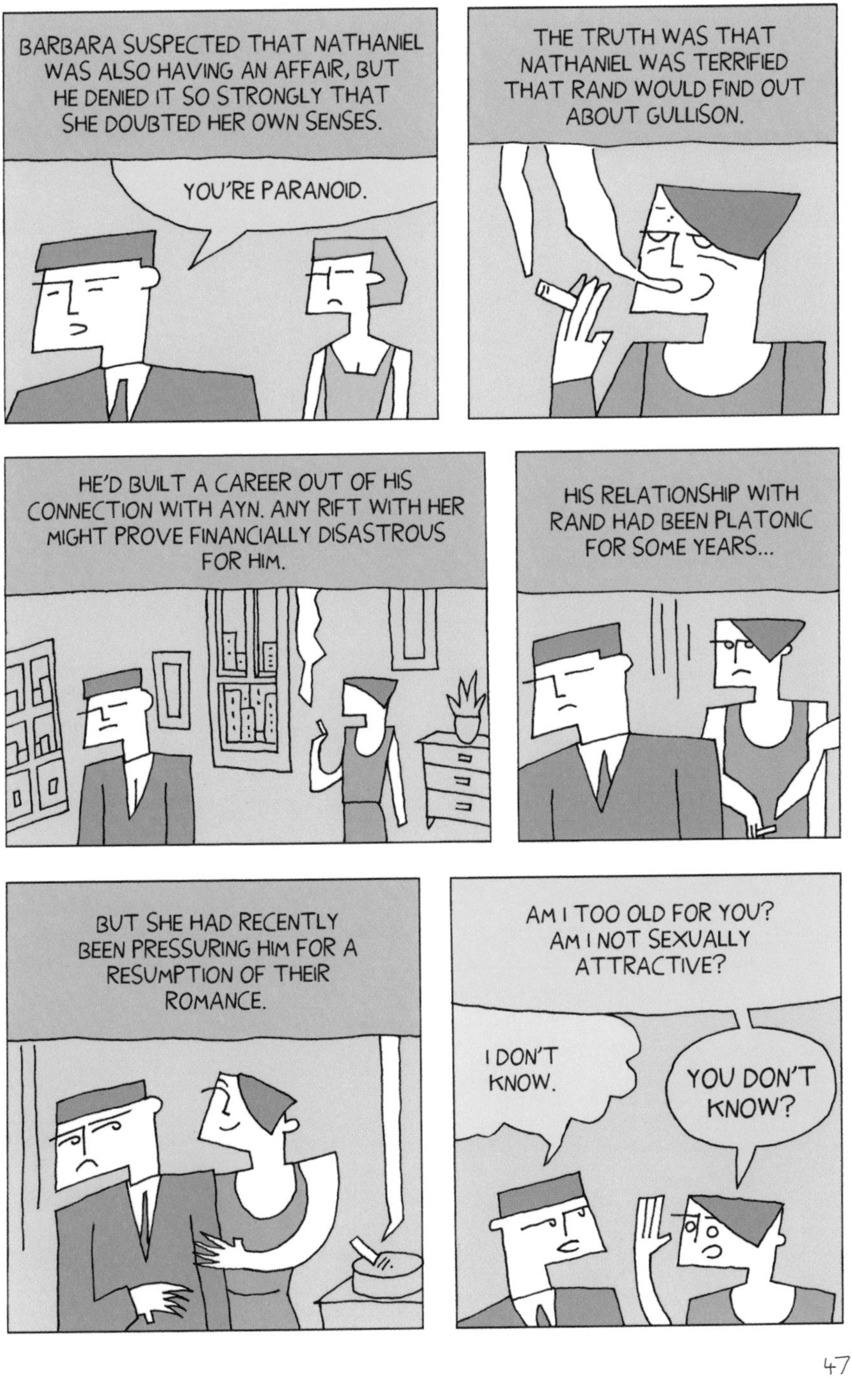
BARBARA SUSPECTED THAT NATHANIEL WAS ALSO HAVING AN AFFAIR, BUT HE DENIED IT SO STRONGLY THAT SHE DOUBTED HER OWN SENSES.
YOU'RE PARANOID.
THE TRUTH WAS THAT NATHANIEL WAS TERRIFIED THAT RAND WOULD FIND OUT ABOUT GULLISON.
HE'D BUILT A CAREER OUT OF HIS CONNECTION WITH AYN. ANY RIFT WITH HER MIGHT PROVE FINANCIALLY DISASTROUS FOR HIM.
HIS RELATIONSHIP WITH RAND HAD BEEN PLATONIC FOR SOME YEARS...
BUT SHE HAD RECENTLY BEEN PRESSURING HIM FOR A RESUMPTION OF THEIR ROMANCE.
AM I TOO OLD FOR YOU? AM I NOT SEXUALLY ATTRACTIVE?
I DON'T KNOW.
YOU DON'T KNOW?

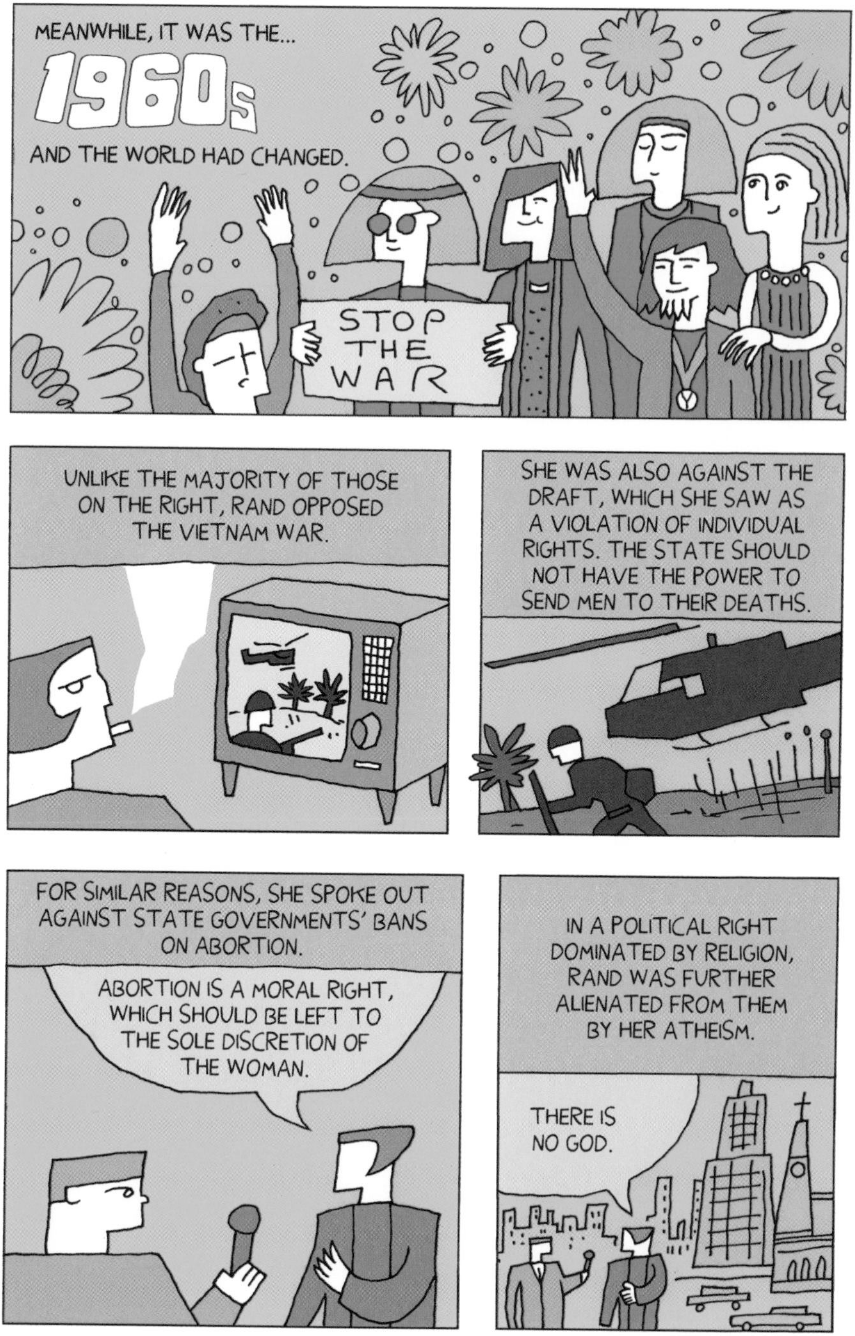
MEANWHILE, IT WAS THE...
1960s
AND THE WORLD HAD CHANGED.
STOP THE WAR
UNLIKE THE MAJORITY OF THOSE ON THE RIGHT, RAND OPPOSED THE VIETNAM WAR.
SHE WAS ALSO AGAINST THE DRAFT, WHICH SHE SAW AS A VIOLATION OF INDIVIDUAL RIGHTS. THE STATE SHOULD NOT HAVE THE POWER TO SEND MEN TO THEIR DEATHS.
FOR SIMILAR REASONS, SHE SPOKE OUT AGAINST STATE GOVERNMENTS' BANS ON ABORTION.
ABORTION IS A MORAL RIGHT, WHICH SHOULD BE LEFT TO THE SOLE DISCRETION OF THE WOMAN.
IN A POLITICAL RIGHT DOMINATED BY RELIGION, RAND WAS FURTHER ALIENATED FROM THEM BY HER ATHEISM.
THERE IS NO GOD.

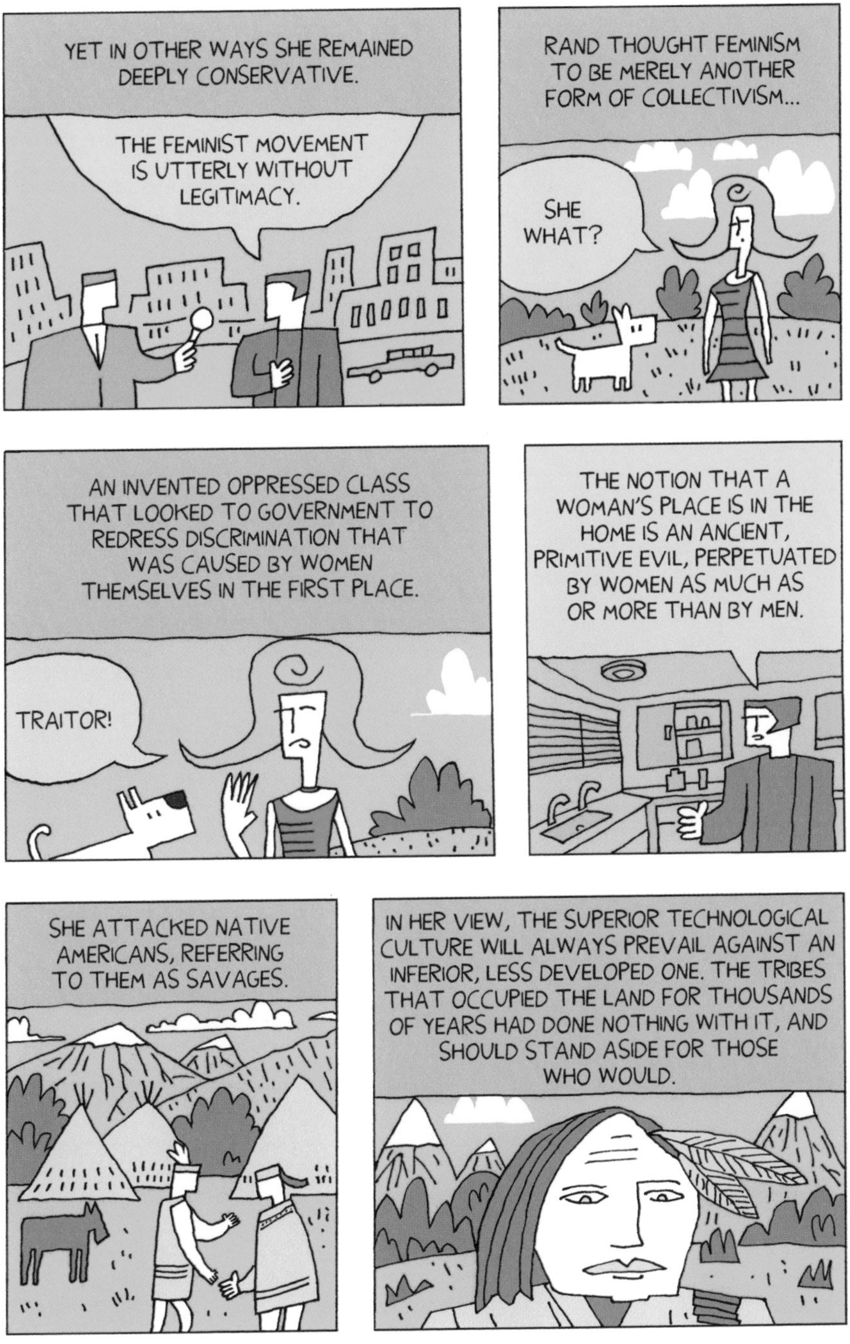
YET IN OTHER WAYS SHE REMAINED DEEPLY CONSERVATIVE.
THE FEMINIST MOVEMENT IS UTTERLY WITHOUT LEGITIMACY.
RAND THOUGHT FEMINISM TO BE MERELY ANOTHER FORM OF COLLECTIVISM...
SHE WHAT?
AN INVENTED OPPRESSED CLASS THAT LOOKED TO GOVERNMENT TO REDRESS DISCRIMINATION THAT WAS CAUSED BY WOMEN THEMSELVES IN THE FIRST PLACE.
TRAITOR!
THE NOTION THAT A WOMAN'S PLACE IS IN THE HOME IS AN ANCIENT, PRIMITIVE EVIL, PERPETUATED BY WOMEN AS MUCH AS OR MORE THAN BY MEN.
SHE ATTACKED NATIVE AMERICANS, REFERRING TO THEM AS SAVAGES.
IN HER VIEW, THE SUPERIOR TECHNOLOGICAL CULTURE WILL ALWAYS PREVAIL AGAINST AN INFERIOR, LESS DEVELOPED ONE. THE TRIBES THAT OCCUPIED THE LAND FOR THOUSANDS OF YEARS HAD DONE NOTHING WITH IT, AND SHOULD STAND ASIDE FOR THOSE WHO WOULD.

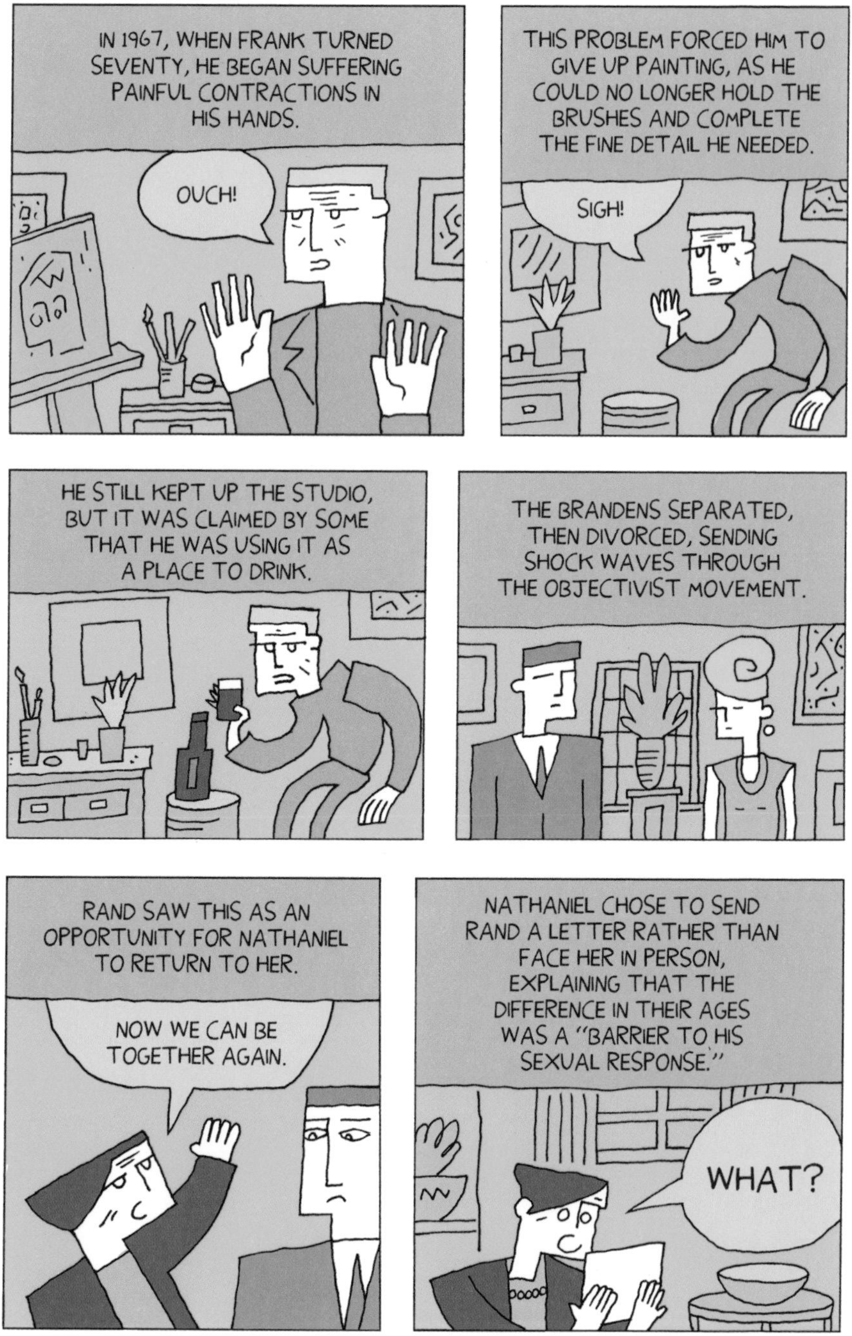
IN 1967, WHEN FRANK TURNED SEVENTY, HE BEGAN SUFFERING PAINFUL CONTRACTIONS IN HIS HANDS.
OUCH!
THIS PROBLEM FORCED HIM TO GIVE UP PAINTING, AS HE COULD NO LONGER HOLD THE BRUSHES AND COMPLETE THE FINE DETAIL HE NEEDED.
SIGH!
HE STILL KEPT UP THE STUDIO, BUT IT WAS CLAIMED BY SOME THAT HE WAS USING IT AS A PLACE TO DRINK.
THE BRANDENS SEPARATED, THEN DIVORCED, SENDING SHOCK WAVES THROUGH THE OBJECTIVIST MOVEMENT.
RAND SAW THIS AS AN OPPORTUNITY FOR NATHANIEL TO RETURN TO HER.
NOW WE CAN BE TOGETHER AGAIN.
NATHANIEL CHOSE TO SEND RAND A LETTER RATHER THAN FACE HER IN PERSON, EXPLAINING THAT THE DIFFERENCE IN THEIR AGES WAS A "BARRIER TO HIS SEXUAL RESPONSE."
WHAT?

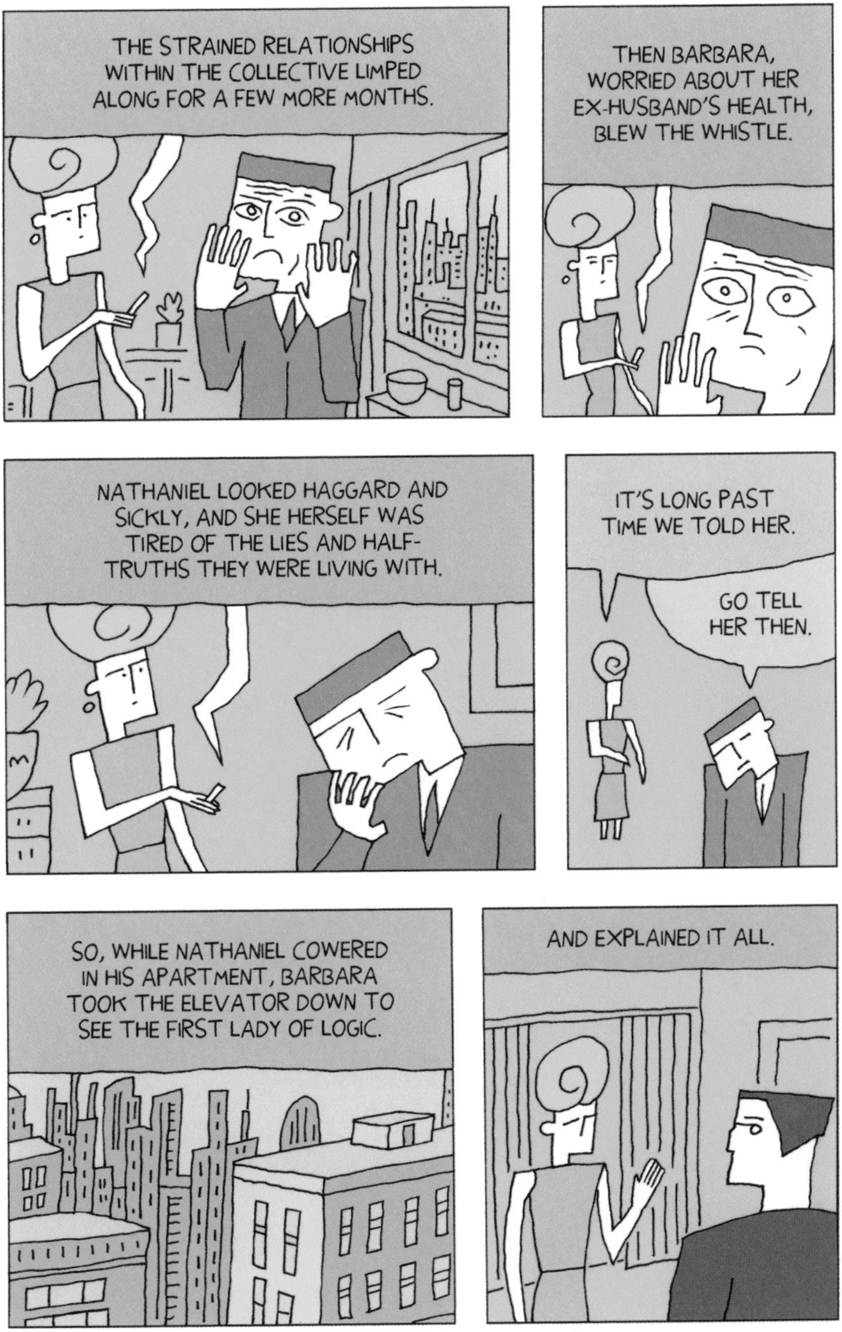
THE STRAINED RELATIONSHIPS WITHIN THE COLLECTIVE LIMPED ALONG FOR A FEW MORE MONTHS.
THEN BARBARA, WORRIED ABOUT HER EX-HUSBAND'S HEALTH, BLEW THE WHISTLE.
NATHANIEL LOOKED HAGGARD AND SICKLY, AND SHE HERSELF WAS TIRED OF THE LIES AND HALF-TRUTHS THEY WERE LIVING WITH.
IT'S LONG PAST TIME WE TOLD HER.
GO TELL HER THEN.
SO, WHILE NATHANIEL COWERED IN HIS APARTMENT, BARBARA TOOK THE ELEVATOR DOWN TO SEE THE FIRST LADY OF LOGIC.
AND EXPLAINED IT ALL.

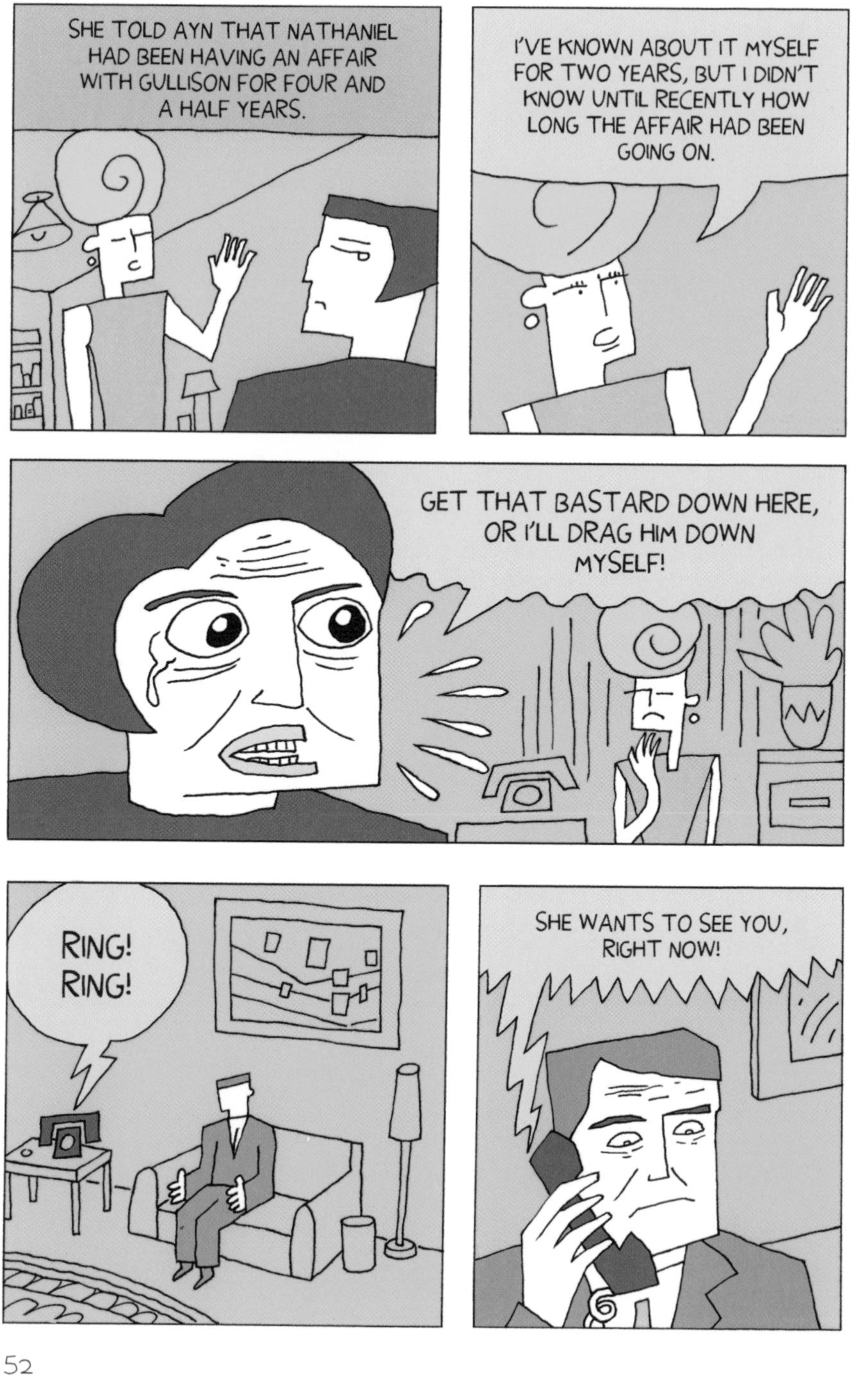
SHE TOLD AYN THAT NATHANIEL HAD BEEN HAVING AN AFFAIR WITH GULLISON FOR FOUR AND A HALF YEARS.
I'VE KNOWN ABOUT IT MYSELF FOR TWO YEARS, BUT I DIDN'T KNOW UNTIL RECENTLY HOW LONG THE AFFAIR HAD BEEN GOING ON.
GET THAT BASTARD DOWN HERE, OR I'LL DRAG HIM DOWN MYSELF!
RING! RING!
SHE WANTS TO SEE YOU, RIGHT NOW!

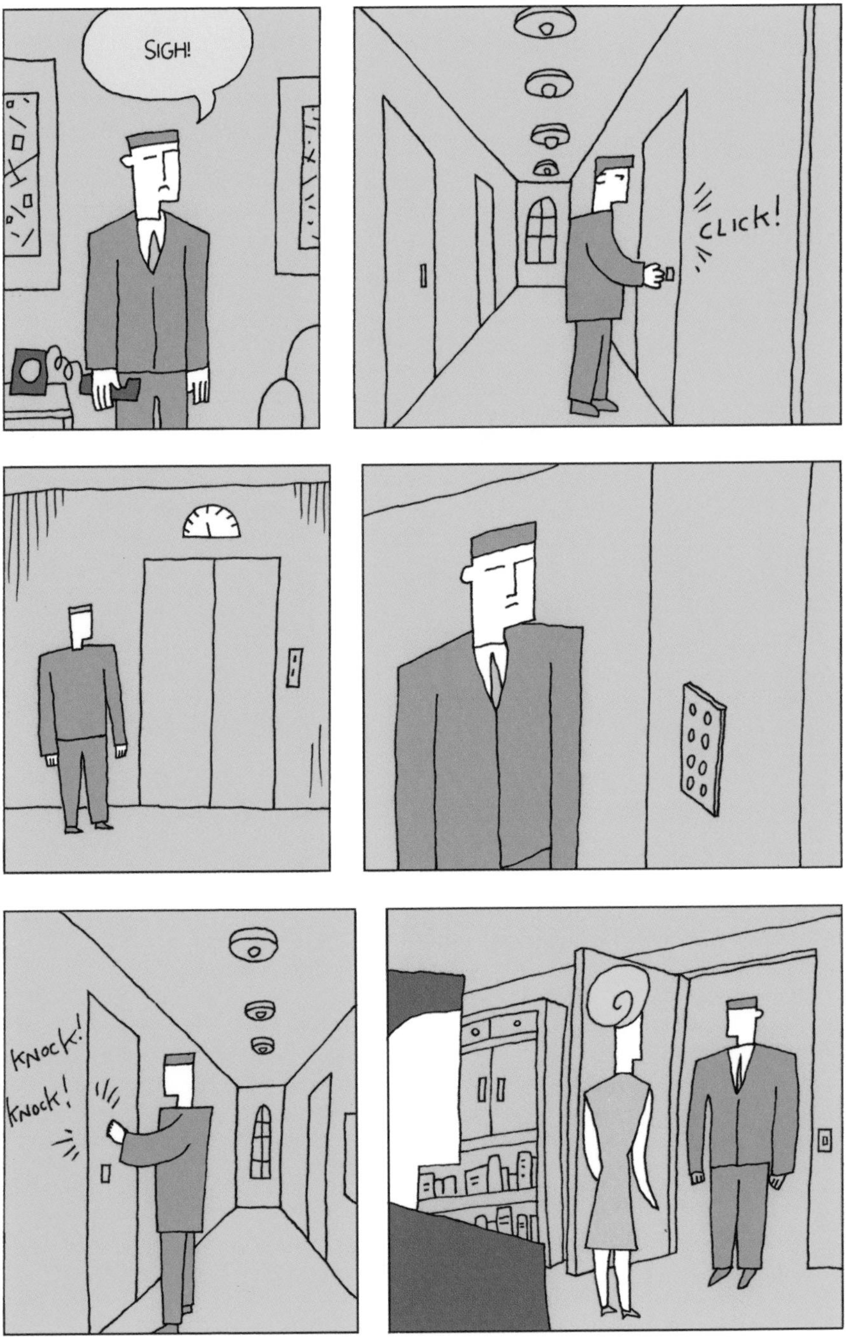
SIGH!
CLICK!
KNOCK!
KNOCK!

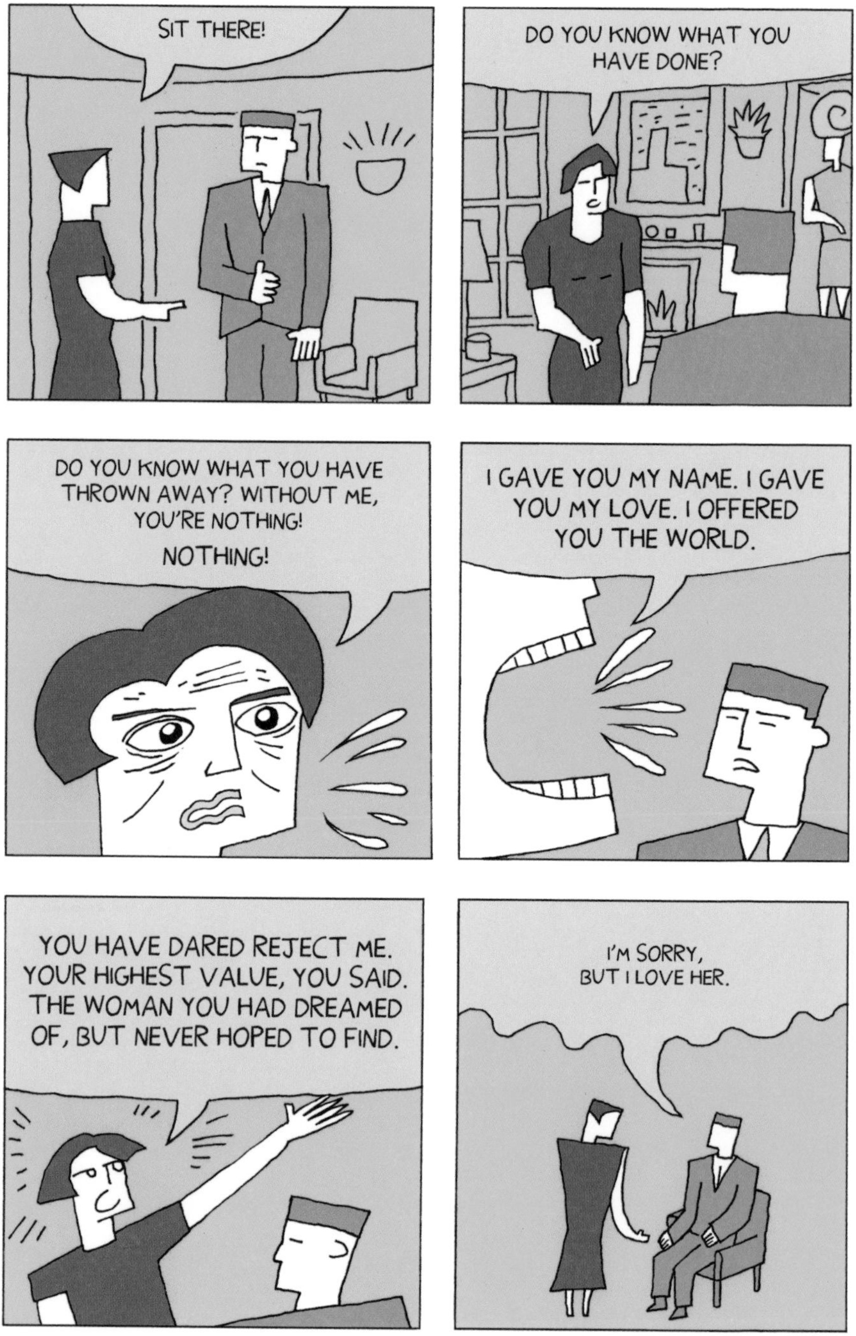
SIT THERE!
DO YOU KNOW WHAT YOU HAVE DONE?
DO YOU KNOW WHAT YOU HAVE THROWN AWAY? WITHOUT ME, YOU'RE NOTHING!
NOTHING!
I GAVE YOU MY NAME. I GAVE YOU MY LOVE. I OFFERED YOU THE WORLD.
YOU HAVE DARED REJECT ME. YOUR HIGHEST VALUE, YOU SAID. THE WOMAN YOU HAD DREAMED OF, BUT NEVER HOPED TO FIND.
I'M SORRY, BUT I LOVE HER.

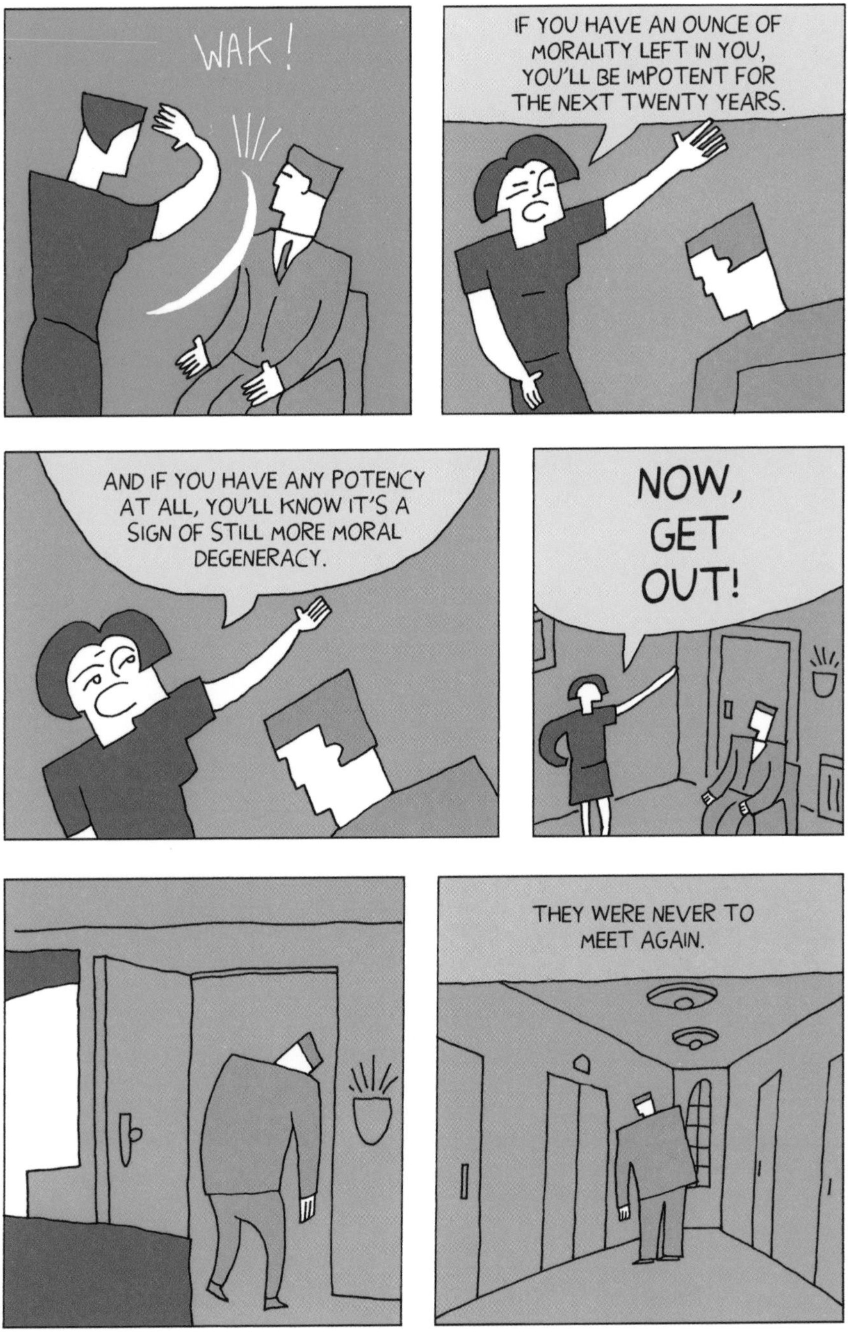
WAK!
IF YOU HAVE AN OUNCE OF MORALITY LEFT IN YOU, YOU'LL BE IMPOTENT FOR THE NEXT TWENTY YEARS.
AND IF YOU HAVE ANY POTENCY AT ALL, YOU'LL KNOW IT'S A SIGN OF STILL MORE MORAL DEGENERACY.
NOW, GET OUT!
THEY WERE NEVER TO MEET AGAIN.

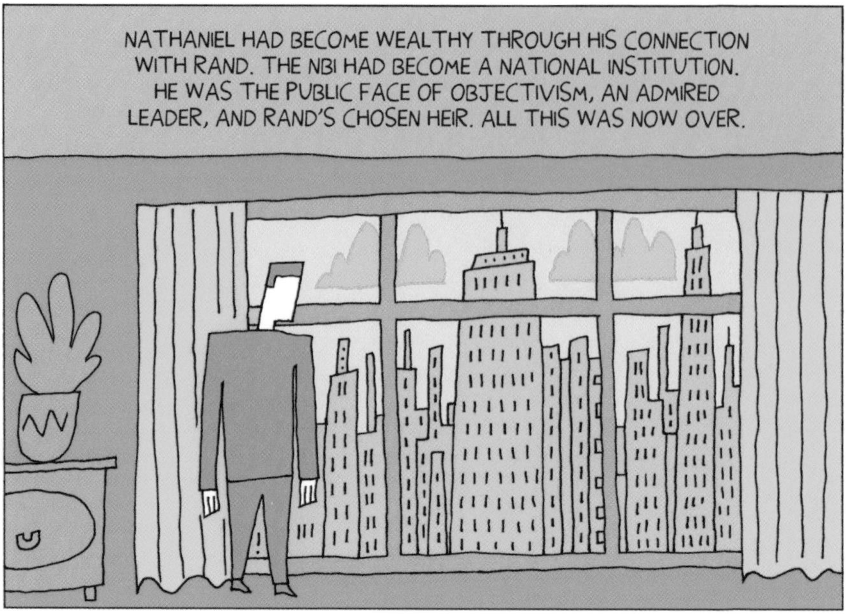
NATHANIEL HAD BECOME WEALTHY THROUGH HIS CONNECTION WITH RAND. THE NBI HAD BECOME A NATIONAL INSTITUTION. HE WAS THE PUBLIC FACE OF OBJECTIVISM, AN ADMIRED LEADER, AND RAND'S CHOSEN HEIR. ALL THIS WAS NOW OVER.

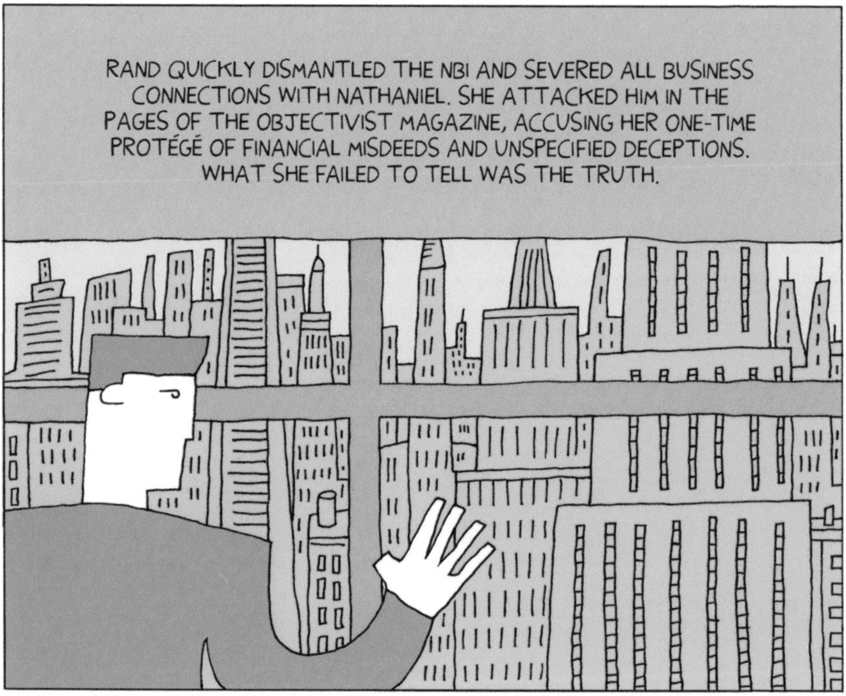
RAND QUICKLY DISMANTLED THE NBI AND SEVERED ALL BUSINESS CONNECTIONS WITH NATHANIEL. SHE ATTACKED HIM IN THE PAGES OF THE OBJECTIVIST MAGAZINE, ACCUSING HER ONE-TIME PROTÉGÉ OF FINANCIAL MISDEEDS AND UNSPECIFIED DECEPTIONS. WHAT SHE FAILED TO TELL WAS THE TRUTH.

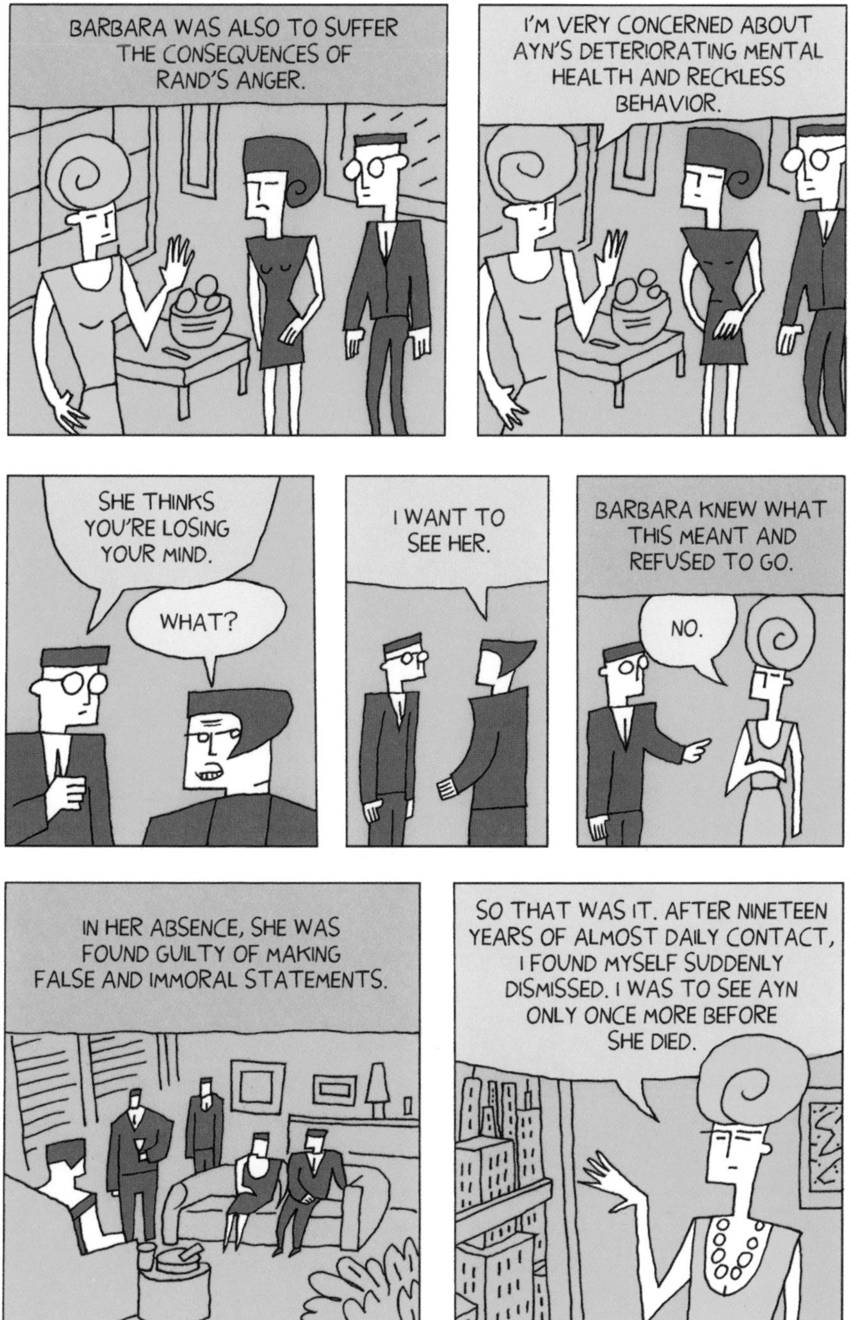
BARBARA WAS ALSO TO SUFFER THE CONSEQUENCES OF RAND'S ANGER.
I'M VERY CONCERNED ABOUT AYN'S DETERIORATING MENTAL HEALTH AND RECKLESS BEHAVIOR.
SHE THINKS YOU'RE LOSING YOUR MIND.
WHAT?
I WANT TO SEE HER.
BARBARA KNEW WHAT THIS MEANT AND REFUSED TO GO.
NO.
IN HER ABSENCE, SHE WAS FOUND GUILTY OF MAKING FALSE AND IMMORAL STATEMENTS.
SO THAT WAS IT. AFTER NINETEEN YEARS OF ALMOST DAILY CONTACT, I FOUND MYSELF SUDDENLY DISMISSED. I WAS TO SEE AYN ONLY ONCE MORE BEFORE SHE DIED.

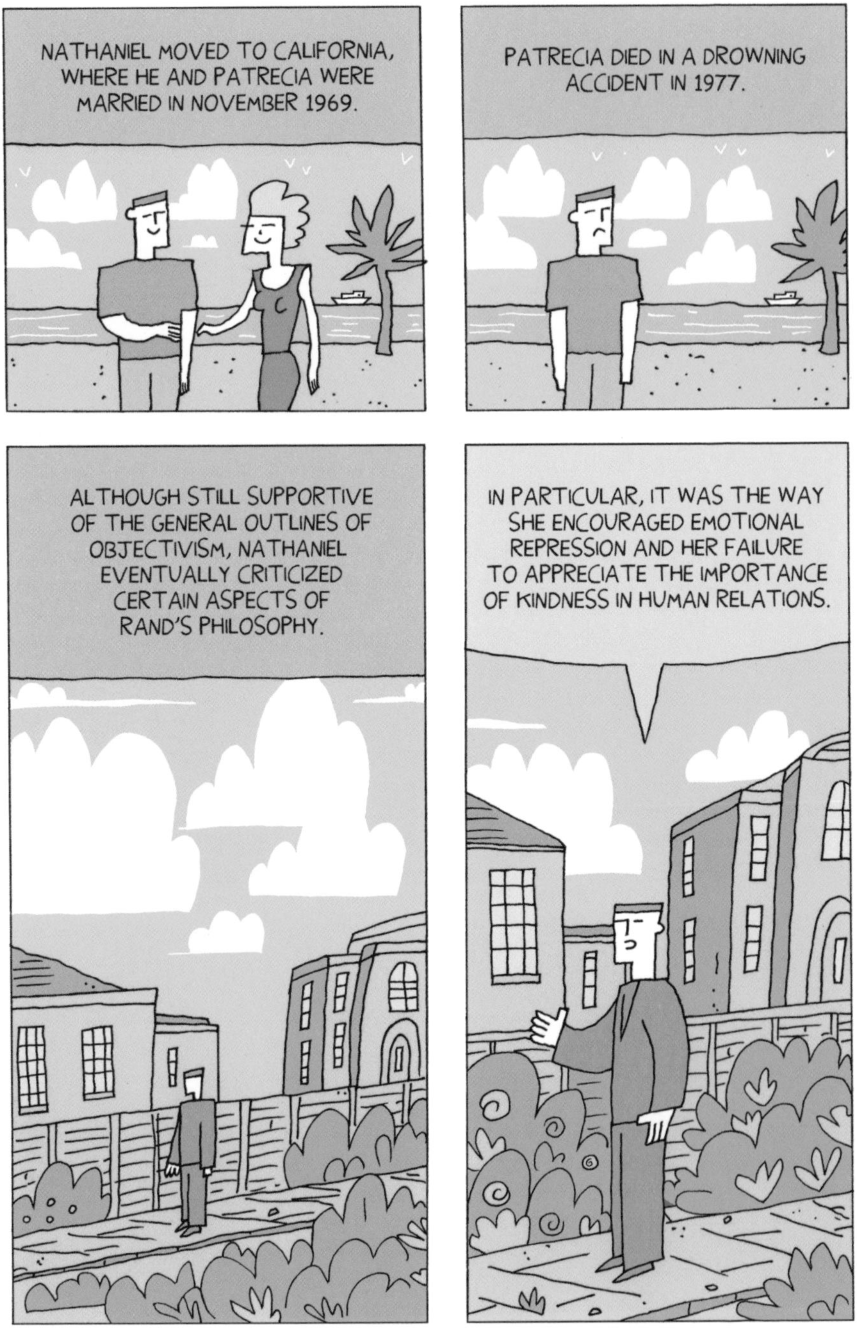
NATHANIEL MOVED TO CALIFORNIA, WHERE HE AND PATRECIA WERE MARRIED IN NOVEMBER 1969.
PATRECIA DIED IN A DROWNING ACCIDENT IN 1977.
ALTHOUGH STILL SUPPORTIVE OF THE GENERAL OUTLINES OF OBJECTIVISM, NATHANIEL EVENTUALLY CRITICIZED CERTAIN ASPECTS OF RAND'S PHILOSOPHY.
IN PARTICULAR, IT WAS THE WAY SHE ENCOURAGED EMOTIONAL REPRESSION AND HER FAILURE TO APPRECIATE THE IMPORTANCE OF KINDNESS IN HUMAN RELATIONS.

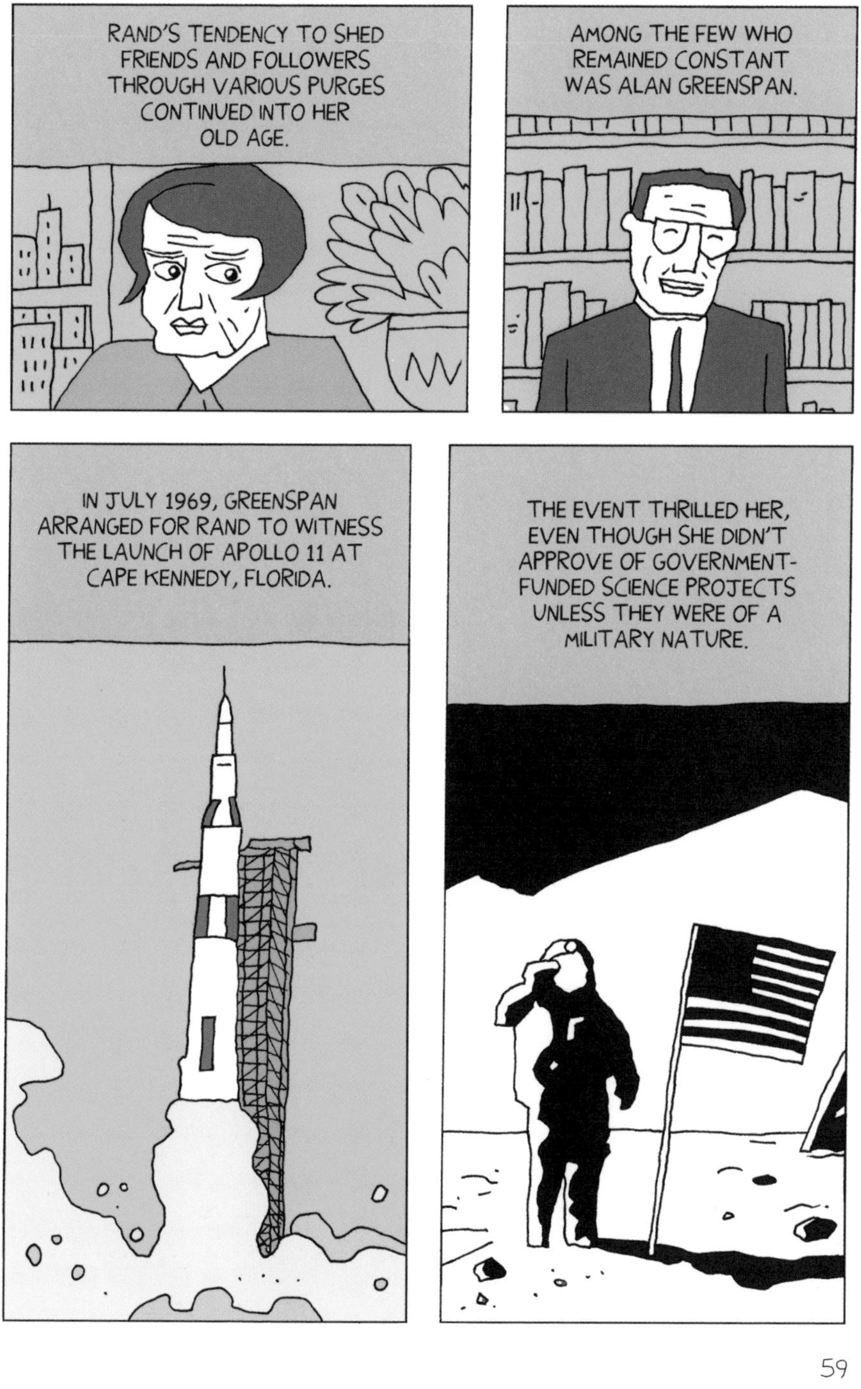
RAND'S TENDENCY TO SHED FRIENDS AND FOLLOWERS THROUGH VARIOUS PURGES CONTINUED INTO HER OLD AGE.
AMONG THE FEW WHO REMAINED CONSTANT WAS ALAN GREENSPAN.
IN JULY 1969, GREENSPAN ARRANGED FOR RAND TO WITNESS THE LAUNCH OF APOLLO 11 AT CAPE KENNEDY, FLORIDA.
THE EVENT THRILLED HER, EVEN THOUGH SHE DIDN'T APPROVE OF GOVERNMENT-FUNDED SCIENCE PROJECTS UNLESS THEY WERE OF A MILITARY NATURE.

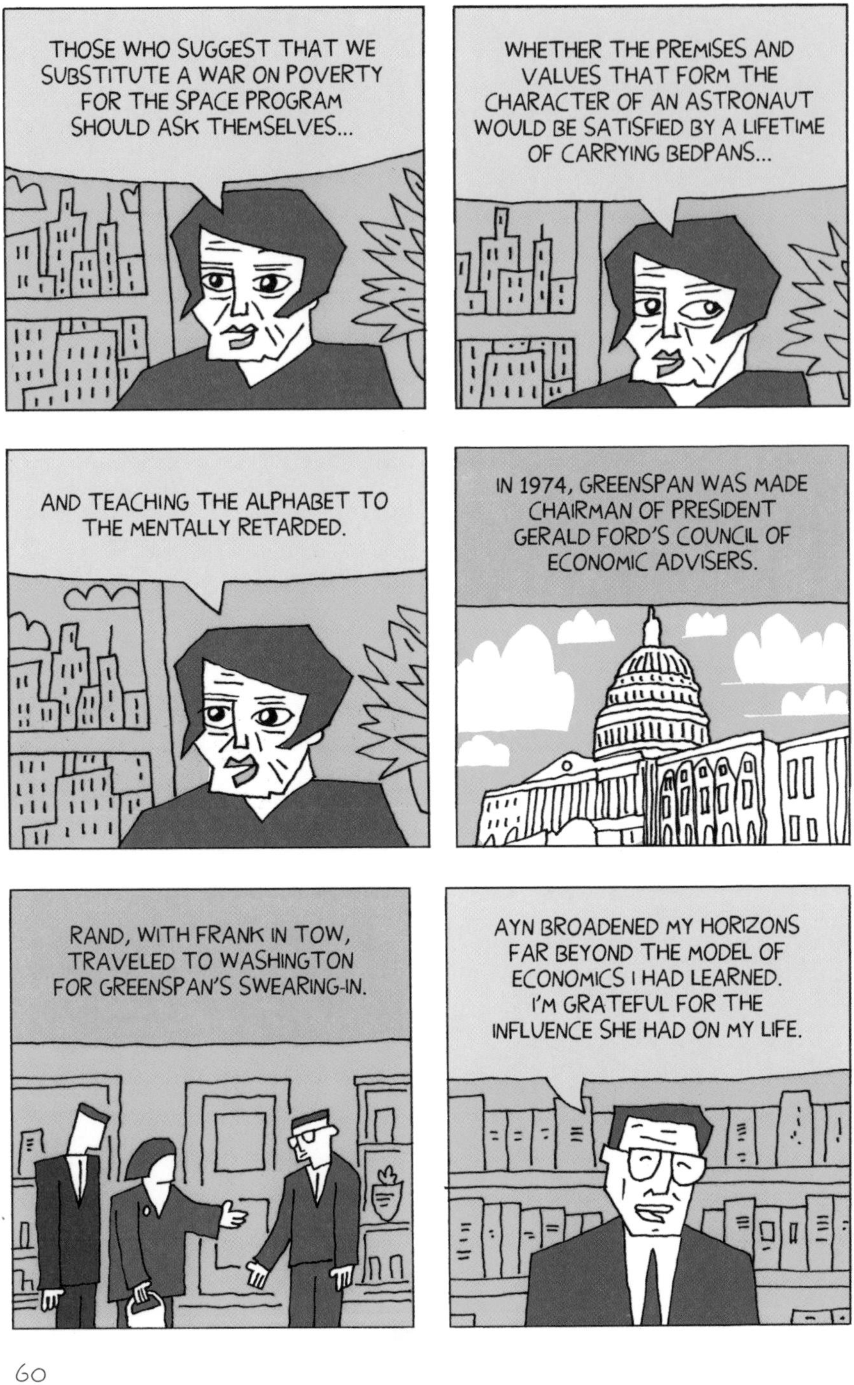
THOSE WHO SUGGEST THAT WE SUBSTITUTE A WAR ON POVERTY FOR THE SPACE PROGRAM SHOULD ASK THEMSELVES...
WHETHER THE PREMISES AND VALUES THAT FORM THE CHARACTER OF AN ASTRONAUT WOULD BE SATISFIED BY A LIFETIME OF CARRYING BEDPANS...
AND TEACHING THE ALPHABET TO THE MENTALLY RETARDED.
IN 1974, GREENSPAN WAS MADE CHAIRMAN OF PRESIDENT GERALD FORD'S COUNCIL OF ECONOMIC ADVISERS.
RAND, WITH FRANK IN TOW, TRAVELED TO WASHINGTON FOR GREENSPAN'S SWEARING-IN.
AYN BROADENED MY HORIZONS FAR BEYOND THE MODEL OF ECONOMICS I HAD LEARNED. I'M GRATEFUL FOR THE INFLUENCE SHE HAD ON MY LIFE.

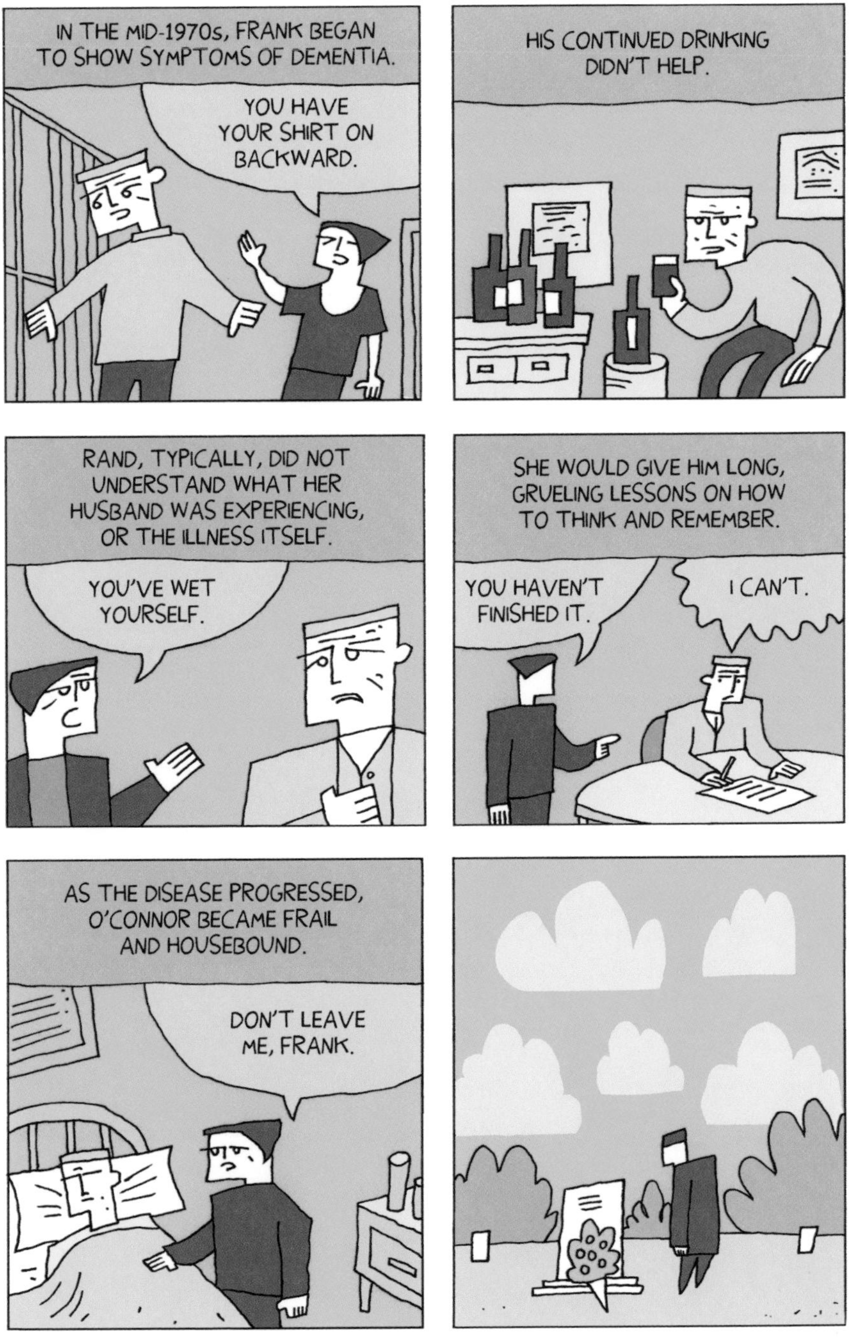
IN THE MID-1970s, FRANK BEGAN TO SHOW SYMPTOMS OF DEMENTIA.
YOU HAVE YOUR SHIRT ON BACKWARD.
HIS CONTINUED DRINKING DIDN'T HELP.
RAND, TYPICALLY, DID NOT UNDERSTAND WHAT HER HUSBAND WAS EXPERIENCING, OR THE ILLNESS ITSELF.
YOU'VE WET YOURSELF.
SHE WOULD GIVE HIM LONG, GRUELING LESSONS ON HOW TO THINK AND REMEMBER.
YOU HAVEN'T FINISHED IT.
I CAN'T.
AS THE DISEASE PROGRESSED, O'CONNOR BECAME FRAIL AND HOUSEBOUND.
DON'T LEAVE ME, FRANK.

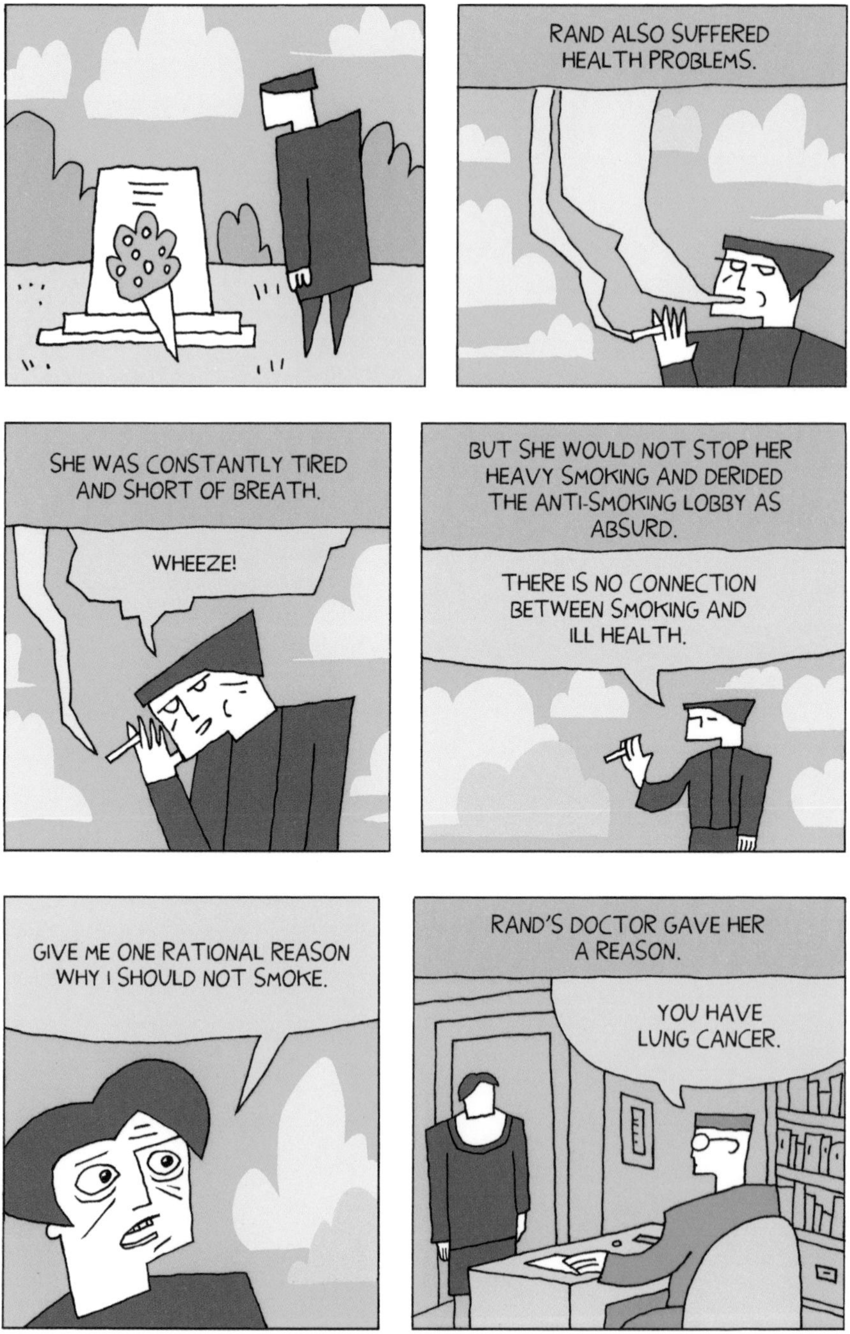
RAND ALSO SUFFERED HEALTH PROBLEMS.
SHE WAS CONSTANTLY TIRED AND SHORT OF BREATH.
WHEEZE!
BUT SHE WOULD NOT STOP HER HEAVY SMOKING AND DERIDED THE ANTI-SMOKING LOBBY AS ABSURD.
THERE IS NO CONNECTION BETWEEN SMOKING AND ILL HEALTH.
GIVE ME ONE RATIONAL REASON WHY I SHOULD NOT SMOKE.
RAND'S DOCTOR GAVE HER A REASON.
YOU HAVE LUNG CANCER.

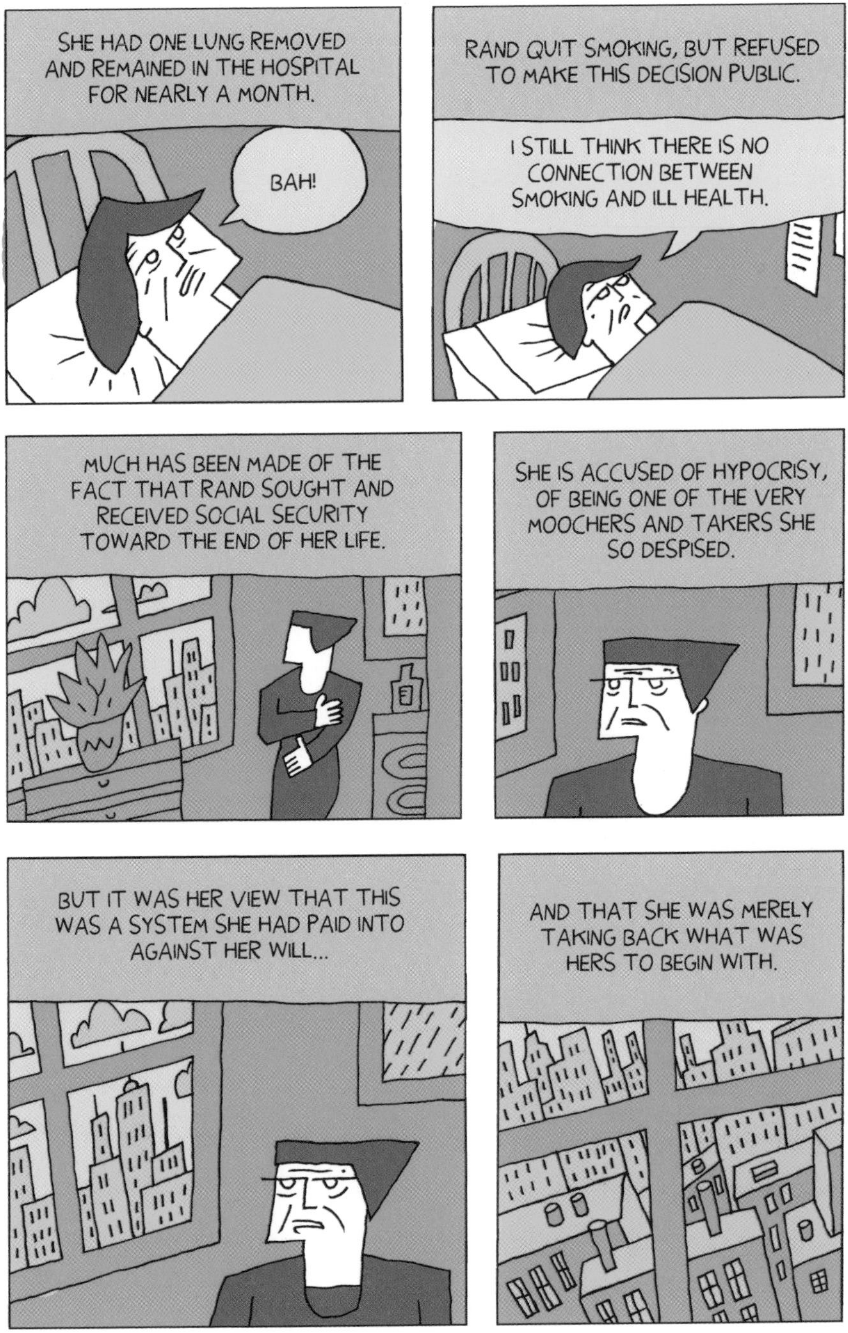
SHE HAD ONE LUNG REMOVED AND REMAINED IN THE HOSPITAL FOR NEARLY A MONTH.
BAH!
RAND QUIT SMOKING, BUT REFUSED TO MAKE THIS DECISION PUBLIC.
I STILL THINK THERE IS NO CONNECTION BETWEEN SMOKING AND ILL HEALTH.
MUCH HAS BEEN MADE OF THE FACT THAT RAND SOUGHT AND RECEIVED SOCIAL SECURITY TOWARD THE END OF HER LIFE.
SHE IS ACCUSED OF HYPOCRISY, OF BEING ONE OF THE VERY MOOCHERS AND TAKERS SHE SO DESPISED.
BUT IT WAS HER VIEW THAT THIS WAS A SYSTEM SHE HAD PAID INTO AGAINST HER WILL...
AND THAT SHE WAS MERELY TAKING BACK WHAT WAS HERS TO BEGIN WITH.

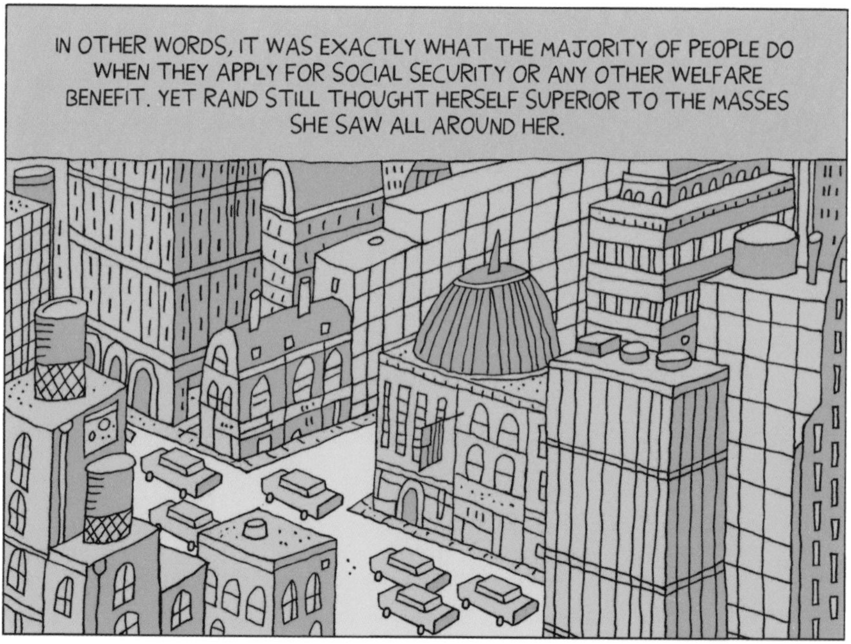
IN OTHER WORDS, IT WAS EXACTLY WHAT THE MAJORITY OF PEOPLE DO WHEN THEY APPLY FOR SOCIAL SECURITY OR ANY OTHER WELFARE BENEFIT. YET RAND STILL THOUGHT HERSELF SUPERIOR TO THE MASSES SHE SAW ALL AROUND HER.

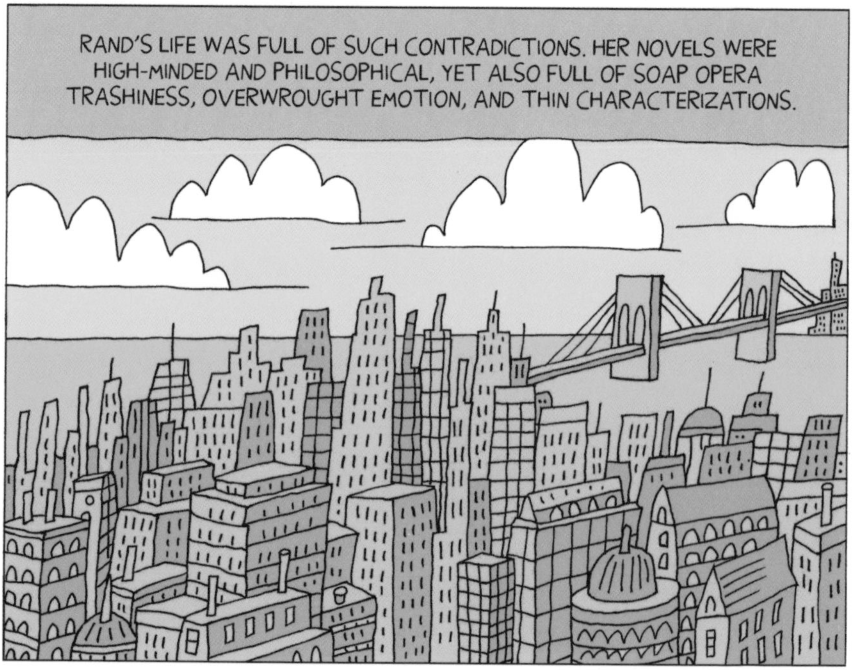
RAND'S LIFE WAS FULL OF SUCH CONTRADICTIONS. HER NOVELS WERE HIGH-MINDED AND PHILOSOPHICAL, YET ALSO FULL OF SOAP OPERA TRASHINESS, OVERWROUGHT EMOTION, AND THIN CHARACTERIZATIONS.

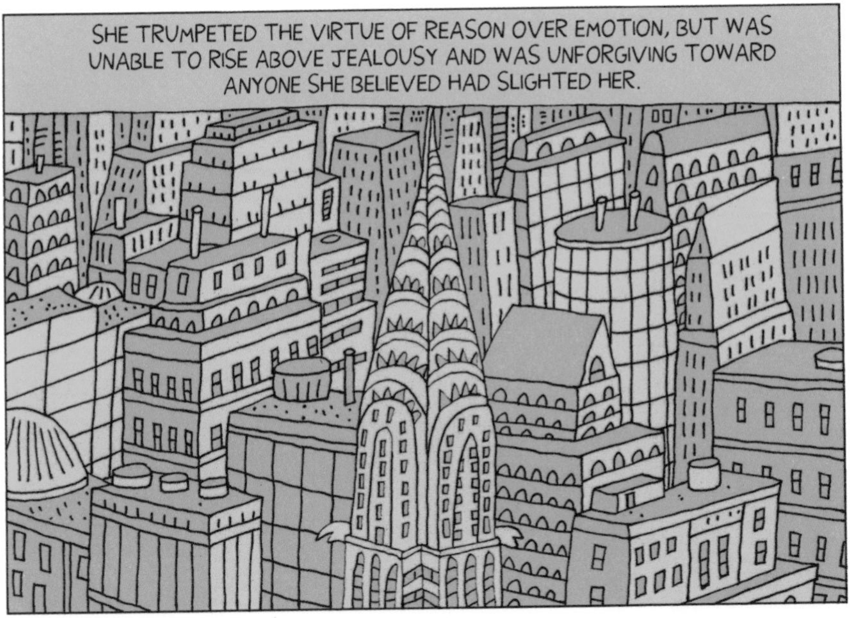
SHE TRUMPETED THE VIRTUE OF REASON OVER EMOTION, BUT WAS UNABLE TO RISE ABOVE JEALOUSY AND WAS UNFORGIVING TOWARD ANYONE SHE BELIEVED HAD SLIGHTED HER.

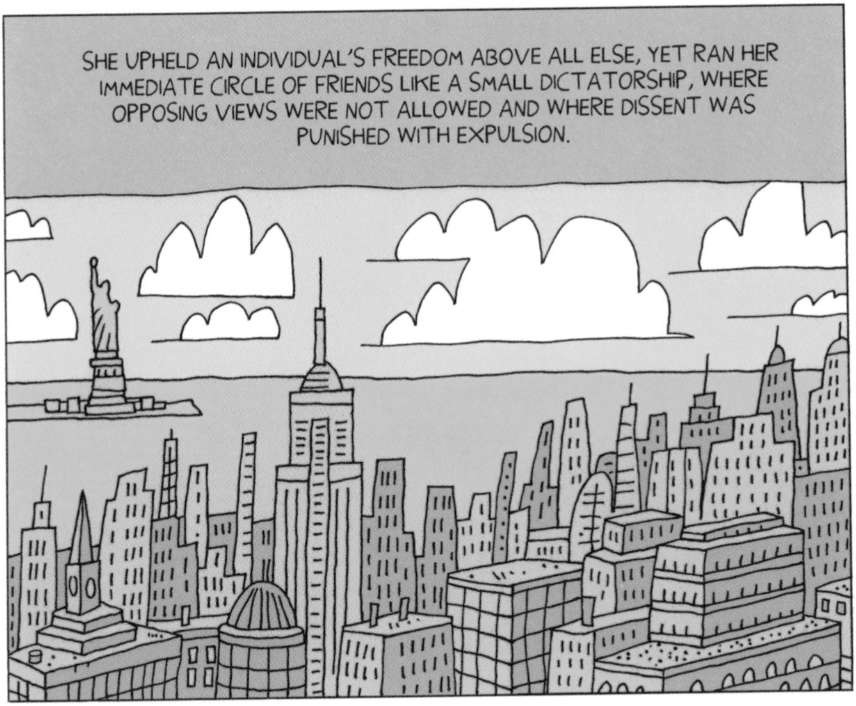
SHE UPHELD AN INDIVIDUAL'S FREEDOM ABOVE ALL ELSE, YET RAN HER IMMEDIATE CIRCLE OF FRIENDS LIKE A SMALL DICTATORSHIP, WHERE OPPOSING VIEWS WERE NOT ALLOWED AND WHERE DISSENT WAS PUNISHED WITH EXPULSION.

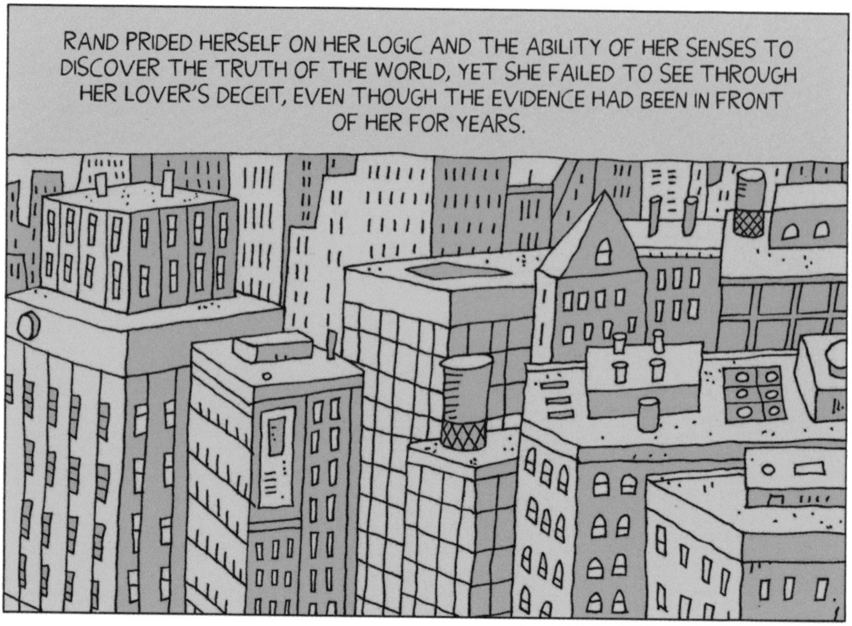
RAND PRIDED HERSELF ON HER LOGIC AND THE ABILITY OF HER SENSES TO DISCOVER THE TRUTH OF THE WORLD, YET SHE FAILED TO SEE THROUGH HER LOVER'S DECEIT, EVEN THOUGH THE EVIDENCE HAD BEEN IN FRONT OF HER FOR YEARS.

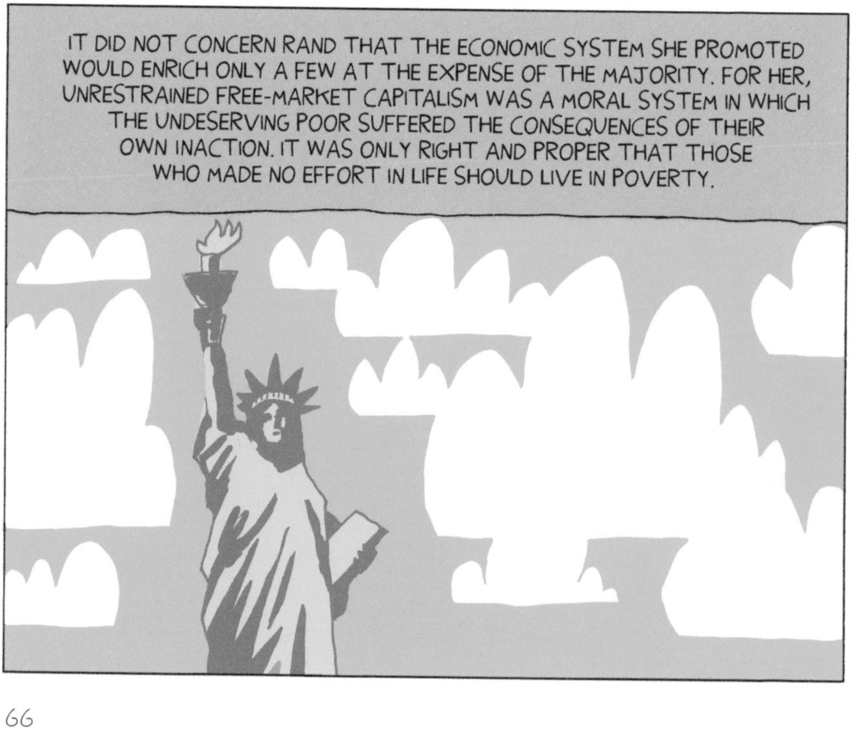
IT DID NOT CONCERN RAND THAT THE ECONOMIC SYSTEM SHE PROMOTED WOULD ENRICH ONLY A FEW AT THE EXPENSE OF THE MAJORITY. FOR HER, UNRESTRAINED FREE-MARKET CAPITALISM WAS A MORAL SYSTEM IN WHICH THE UNDESERVING POOR SUFFERED THE CONSEQUENCES OF THEIR OWN INACTION. IT WAS ONLY RIGHT AND PROPER THAT THOSE WHO MADE NO EFFORT IN LIFE SHOULD LIVE IN POVERTY.

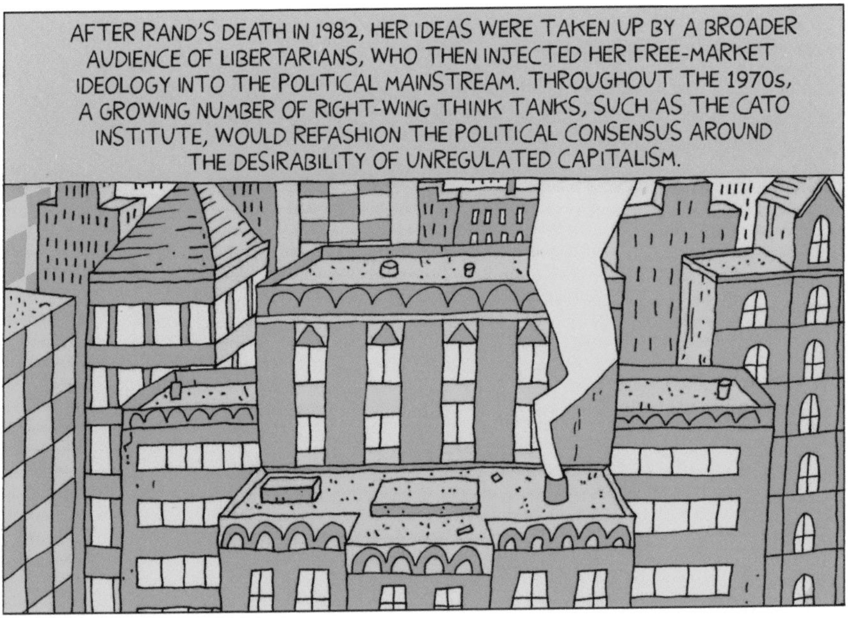
AFTER RAND'S DEATH IN 1982, HER IDEAS WERE TAKEN UP BY A BROADER AUDIENCE OF LIBERTARIANS, WHO THEN INJECTED HER FREE-MARKET IDEOLOGY INTO THE POLITICAL MAINSTREAM. THROUGHOUT THE 1970s, A GROWING NUMBER OF RIGHT-WING THINK TANKS, SUCH AS THE CATO INSTITUTE, WOULD REFASHION THE POLITICAL CONSENSUS AROUND THE DESIRABILITY OF UNREGULATED CAPITALISM.

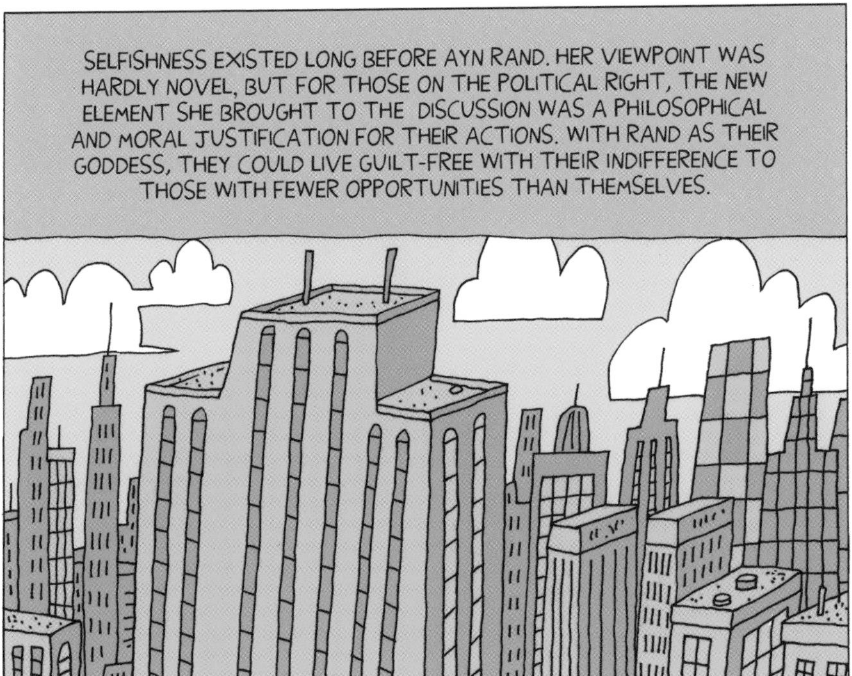
SELFISHNESS EXISTED LONG BEFORE AYN RAND. HER VIEWPOINT WAS HARDLY NOVEL, BUT FOR THOSE ON THE POLITICAL RIGHT, THE NEW ELEMENT SHE BROUGHT TO THE DISCUSSION WAS A PHILOSOPHICAL AND MORAL JUSTIFICATION FOR THEIR ACTIONS. WITH RAND AS THEIR GODDESS, THEY COULD LIVE GUILT-FREE WITH THEIR INDIFFERENCE TO THOSE WITH FEWER OPPORTUNITIES THAN THEMSELVES.

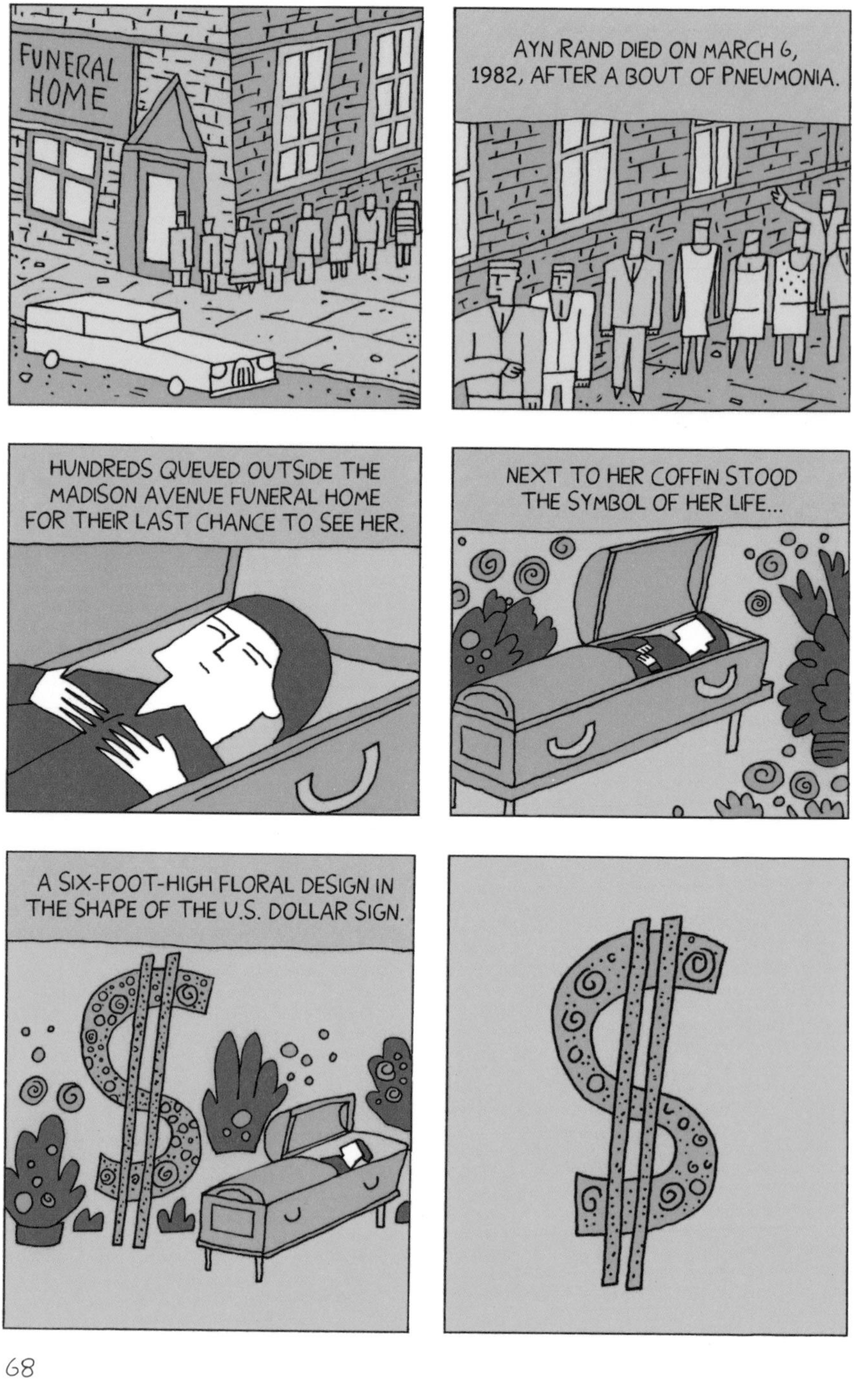
FUNERAL HOME
AYN RAND DIED ON MARCH 6, 1982, AFTER A BOUT OF PNEUMONIA.
HUNDREDS QUEUED OUTSIDE THE MADISON AVENUE FUNERAL HOME FOR THEIR LAST CHANCE TO SEE HER.
NEXT TO HER COFFIN STOOD THE SYMBOL OF HER LIFE...
A SIX-FOOT-HIGH FLORAL DESIGN IN THE SHAPE OF THE U.S. DOLLAR SIGN.

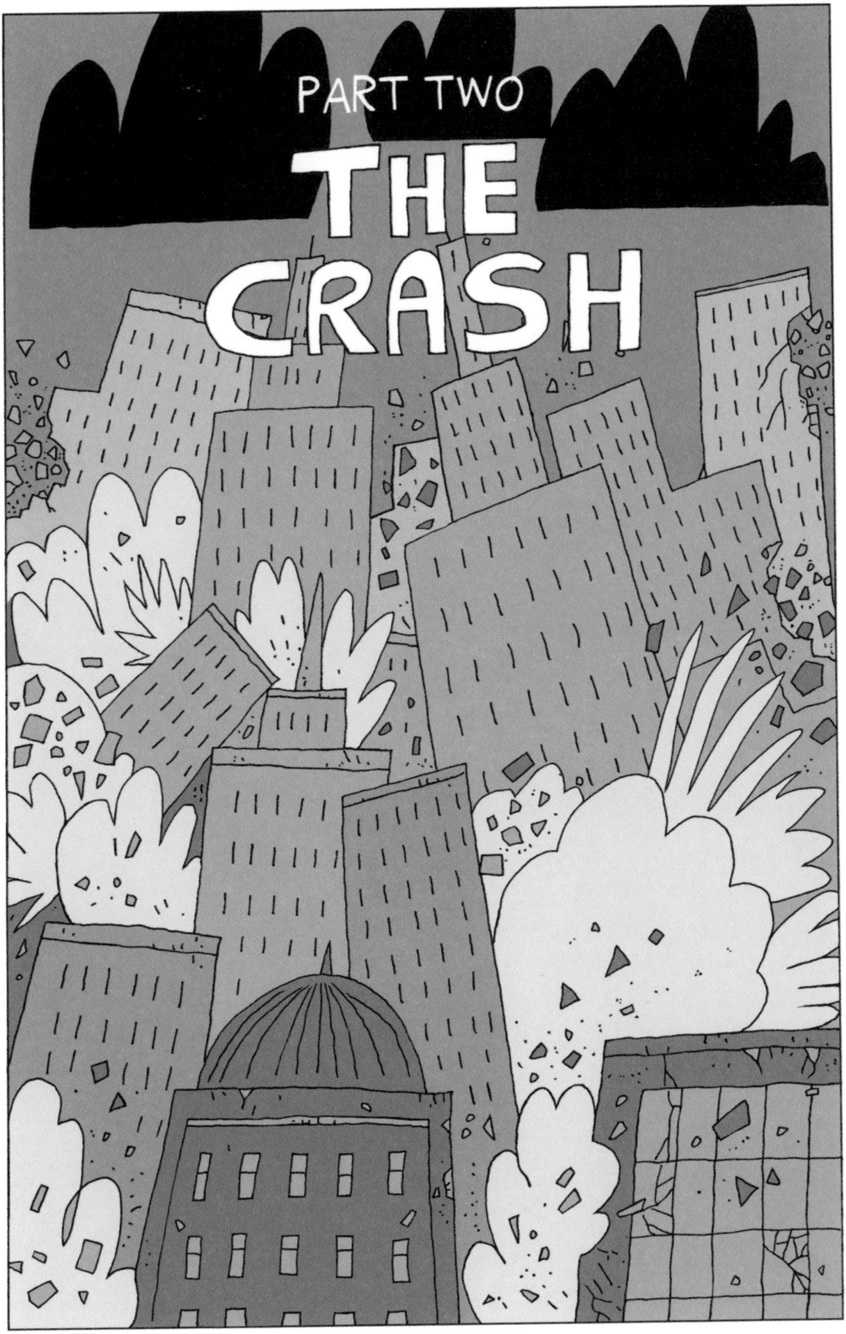
PART TWO
THE CRASH

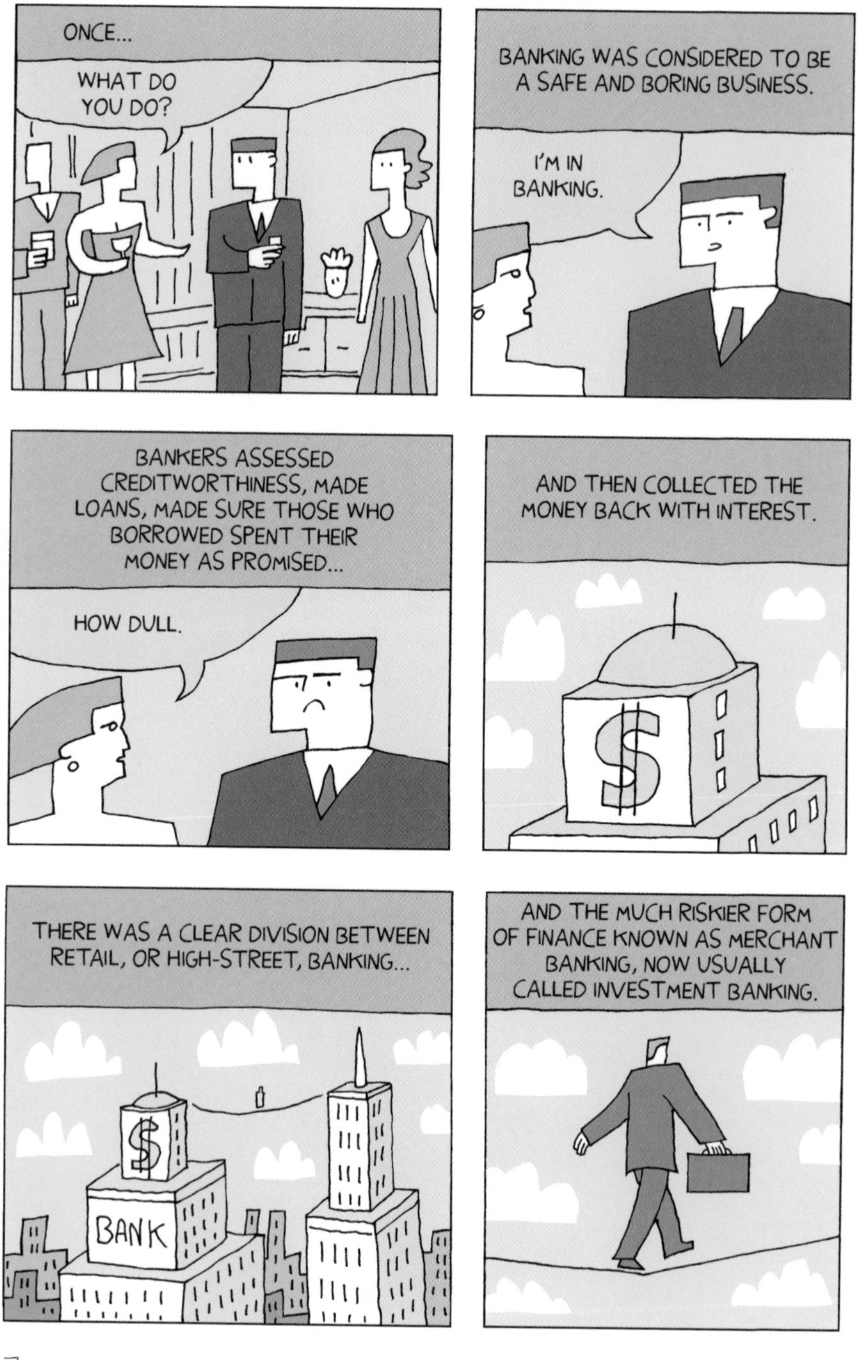
ONCE...
WHAT DO YOU DO?
BANKING WAS CONSIDERED TO BE A SAFE AND BORING BUSINESS.
I'M IN BANKING.
BANKERS ASSESSED CREDITWORTHINESS, MADE LOANS, MADE SURE THOSE WHO BORROWED SPENT THEIR MONEY AS PROMISED...
HOW DULL.
AND THEN COLLECTED THE MONEY BACK WITH INTEREST.
$
THERE WAS A CLEAR DIVISION BETWEEN RETAIL, OR HIGH-STREET, BANKING...
$
BANK
AND THE MUCH RISKIER FORM OF FINANCE KNOWN AS MERCHANT BANKING, NOW USUALLY CALLED INVESTMENT BANKING.

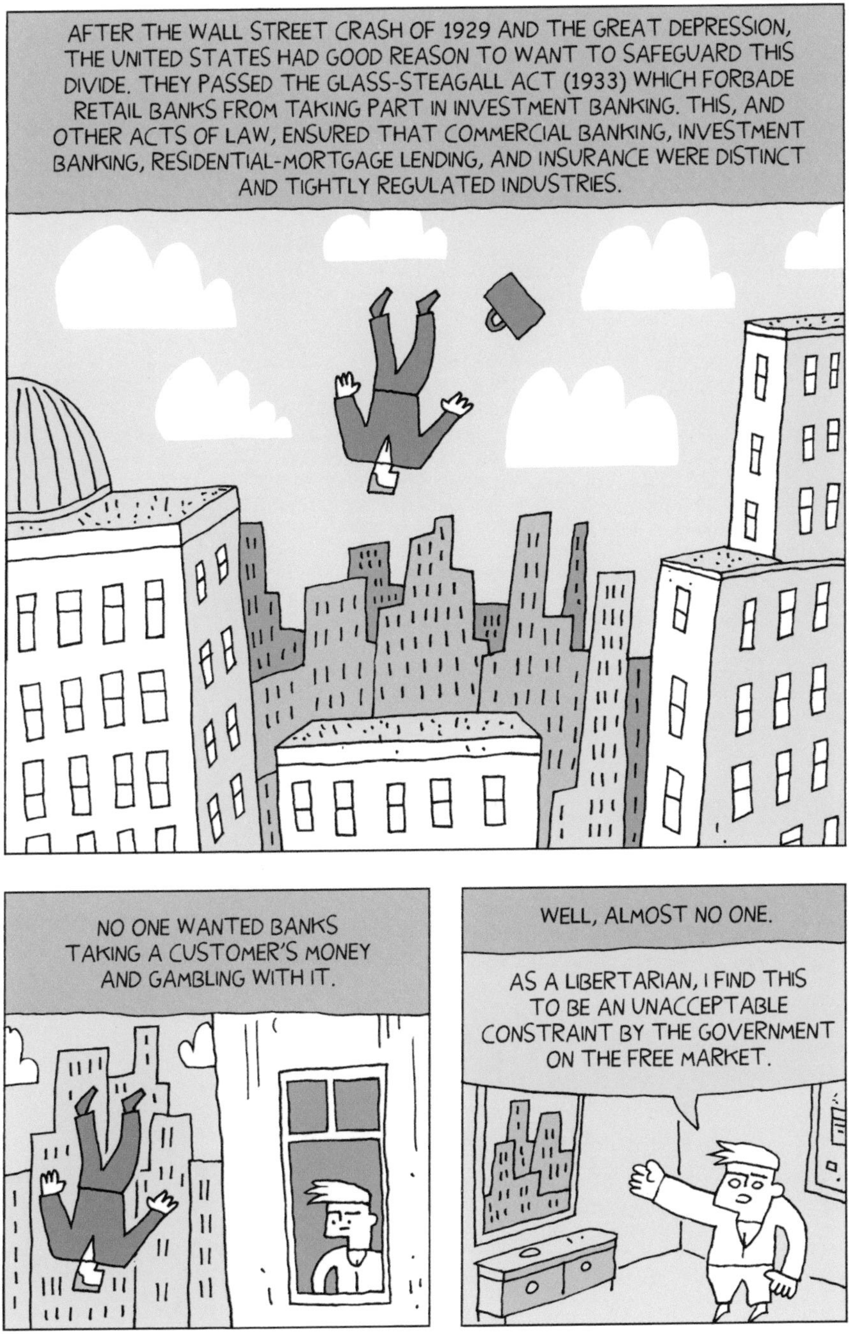
AFTER THE WALL STREET CRASH OF 1929 AND THE GREAT DEPRESSION, THE UNITED STATES HAD GOOD REASON TO WANT TO SAFEGUARD THIS DIVIDE. THEY PASSED THE GLASS-STEAGALL ACT (1933) WHICH FORBADE RETAIL BANKS FROM TAKING PART IN INVESTMENT BANKING. THIS, AND OTHER ACTS OF LAW, ENSURED THAT COMMERCIAL BANKING, INVESTMENT BANKING, RESIDENTIAL-MORTGAGE LENDING, AND INSURANCE WERE DISTINCT AND TIGHTLY REGULATED INDUSTRIES.
NO ONE WANTED BANKS TAKING A CUSTOMER'S MONEY AND GAMBLING WITH IT.
WELL, ALMOST NO ONE.
AS A LIBERTARIAN, I FIND THIS TO BE AN UNACCEPTABLE CONSTRAINT BY THE GOVERNMENT ON THE FREE MARKET.

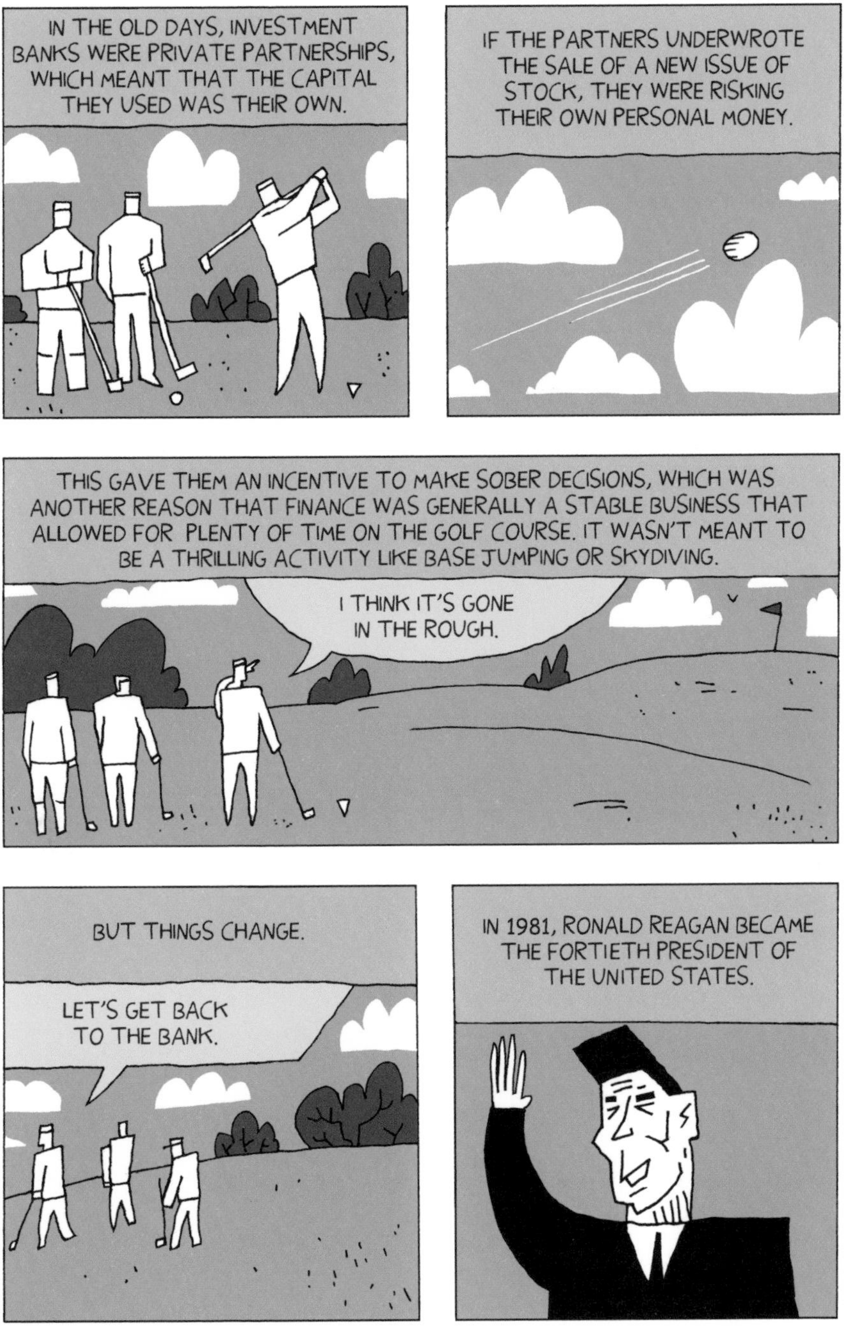
IN THE OLD DAYS, INVESTMENT BANKS WERE PRIVATE PARTNERSHIPS, WHICH MEANT THAT THE CAPITAL THEY USED WAS THEIR OWN.
IF THE PARTNERS UNDERWROTE THE SALE OF A NEW ISSUE OF STOCK, THEY WERE RISKING THEIR OWN PERSONAL MONEY.
THIS GAVE THEM AN INCENTIVE TO MAKE SOBER DECISIONS, WHICH WAS ANOTHER REASON THAT FINANCE WAS GENERALLY A STABLE BUSINESS THAT ALLOWED FOR PLENTY OF TIME ON THE GOLF COURSE. IT WASN'T MEANT TO BE A THRILLING ACTIVITY LIKE BASE JUMPING OR SKYDIVING.
I THINK IT'S GONE IN THE ROUGH.
BUT THINGS CHANGE.
LET'S GET BACK TO THE BANK.
IN 1981, RONALD REAGAN BECAME THE FORTIETH PRESIDENT OF THE UNITED STATES.

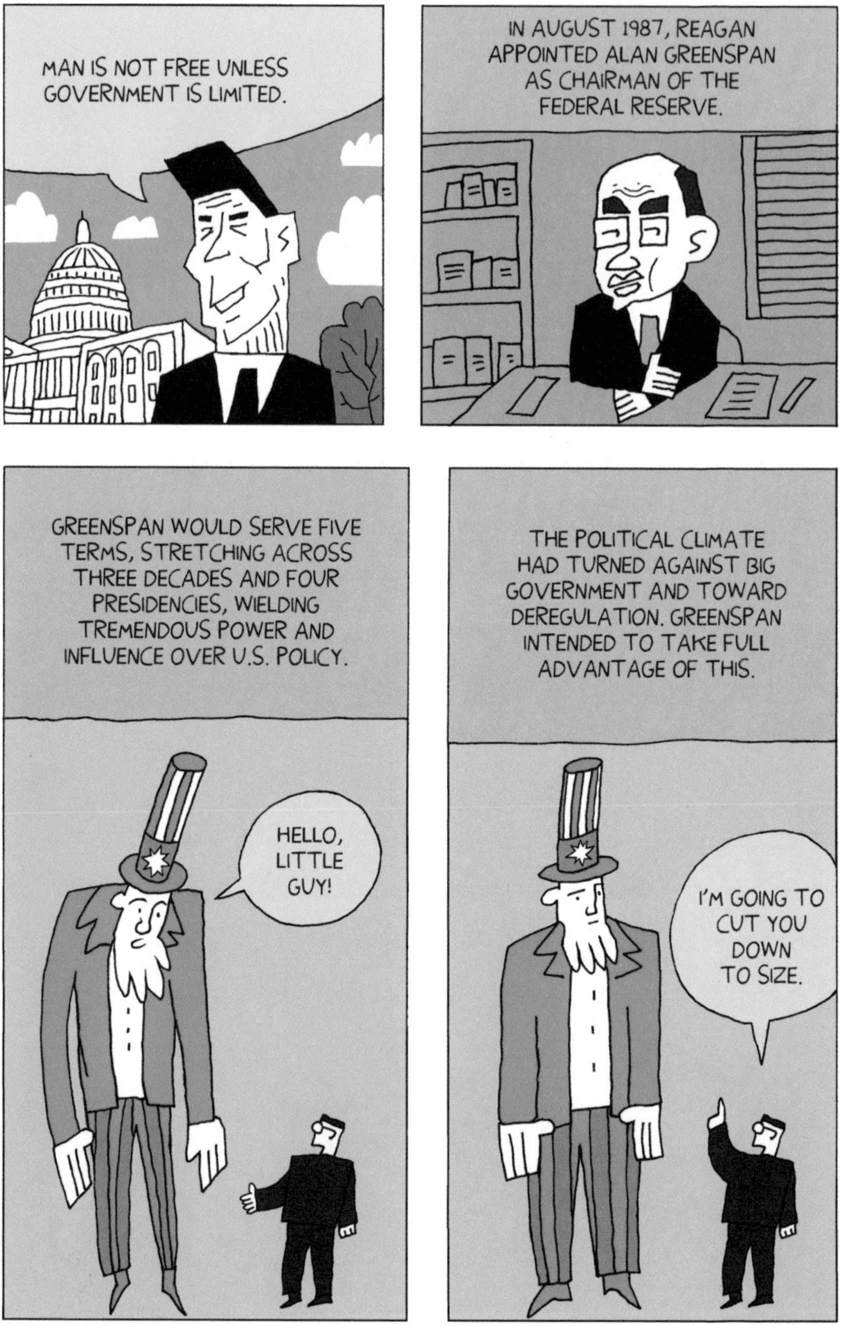
MAN IS NOT FREE UNLESS GOVERNMENT IS LIMITED.
IN AUGUST 1987, REAGAN APPOINTED ALAN GREENSPAN AS CHAIRMAN OF THE FEDERAL RESERVE.
GREENSPAN WOULD SERVE FIVE TERMS, STRETCHING ACROSS THREE DECADES AND FOUR PRESIDENCIES, WIELDING TREMENDOUS POWER AND INFLUENCE OVER U.S. POLICY.
HELLO, LITTLE GUY!
THE POLITICAL CLIMATE HAD TURNED AGAINST BIG GOVERNMENT AND TOWARD DEREGULATION. GREENSPAN INTENDED TO TAKE FULL ADVANTAGE OF THIS.
I'M GOING TO CUT YOU DOWN TO SIZE.

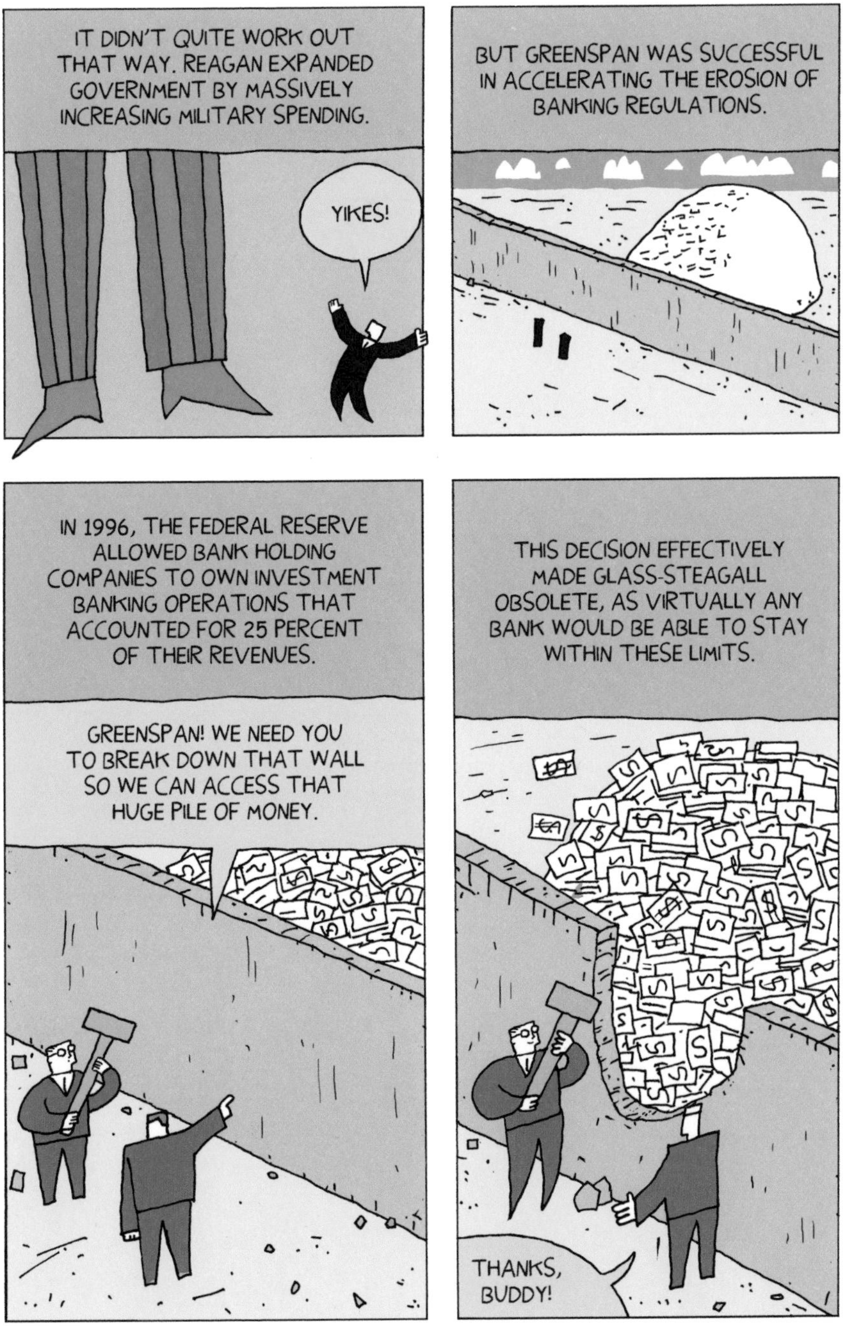
IT DIDN'T QUITE WORK OUT THAT WAY. REAGAN EXPANDED GOVERNMENT BY MASSIVELY INCREASING MILITARY SPENDING.
YIKES!
BUT GREENSPAN WAS SUCCESSFUL IN ACCELERATING THE EROSION OF BANKING REGULATIONS.
IN 1996, THE FEDERAL RESERVE ALLOWED BANK HOLDING COMPANIES TO OWN INVESTMENT BANKING OPERATIONS THAT ACCOUNTED FOR 25 PERCENT OF THEIR REVENUES.
GREENSPAN! WE NEED YOU TO BREAK DOWN THAT WALL SO WE CAN ACCESS THAT HUGE PILE OF MONEY.
THIS DECISION EFFECTIVELY MADE GLASS-STEAGALL OBSOLETE, AS VIRTUALLY ANY BANK WOULD BE ABLE TO STAY WITHIN THESE LIMITS.
THANKS, BUDDY!

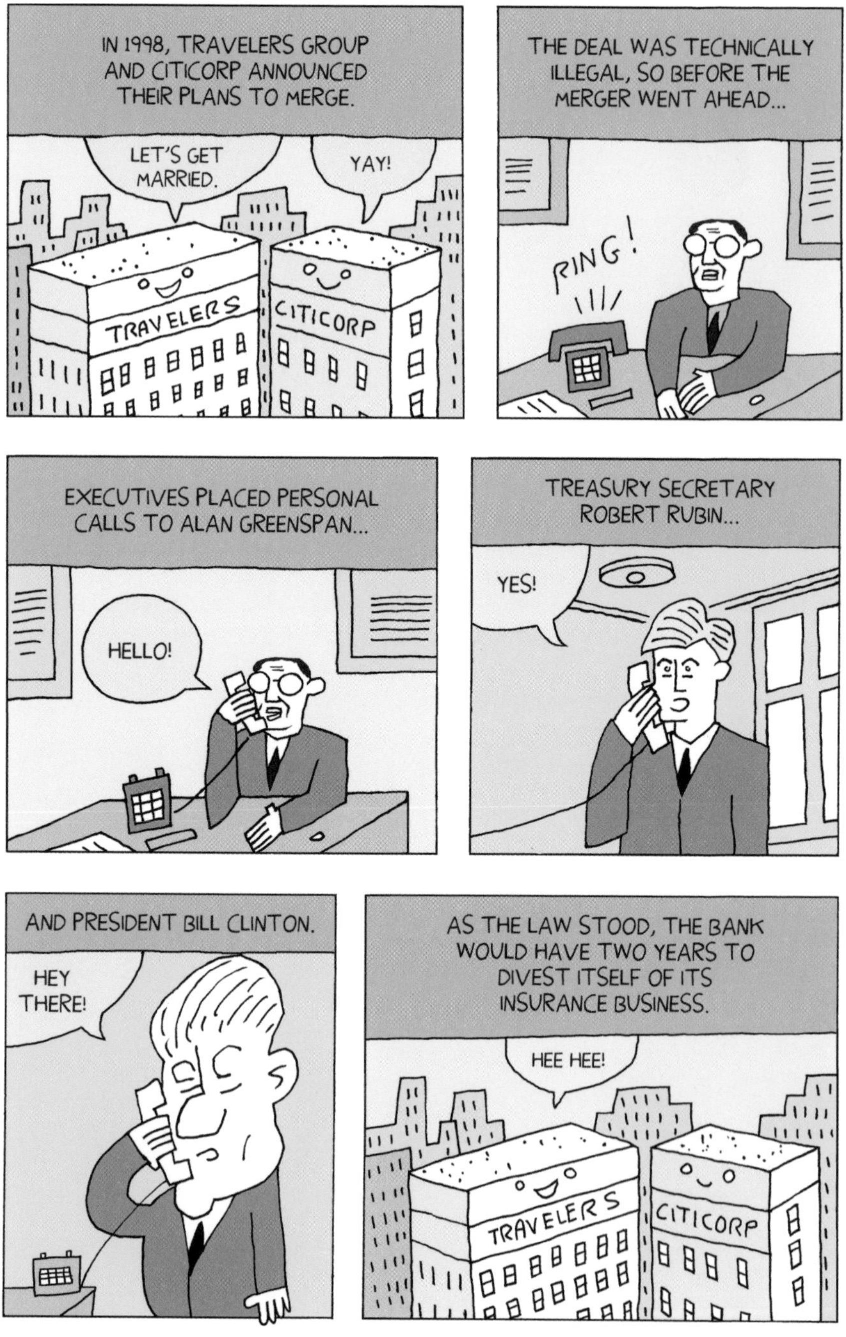
IN 1998, TRAVELERS GROUP AND CITICORP ANNOUNCED THEIR PLANS TO MERGE.
LET'S GET MARRIED.
YAY!
TRAVELERS
CITICORP
THE DEAL WAS TECHNICALLY ILLEGAL, SO BEFORE THE MERGER WENT AHEAD...
RING!
EXECUTIVES PLACED PERSONAL CALLS TO ALAN GREENSPAN...
HELLO!
TREASURY SECRETARY ROBERT RUBIN...
YES!
AND PRESIDENT BILL CLINTON.
HEY THERE!
AS THE LAW STOOD, THE BANK WOULD HAVE TWO YEARS TO DIVEST ITSELF OF ITS INSURANCE BUSINESS.
HEE HEE!
TRAVELERS
CITICORP

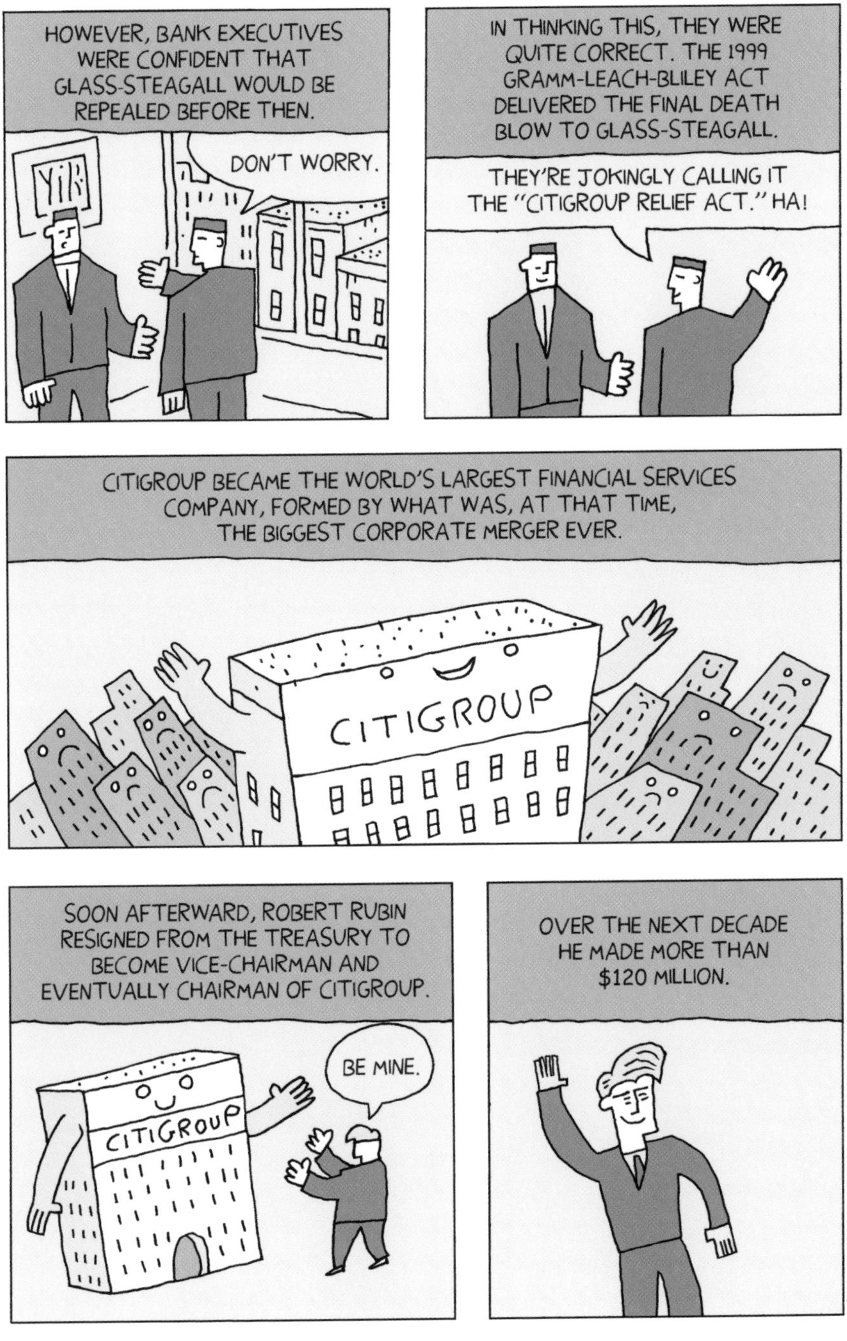
HOWEVER, BANK EXECUTIVES WERE CONFIDENT THAT GLASS-STEAGALL WOULD BE REPEALED BEFORE THEN.
DON'T WORRY.
IN THINKING THIS, THEY WERE QUITE CORRECT. THE 1999 GRAMM-LEACH-BLILEY ACT DELIVERED THE FINAL DEATH BLOW TO GLASS-STEAGALL.
THEY'RE JOKINGLY CALLING IT THE "CITIGROUP RELIEF ACT." HA!
CITIGROUP BECAME THE WORLD'S LARGEST FINANCIAL SERVICES COMPANY, FORMED BY WHAT WAS, AT THAT TIME, THE BIGGEST CORPORATE MERGER EVER.
CITIGROUP
SOON AFTERWARD, ROBERT RUBIN RESIGNED FROM THE TREASURY TO BECOME VICE-CHAIRMAN AND EVENTUALLY CHAIRMAN OF CITIGROUP.
CITIGROUP
BE MINE.
OVER THE NEXT DECADE HE MADE MORE THAN $120 MILLION.

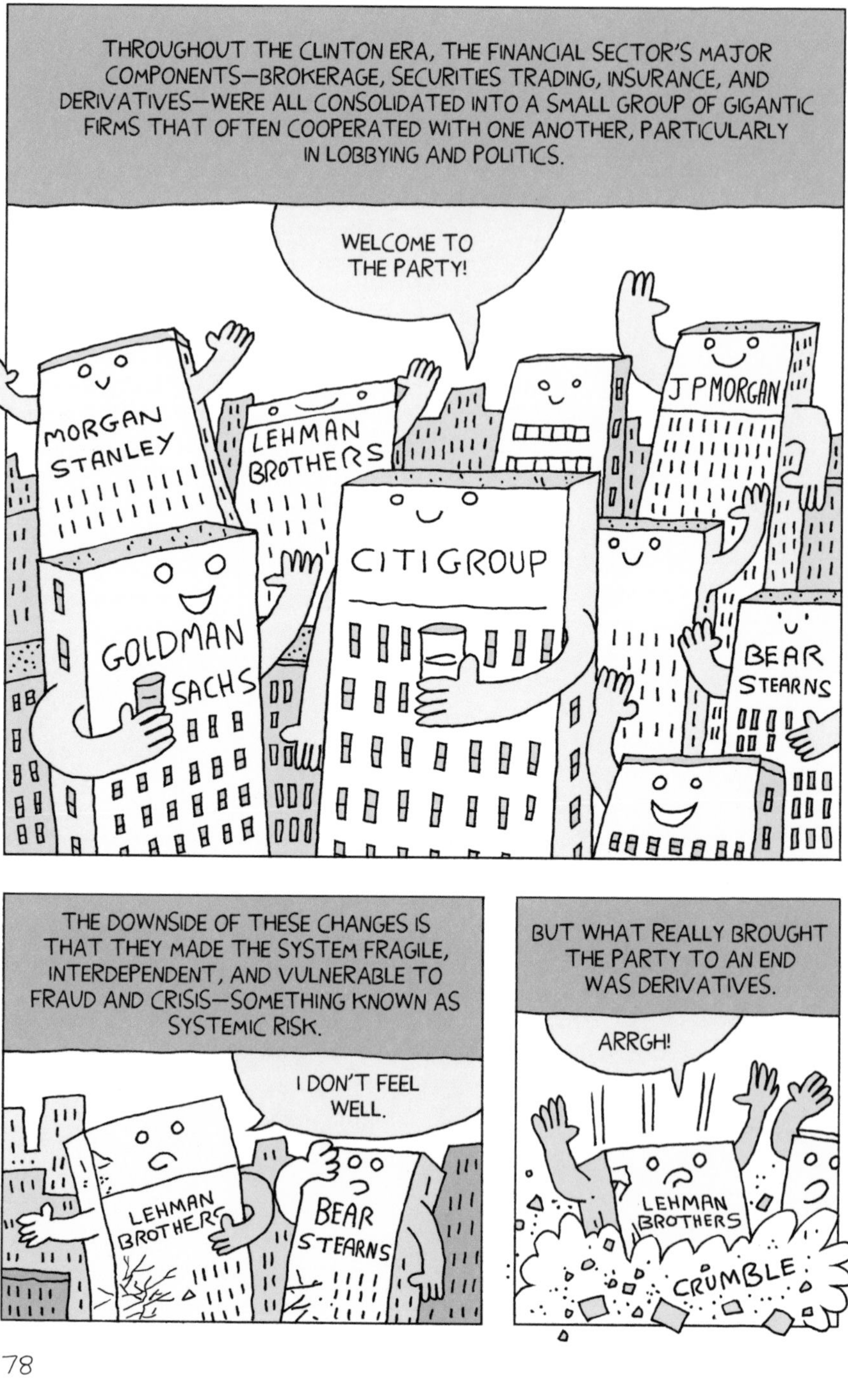
THROUGHOUT THE CLINTON ERA, THE FINANCIAL SECTOR'S MAJOR COMPONENTS—BROKERAGE, SECURITIES TRADING, INSURANCE, AND DERIVATIVES—WERE ALL CONSOLIDATED INTO A SMALL GROUP OF GIGANTIC FIRMS THAT OFTEN COOPERATED WITH ONE ANOTHER, PARTICULARLY IN LOBBYING AND POLITICS.
WELCOME TO THE PARTY!
MORGAN STANLEY
LEHMAN BROTHERS
JPMORGAN
CITIGROUP
GOLDMAN SACHS
BEAR STEARNS
THE DOWNSIDE OF THESE CHANGES IS THAT THEY MADE THE SYSTEM FRAGILE, INTERDEPENDENT, AND VULNERABLE TO FRAUD AND CRISIS—SOMETHING KNOWN AS SYSTEMIC RISK.
I DON'T FEEL WELL.
LEHMAN BROTHERS
BEAR STEARNS
BUT WHAT REALLY BROUGHT THE PARTY TO AN END WAS DERIVATIVES.
ARRGH!
LEHMAN BROTHERS
CRUMBLE

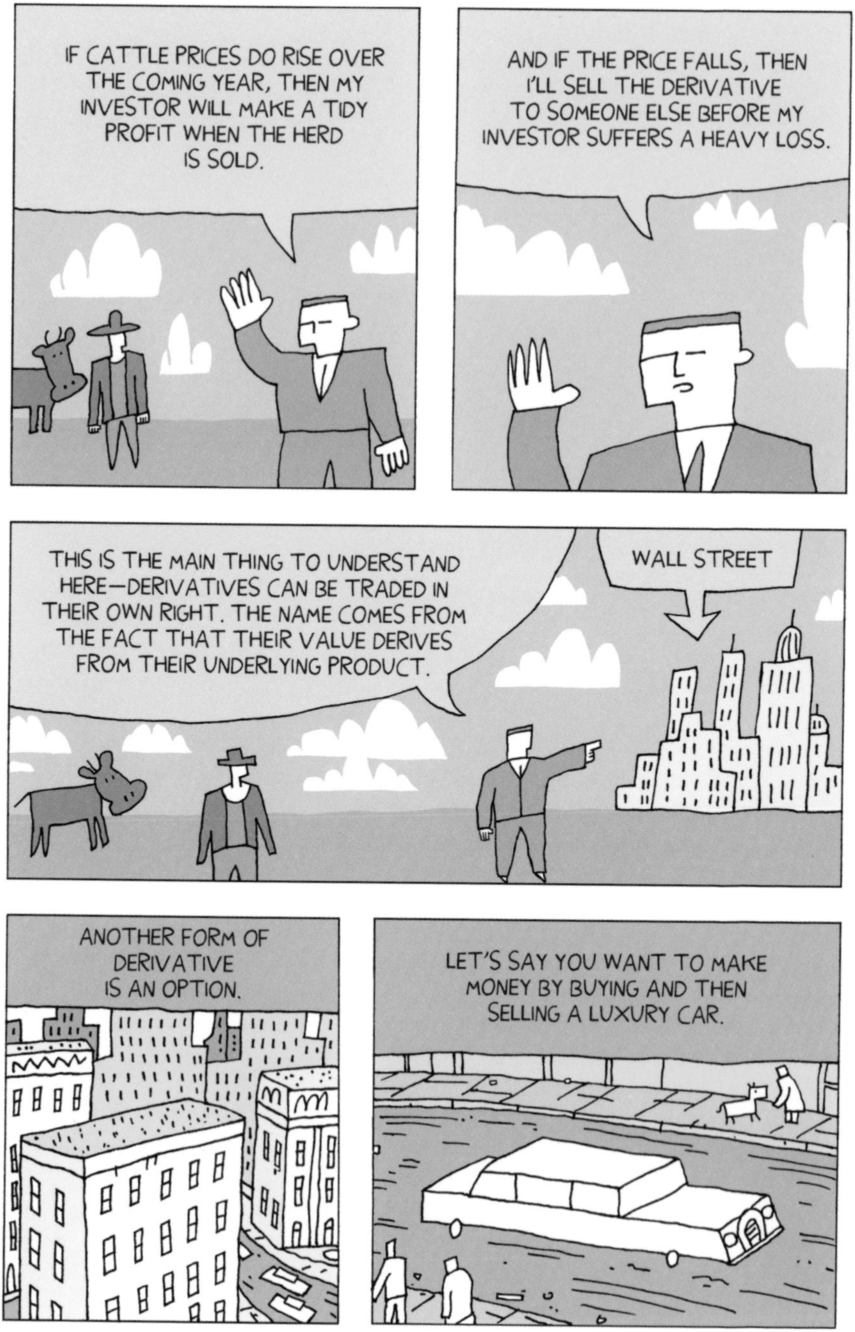
IF CATTLE PRICES DO RISE OVER THE COMING YEAR, THEN MY INVESTOR WILL MAKE A TIDY PROFIT WHEN THE HERD IS SOLD.
AND IF THE PRICE FALLS, THEN I'LL SELL THE DERIVATIVE TO SOMEONE ELSE BEFORE MY INVESTOR SUFFERS A HEAVY LOSS.
THIS IS THE MAIN THING TO UNDERSTAND HERE—DERIVATIVES CAN BE TRADED IN THEIR OWN RIGHT. THE NAME COMES FROM THE FACT THAT THEIR VALUE DERIVES FROM THEIR UNDERLYING PRODUCT.
WALL STREET
ANOTHER FORM OF DERIVATIVE IS AN OPTION.
LET'S SAY YOU WANT TO MAKE MONEY BY BUYING AND THEN SELLING A LUXURY CAR.

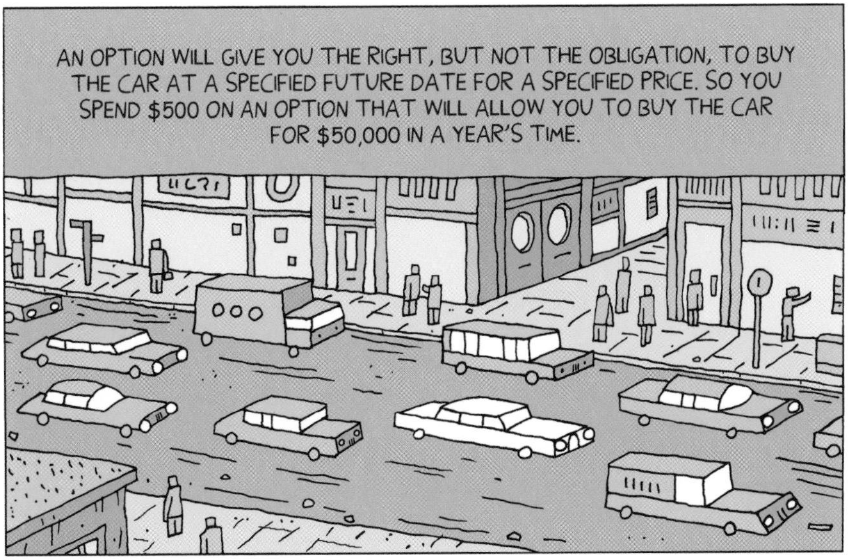
AN OPTION WILL GIVE YOU THE RIGHT, BUT NOT THE OBLIGATION, TO BUY THE CAR AT A SPECIFIED FUTURE DATE FOR A SPECIFIED PRICE. SO YOU SPEND $500 ON AN OPTION THAT WILL ALLOW YOU TO BUY THE CAR FOR $50,000 IN A YEAR'S TIME.

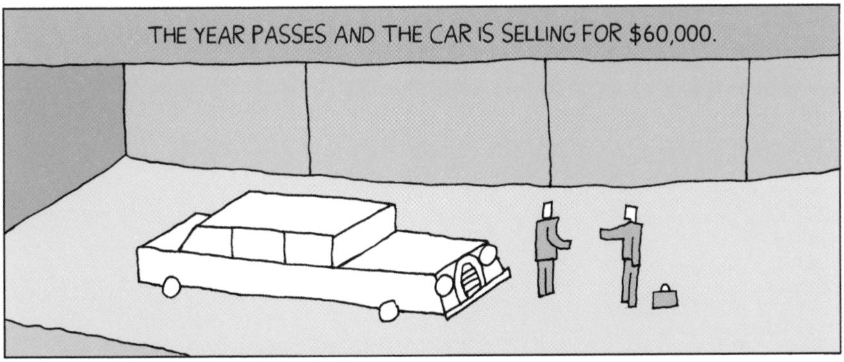
THE YEAR PASSES AND THE CAR IS SELLING FOR $60,000.

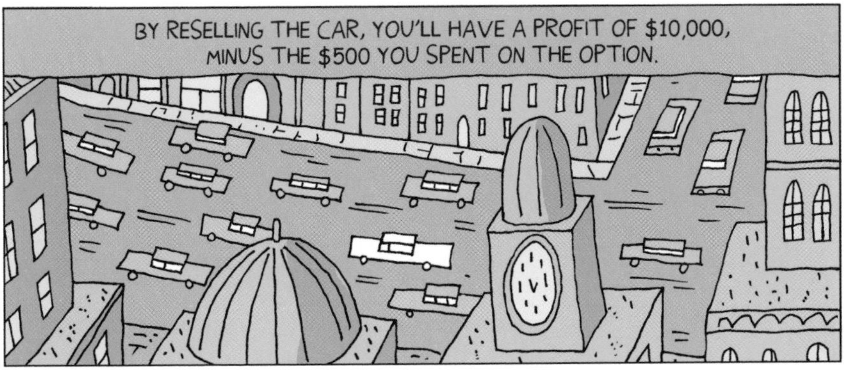
BY RESELLING THE CAR, YOU'LL HAVE A PROFIT OF $10,000, MINUS THE $500 YOU SPENT ON THE OPTION.

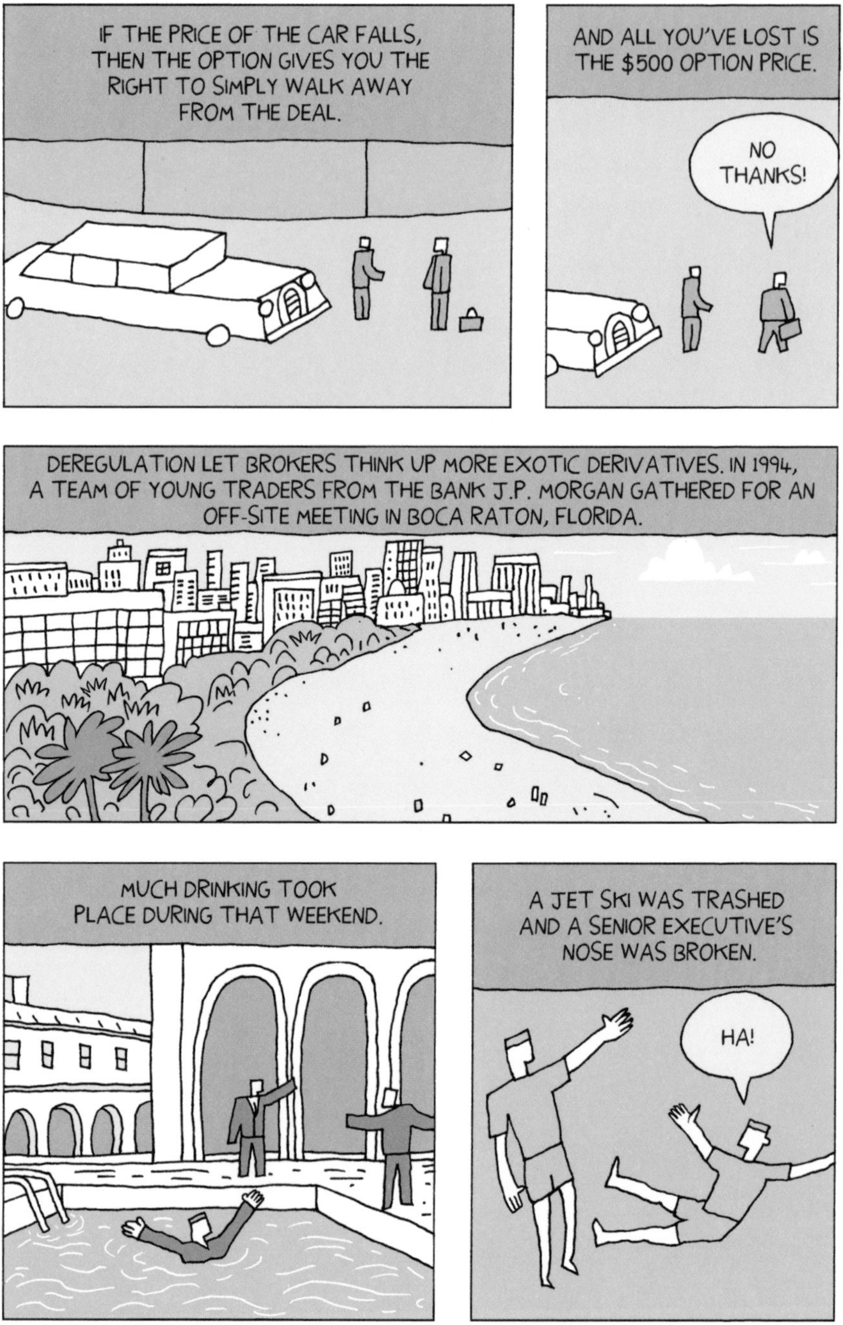
IF THE PRICE OF THE CAR FALLS, THEN THE OPTION GIVES YOU THE RIGHT TO SIMPLY WALK AWAY FROM THE DEAL.
AND ALL YOU'VE LOST IS THE $500 OPTION PRICE.
NO THANKS!
DEREGULATION LET BROKERS THINK UP MORE EXOTIC DERIVATIVES. IN 1994, A TEAM OF YOUNG TRADERS FROM THE BANK J.P. MORGAN GATHERED FOR AN OFF-SITE MEETING IN BOCA RATON, FLORIDA.
MUCH DRINKING TOOK PLACE DURING THAT WEEKEND.
A JET SKI WAS TRASHED AND A SENIOR EXECUTIVE'S NOSE WAS BROKEN.
HA!

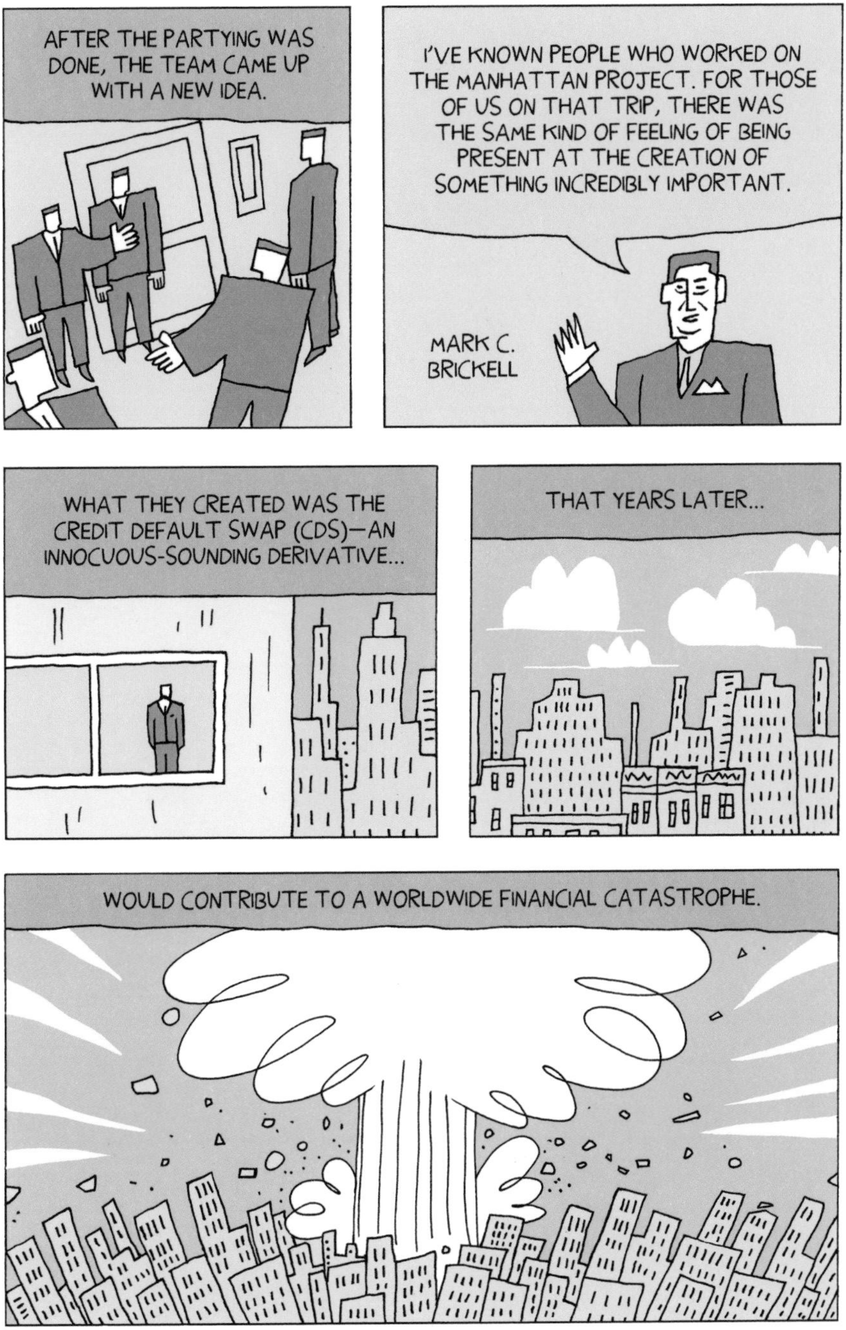
AFTER THE PARTYING WAS DONE, THE TEAM CAME UP WITH A NEW IDEA.
I'VE KNOWN PEOPLE WHO WORKED ON THE MANHATTAN PROJECT. FOR THOSE OF US ON THAT TRIP, THERE WAS THE SAME KIND OF FEELING OF BEING PRESENT AT THE CREATION OF SOMETHING INCREDIBLY IMPORTANT.
MARK C. BRICKELL
WHAT THEY CREATED WAS THE CREDIT DEFAULT SWAP (CDS)—AN INNOCUOUS-SOUNDING DERIVATIVE...
THAT YEARS LATER...
WOULD CONTRIBUTE TO A WORLDWIDE FINANCIAL CATASTROPHE.

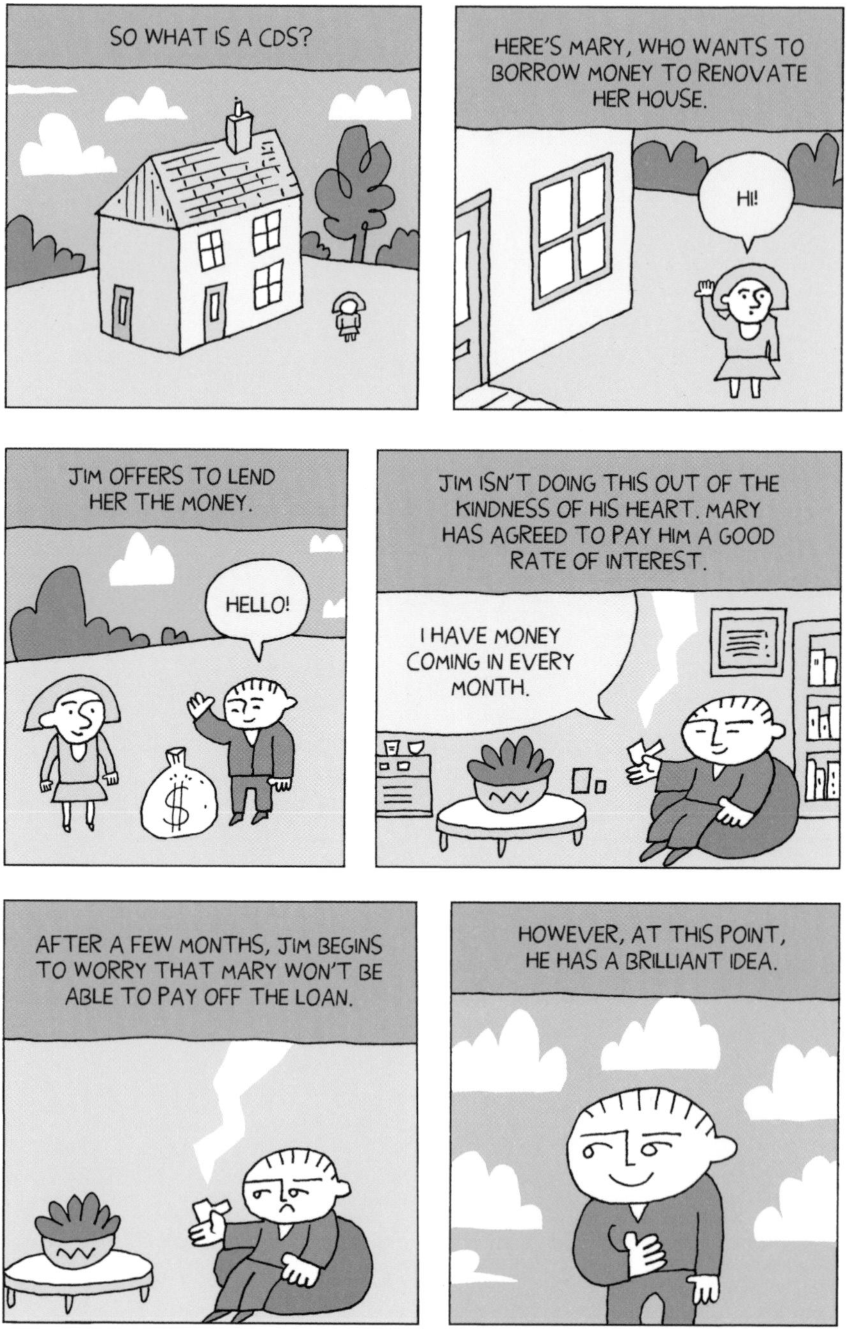
SO WHAT IS A CDS?
HERE'S MARY, WHO WANTS TO BORROW MONEY TO RENOVATE HER HOUSE.
HI!
JIM OFFERS TO LEND HER THE MONEY.
HELLO!
JIM ISN'T DOING THIS OUT OF THE KINDNESS OF HIS HEART. MARY HAS AGREED TO PAY HIM A GOOD RATE OF INTEREST.
I HAVE MONEY COMING IN EVERY MONTH.
AFTER A FEW MONTHS, JIM BEGINS TO WORRY THAT MARY WON'T BE ABLE TO PAY OFF THE LOAN.
HOWEVER, AT THIS POINT, HE HAS A BRILLIANT IDEA.

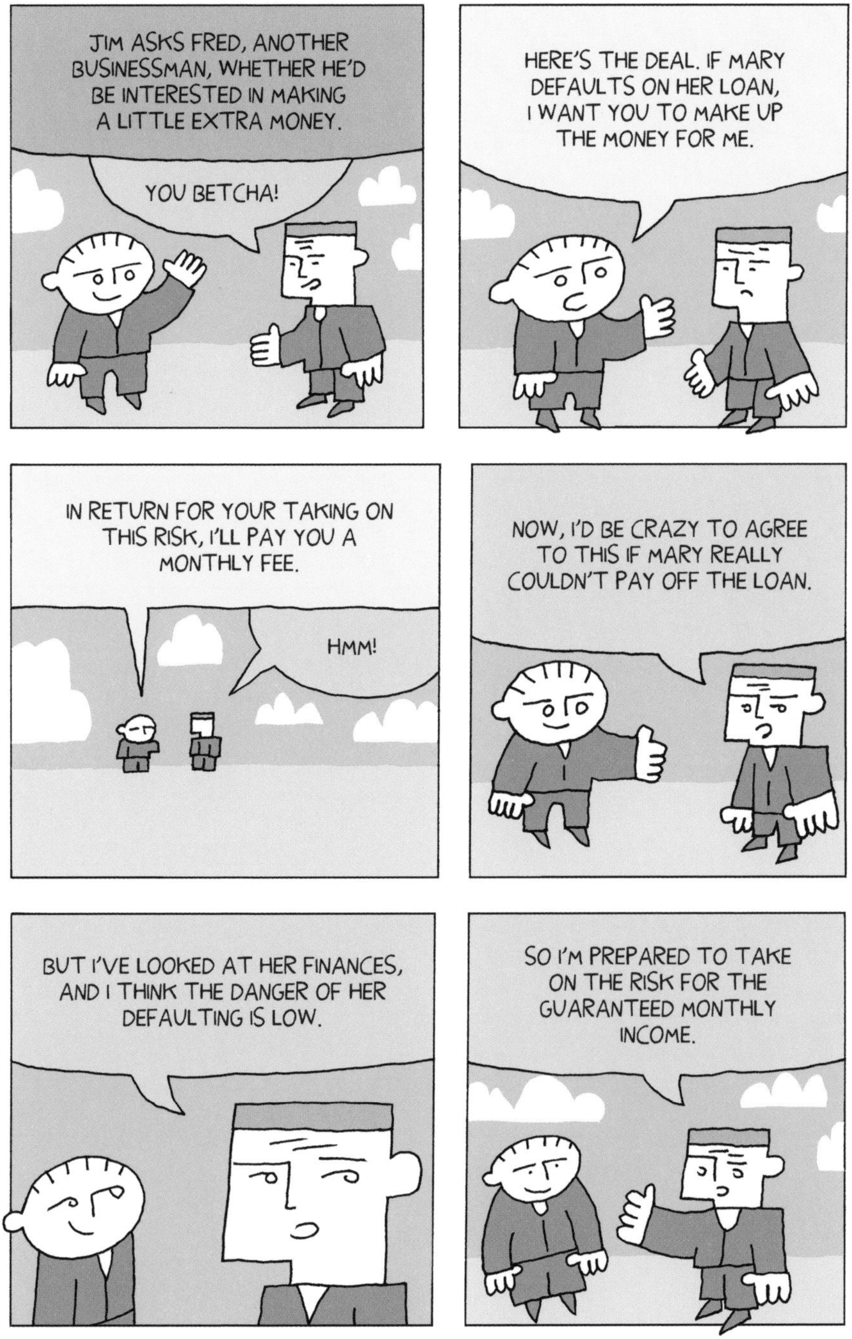
JIM ASKS FRED, ANOTHER BUSINESSMAN, WHETHER HE'D BE INTERESTED IN MAKING A LITTLE EXTRA MONEY.
YOU BETCHA!
HERE'S THE DEAL. IF MARY DEFAULTS ON HER LOAN, I WANT YOU TO MAKE UP THE MONEY FOR ME.
IN RETURN FOR YOUR TAKING ON THIS RISK, I'LL PAY YOU A MONTHLY FEE.
HMM!
NOW, I'D BE CRAZY TO AGREE TO THIS IF MARY REALLY COULDN'T PAY OFF THE LOAN.
BUT I'VE LOOKED AT HER FINANCES, AND I THINK THE DANGER OF HER DEFAULTING IS LOW.
SO I'M PREPARED TO TAKE ON THE RISK FOR THE GUARANTEED MONTHLY INCOME.

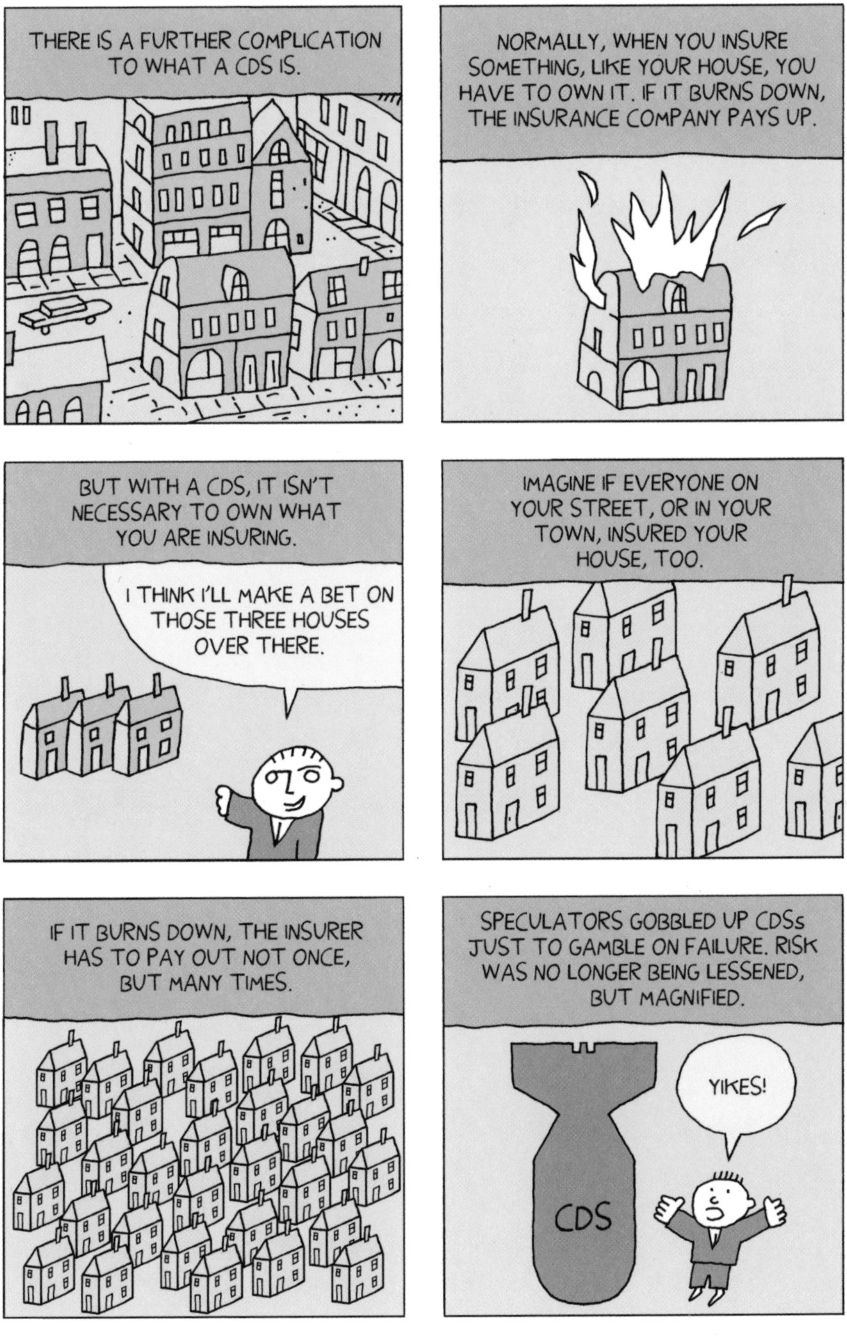
THERE IS A FURTHER COMPLICATION TO WHAT A CDS IS.
NORMALLY, WHEN YOU INSURE SOMETHING, LIKE YOUR HOUSE, YOU HAVE TO OWN IT. IF IT BURNS DOWN, THE INSURANCE COMPANY PAYS UP.
BUT WITH A CDS, IT ISN'T NECESSARY TO OWN WHAT YOU ARE INSURING.
I THINK I'LL MAKE A BET ON THOSE THREE HOUSES OVER THERE.
IMAGINE IF EVERYONE ON YOUR STREET, OR IN YOUR TOWN, INSURED YOUR HOUSE, TOO.
IF IT BURNS DOWN, THE INSURER HAS TO PAY OUT NOT ONCE, BUT MANY TIMES.
SPECULATORS GOBBLED UP CDSs JUST TO GAMBLE ON FAILURE. RISK WAS NO LONGER BEING LESSENED, BUT MAGNIFIED.
YIKES!
CDS

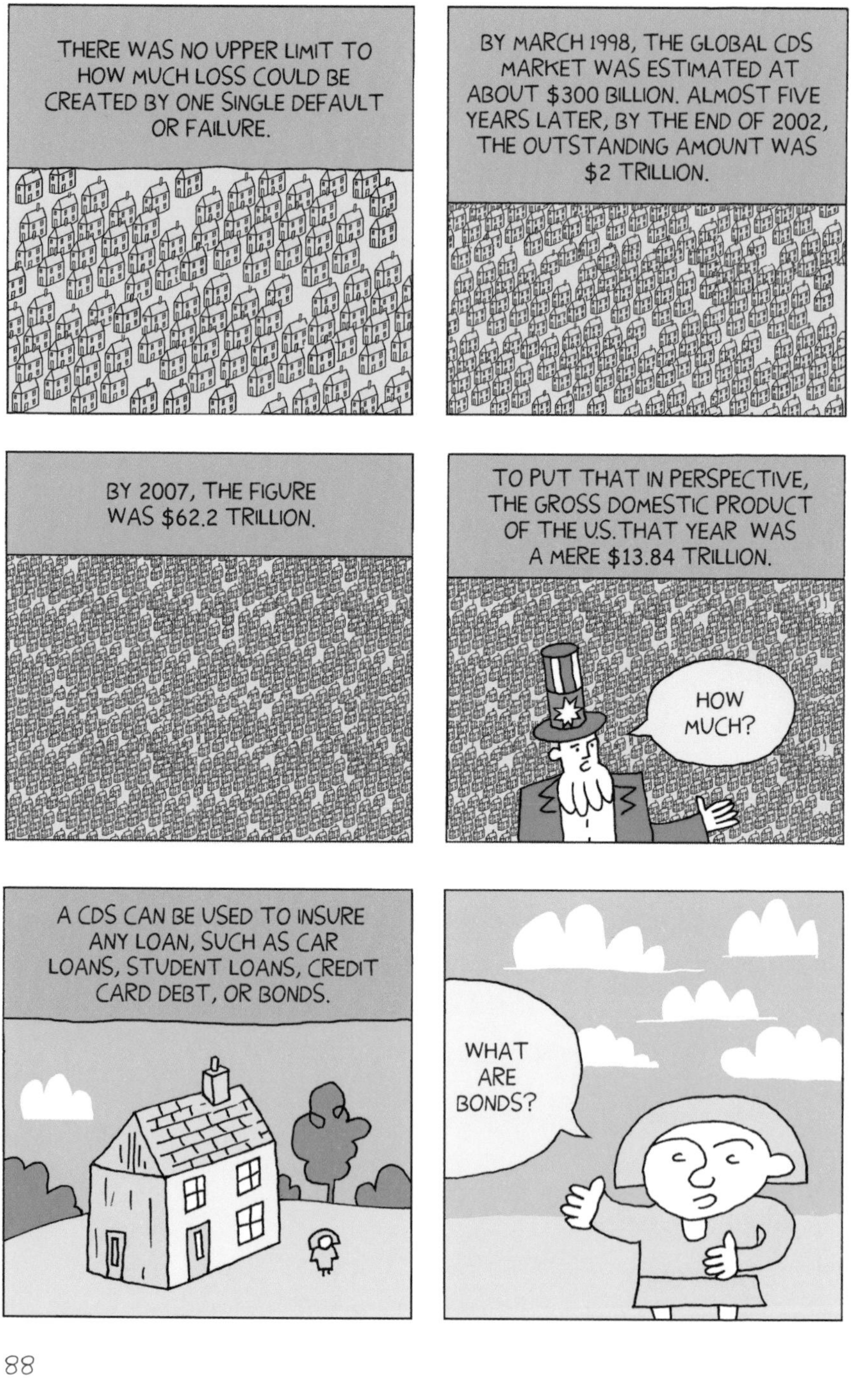
THERE WAS NO UPPER LIMIT TO HOW MUCH LOSS COULD BE CREATED BY ONE SINGLE DEFAULT OR FAILURE.
BY MARCH 1998, THE GLOBAL CDS MARKET WAS ESTIMATED AT ABOUT $300 BILLION. ALMOST FIVE YEARS LATER, BY THE END OF 2002, THE OUTSTANDING AMOUNT WAS $2 TRILLION.
BY 2007, THE FIGURE WAS $62.2 TRILLION.
TO PUT THAT IN PERSPECTIVE, THE GROSS DOMESTIC PRODUCT OF THE U.S. THAT YEAR WAS A MERE $13.84 TRILLION.
HOW MUCH?
A CDS CAN BE USED TO INSURE ANY LOAN, SUCH AS CAR LOANS, STUDENT LOANS, CREDIT CARD DEBT, OR BONDS.
WHAT ARE BONDS?

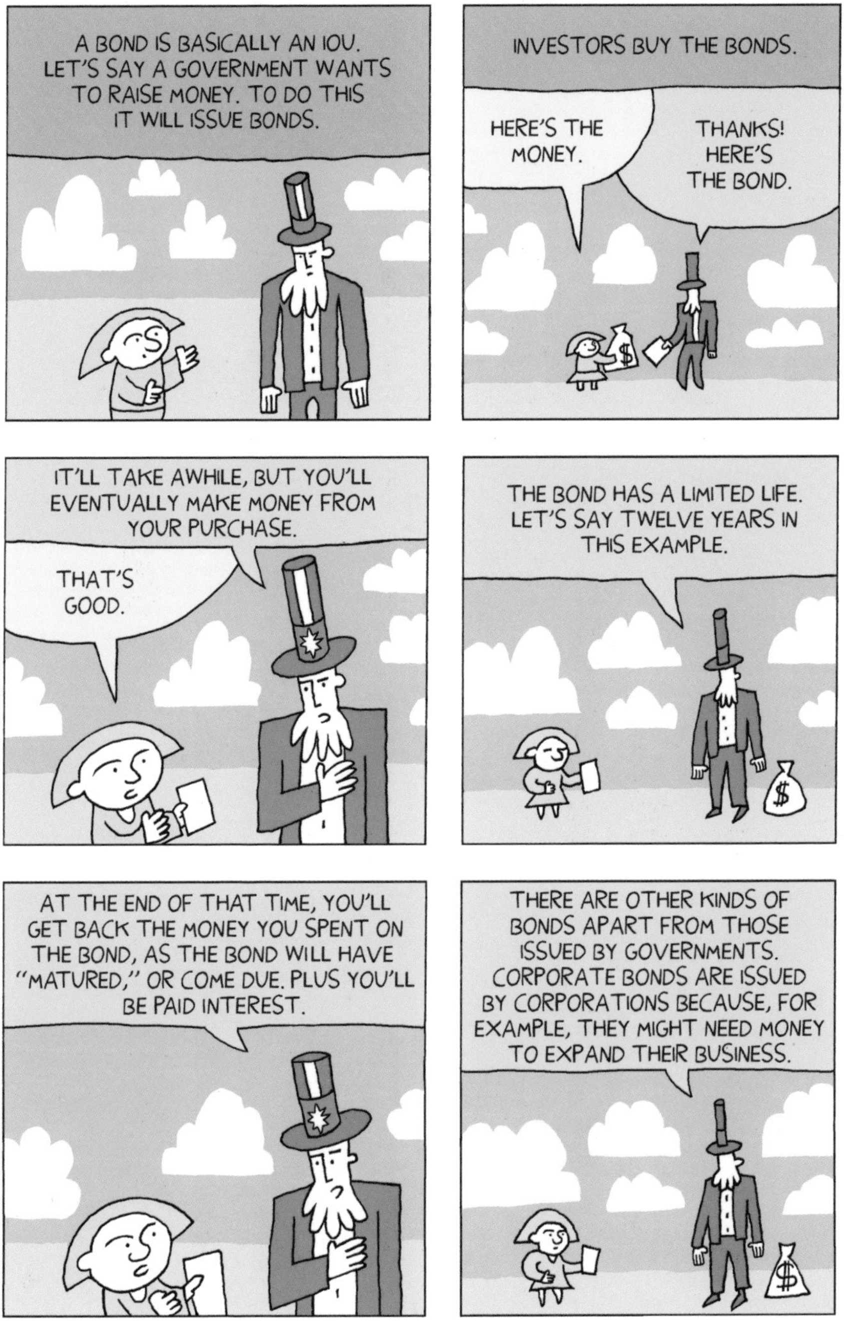
A BOND IS BASICALLY AN IOU. LET'S SAY A GOVERNMENT WANTS TO RAISE MONEY. TO DO THIS IT WILL ISSUE BONDS.
INVESTORS BUY THE BONDS.
HERE'S THE MONEY.
THANKS! HERE'S THE BOND.
IT'LL TAKE AWHILE, BUT YOU'LL EVENTUALLY MAKE MONEY FROM YOUR PURCHASE.
THAT'S GOOD.
THE BOND HAS A LIMITED LIFE. LET'S SAY TWELVE YEARS IN THIS EXAMPLE.
AT THE END OF THAT TIME, YOU'LL GET BACK THE MONEY YOU SPENT ON THE BOND, AS THE BOND WILL HAVE "MATURED," OR COME DUE. PLUS YOU'LL BE PAID INTEREST.
THERE ARE OTHER KINDS OF BONDS APART FROM THOSE ISSUED BY GOVERNMENTS. CORPORATE BONDS ARE ISSUED BY CORPORATIONS BECAUSE, FOR EXAMPLE, THEY MIGHT NEED MONEY TO EXPAND THEIR BUSINESS.

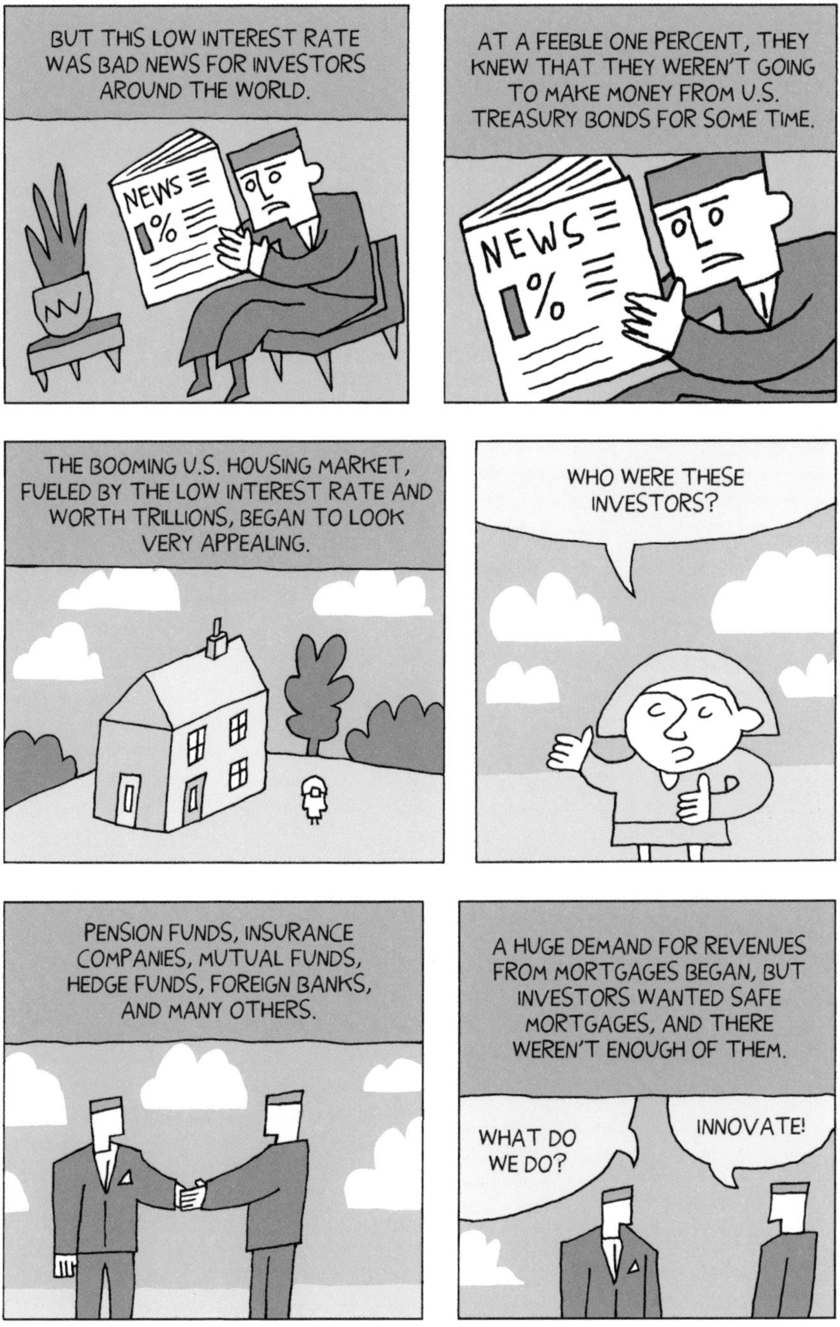
BUT THIS LOW INTEREST RATE WAS BAD NEWS FOR INVESTORS AROUND THE WORLD.
NEWS
1%
AT A FEEBLE ONE PERCENT, THEY KNEW THAT THEY WEREN'T GOING TO MAKE MONEY FROM U.S. TREASURY BONDS FOR SOME TIME.
NEWS
1%
THE BOOMING U.S. HOUSING MARKET, FUELED BY THE LOW INTEREST RATE AND WORTH TRILLIONS, BEGAN TO LOOK VERY APPEALING.
WHO WERE THESE INVESTORS?
PENSION FUNDS, INSURANCE COMPANIES, MUTUAL FUNDS, HEDGE FUNDS, FOREIGN BANKS, AND MANY OTHERS.
A HUGE DEMAND FOR REVENUES FROM MORTGAGES BEGAN, BUT INVESTORS WANTED SAFE MORTGAGES, AND THERE WEREN'T ENOUGH OF THEM.
WHAT DO WE DO?
INNOVATE!

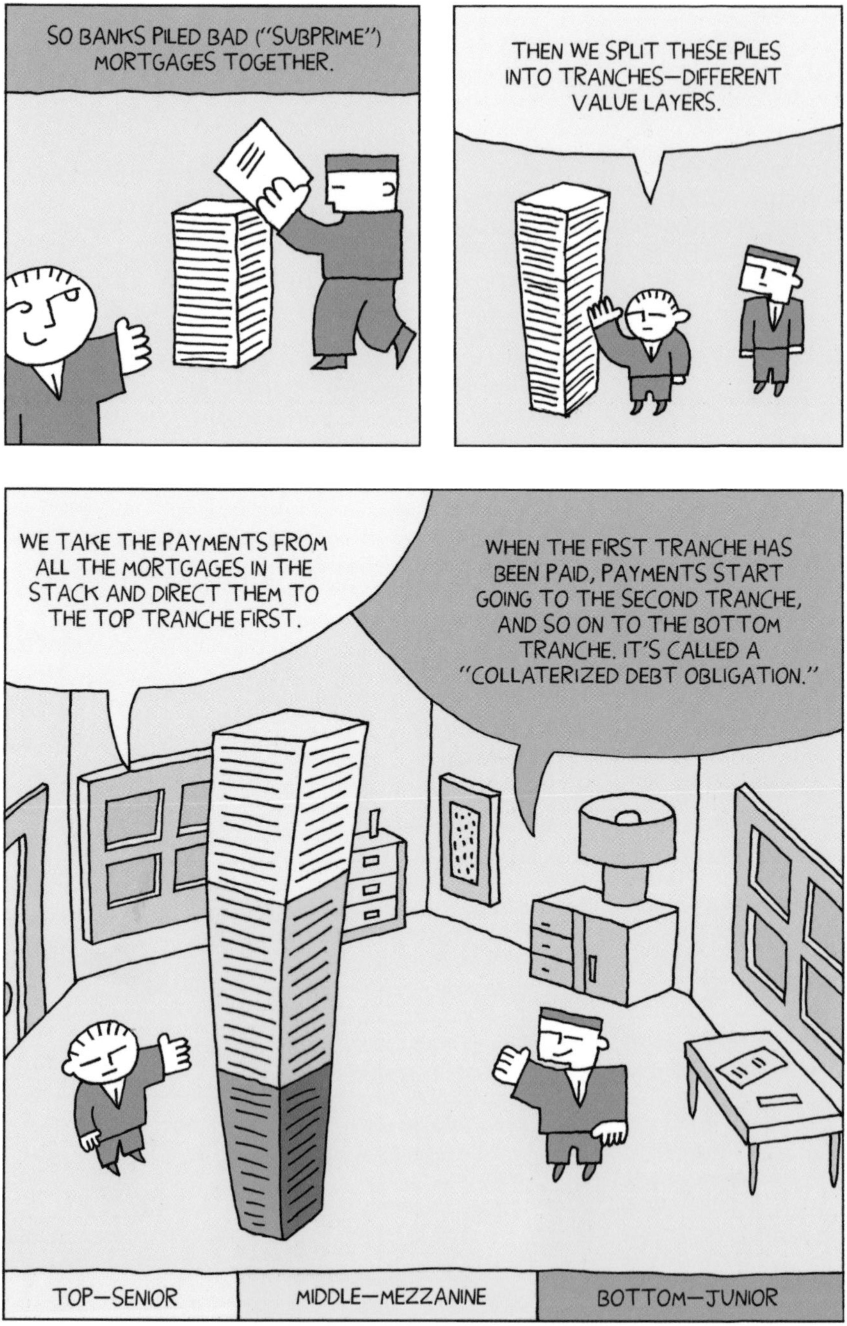
SO BANKS PILED BAD ("SUBPRIME") MORTGAGES TOGETHER.
THEN WE SPLIT THESE PILES INTO TRANCHES—DIFFERENT VALUE LAYERS.
WE TAKE THE PAYMENTS FROM ALL THE MORTGAGES IN THE STACK AND DIRECT THEM TO THE TOP TRANCHE FIRST.
WHEN THE FIRST TRANCHE HAS BEEN PAID, PAYMENTS START GOING TO THE SECOND TRANCHE, AND SO ON TO THE BOTTOM TRANCHE. IT'S CALLED A "COLLATERIZED DEBT OBLIGATION."
TOP—SENIOR
MIDDLE—MEZZANINE
BOTTOM—JUNIOR

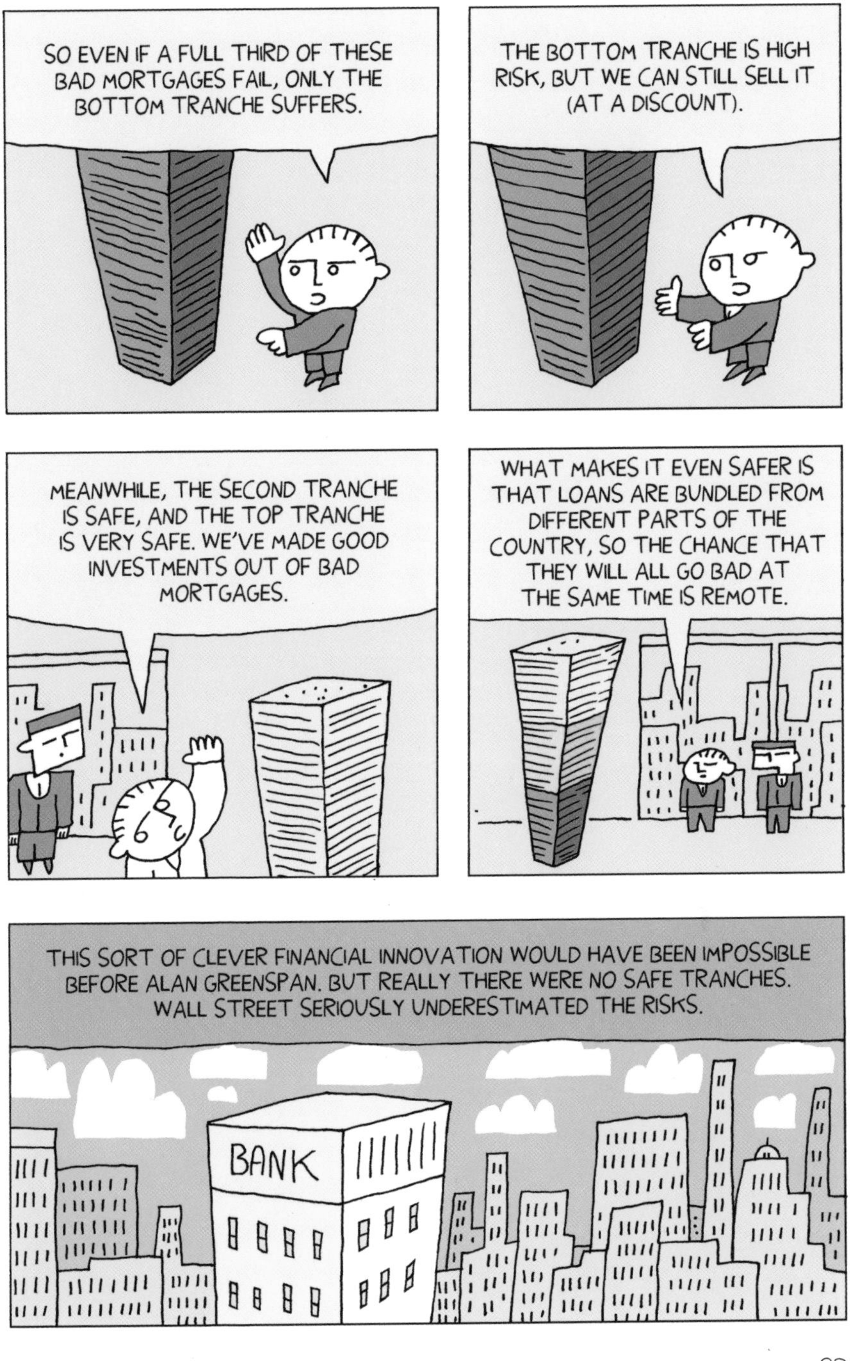
SO EVEN IF A FULL THIRD OF THESE BAD MORTGAGES FAIL, ONLY THE BOTTOM TRANCHE SUFFERS.
THE BOTTOM TRANCHE IS HIGH RISK, BUT WE CAN STILL SELL IT (AT A DISCOUNT).
MEANWHILE, THE SECOND TRANCHE IS SAFE, AND THE TOP TRANCHE IS VERY SAFE. WE'VE MADE GOOD INVESTMENTS OUT OF BAD MORTGAGES.
WHAT MAKES IT EVEN SAFER IS THAT LOANS ARE BUNDLED FROM DIFFERENT PARTS OF THE COUNTRY, SO THE CHANCE THAT THEY WILL ALL GO BAD AT THE SAME TIME IS REMOTE.
THIS SORT OF CLEVER FINANCIAL INNOVATION WOULD HAVE BEEN IMPOSSIBLE BEFORE ALAN GREENSPAN. BUT REALLY THERE WERE NO SAFE TRANCHES. WALL STREET SERIOUSLY UNDERESTIMATED THE RISKS.
BANK

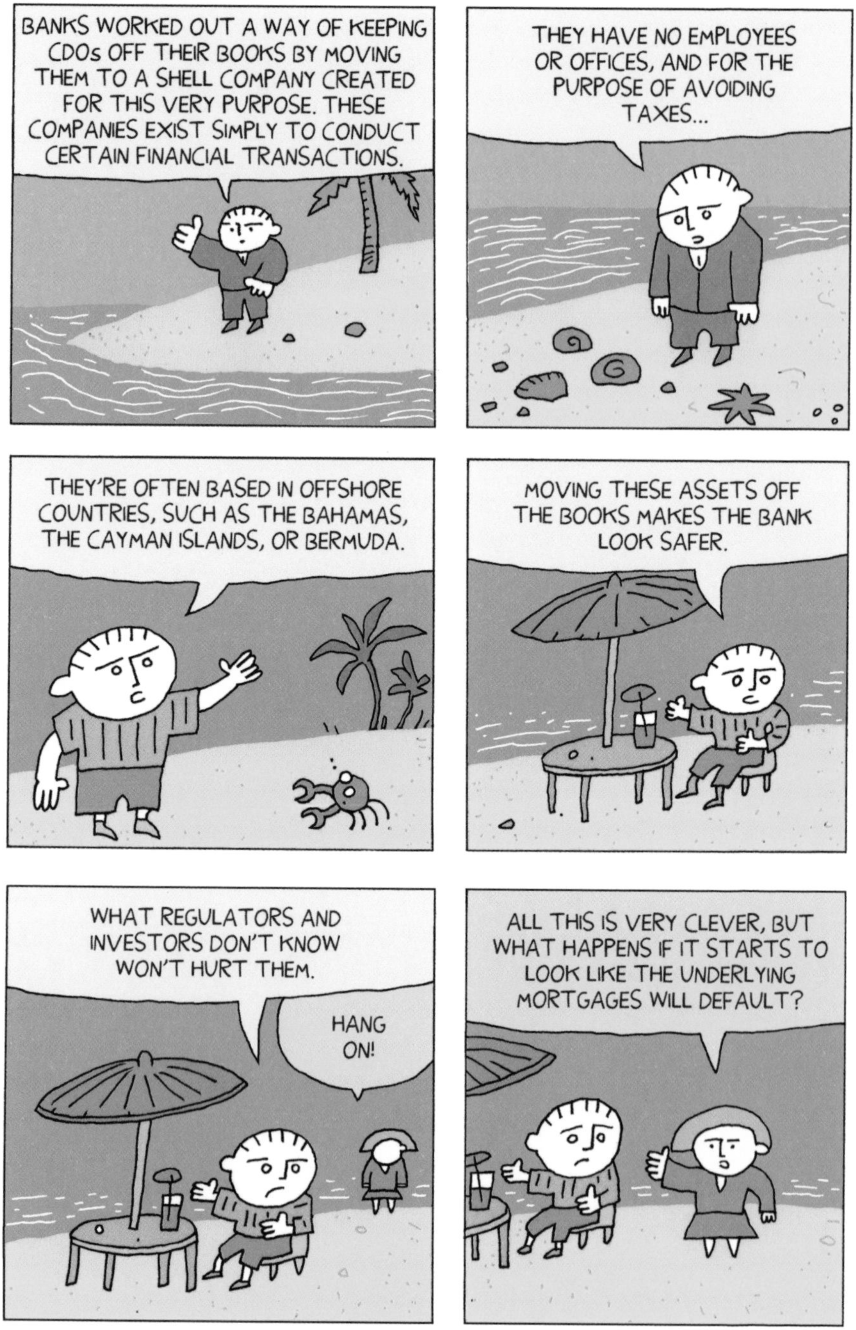
BANKS WORKED OUT A WAY OF KEEPING CDOs OFF THEIR BOOKS BY MOVING THEM TO A SHELL COMPANY CREATED FOR THIS VERY PURPOSE. THESE COMPANIES EXIST SIMPLY TO CONDUCT CERTAIN FINANCIAL TRANSACTIONS.
THEY HAVE NO EMPLOYEES OR OFFICES, AND FOR THE PURPOSE OF AVOIDING TAXES...
THEY'RE OFTEN BASED IN OFFSHORE COUNTRIES, SUCH AS THE BAHAMAS, THE CAYMAN ISLANDS, OR BERMUDA.
MOVING THESE ASSETS OFF THE BOOKS MAKES THE BANK LOOK SAFER.
WHAT REGULATORS AND INVESTORS DON'T KNOW WON'T HURT THEM.
HANG ON!
ALL THIS IS VERY CLEVER, BUT WHAT HAPPENS IF IT STARTS TO LOOK LIKE THE UNDERLYING MORTGAGES WILL DEFAULT?

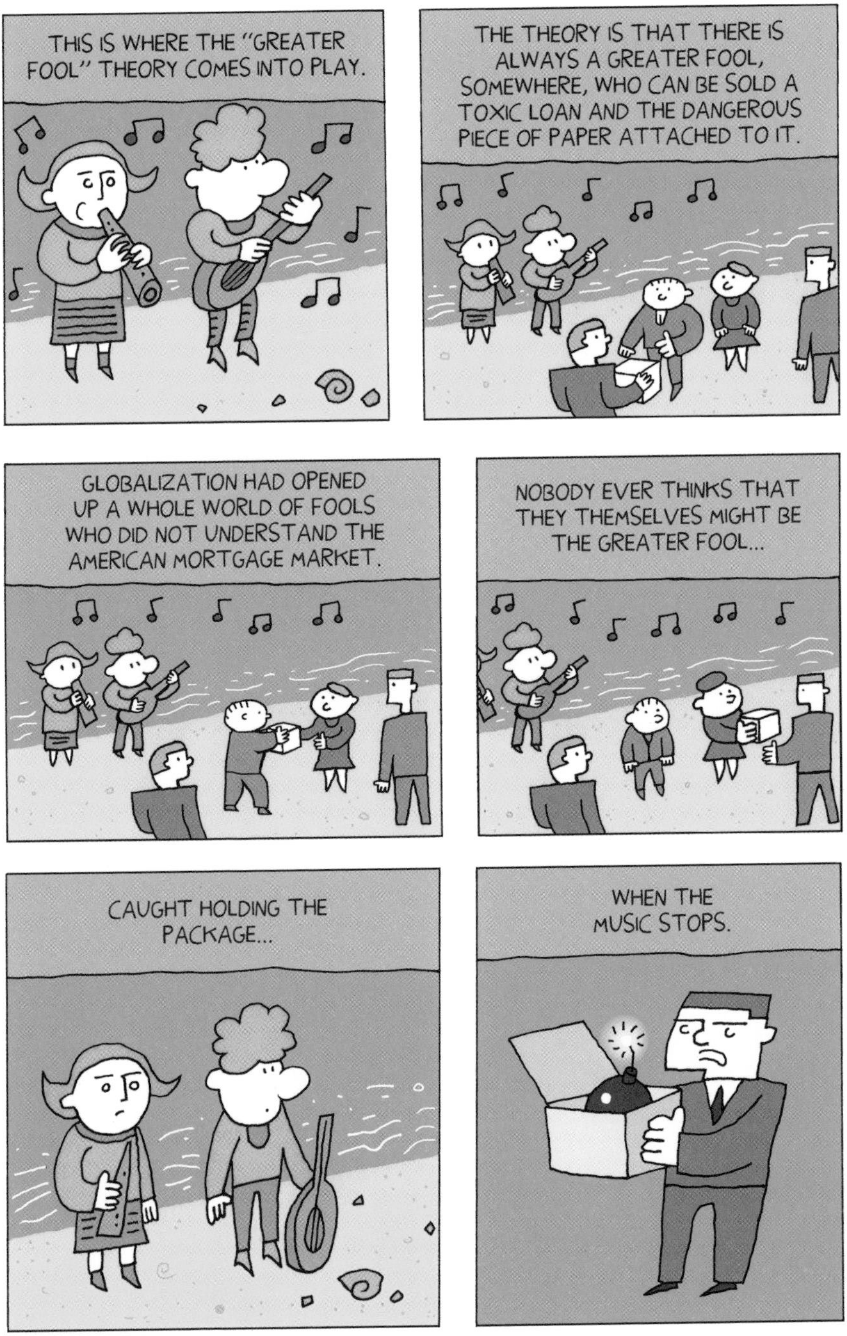
THIS IS WHERE THE "GREATER FOOL" THEORY COMES INTO PLAY.
THE THEORY IS THAT THERE IS ALWAYS A GREATER FOOL, SOMEWHERE, WHO CAN BE SOLD A TOXIC LOAN AND THE DANGEROUS PIECE OF PAPER ATTACHED TO IT.
GLOBALIZATION HAD OPENED UP A WHOLE WORLD OF FOOLS WHO DID NOT UNDERSTAND THE AMERICAN MORTGAGE MARKET.
NOBODY EVER THINKS THAT THEY THEMSELVES MIGHT BE THE GREATER FOOL...
CAUGHT HOLDING THE PACKAGE...
WHEN THE MUSIC STOPS.

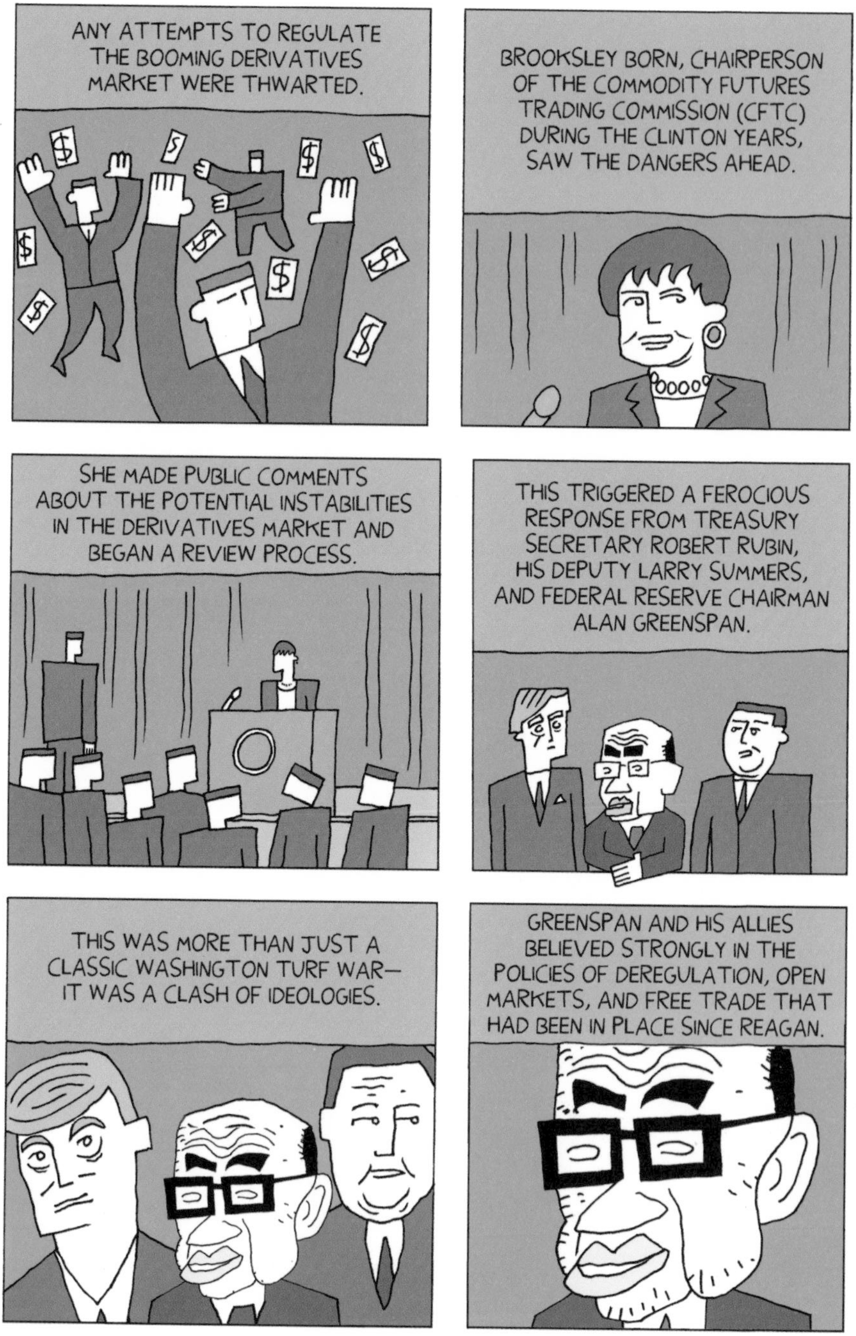
ANY ATTEMPTS TO REGULATE THE BOOMING DERIVATIVES MARKET WERE THWARTED.
BROOKSLEY BORN, CHAIRPERSON OF THE COMMODITY FUTURES TRADING COMMISSION (CFTC) DURING THE CLINTON YEARS, SAW THE DANGERS AHEAD.
SHE MADE PUBLIC COMMENTS ABOUT THE POTENTIAL INSTABILITIES IN THE DERIVATIVES MARKET AND BEGAN A REVIEW PROCESS.
THIS TRIGGERED A FEROCIOUS RESPONSE FROM TREASURY SECRETARY ROBERT RUBIN, HIS DEPUTY LARRY SUMMERS, AND FEDERAL RESERVE CHAIRMAN ALAN GREENSPAN.
THIS WAS MORE THAN JUST A CLASSIC WASHINGTON TURF WAR— IT WAS A CLASH OF IDEOLOGIES.
GREENSPAN AND HIS ALLIES BELIEVED STRONGLY IN THE POLICIES OF DEREGULATION, OPEN MARKETS, AND FREE TRADE THAT HAD BEEN IN PLACE SINCE REAGAN.

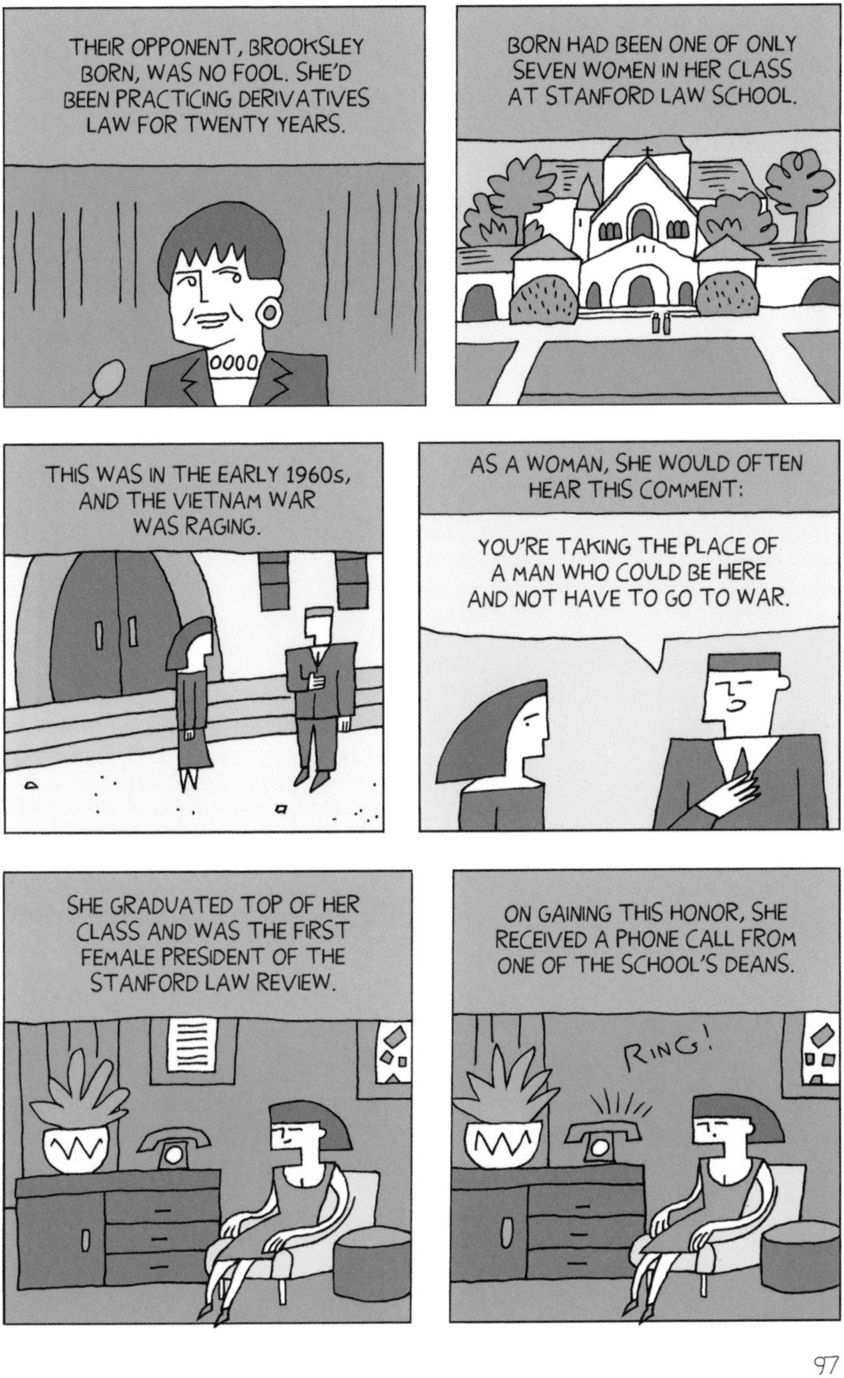
THEIR OPPONENT, BROOKSLEY BORN, WAS NO FOOL. SHE'D BEEN PRACTICING DERIVATIVES LAW FOR TWENTY YEARS.
BORN HAD BEEN ONE OF ONLY SEVEN WOMEN IN HER CLASS AT STANFORD LAW SCHOOL.
THIS WAS IN THE EARLY 1960s, AND THE VIETNAM WAR WAS RAGING.
AS A WOMAN, SHE WOULD OFTEN HEAR THIS COMMENT:
YOU'RE TAKING THE PLACE OF A MAN WHO COULD BE HERE AND NOT HAVE TO GO TO WAR.
SHE GRADUATED TOP OF HER CLASS AND WAS THE FIRST FEMALE PRESIDENT OF THE STANFORD LAW REVIEW.
ON GAINING THIS HONOR, SHE RECEIVED A PHONE CALL FROM ONE OF THE SCHOOL'S DEANS.
RING!

IN GREENSPAN'S MEMOIR, "THE AGE OF TURBULENCE," PUBLISHED IN 2007, HE BARELY MENTIONS AYN RAND OR THE THIRTY-YEAR INFLUENCE SHE HAD ON HIS LIFE.

IT'S PERHAPS UNDERSTANDABLE THAT HE'D WANT TO DISTANCE HIMSELF FROM HER ONCE HE'D REACHED HIGH OFFICE, CONSIDERING THE EXTREME POSITIONS HE'D ADVANCED AS A MEMBER OF HER COLLECTIVE.

IN 1957 HE WROTE TO THE EDITOR OF THE NEW YORK TIMES BOOK REVIEW, PRAISING "ATLAS SHRUGGED."

"ATLAS SHRUGGED" IS A CELEBRATION OF LIFE AND HAPPINESS. JUSTICE IS UNRELENTING. CREATIVE INDIVIDUALS AND UNDEVIATING PURPOSE AND RATIONALITY ACHIEVE JOY... PARASITES WHO PERSISTENTLY AVOID EITHER PURPOSE OR REASON PERISH AS THEY SHOULD.

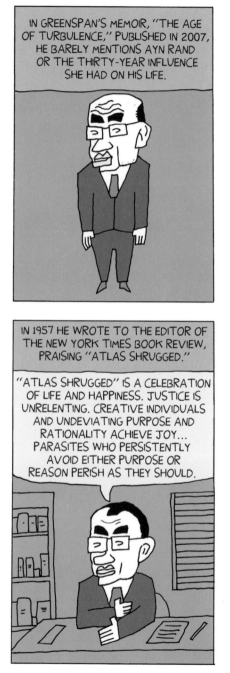

IN 1966, GREENSPAN WROTE THREE ESSAYS FOR THE RAND ANTHOLOGY "CAPITALISM: THE UNKNOWN IDEAL" IN WHICH HE EQUATED GOVERNMENT REGULATION WITH A BREAKDOWN OF SOCIETY'S MORALS. IN HIS VIEW, THERE WAS NO NEED FOR THE SECURITIES AND EXCHANGE COMMISSION, OR THE FOOD AND DRUG ADMINISTRATION.

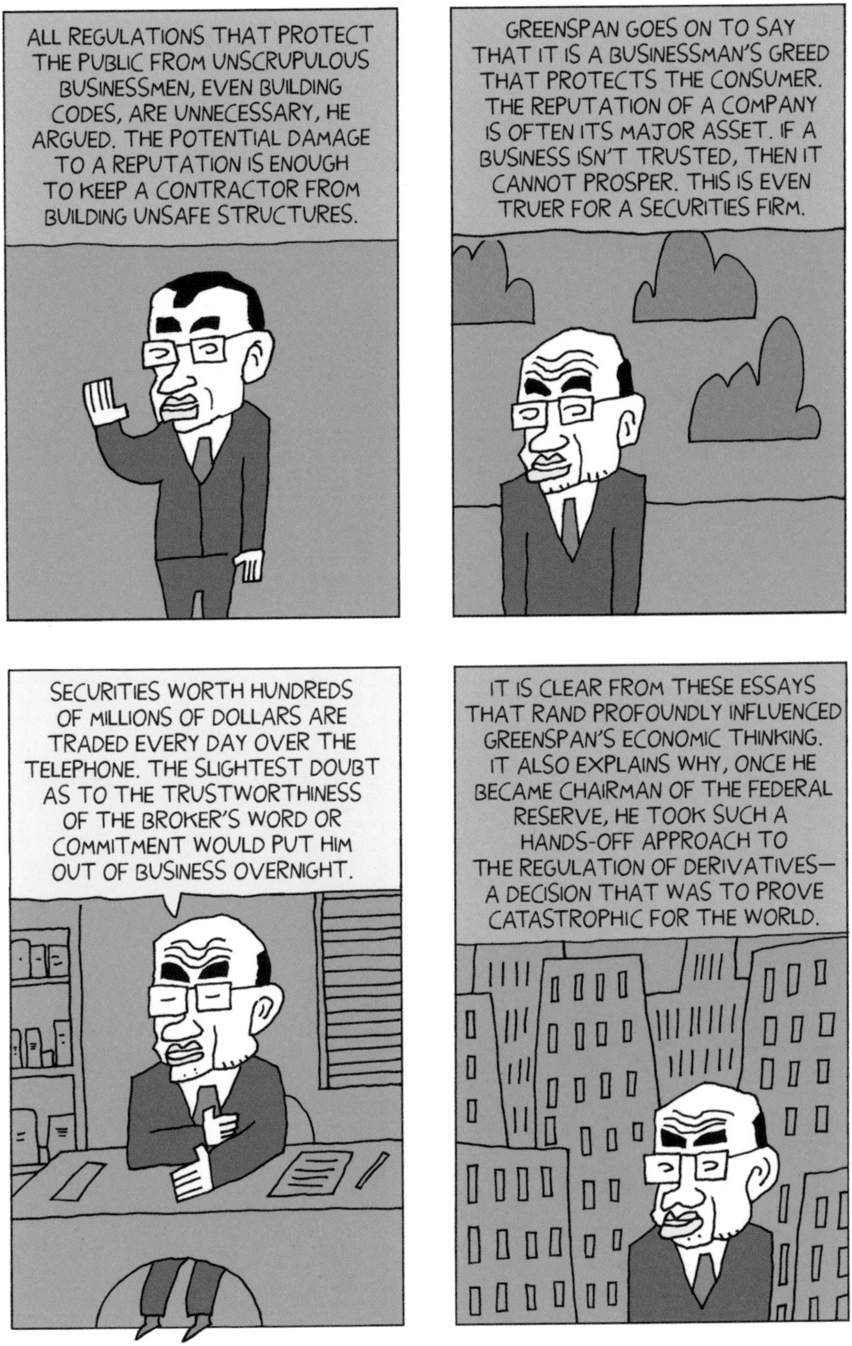
ALL REGULATIONS THAT PROTECT THE PUBLIC FROM UNSCRUPULOUS BUSINESSMEN, EVEN BUILDING CODES, ARE UNNECESSARY, HE ARGUED. THE POTENTIAL DAMAGE TO A REPUTATION IS ENOUGH TO KEEP A CONTRACTOR FROM BUILDING UNSAFE STRUCTURES.
GREENSPAN GOES ON TO SAY THAT IT IS A BUSINESSMAN'S GREED THAT PROTECTS THE CONSUMER. THE REPUTATION OF A COMPANY IS OFTEN ITS MAJOR ASSET. IF A BUSINESS ISN'T TRUSTED, THEN IT CANNOT PROSPER. THIS IS EVEN TRUER FOR A SECURITIES FIRM.
SECURITIES WORTH HUNDREDS OF MILLIONS OF DOLLARS ARE TRADED EVERY DAY OVER THE TELEPHONE. THE SLIGHTEST DOUBT AS TO THE TRUSTWORTHINESS OF THE BROKER'S WORD OR COMMITMENT WOULD PUT HIM OUT OF BUSINESS OVERNIGHT.
IT IS CLEAR FROM THESE ESSAYS THAT RAND PROFOUNDLY INFLUENCED GREENSPAN'S ECONOMIC THINKING. IT ALSO EXPLAINS WHY, ONCE HE BECAME CHAIRMAN OF THE FEDERAL RESERVE, HE TOOK SUCH A HANDS-OFF APPROACH TO THE REGULATION OF DERIVATIVES—A DECISION THAT WAS TO PROVE CATASTROPHIC FOR THE WORLD.

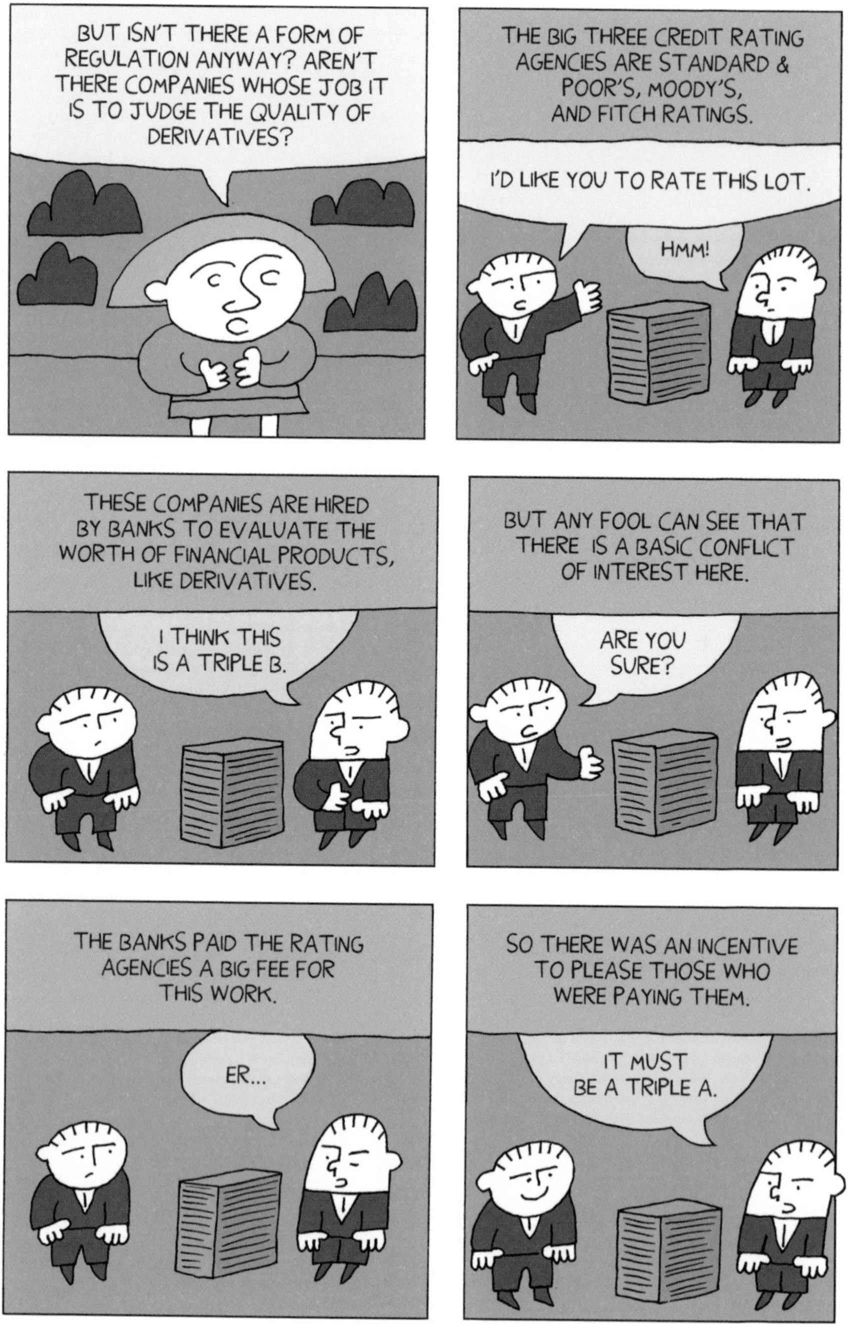
BUT ISN'T THERE A FORM OF REGULATION ANYWAY? AREN'T THERE COMPANIES WHOSE JOB IT IS TO JUDGE THE QUALITY OF DERIVATIVES?
THE BIG THREE CREDIT RATING AGENCIES ARE STANDARD & POOR'S, MOODY'S, AND FITCH RATINGS.
I'D LIKE YOU TO RATE THIS LOT.
HMM!
THESE COMPANIES ARE HIRED BY BANKS TO EVALUATE THE WORTH OF FINANCIAL PRODUCTS, LIKE DERIVATIVES.
I THINK THIS IS A TRIPLE B.
BUT ANY FOOL CAN SEE THAT THERE IS A BASIC CONFLICT OF INTEREST HERE.
ARE YOU SURE?
THE BANKS PAID THE RATING AGENCIES A BIG FEE FOR THIS WORK.
ER...
SO THERE WAS AN INCENTIVE TO PLEASE THOSE WHO WERE PAYING THEM.
IT MUST BE A TRIPLE A.

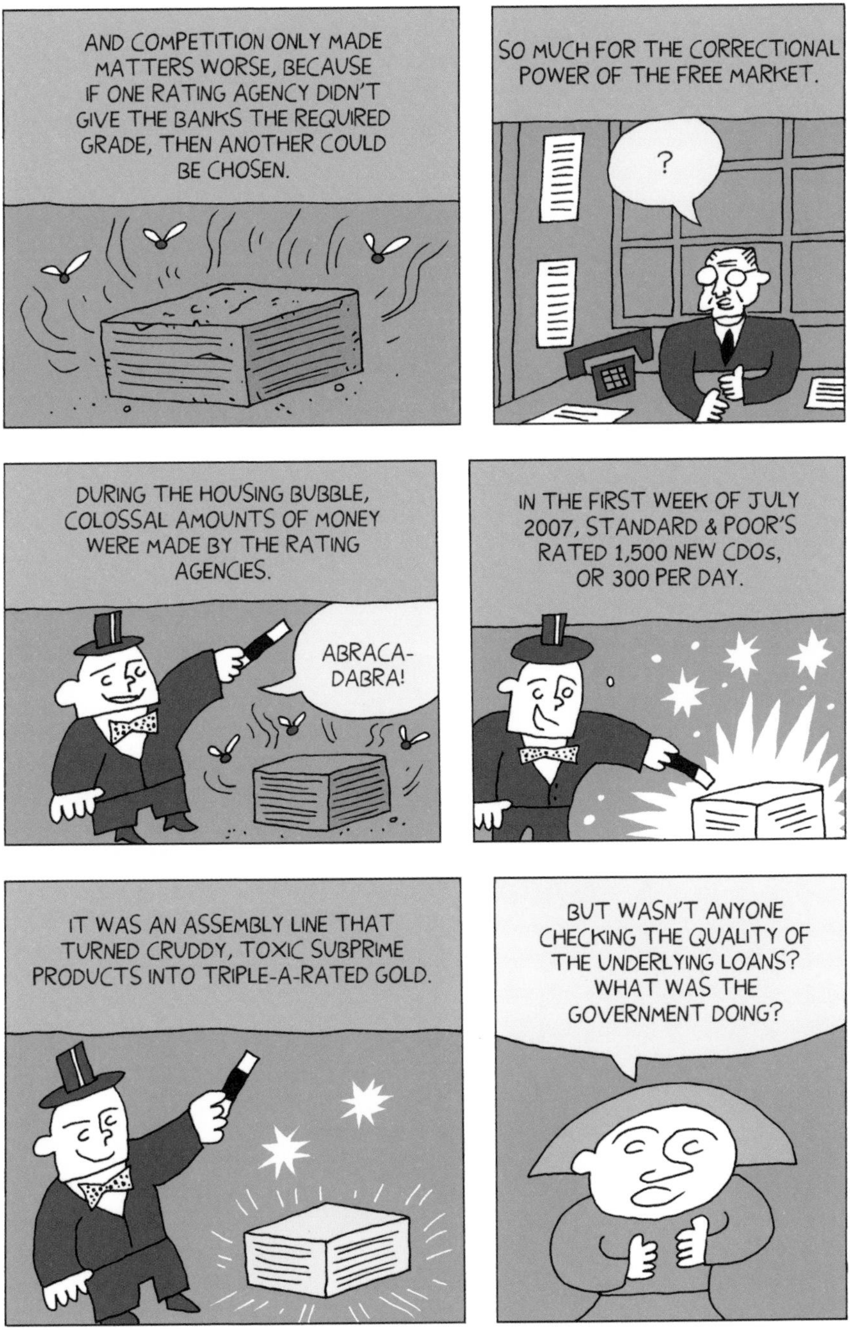
AND COMPETITION ONLY MADE MATTERS WORSE, BECAUSE IF ONE RATING AGENCY DIDN'T GIVE THE BANKS THE REQUIRED GRADE, THEN ANOTHER COULD BE CHOSEN.
SO MUCH FOR THE CORRECTIONAL POWER OF THE FREE MARKET.
?
DURING THE HOUSING BUBBLE, COLOSSAL AMOUNTS OF MONEY WERE MADE BY THE RATING AGENCIES.
ABRACA-DABRA!
IN THE FIRST WEEK OF JULY 2007, STANDARD & POOR'S RATED 1,500 NEW CDOs, OR 300 PER DAY.
IT WAS AN ASSEMBLY LINE THAT TURNED CRUDDY, TOXIC SUBPRIME PRODUCTS INTO TRIPLE-A-RATED GOLD.
BUT WASN'T ANYONE CHECKING THE QUALITY OF THE UNDERLYING LOANS? WHAT WAS THE GOVERNMENT DOING?

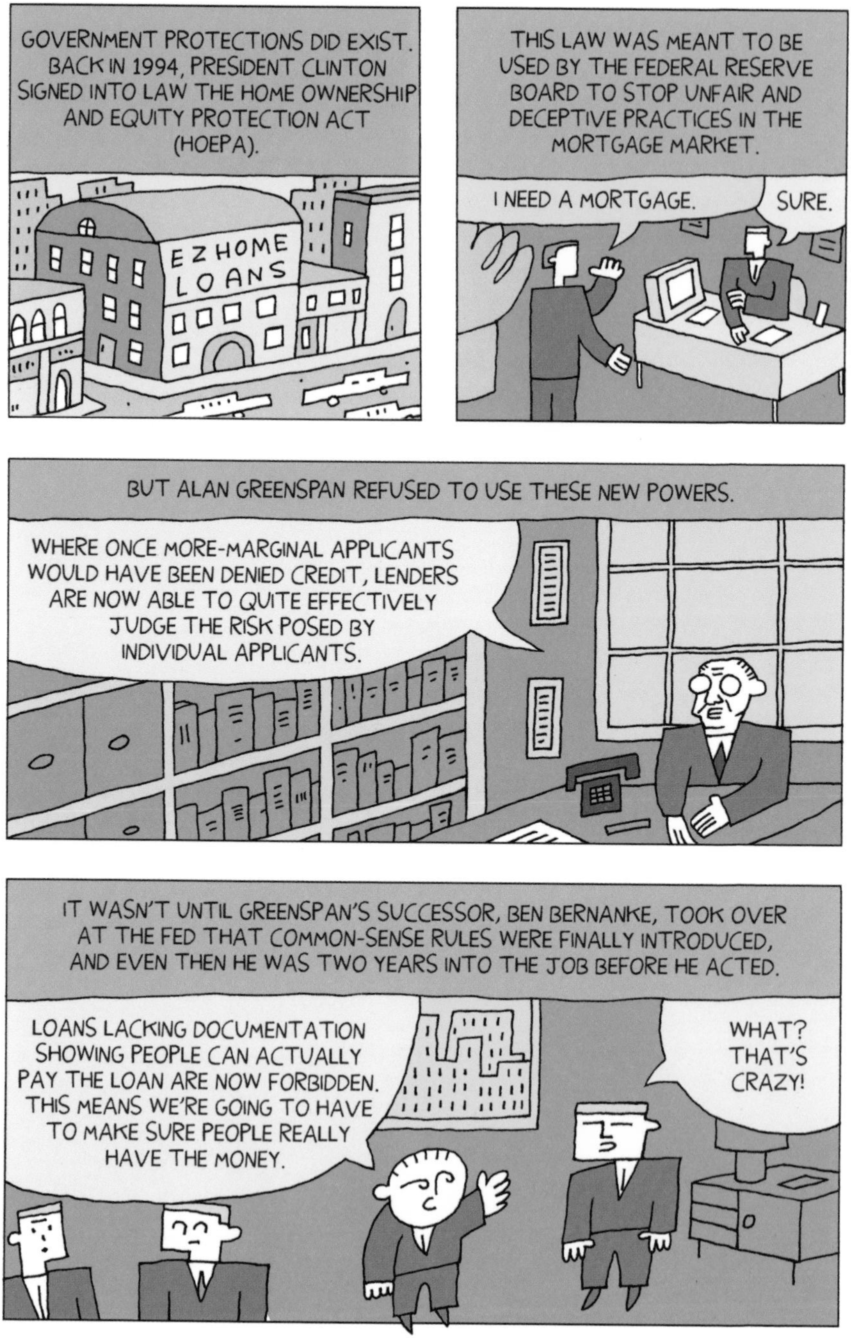
GOVERNMENT PROTECTIONS DID EXIST. BACK IN 1994, PRESIDENT CLINTON SIGNED INTO LAW THE HOME OWNERSHIP AND EQUITY PROTECTION ACT (HOEPA).
EZ HOME LOANS
THIS LAW WAS MEANT TO BE USED BY THE FEDERAL RESERVE BOARD TO STOP UNFAIR AND DECEPTIVE PRACTICES IN THE MORTGAGE MARKET.
I NEED A MORTGAGE.
SURE.
BUT ALAN GREENSPAN REFUSED TO USE THESE NEW POWERS.
WHERE ONCE MORE-MARGINAL APPLICANTS WOULD HAVE BEEN DENIED CREDIT, LENDERS ARE NOW ABLE TO QUITE EFFECTIVELY JUDGE THE RISK POSED BY INDIVIDUAL APPLICANTS.
IT WASN'T UNTIL GREENSPAN'S SUCCESSOR, BEN BERNANKE, TOOK OVER AT THE FED THAT COMMON-SENSE RULES WERE FINALLY INTRODUCED, AND EVEN THEN HE WAS TWO YEARS INTO THE JOB BEFORE HE ACTED.
LOANS LACKING DOCUMENTATION SHOWING PEOPLE CAN ACTUALLY PAY THE LOAN ARE NOW FORBIDDEN. THIS MEANS WE'RE GOING TO HAVE TO MAKE SURE PEOPLE REALLY HAVE THE MONEY.
WHAT? THAT'S CRAZY!

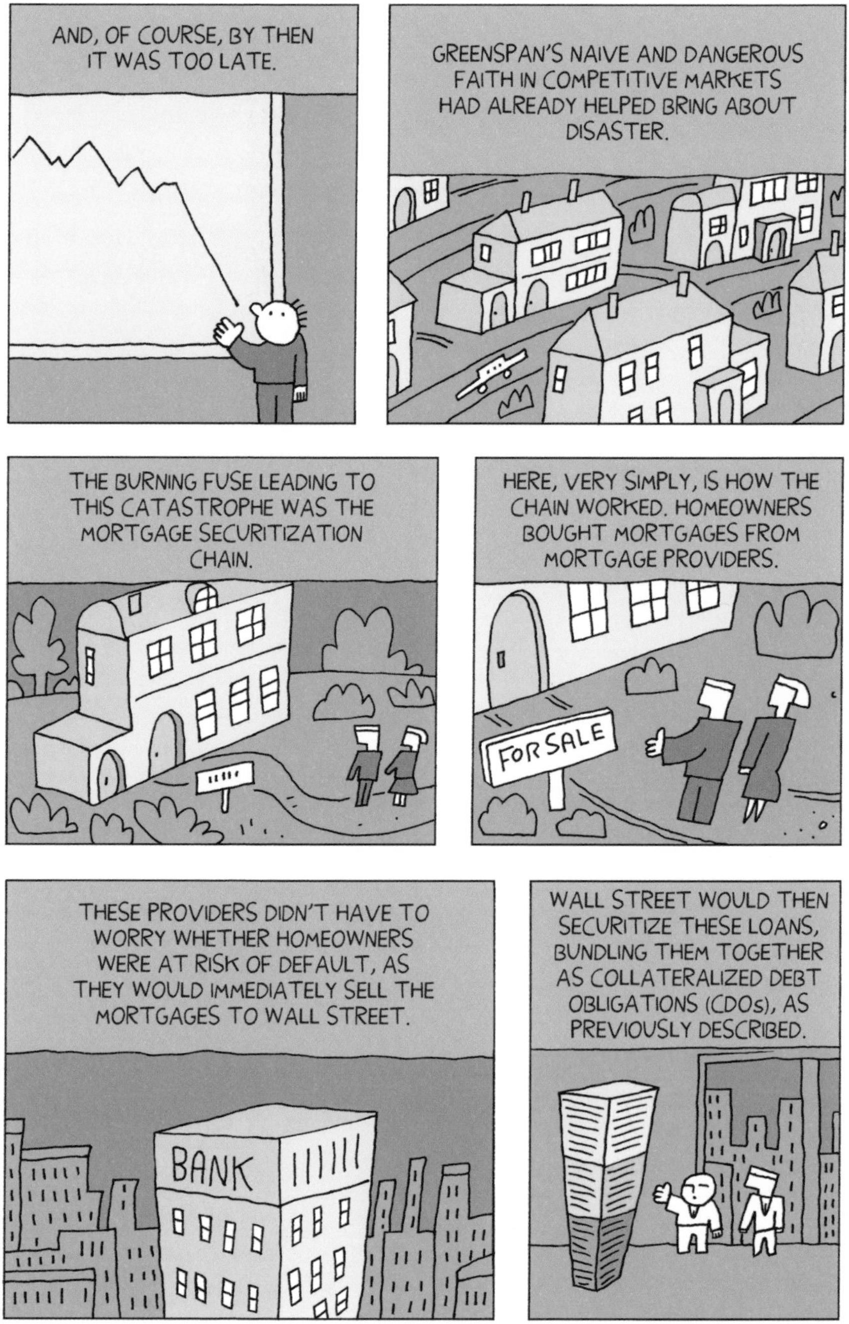
AND, OF COURSE, BY THEN IT WAS TOO LATE.
GREENSPAN'S NAIVE AND DANGEROUS FAITH IN COMPETITIVE MARKETS HAD ALREADY HELPED BRING ABOUT DISASTER.
THE BURNING FUSE LEADING TO THIS CATASTROPHE WAS THE MORTGAGE SECURITIZATION CHAIN.
HERE, VERY SIMPLY, IS HOW THE CHAIN WORKED. HOMEOWNERS BOUGHT MORTGAGES FROM MORTGAGE PROVIDERS.
FOR SALE
THESE PROVIDERS DIDN'T HAVE TO WORRY WHETHER HOMEOWNERS WERE AT RISK OF DEFAULT, AS THEY WOULD IMMEDIATELY SELL THE MORTGAGES TO WALL STREET.
BANK
WALL STREET WOULD THEN SECURITIZE THESE LOANS, BUNDLING THEM TOGETHER AS COLLATERALIZED DEBT OBLIGATIONS (CDOs), AS PREVIOUSLY DESCRIBED.

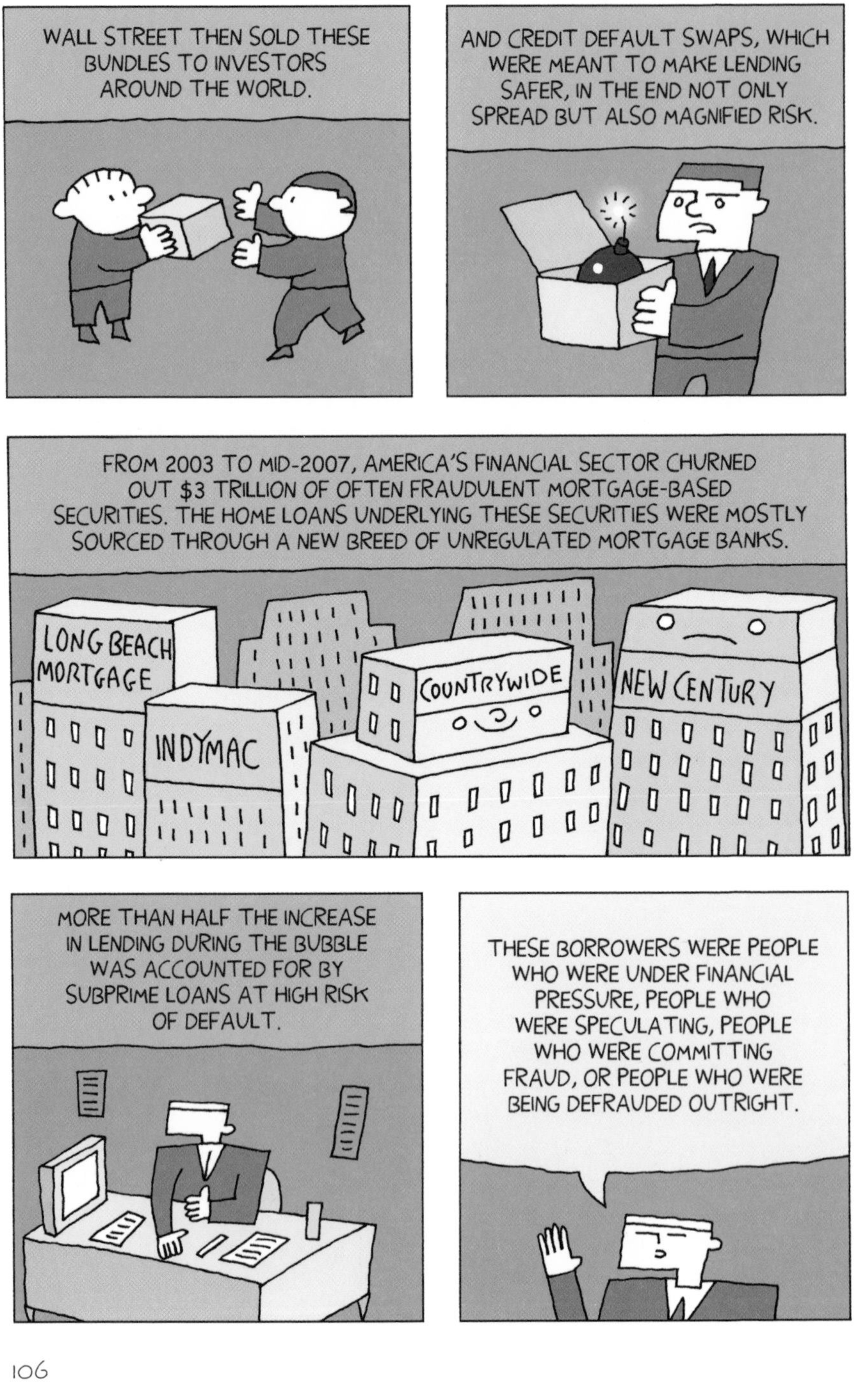
WALL STREET THEN SOLD THESE BUNDLES TO INVESTORS AROUND THE WORLD.
AND CREDIT DEFAULT SWAPS, WHICH WERE MEANT TO MAKE LENDING SAFER, IN THE END NOT ONLY SPREAD BUT ALSO MAGNIFIED RISK.
FROM 2003 TO MID-2007, AMERICA'S FINANCIAL SECTOR CHURNED OUT $3 TRILLION OF OFTEN FRAUDULENT MORTGAGE-BASED SECURITIES. THE HOME LOANS UNDERLYING THESE SECURITIES WERE MOSTLY SOURCED THROUGH A NEW BREED OF UNREGULATED MORTGAGE BANKS.
LONG BEACH MORTGAGE
INDYMAC
COUNTRYWIDE
NEW CENTURY
MORE THAN HALF THE INCREASE IN LENDING DURING THE BUBBLE WAS ACCOUNTED FOR BY SUBPRIME LOANS AT HIGH RISK OF DEFAULT.
THESE BORROWERS WERE PEOPLE WHO WERE UNDER FINANCIAL PRESSURE, PEOPLE WHO WERE SPECULATING, PEOPLE WHO WERE COMMITTING FRAUD, OR PEOPLE WHO WERE BEING DEFRAUDED OUTRIGHT.

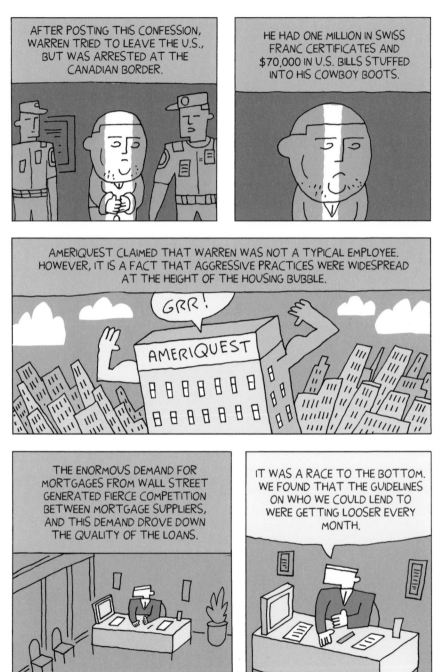

AFTER POSTING THIS CONFESSION, WARREN TRIED TO LEAVE THE U.S., BUT WAS ARRESTED AT THE CANADIAN BORDER.

HE HAD ONE MILLION IN SWISS FRANC CERTIFICATES AND $70,000 IN U.S. BILLS STUFFED INTO HIS COWBOY BOOTS.

AMERIQUEST CLAIMED THAT WARREN WAS NOT A TYPICAL EMPLOYEE. HOWEVER, IT IS A FACT THAT AGGRESSIVE PRACTICES WERE WIDESPREAD AT THE HEIGHT OF THE HOUSING BUBBLE.

GRR!

AMERIQUEST

THE ENORMOUS DEMAND FOR MORTGAGES FROM WALL STREET GENERATED FIERCE COMPETITION BETWEEN MORTGAGE SUPPLIERS, AND THIS DEMAND DROVE DOWN THE QUALITY OF THE LOANS.

IT WAS A RACE TO THE BOTTOM. WE FOUND THAT THE GUIDELINES ON WHO WE COULD LEND TO WERE GETTING LOOSER EVERY MONTH.

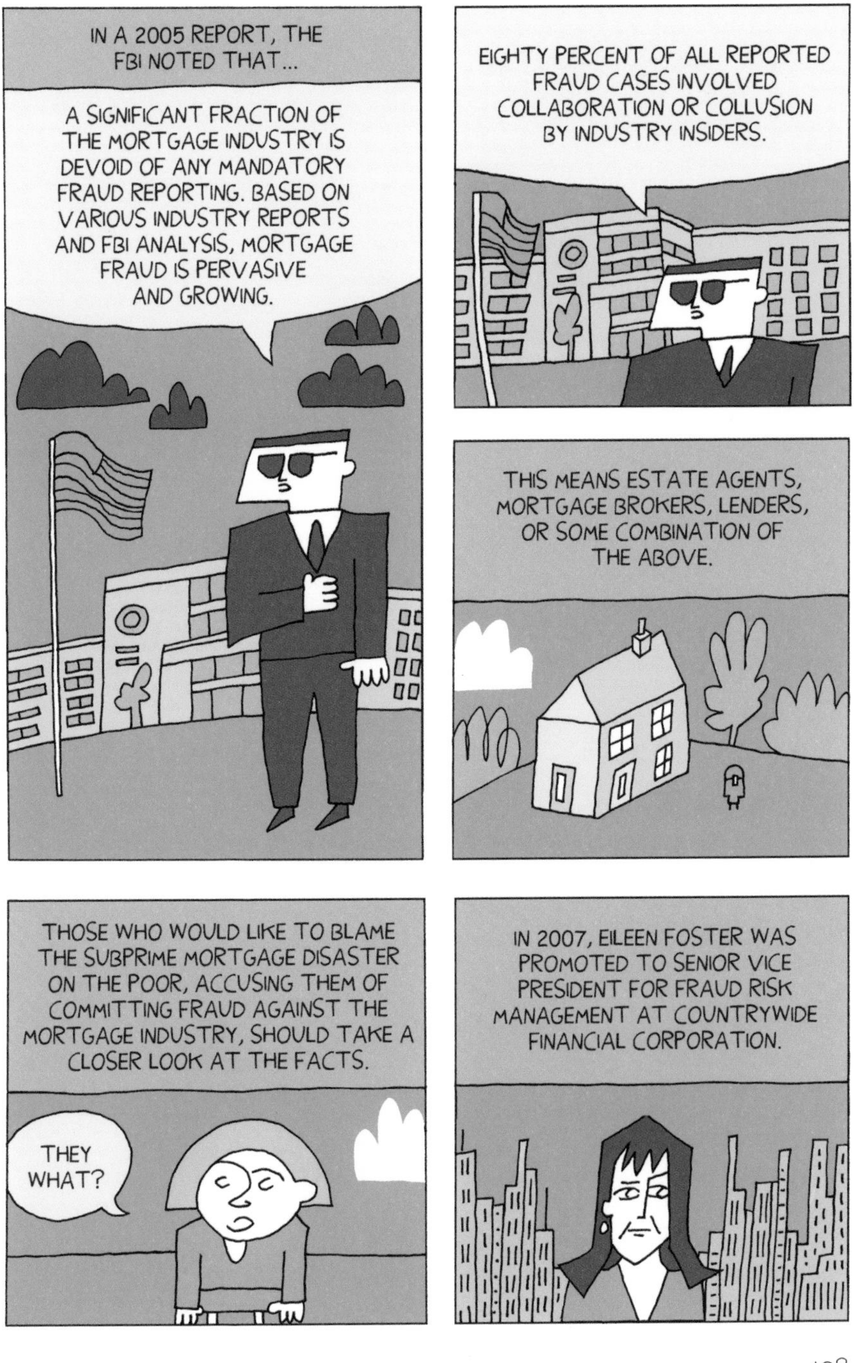
IN A 2005 REPORT, THE FBI NOTED THAT...
A SIGNIFICANT FRACTION OF THE MORTGAGE INDUSTRY IS DEVOID OF ANY MANDATORY FRAUD REPORTING. BASED ON VARIOUS INDUSTRY REPORTS AND FBI ANALYSIS, MORTGAGE FRAUD IS PERVASIVE AND GROWING.
EIGHTY PERCENT OF ALL REPORTED FRAUD CASES INVOLVED COLLABORATION OR COLLUSION BY INDUSTRY INSIDERS.
THIS MEANS ESTATE AGENTS, MORTGAGE BROKERS, LENDERS, OR SOME COMBINATION OF THE ABOVE.
THOSE WHO WOULD LIKE TO BLAME THE SUBPRIME MORTGAGE DISASTER ON THE POOR, ACCUSING THEM OF COMMITTING FRAUD AGAINST THE MORTGAGE INDUSTRY, SHOULD TAKE A CLOSER LOOK AT THE FACTS.
THEY WHAT?
IN 2007, EILEEN FOSTER WAS PROMOTED TO SENIOR VICE PRESIDENT FOR FRAUD RISK MANAGEMENT AT COUNTRYWIDE FINANCIAL CORPORATION.

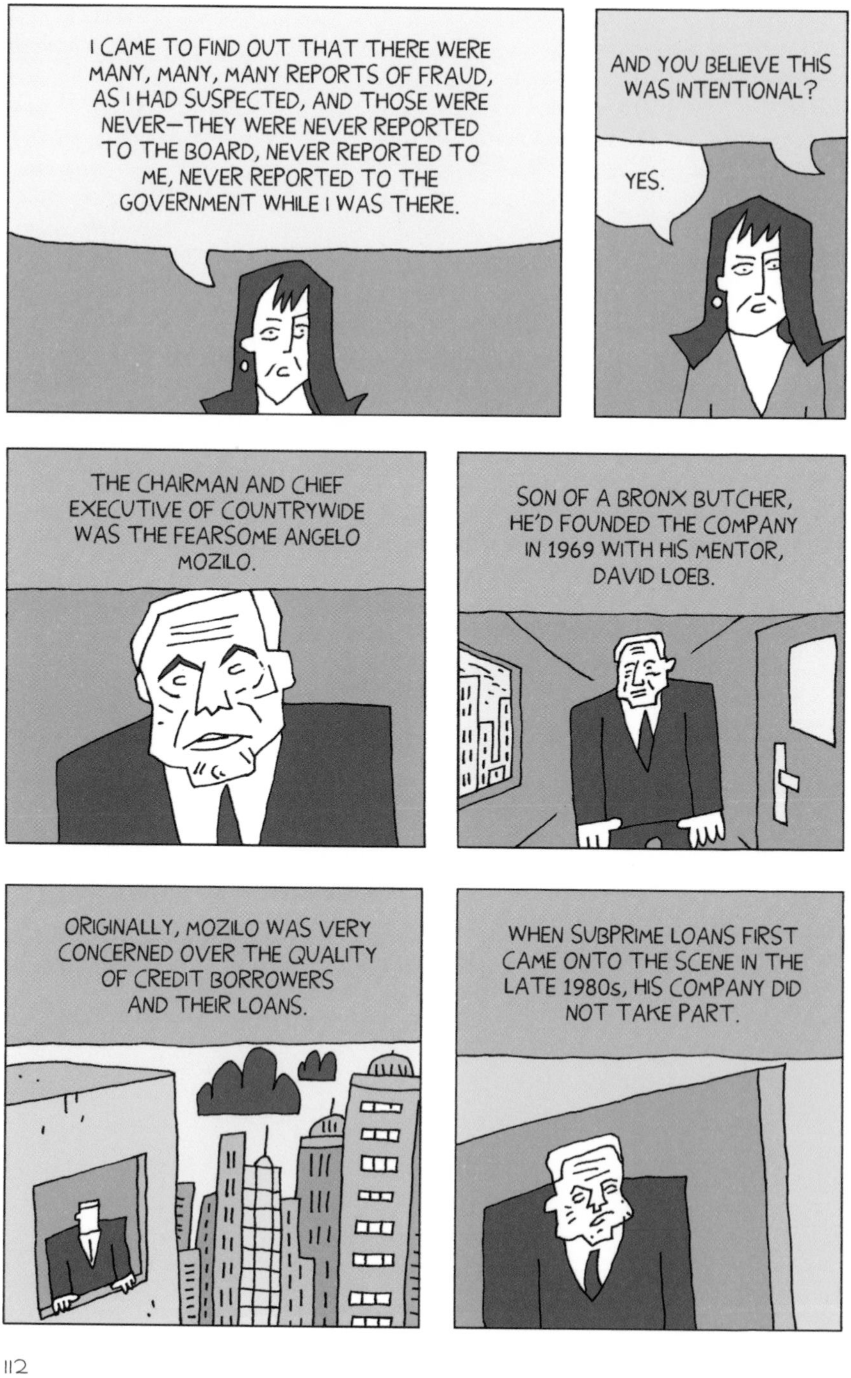
I CAME TO FIND OUT THAT THERE WERE MANY, MANY, MANY REPORTS OF FRAUD, AS I HAD SUSPECTED, AND THOSE WERE NEVER—THEY WERE NEVER REPORTED TO THE BOARD, NEVER REPORTED TO ME, NEVER REPORTED TO THE GOVERNMENT WHILE I WAS THERE.
AND YOU BELIEVE THIS WAS INTENTIONAL?
YES.
THE CHAIRMAN AND CHIEF EXECUTIVE OF COUNTRYWIDE WAS THE FEARSOME ANGELO MOZILO.
SON OF A BRONX BUTCHER, HE'D FOUNDED THE COMPANY IN 1969 WITH HIS MENTOR, DAVID LOEB.
ORIGINALLY, MOZILO WAS VERY CONCERNED OVER THE QUALITY OF CREDIT BORROWERS AND THEIR LOANS.
WHEN SUBPRIME LOANS FIRST CAME ONTO THE SCENE IN THE LATE 1980s, HIS COMPANY DID NOT TAKE PART.

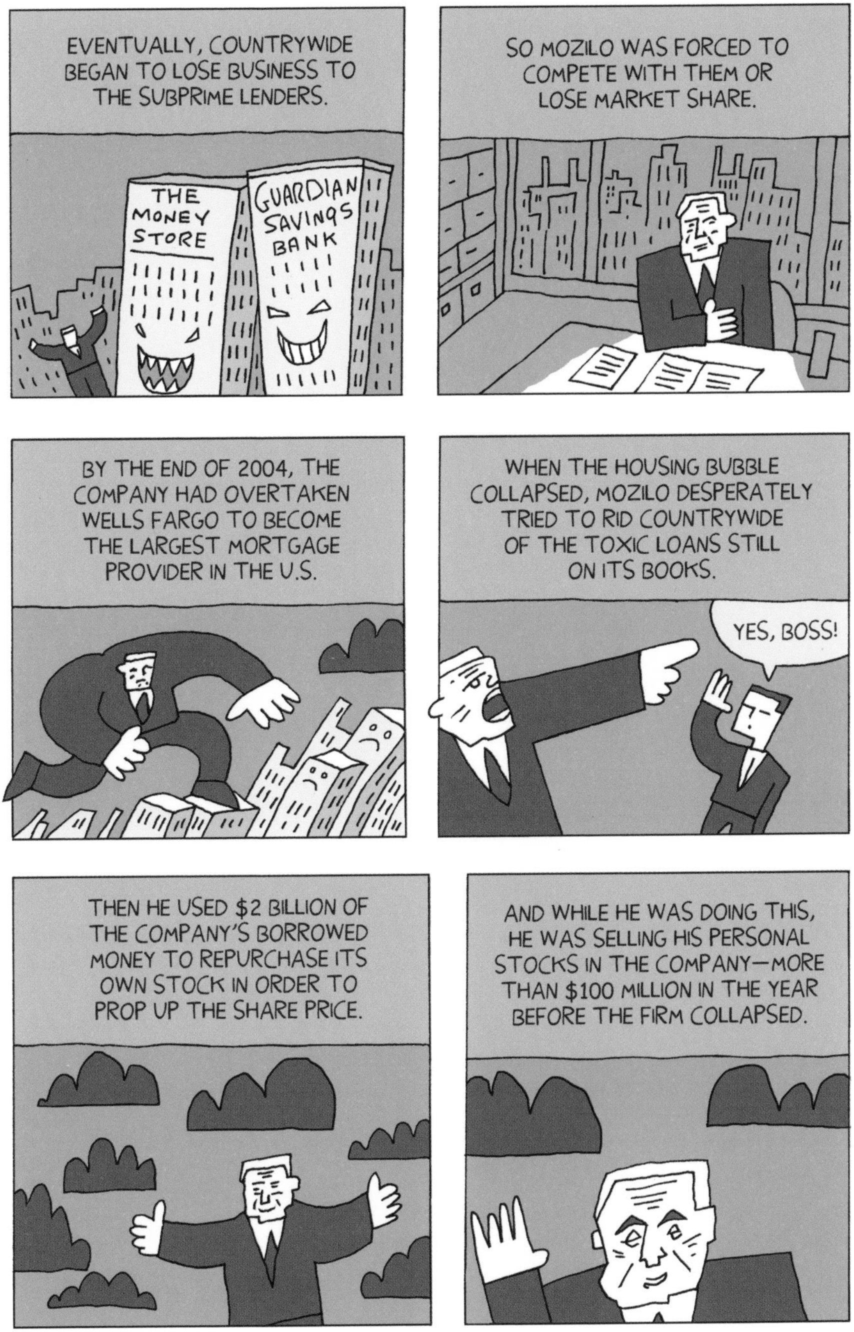
EVENTUALLY, COUNTRYWIDE BEGAN TO LOSE BUSINESS TO THE SUBPRIME LENDERS.
THE MONEY STORE
GUARDIAN SAVINGS BANK
SO MOZILO WAS FORCED TO COMPETE WITH THEM OR LOSE MARKET SHARE.
BY THE END OF 2004, THE COMPANY HAD OVERTAKEN WELLS FARGO TO BECOME THE LARGEST MORTGAGE PROVIDER IN THE U.S.
WHEN THE HOUSING BUBBLE COLLAPSED, MOZILO DESPERATELY TRIED TO RID COUNTRYWIDE OF THE TOXIC LOANS STILL ON ITS BOOKS.
YES, BOSS!
THEN HE USED $2 BILLION OF THE COMPANY'S BORROWED MONEY TO REPURCHASE ITS OWN STOCK IN ORDER TO PROP UP THE SHARE PRICE.
AND WHILE HE WAS DOING THIS, HE WAS SELLING HIS PERSONAL STOCKS IN THE COMPANY—MORE THAN $100 MILLION IN THE YEAR BEFORE THE FIRM COLLAPSED.

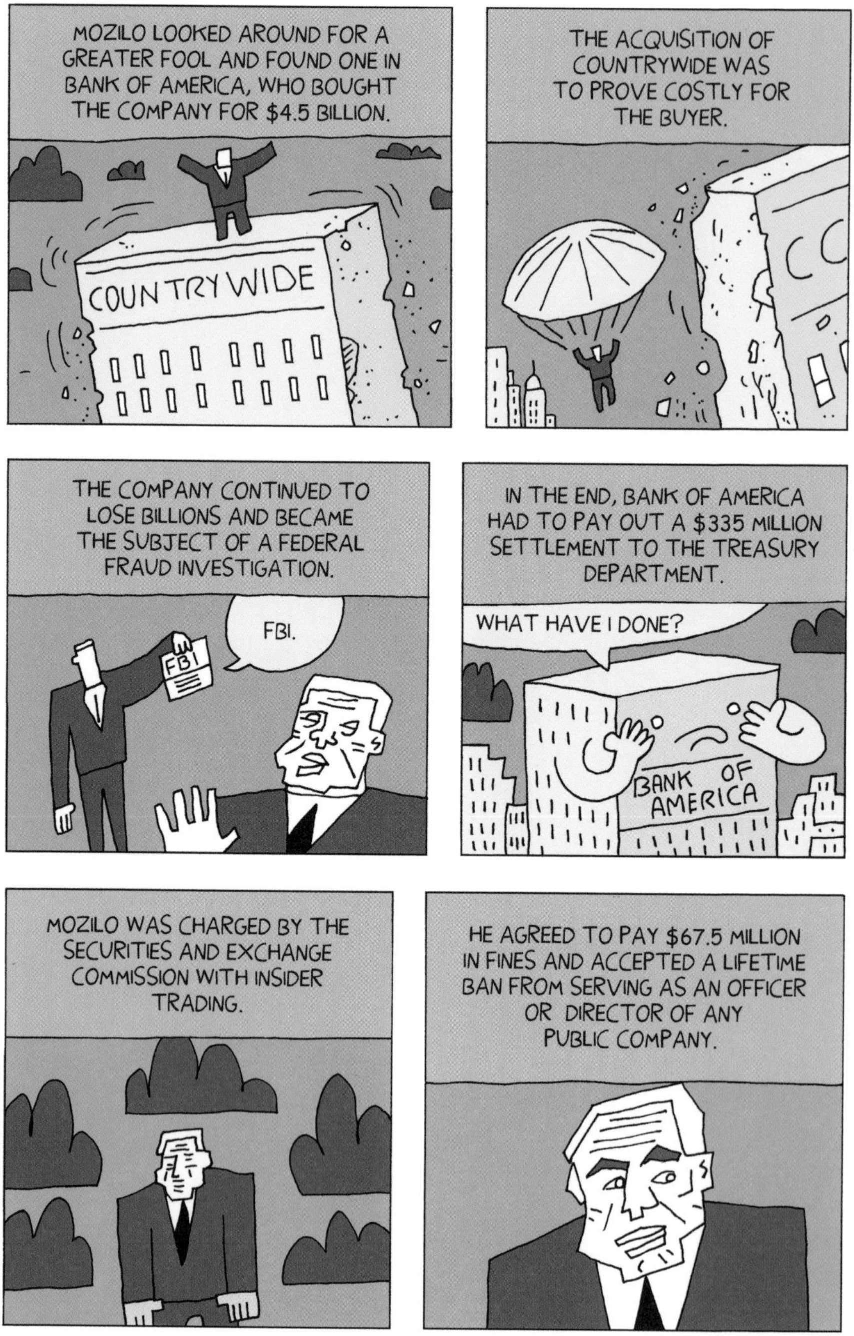
MOZILO LOOKED AROUND FOR A GREATER FOOL AND FOUND ONE IN BANK OF AMERICA, WHO BOUGHT THE COMPANY FOR $4.5 BILLION.
COUNTRYWIDE
THE ACQUISITION OF COUNTRYWIDE WAS TO PROVE COSTLY FOR THE BUYER.
THE COMPANY CONTINUED TO LOSE BILLIONS AND BECAME THE SUBJECT OF A FEDERAL FRAUD INVESTIGATION.
FBI
FBI.
IN THE END, BANK OF AMERICA HAD TO PAY OUT A $335 MILLION SETTLEMENT TO THE TREASURY DEPARTMENT.
WHAT HAVE I DONE?
BANK OF AMERICA
MOZILO WAS CHARGED BY THE SECURITIES AND EXCHANGE COMMISSION WITH INSIDER TRADING.
HE AGREED TO PAY $67.5 MILLION IN FINES AND ACCEPTED A LIFETIME BAN FROM SERVING AS AN OFFICER OR DIRECTOR OF ANY PUBLIC COMPANY.

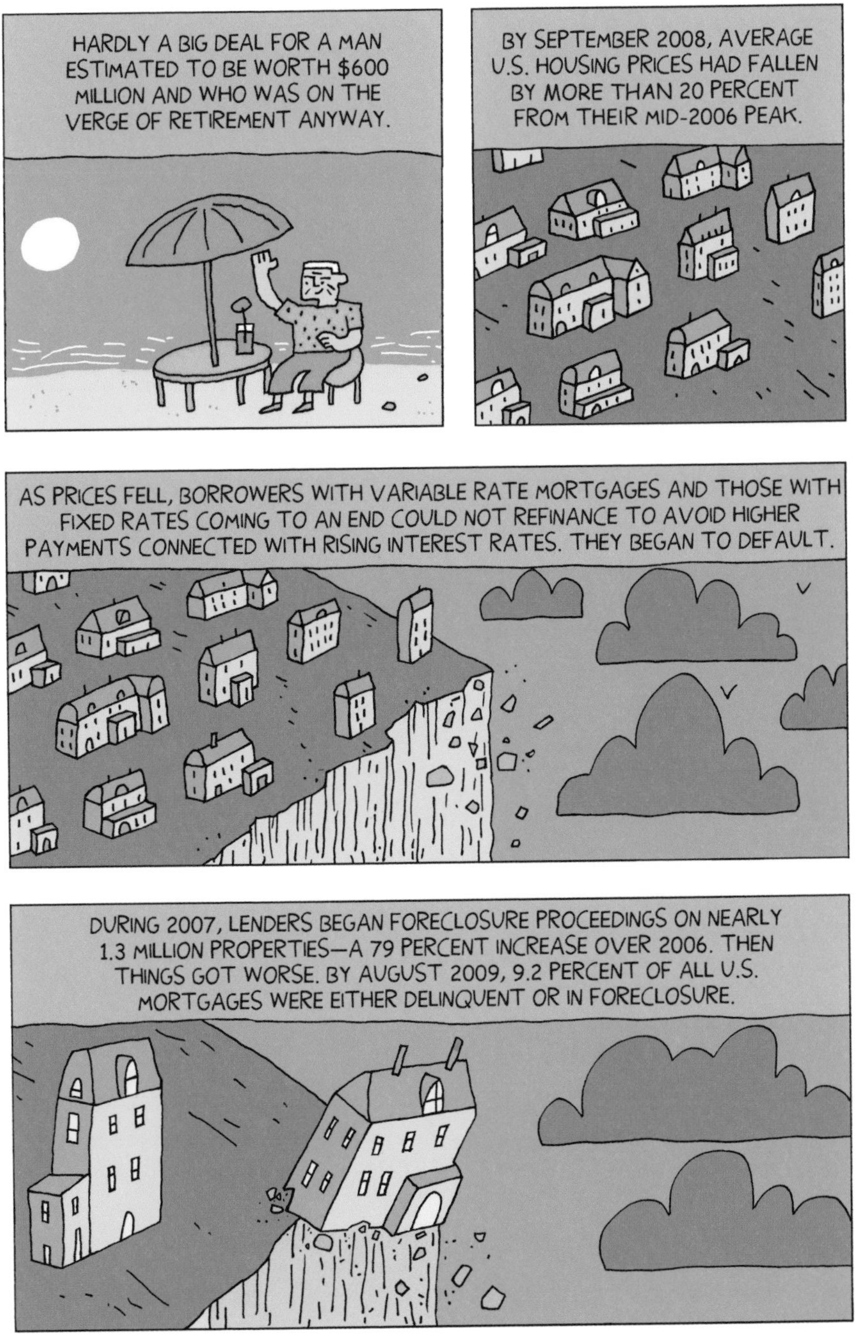
HARDLY A BIG DEAL FOR A MAN ESTIMATED TO BE WORTH $600 MILLION AND WHO WAS ON THE VERGE OF RETIREMENT ANYWAY.
BY SEPTEMBER 2008, AVERAGE U.S. HOUSING PRICES HAD FALLEN BY MORE THAN 20 PERCENT FROM THEIR MID-2006 PEAK.
AS PRICES FELL, BORROWERS WITH VARIABLE RATE MORTGAGES AND THOSE WITH FIXED RATES COMING TO AN END COULD NOT REFINANCE TO AVOID HIGHER PAYMENTS CONNECTED WITH RISING INTEREST RATES. THEY BEGAN TO DEFAULT.
DURING 2007, LENDERS BEGAN FORECLOSURE PROCEEDINGS ON NEARLY 1.3 MILLION PROPERTIES—A 79 PERCENT INCREASE OVER 2006. THEN THINGS GOT WORSE. BY AUGUST 2009, 9.2 PERCENT OF ALL U.S. MORTGAGES WERE EITHER DELINQUENT OR IN FORECLOSURE.

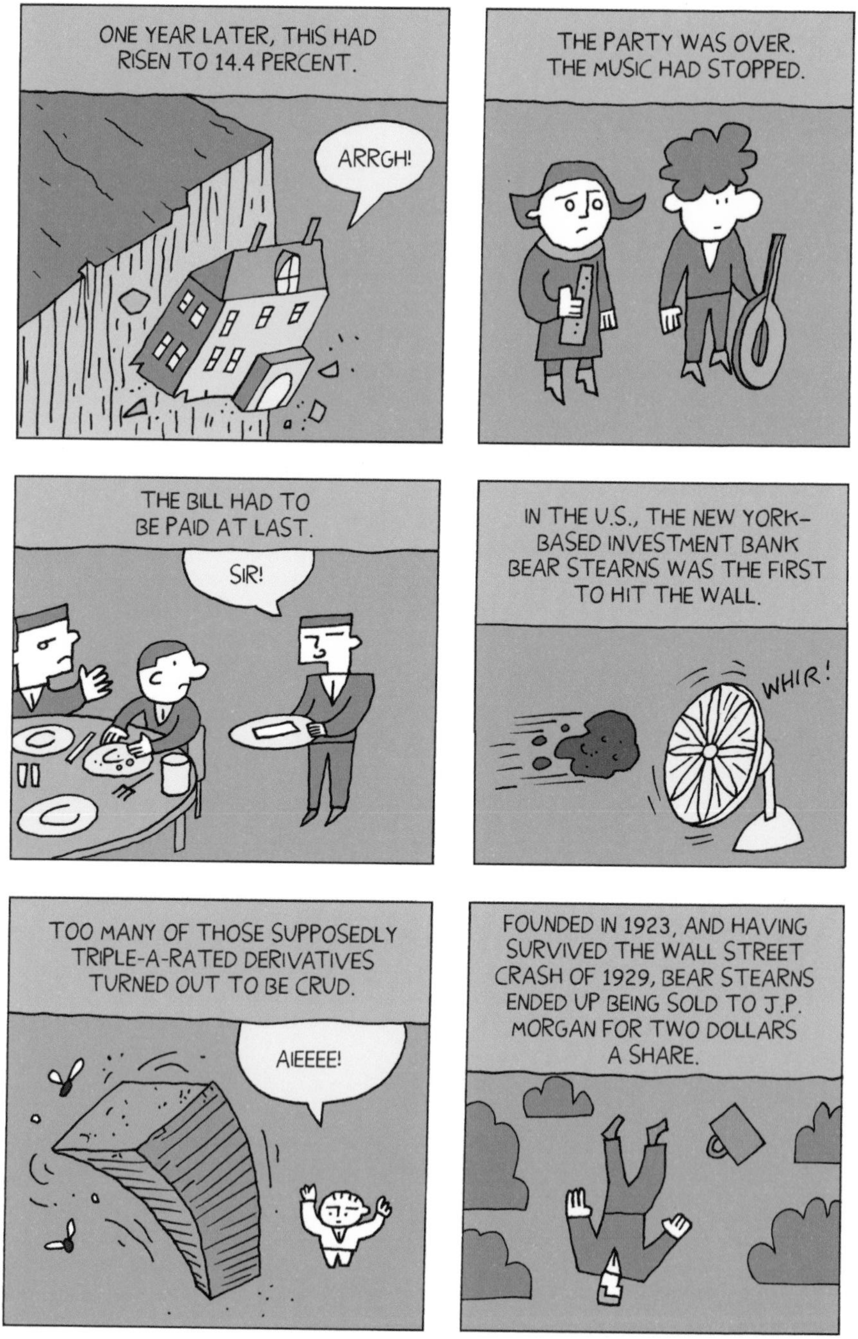
ONE YEAR LATER, THIS HAD RISEN TO 14.4 PERCENT.
ARRGH!
THE PARTY WAS OVER. THE MUSIC HAD STOPPED.
THE BILL HAD TO BE PAID AT LAST.
SIR!
IN THE U.S., THE NEW YORK-BASED INVESTMENT BANK BEAR STEARNS WAS THE FIRST TO HIT THE WALL.
WHIR!
TOO MANY OF THOSE SUPPOSEDLY TRIPLE-A-RATED DERIVATIVES TURNED OUT TO BE CRUD.
AIEEEE!
FOUNDED IN 1923, AND HAVING SURVIVED THE WALL STREET CRASH OF 1929, BEAR STEARNS ENDED UP BEING SOLD TO J.P. MORGAN FOR TWO DOLLARS A SHARE.

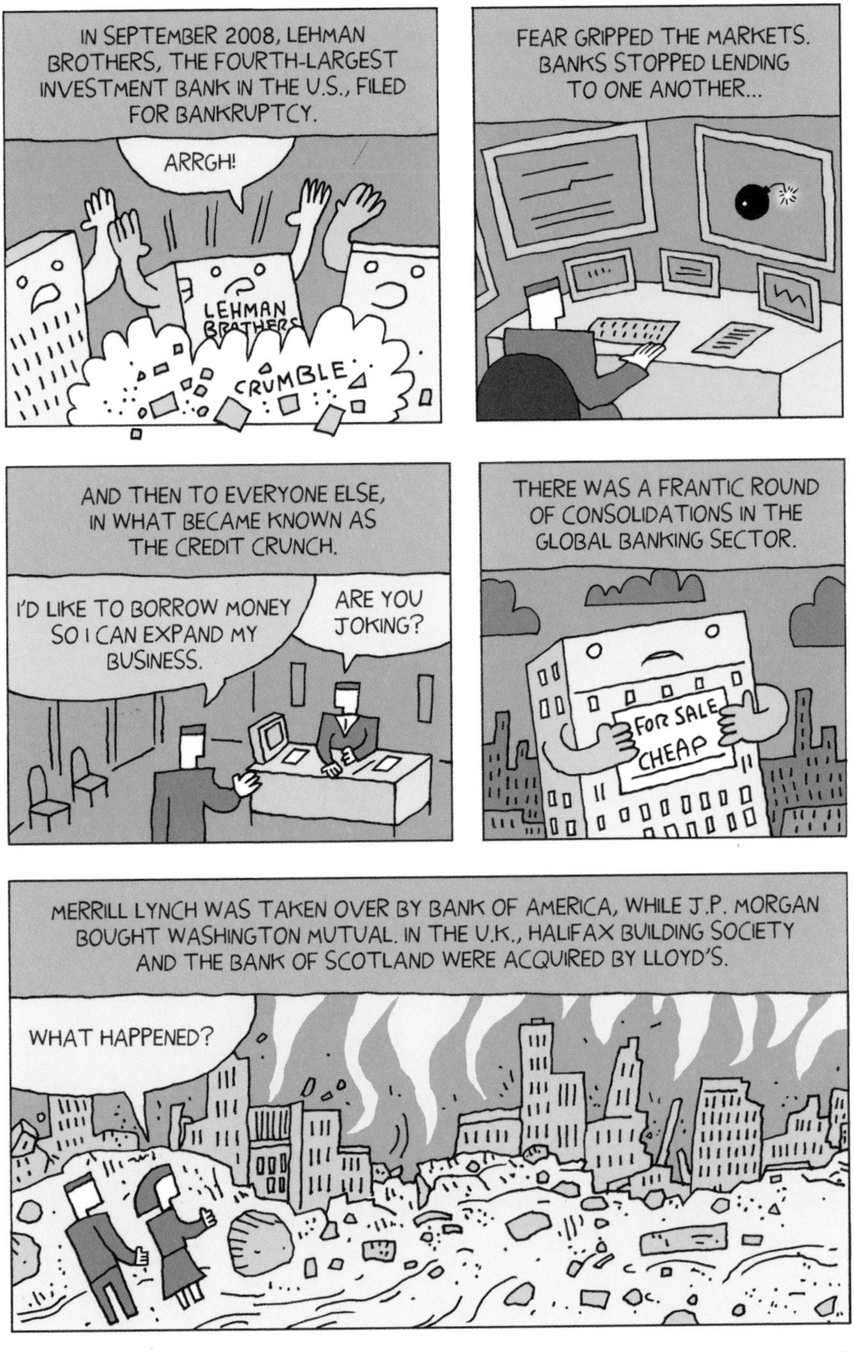
IN SEPTEMBER 2008, LEHMAN BROTHERS, THE FOURTH-LARGEST INVESTMENT BANK IN THE U.S., FILED FOR BANKRUPTCY.
ARRGH!
LEHMAN BROTHERS
CRUMBLE
FEAR GRIPPED THE MARKETS. BANKS STOPPED LENDING TO ONE ANOTHER...
AND THEN TO EVERYONE ELSE, IN WHAT BECAME KNOWN AS THE CREDIT CRUNCH.
I'D LIKE TO BORROW MONEY SO I CAN EXPAND MY BUSINESS.
ARE YOU JOKING?
THERE WAS A FRANTIC ROUND OF CONSOLIDATIONS IN THE GLOBAL BANKING SECTOR.
FOR SALE CHEAP
MERRILL LYNCH WAS TAKEN OVER BY BANK OF AMERICA, WHILE J.P. MORGAN BOUGHT WASHINGTON MUTUAL. IN THE U.K., HALIFAX BUILDING SOCIETY AND THE BANK OF SCOTLAND WERE ACQUIRED BY LLOYD'S.
WHAT HAPPENED?

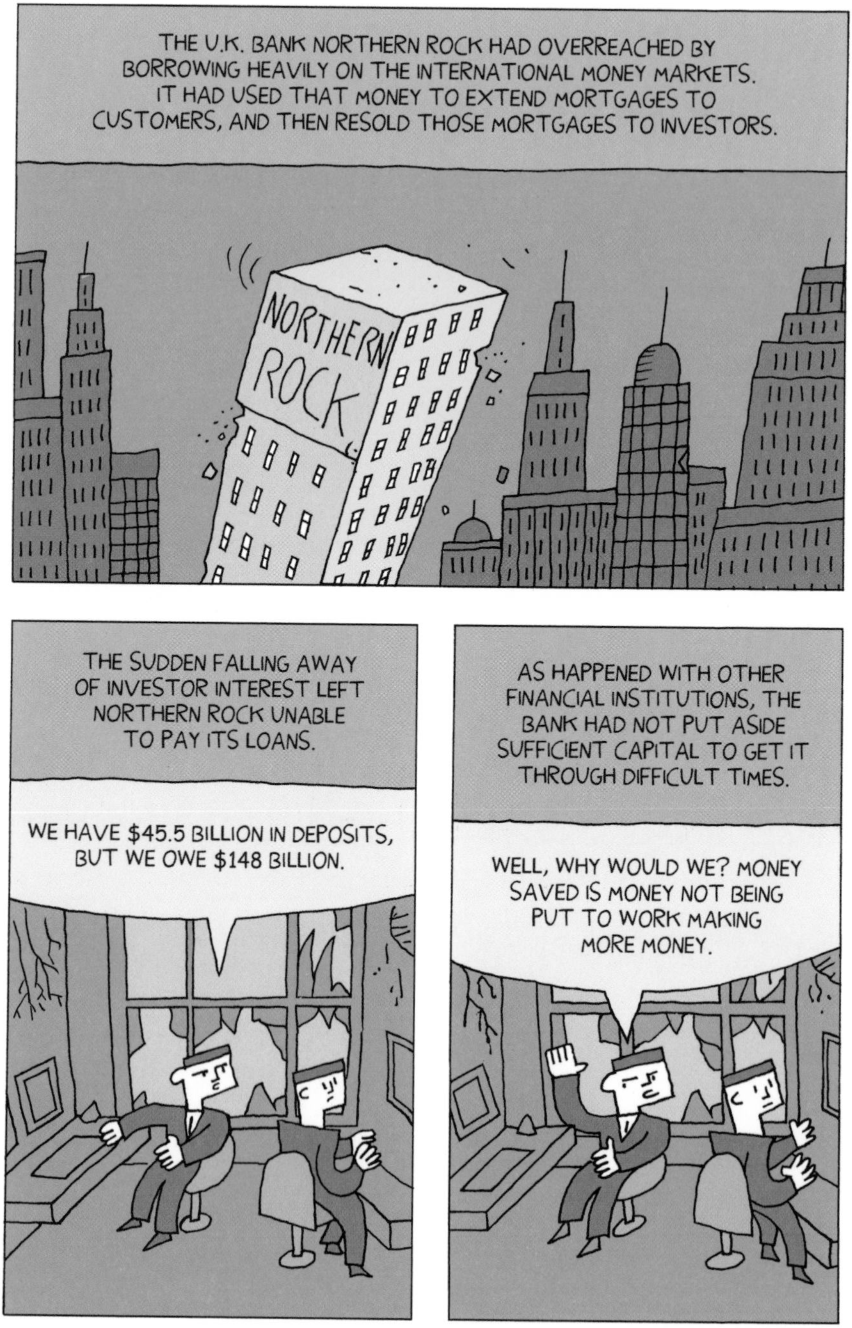
THE U.K. BANK NORTHERN ROCK HAD OVERREACHED BY BORROWING HEAVILY ON THE INTERNATIONAL MONEY MARKETS. IT HAD USED THAT MONEY TO EXTEND MORTGAGES TO CUSTOMERS, AND THEN RESOLD THOSE MORTGAGES TO INVESTORS.
NORTHERN ROCK
THE SUDDEN FALLING AWAY OF INVESTOR INTEREST LEFT NORTHERN ROCK UNABLE TO PAY ITS LOANS.
WE HAVE $45.5 BILLION IN DEPOSITS, BUT WE OWE $148 BILLION.
AS HAPPENED WITH OTHER FINANCIAL INSTITUTIONS, THE BANK HAD NOT PUT ASIDE SUFFICIENT CAPITAL TO GET IT THROUGH DIFFICULT TIMES.
WELL, WHY WOULD WE? MONEY SAVED IS MONEY NOT BEING PUT TO WORK MAKING MORE MONEY.

WHEN CUSTOMERS HEARD THAT NORTHERN ROCK HAD APPROACHED THE BANK OF ENGLAND FOR A LOAN...

PLEASE!

IT CAUSED THE FIRST RUN ON A BRITISH BANK IN 150 YEARS.

NORTHERN ROCK

THE STRUGGLING BANK WAS THEN TAKEN OVER BY THE GOVERNMENT. IT WOULD BE FOUR YEARS BEFORE IT RETURNED TO PRIVATE OWNERSHIP.

NORTHERN ROCK

BACK IN THE U.S., HANK PAULSON, FORMER CHAIRMAN OF GOLDMAN SACHS, WAS NOW TREASURY SECRETARY.

HI!

PAULSON WAS ANOTHER STRONG ADVOCATE OF UNFETTERED FREE MARKETS, YET DESPITE THIS, HE THOUGHT THAT ONLY A MASSIVE INTERVENTION BY THE GOVERNMENT WAS GOING TO HALT THE CRISIS.

ALONG WITH FED CHAIRMAN BEN BERNANKE, PAULSON PLEADED WITH CONGRESS TO GIVE THE TREASURY $700 BILLION, WHICH HE WOULD USE TO SHORE UP THE SYSTEM.

PLEASE!

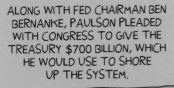

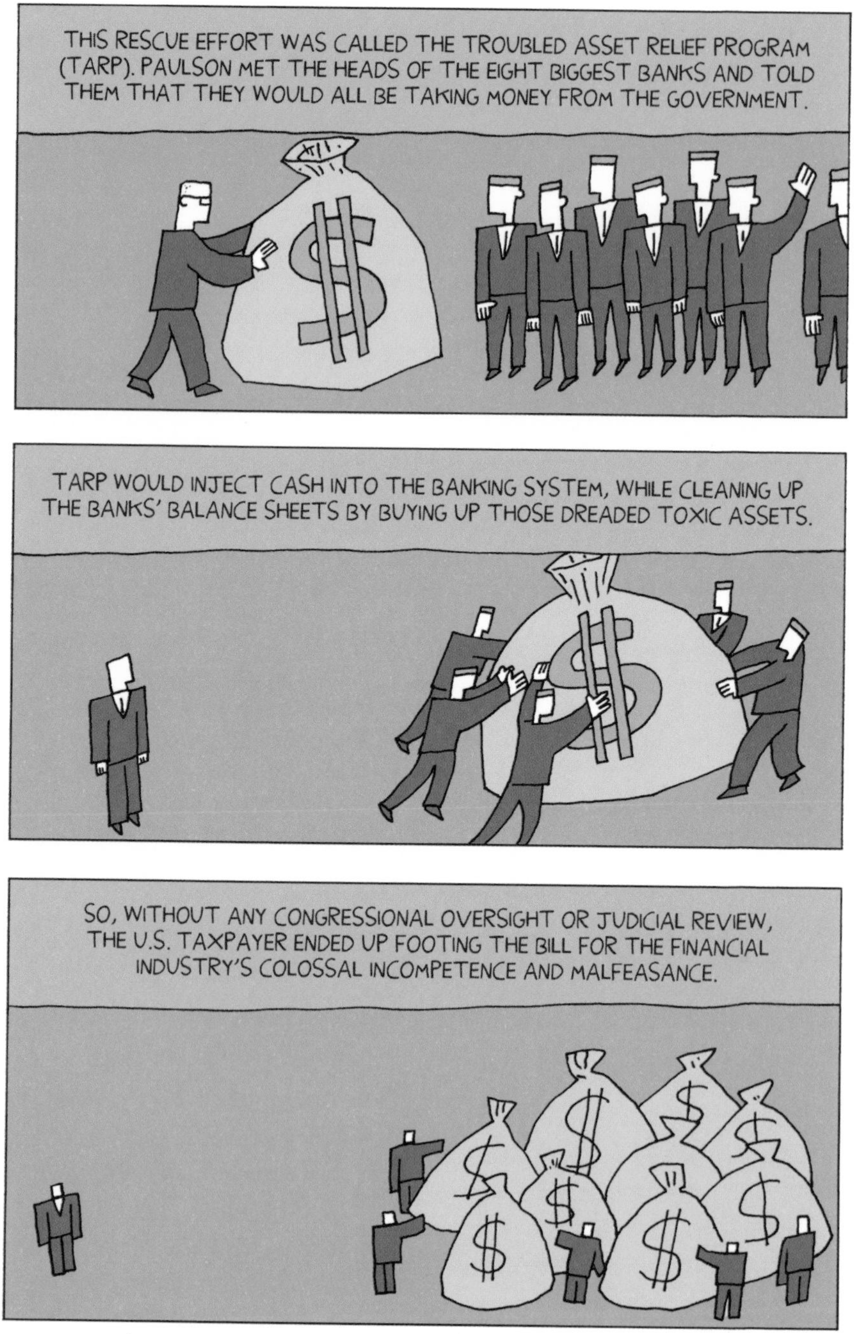
THIS RESCUE EFFORT WAS CALLED THE TROUBLED ASSET RELIEF PROGRAM (TARP). PAULSON MET THE HEADS OF THE EIGHT BIGGEST BANKS AND TOLD THEM THAT THEY WOULD ALL BE TAKING MONEY FROM THE GOVERNMENT.
TARP WOULD INJECT CASH INTO THE BANKING SYSTEM, WHILE CLEANING UP THE BANKS' BALANCE SHEETS BY BUYING UP THOSE DREADED TOXIC ASSETS.
SO, WITHOUT ANY CONGRESSIONAL OVERSIGHT OR JUDICIAL REVIEW, THE U.S. TAXPAYER ENDED UP FOOTING THE BILL FOR THE FINANCIAL INDUSTRY'S COLOSSAL INCOMPETENCE AND MALFEASANCE.

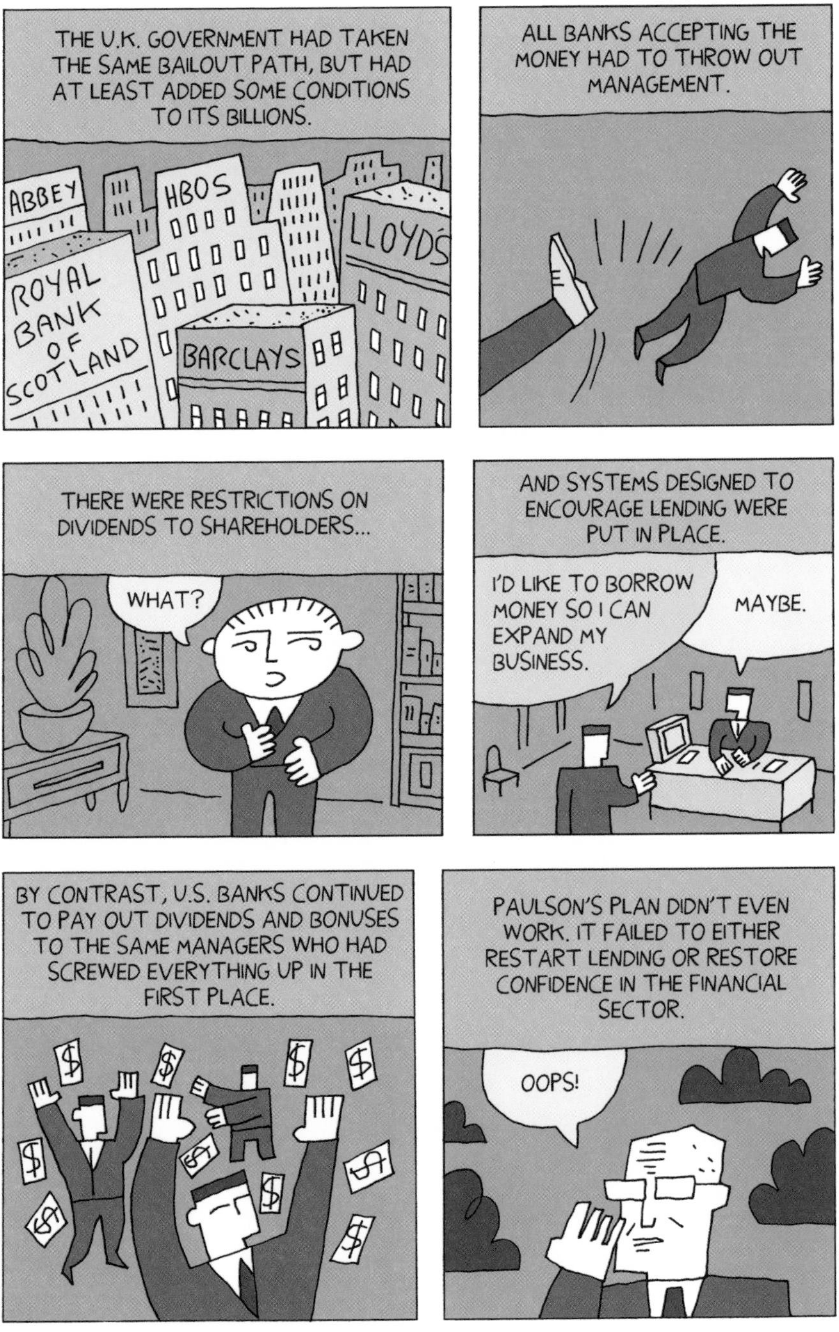
THE U.K. GOVERNMENT HAD TAKEN THE SAME BAILOUT PATH, BUT HAD AT LEAST ADDED SOME CONDITIONS TO ITS BILLIONS.
ABBEY
HBOS
LLOYD'S
ROYAL BANK OF SCOTLAND
BARCLAYS
ALL BANKS ACCEPTING THE MONEY HAD TO THROW OUT MANAGEMENT.
THERE WERE RESTRICTIONS ON DIVIDENDS TO SHAREHOLDERS...
WHAT?
AND SYSTEMS DESIGNED TO ENCOURAGE LENDING WERE PUT IN PLACE.
I'D LIKE TO BORROW MONEY SO I CAN EXPAND MY BUSINESS.
MAYBE.
BY CONTRAST, U.S. BANKS CONTINUED TO PAY OUT DIVIDENDS AND BONUSES TO THE SAME MANAGERS WHO HAD SCREWED EVERYTHING UP IN THE FIRST PLACE.
PAULSON'S PLAN DIDN'T EVEN WORK. IT FAILED TO EITHER RESTART LENDING OR RESTORE CONFIDENCE IN THE FINANCIAL SECTOR.
OOPS!

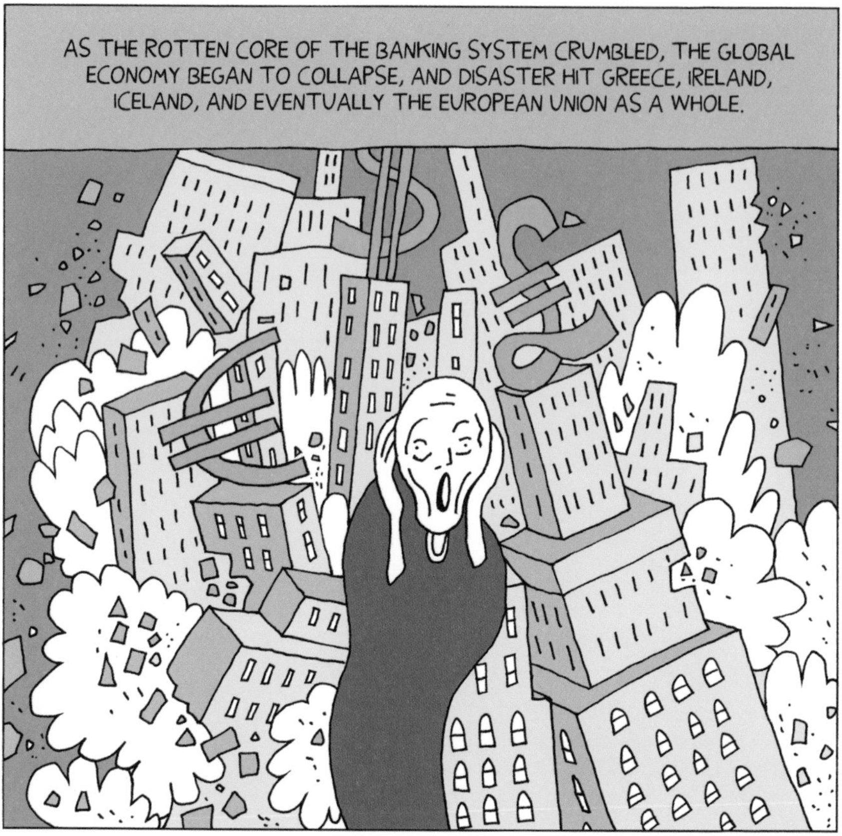
AS THE ROTTEN CORE OF THE BANKING SYSTEM CRUMBLED, THE GLOBAL ECONOMY BEGAN TO COLLAPSE, AND DISASTER HIT GREECE, IRELAND, ICELAND, AND EVENTUALLY THE EUROPEAN UNION AS A WHOLE.

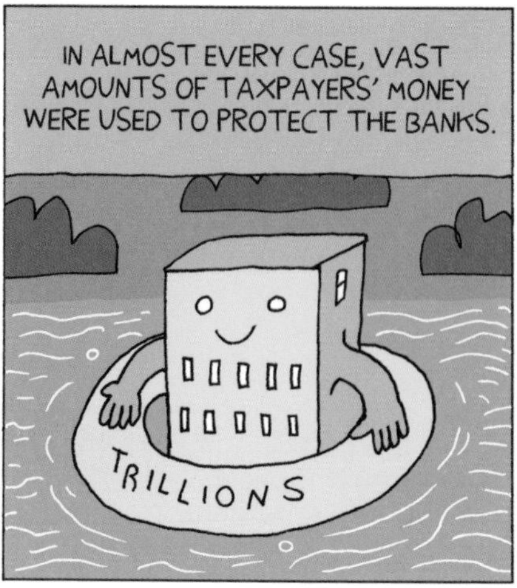
IN ALMOST EVERY CASE, VAST AMOUNTS OF TAXPAYERS' MONEY WERE USED TO PROTECT THE BANKS.
TRILLIONS

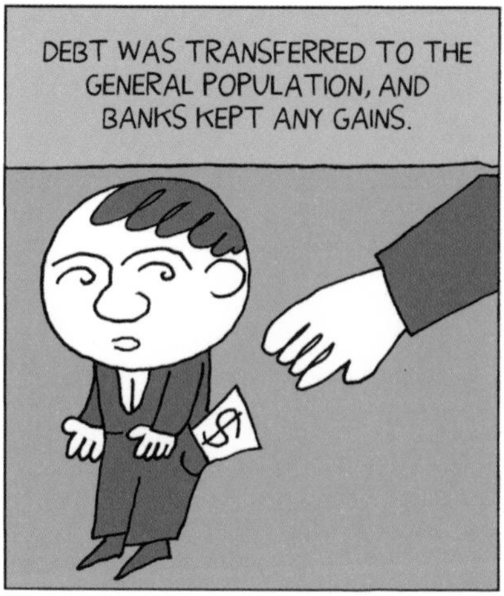
DEBT WAS TRANSFERRED TO THE GENERAL POPULATION, AND BANKS KEPT ANY GAINS.

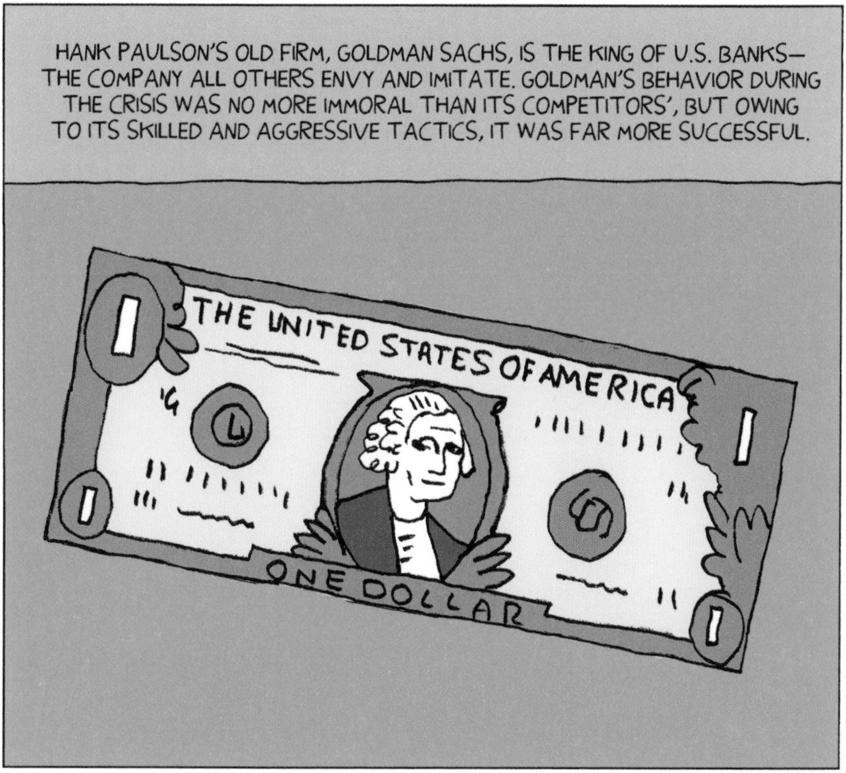
HANK PAULSON'S OLD FIRM, GOLDMAN SACHS, IS THE KING OF U.S. BANKS—THE COMPANY ALL OTHERS ENVY AND IMITATE. GOLDMAN'S BEHAVIOR DURING THE CRISIS WAS NO MORE IMMORAL THAN ITS COMPETITORS', BUT OWING TO ITS SKILLED AND AGGRESSIVE TACTICS, IT WAS FAR MORE SUCCESSFUL.
THE UNITED STATES OF AMERICA
ONE DOLLAR

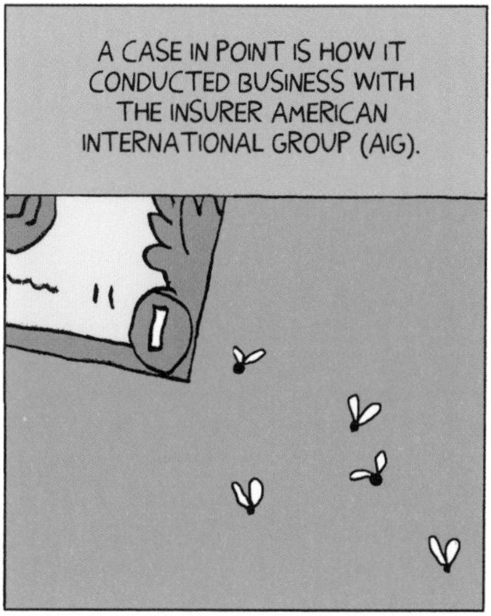
A CASE IN POINT IS HOW IT CONDUCTED BUSINESS WITH THE INSURER AMERICAN INTERNATIONAL GROUP (AIG).

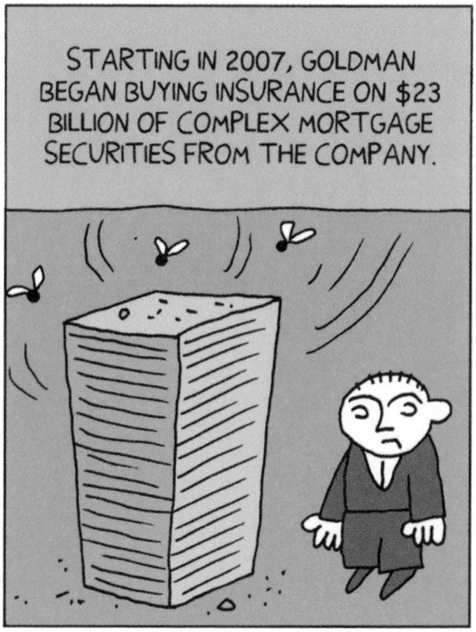
STARTING IN 2007, GOLDMAN BEGAN BUYING INSURANCE ON $23 BILLION OF COMPLEX MORTGAGE SECURITIES FROM THE COMPANY.

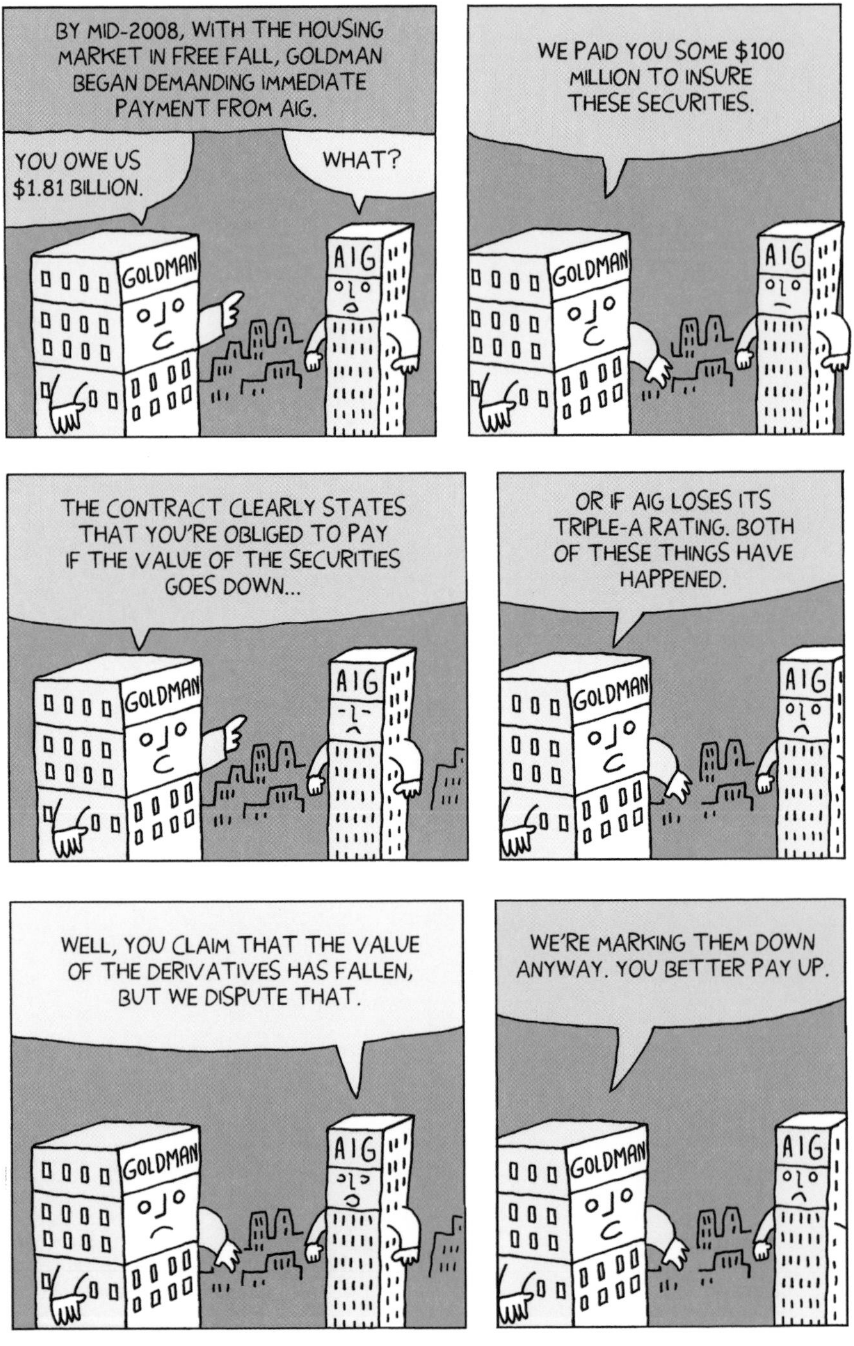
BY MID-2008, WITH THE HOUSING MARKET IN FREE FALL, GOLDMAN BEGAN DEMANDING IMMEDIATE PAYMENT FROM AIG.
YOU OWE US $1.81 BILLION.
WHAT?
GOLDMAN
AIG
WE PAID YOU SOME $100 MILLION TO INSURE THESE SECURITIES.
GOLDMAN
AIG
THE CONTRACT CLEARLY STATES THAT YOU'RE OBLIGED TO PAY IF THE VALUE OF THE SECURITIES GOES DOWN...
GOLDMAN
AIG
OR IF AIG LOSES ITS TRIPLE-A RATING. BOTH OF THESE THINGS HAVE HAPPENED.
GOLDMAN
AIG
WELL, YOU CLAIM THAT THE VALUE OF THE DERIVATIVES HAS FALLEN, BUT WE DISPUTE THAT.
GOLDMAN
AIG
WE'RE MARKING THEM DOWN ANYWAY. YOU BETTER PAY UP.
GOLDMAN
AIG

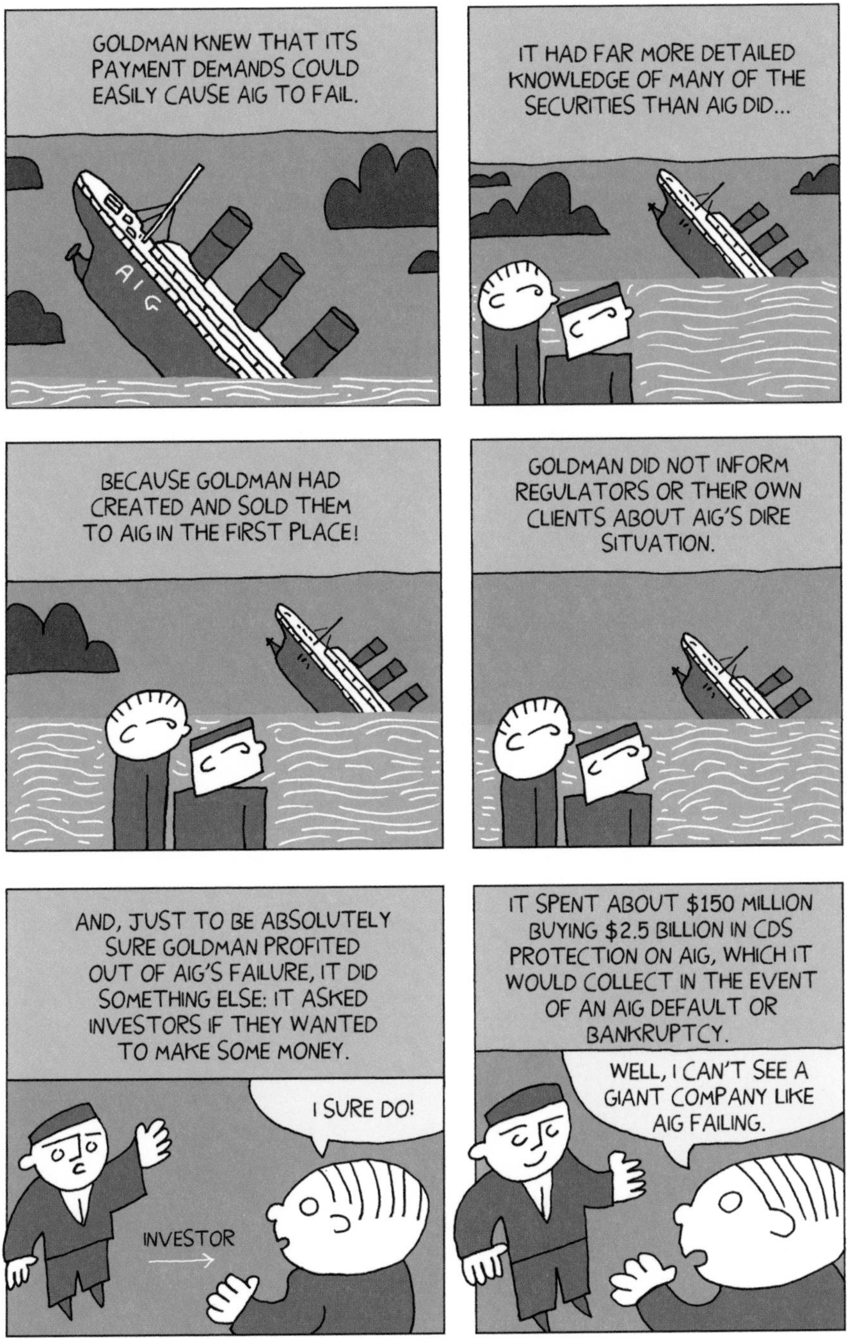
GOLDMAN KNEW THAT ITS PAYMENT DEMANDS COULD EASILY CAUSE AIG TO FAIL.
AIG
IT HAD FAR MORE DETAILED KNOWLEDGE OF MANY OF THE SECURITIES THAN AIG DID...
BECAUSE GOLDMAN HAD CREATED AND SOLD THEM TO AIG IN THE FIRST PLACE!
GOLDMAN DID NOT INFORM REGULATORS OR THEIR OWN CLIENTS ABOUT AIG'S DIRE SITUATION.
AND, JUST TO BE ABSOLUTELY SURE GOLDMAN PROFITED OUT OF AIG'S FAILURE, IT DID SOMETHING ELSE: IT ASKED INVESTORS IF THEY WANTED TO MAKE SOME MONEY.
I SURE DO!
INVESTOR
IT SPENT ABOUT $150 MILLION BUYING $2.5 BILLION IN CDS PROTECTION ON AIG, WHICH IT WOULD COLLECT IN THE EVENT OF AN AIG DEFAULT OR BANKRUPTCY.
WELL, I CAN'T SEE A GIANT COMPANY LIKE AIG FAILING.

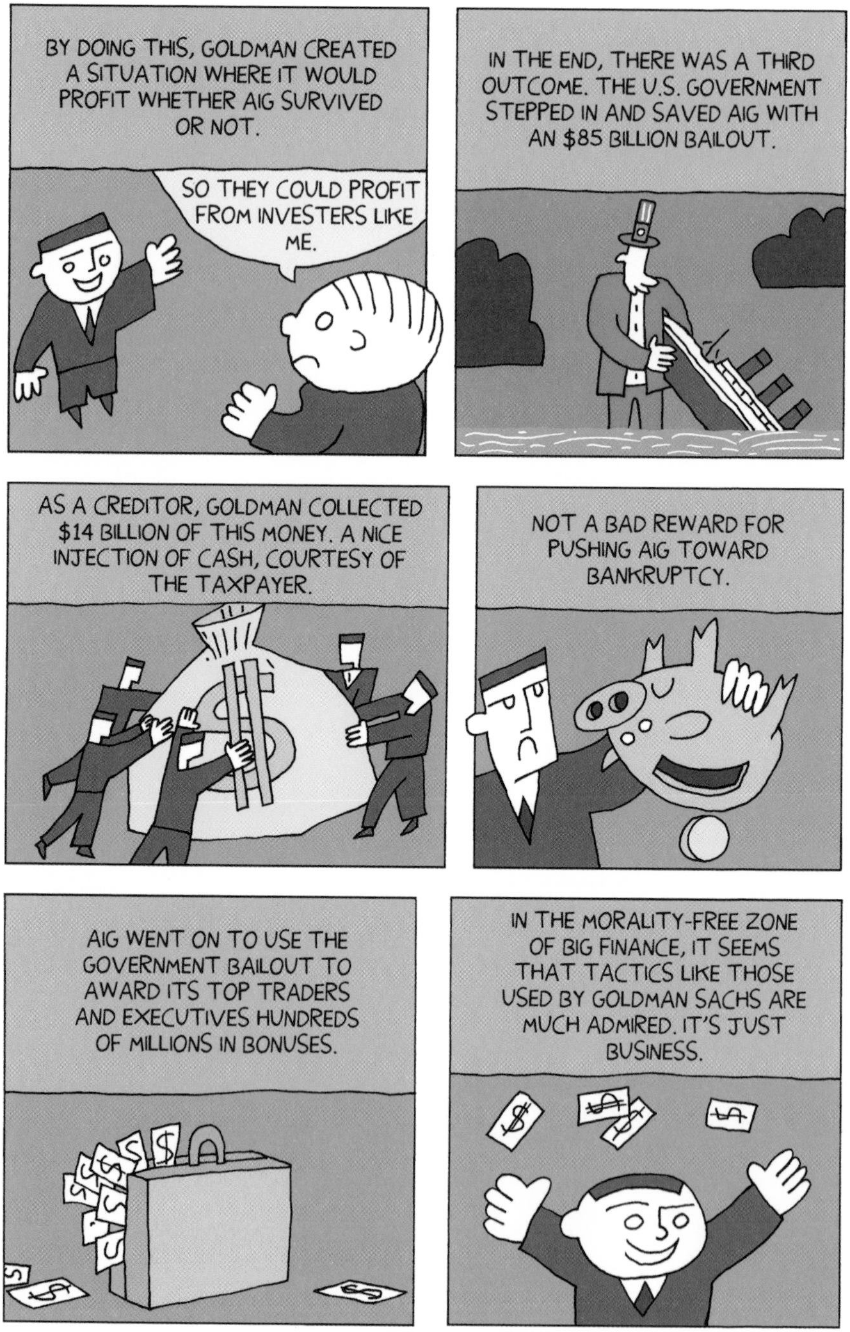
BY DOING THIS, GOLDMAN CREATED A SITUATION WHERE IT WOULD PROFIT WHETHER AIG SURVIVED OR NOT.
SO THEY COULD PROFIT FROM INVESTERS LIKE ME.
IN THE END, THERE WAS A THIRD OUTCOME. THE U.S. GOVERNMENT STEPPED IN AND SAVED AIG WITH AN $85 BILLION BAILOUT.
AS A CREDITOR, GOLDMAN COLLECTED $14 BILLION OF THIS MONEY. A NICE INJECTION OF CASH, COURTESY OF THE TAXPAYER.
NOT A BAD REWARD FOR PUSHING AIG TOWARD BANKRUPTCY.
AIG WENT ON TO USE THE GOVERNMENT BAILOUT TO AWARD ITS TOP TRADERS AND EXECUTIVES HUNDREDS OF MILLIONS IN BONUSES.
IN THE MORALITY-FREE ZONE OF BIG FINANCE, IT SEEMS THAT TACTICS LIKE THOSE USED BY GOLDMAN SACHS ARE MUCH ADMIRED. IT'S JUST BUSINESS.

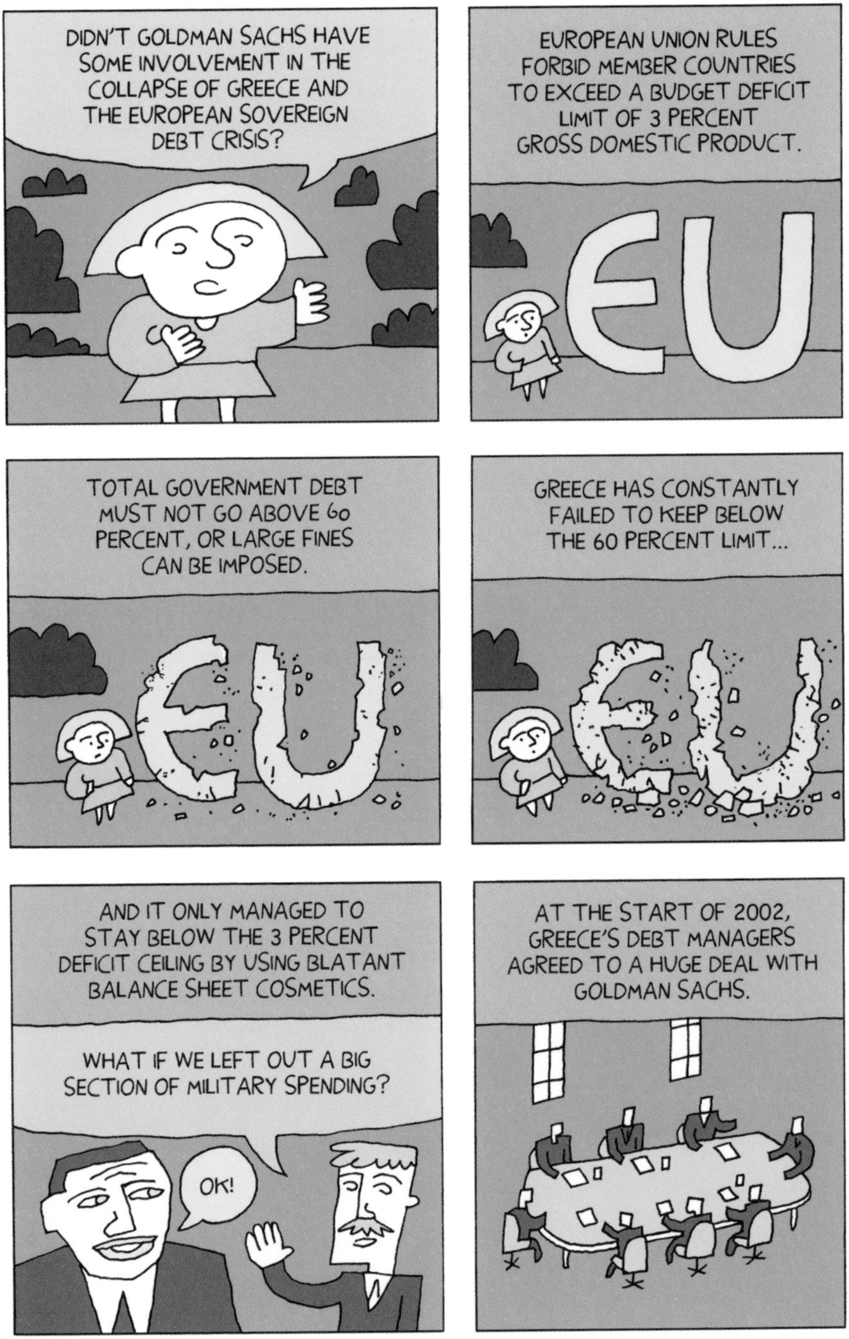
DIDN'T GOLDMAN SACHS HAVE SOME INVOLVEMENT IN THE COLLAPSE OF GREECE AND THE EUROPEAN SOVEREIGN DEBT CRISIS?
EUROPEAN UNION RULES FORBID MEMBER COUNTRIES TO EXCEED A BUDGET DEFICIT LIMIT OF 3 PERCENT GROSS DOMESTIC PRODUCT.
EU
TOTAL GOVERNMENT DEBT MUST NOT GO ABOVE 60 PERCENT, OR LARGE FINES CAN BE IMPOSED.
EU
GREECE HAS CONSTANTLY FAILED TO KEEP BELOW THE 60 PERCENT LIMIT...
EU
AND IT ONLY MANAGED TO STAY BELOW THE 3 PERCENT DEFICIT CEILING BY USING BLATANT BALANCE SHEET COSMETICS.
WHAT IF WE LEFT OUT A BIG SECTION OF MILITARY SPENDING?
OK!
AT THE START OF 2002, GREECE'S DEBT MANAGERS AGREED TO A HUGE DEAL WITH GOLDMAN SACHS.

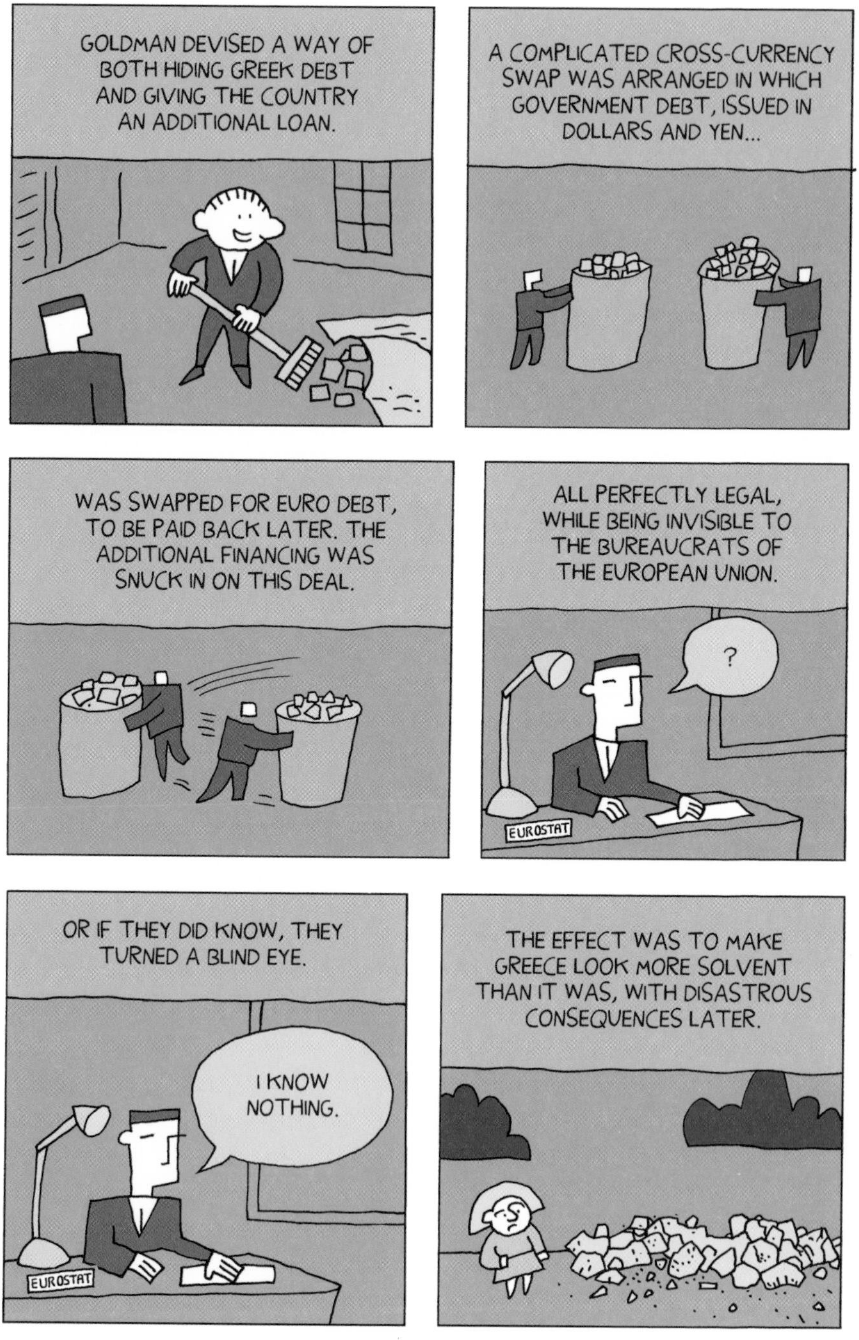
GOLDMAN DEVISED A WAY OF BOTH HIDING GREEK DEBT AND GIVING THE COUNTRY AN ADDITIONAL LOAN.
A COMPLICATED CROSS-CURRENCY SWAP WAS ARRANGED IN WHICH GOVERNMENT DEBT, ISSUED IN DOLLARS AND YEN...
WAS SWAPPED FOR EURO DEBT, TO BE PAID BACK LATER. THE ADDITIONAL FINANCING WAS SNUCK IN ON THIS DEAL.
ALL PERFECTLY LEGAL, WHILE BEING INVISIBLE TO THE BUREAUCRATS OF THE EUROPEAN UNION.
?
EUROSTAT
OR IF THEY DID KNOW, THEY TURNED A BLIND EYE.
I KNOW NOTHING.
EUROSTAT
THE EFFECT WAS TO MAKE GREECE LOOK MORE SOLVENT THAN IT WAS, WITH DISASTROUS CONSEQUENCES LATER.

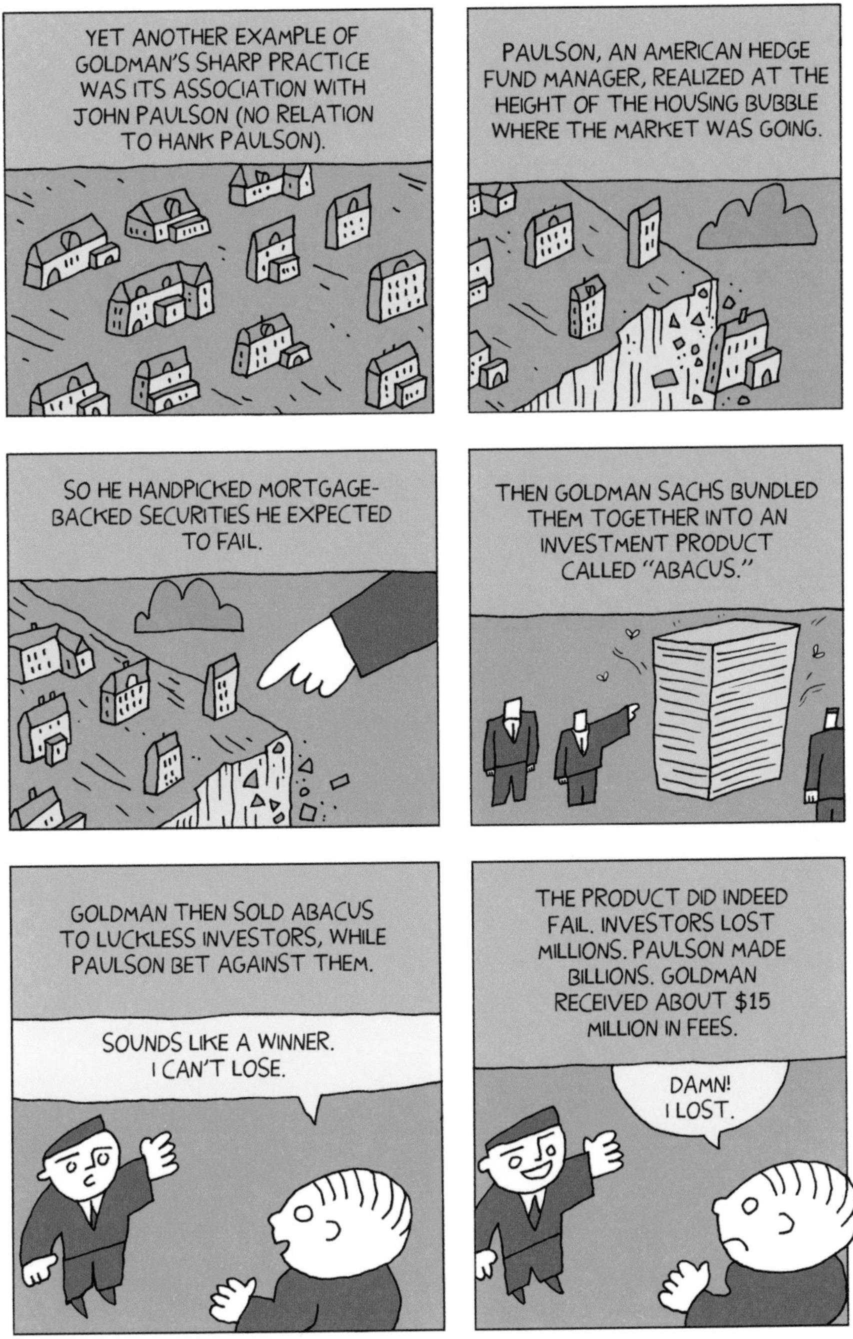
YET ANOTHER EXAMPLE OF GOLDMAN'S SHARP PRACTICE WAS ITS ASSOCIATION WITH JOHN PAULSON (NO RELATION TO HANK PAULSON).
PAULSON, AN AMERICAN HEDGE FUND MANAGER, REALIZED AT THE HEIGHT OF THE HOUSING BUBBLE WHERE THE MARKET WAS GOING.
SO HE HANDPICKED MORTGAGE-BACKED SECURITIES HE EXPECTED TO FAIL.
THEN GOLDMAN SACHS BUNDLED THEM TOGETHER INTO AN INVESTMENT PRODUCT CALLED "ABACUS."
GOLDMAN THEN SOLD ABACUS TO LUCKLESS INVESTORS, WHILE PAULSON BET AGAINST THEM.
SOUNDS LIKE A WINNER. I CAN'T LOSE.
THE PRODUCT DID INDEED FAIL. INVESTORS LOST MILLIONS. PAULSON MADE BILLIONS. GOLDMAN RECEIVED ABOUT $15 MILLION IN FEES.
DAMN! I LOST.

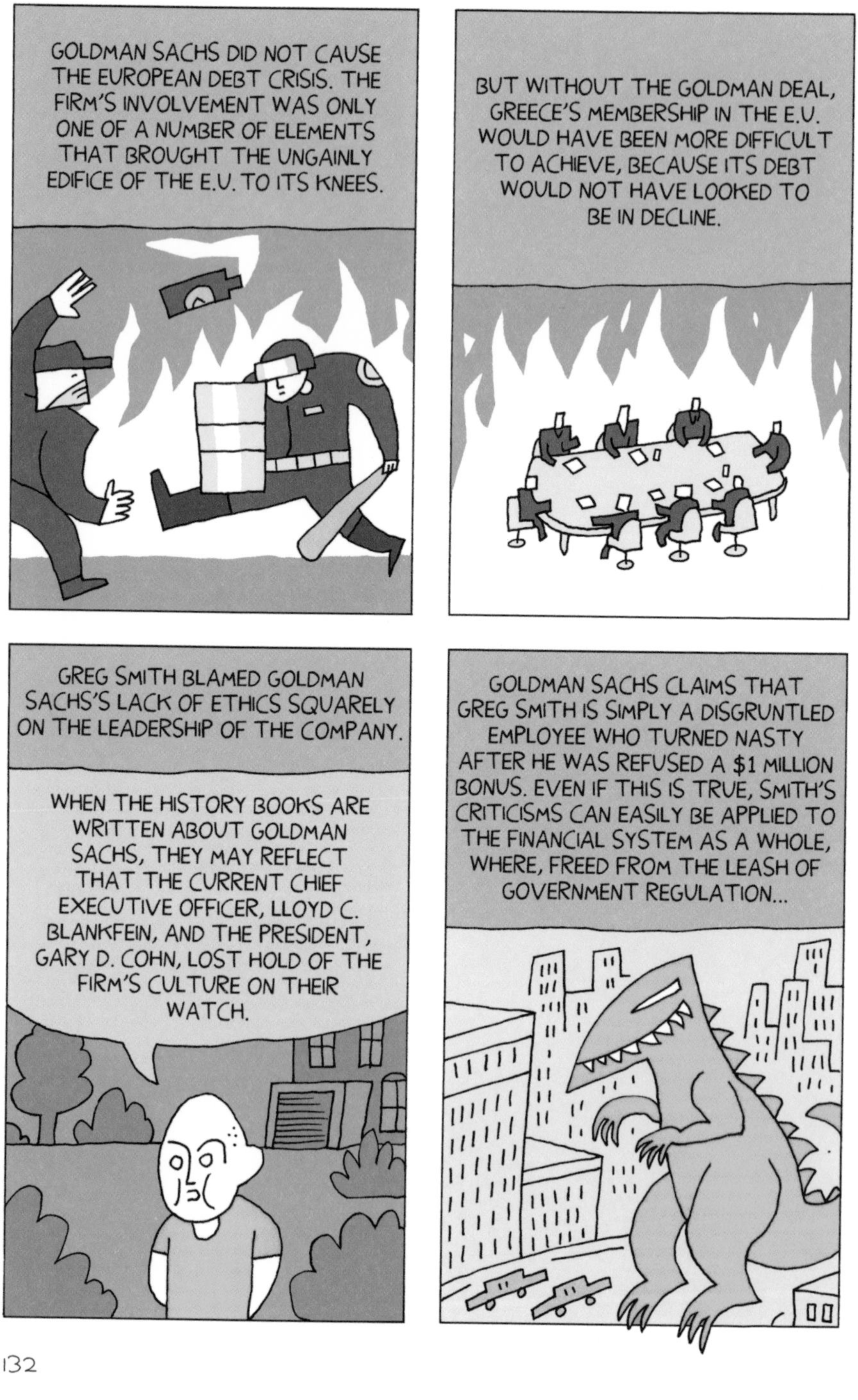
GOLDMAN SACHS DID NOT CAUSE THE EUROPEAN DEBT CRISIS. THE FIRM'S INVOLVEMENT WAS ONLY ONE OF A NUMBER OF ELEMENTS THAT BROUGHT THE UNGAINLY EDIFICE OF THE E.U. TO ITS KNEES.
BUT WITHOUT THE GOLDMAN DEAL, GREECE'S MEMBERSHIP IN THE E.U. WOULD HAVE BEEN MORE DIFFICULT TO ACHIEVE, BECAUSE ITS DEBT WOULD NOT HAVE LOOKED TO BE IN DECLINE.
GREG SMITH BLAMED GOLDMAN SACHS'S LACK OF ETHICS SQUARELY ON THE LEADERSHIP OF THE COMPANY.
WHEN THE HISTORY BOOKS ARE WRITTEN ABOUT GOLDMAN SACHS, THEY MAY REFLECT THAT THE CURRENT CHIEF EXECUTIVE OFFICER, LLOYD C. BLANKFEIN, AND THE PRESIDENT, GARY D. COHN, LOST HOLD OF THE FIRM'S CULTURE ON THEIR WATCH.
GOLDMAN SACHS CLAIMS THAT GREG SMITH IS SIMPLY A DISGRUNTLED EMPLOYEE WHO TURNED NASTY AFTER HE WAS REFUSED A $1 MILLION BONUS. EVEN IF THIS IS TRUE, SMITH'S CRITICISMS CAN EASILY BE APPLIED TO THE FINANCIAL SYSTEM AS A WHOLE, WHERE, FREED FROM THE LEASH OF GOVERNMENT REGULATION...

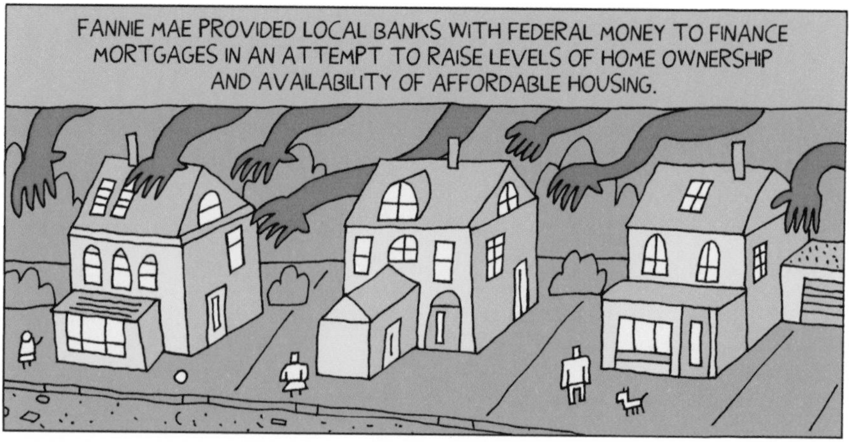
FANNIE MAE PROVIDED LOCAL BANKS WITH FEDERAL MONEY TO FINANCE MORTGAGES IN AN ATTEMPT TO RAISE LEVELS OF HOME OWNERSHIP AND AVAILABILITY OF AFFORDABLE HOUSING.

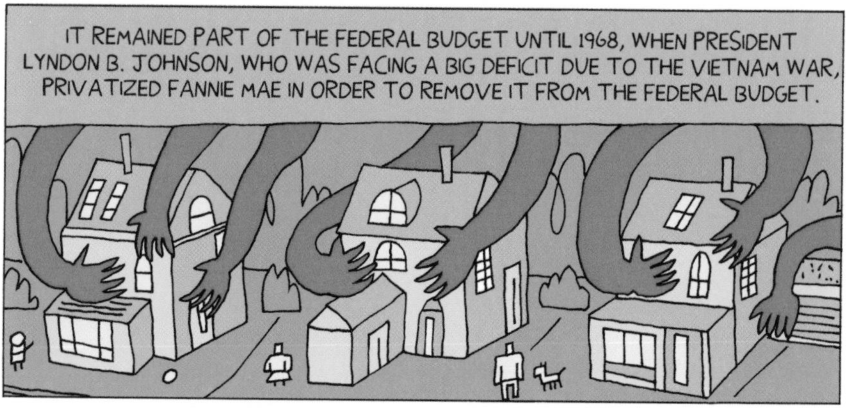
IT REMAINED PART OF THE FEDERAL BUDGET UNTIL 1968, WHEN PRESIDENT LYNDON B. JOHNSON, WHO WAS FACING A BIG DEFICIT DUE TO THE VIETNAM WAR, PRIVATIZED FANNIE MAE IN ORDER TO REMOVE IT FROM THE FEDERAL BUDGET.

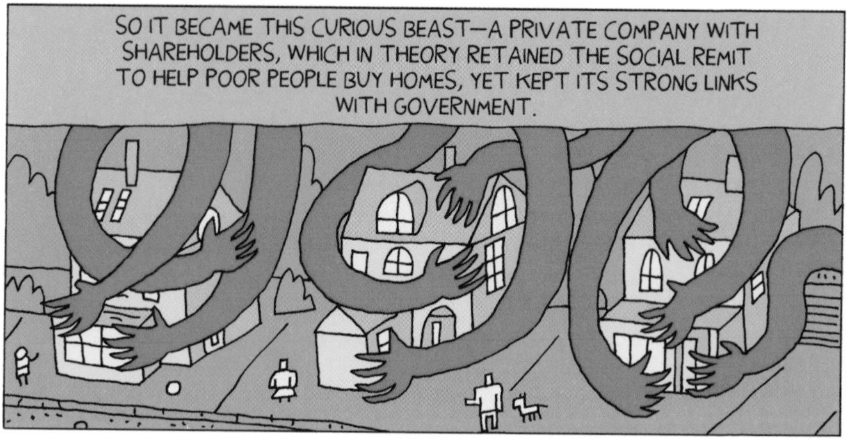
SO IT BECAME THIS CURIOUS BEAST—A PRIVATE COMPANY WITH SHAREHOLDERS, WHICH IN THEORY RETAINED THE SOCIAL REMIT TO HELP POOR PEOPLE BUY HOMES, YET KEPT ITS STRONG LINKS WITH GOVERNMENT.

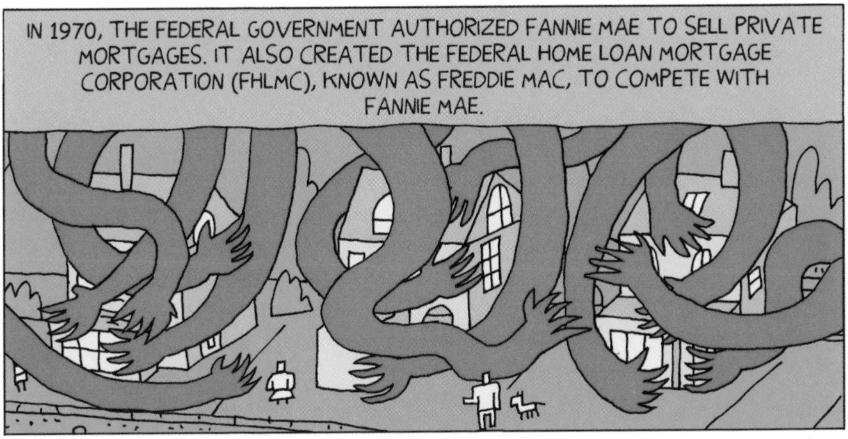
IN 1970, THE FEDERAL GOVERNMENT AUTHORIZED FANNIE MAE TO SELL PRIVATE MORTGAGES. IT ALSO CREATED THE FEDERAL HOME LOAN MORTGAGE CORPORATION (FHLMC), KNOWN AS FREDDIE MAC, TO COMPETE WITH FANNIE MAE.

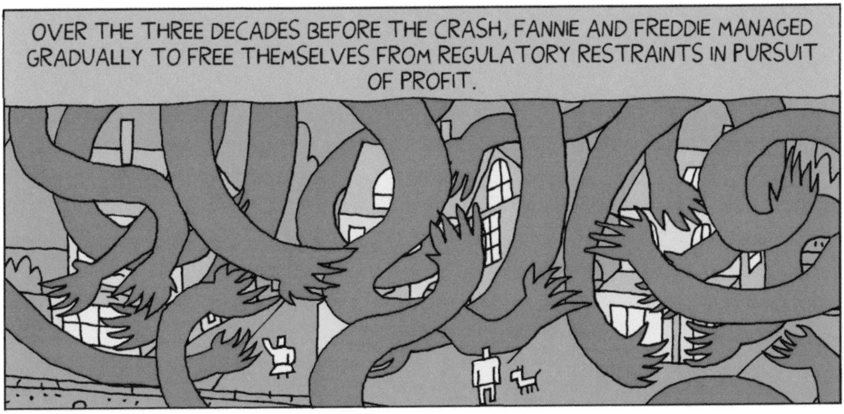
OVER THE THREE DECADES BEFORE THE CRASH, FANNIE AND FREDDIE MANAGED GRADUALLY TO FREE THEMSELVES FROM REGULATORY RESTRAINTS IN PURSUIT OF PROFIT.

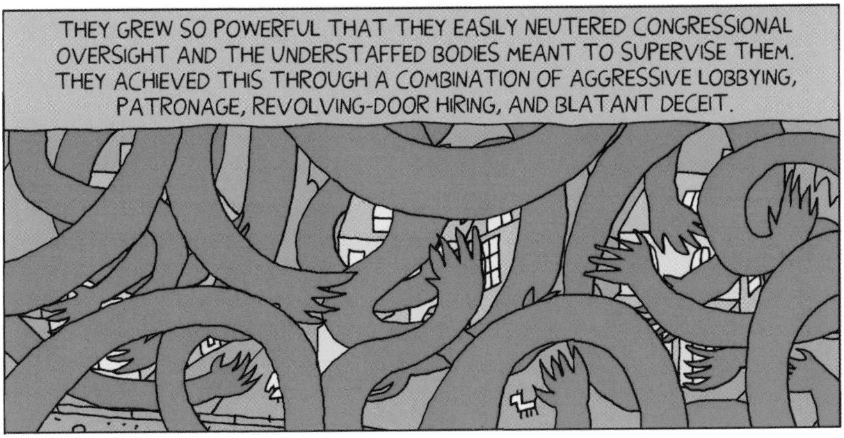
THEY GREW SO POWERFUL THAT THEY EASILY NEUTERED CONGRESSIONAL OVERSIGHT AND THE UNDERSTAFFED BODIES MEANT TO SUPERVISE THEM. THEY ACHIEVED THIS THROUGH A COMBINATION OF AGGRESSIVE LOBBYING, PATRONAGE, REVOLVING-DOOR HIRING, AND BLATANT DECEIT.

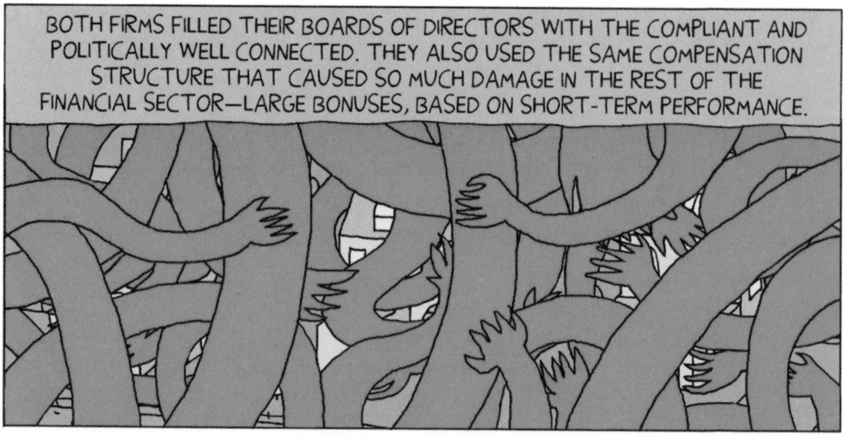
BOTH FIRMS FILLED THEIR BOARDS OF DIRECTORS WITH THE COMPLIANT AND POLITICALLY WELL CONNECTED. THEY ALSO USED THE SAME COMPENSATION STRUCTURE THAT CAUSED SO MUCH DAMAGE IN THE REST OF THE FINANCIAL SECTOR—LARGE BONUSES, BASED ON SHORT-TERM PERFORMANCE.

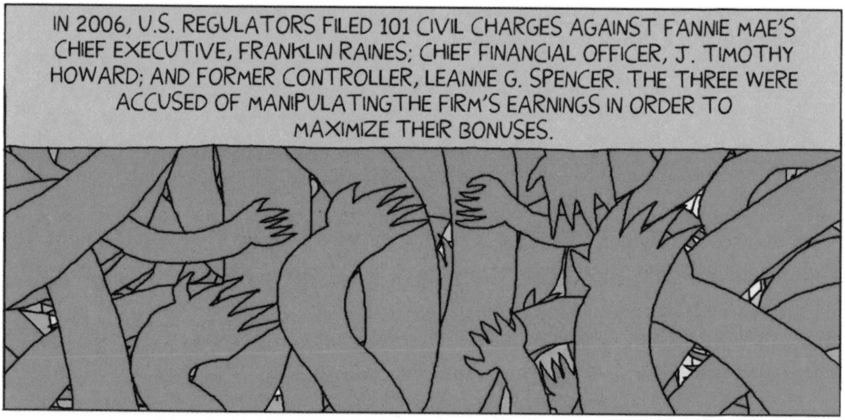
IN 2006, U.S. REGULATORS FILED 101 CIVIL CHARGES AGAINST FANNIE MAE'S CHIEF EXECUTIVE, FRANKLIN RAINES; CHIEF FINANCIAL OFFICER, J. TIMOTHY HOWARD; AND FORMER CONTROLLER, LEANNE G. SPENCER. THE THREE WERE ACCUSED OF MANIPULATING THE FIRM'S EARNINGS IN ORDER TO MAXIMIZE THEIR BONUSES.

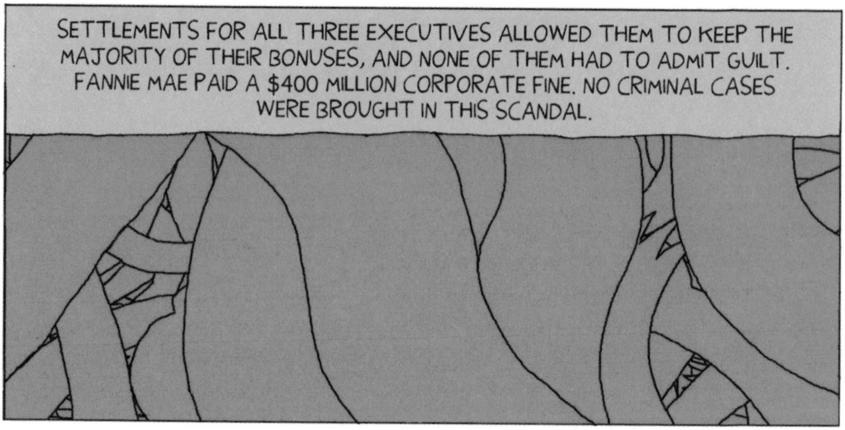
SETTLEMENTS FOR ALL THREE EXECUTIVES ALLOWED THEM TO KEEP THE MAJORITY OF THEIR BONUSES, AND NONE OF THEM HAD TO ADMIT GUILT. FANNIE MAE PAID A $400 MILLION CORPORATE FINE. NO CRIMINAL CASES WERE BROUGHT IN THIS SCANDAL.

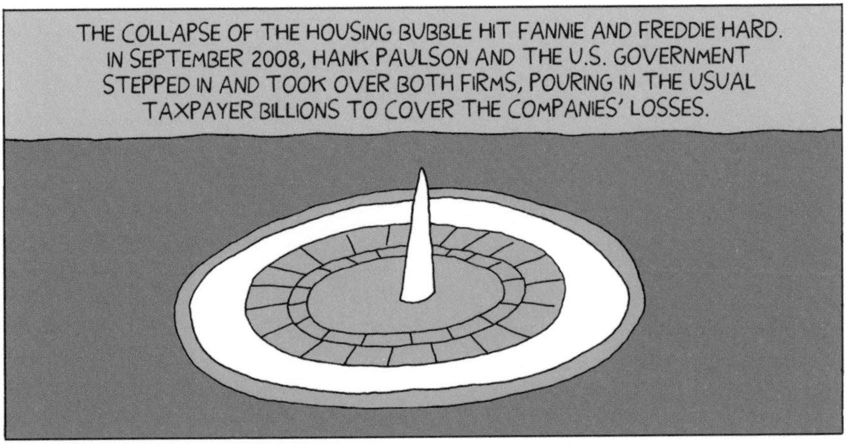
THE COLLAPSE OF THE HOUSING BUBBLE HIT FANNIE AND FREDDIE HARD. IN SEPTEMBER 2008, HANK PAULSON AND THE U.S. GOVERNMENT STEPPED IN AND TOOK OVER BOTH FIRMS, POURING IN THE USUAL TAXPAYER BILLIONS TO COVER THE COMPANIES' LOSSES.

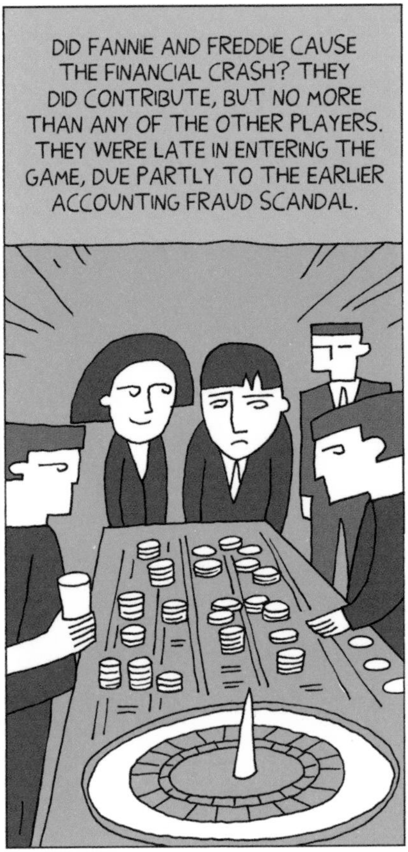
DID FANNIE AND FREDDIE CAUSE THE FINANCIAL CRASH? THEY DID CONTRIBUTE, BUT NO MORE THAN ANY OF THE OTHER PLAYERS. THEY WERE LATE IN ENTERING THE GAME, DUE PARTLY TO THE EARLIER ACCOUNTING FRAUD SCANDAL.

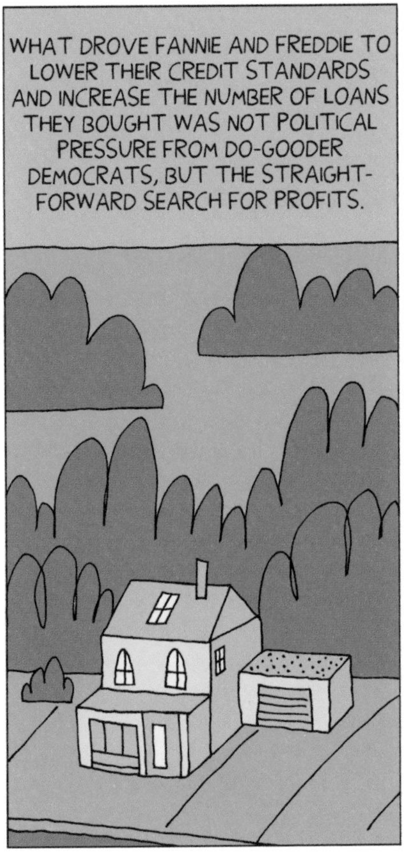
WHAT DROVE FANNIE AND FREDDIE TO LOWER THEIR CREDIT STANDARDS AND INCREASE THE NUMBER OF LOANS THEY BOUGHT WAS NOT POLITICAL PRESSURE FROM DO-GOODER DEMOCRATS, BUT THE STRAIGHT-FORWARD SEARCH FOR PROFITS.

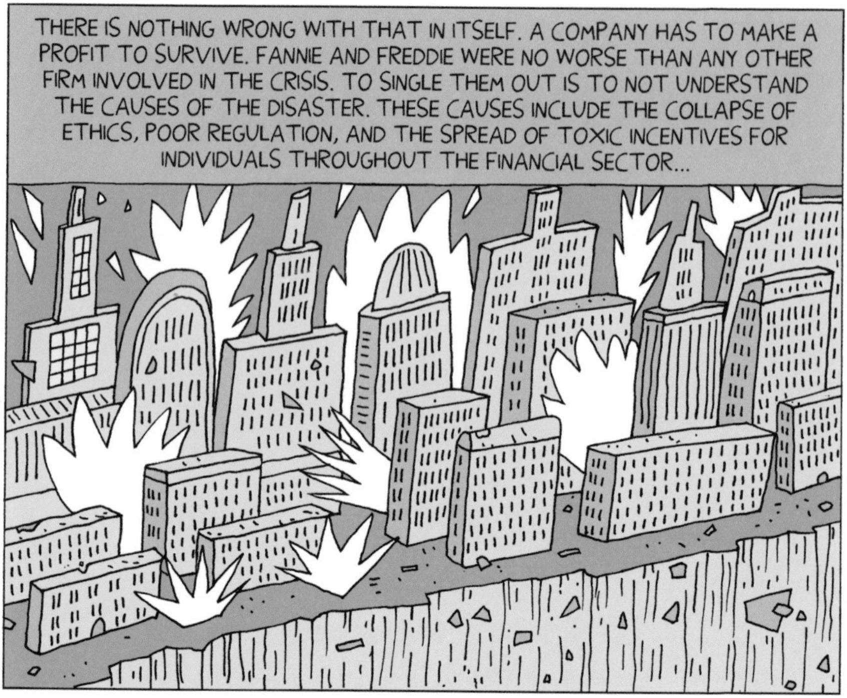
THERE IS NOTHING WRONG WITH THAT IN ITSELF. A COMPANY HAS TO MAKE A PROFIT TO SURVIVE. FANNIE AND FREDDIE WERE NO WORSE THAN ANY OTHER FIRM INVOLVED IN THE CRISIS. TO SINGLE THEM OUT IS TO NOT UNDERSTAND THE CAUSES OF THE DISASTER. THESE CAUSES INCLUDE THE COLLAPSE OF ETHICS, POOR REGULATION, AND THE SPREAD OF TOXIC INCENTIVES FOR INDIVIDUALS THROUGHOUT THE FINANCIAL SECTOR...

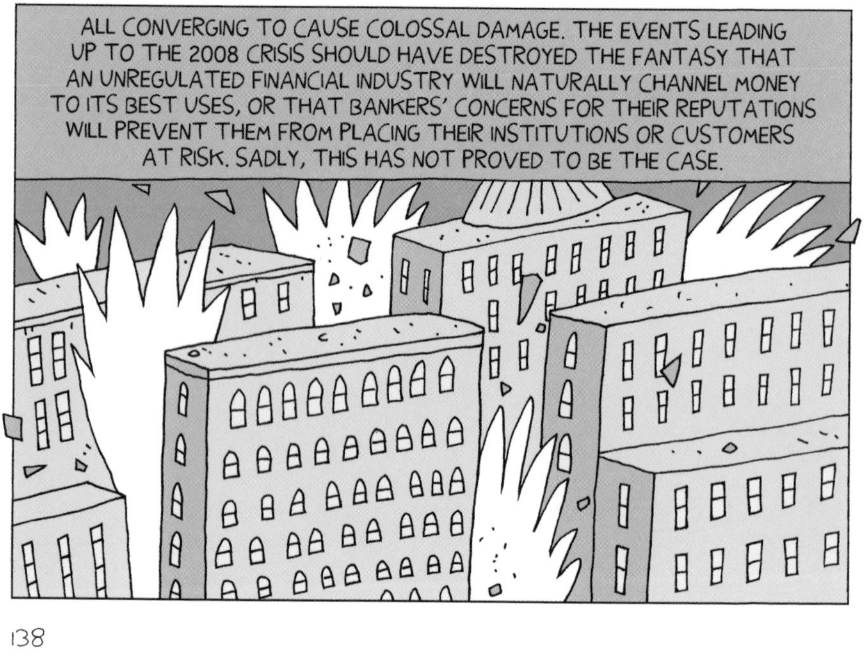
ALL CONVERGING TO CAUSE COLOSSAL DAMAGE. THE EVENTS LEADING UP TO THE 2008 CRISIS SHOULD HAVE DESTROYED THE FANTASY THAT AN UNREGULATED FINANCIAL INDUSTRY WILL NATURALLY CHANNEL MONEY TO ITS BEST USES, OR THAT BANKERS' CONCERNS FOR THEIR REPUTATIONS WILL PREVENT THEM FROM PLACING THEIR INSTITUTIONS OR CUSTOMERS AT RISK. SADLY, THIS HAS NOT PROVED TO BE THE CASE.

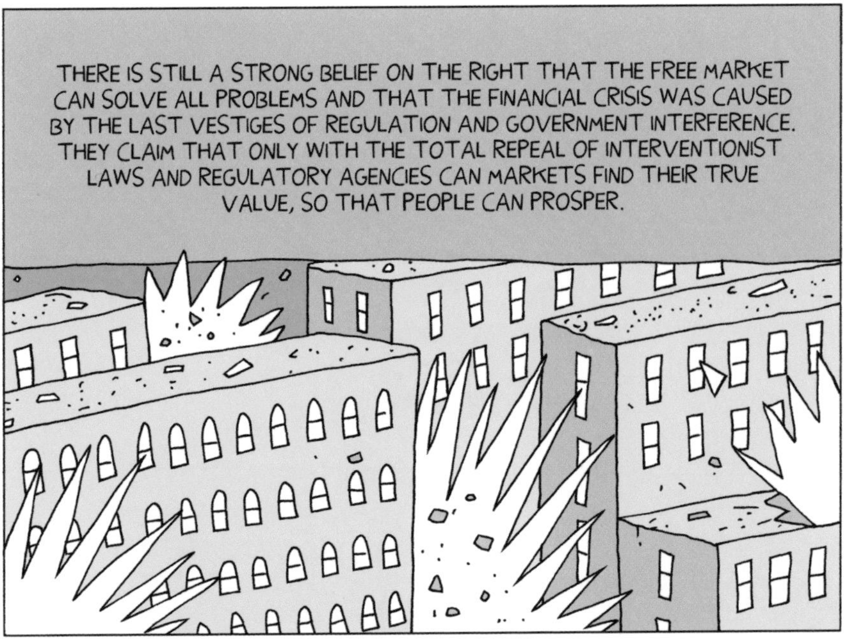
THERE IS STILL A STRONG BELIEF ON THE RIGHT THAT THE FREE MARKET CAN SOLVE ALL PROBLEMS AND THAT THE FINANCIAL CRISIS WAS CAUSED BY THE LAST VESTIGES OF REGULATION AND GOVERNMENT INTERFERENCE. THEY CLAIM THAT ONLY WITH THE TOTAL REPEAL OF INTERVENTIONIST LAWS AND REGULATORY AGENCIES CAN MARKETS FIND THEIR TRUE VALUE, SO THAT PEOPLE CAN PROSPER.

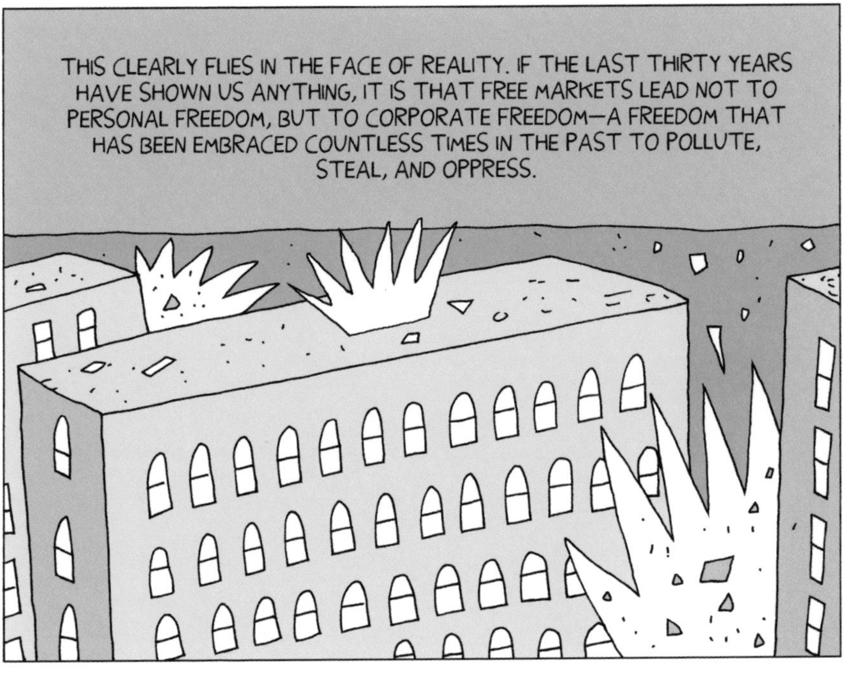
THIS CLEARLY FLIES IN THE FACE OF REALITY. IF THE LAST THIRTY YEARS HAVE SHOWN US ANYTHING, IT IS THAT FREE MARKETS LEAD NOT TO PERSONAL FREEDOM, BUT TO CORPORATE FREEDOM—A FREEDOM THAT HAS BEEN EMBRACED COUNTLESS TIMES IN THE PAST TO POLLUTE, STEAL, AND OPPRESS.

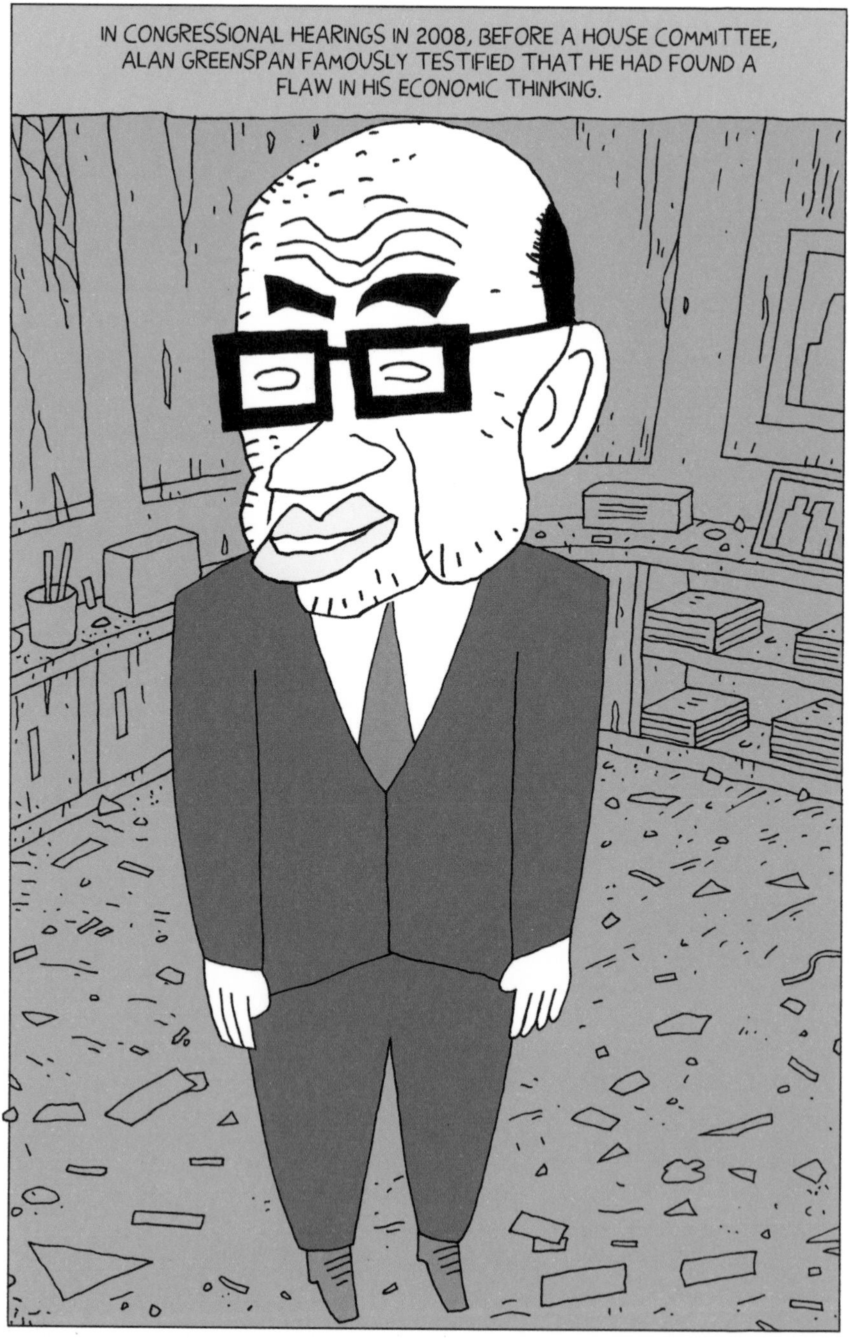
IN CONGRESSIONAL HEARINGS IN 2008, BEFORE A HOUSE COMMITTEE, ALAN GREENSPAN FAMOUSLY TESTIFIED THAT HE HAD FOUND A FLAW IN HIS ECONOMIC THINKING.

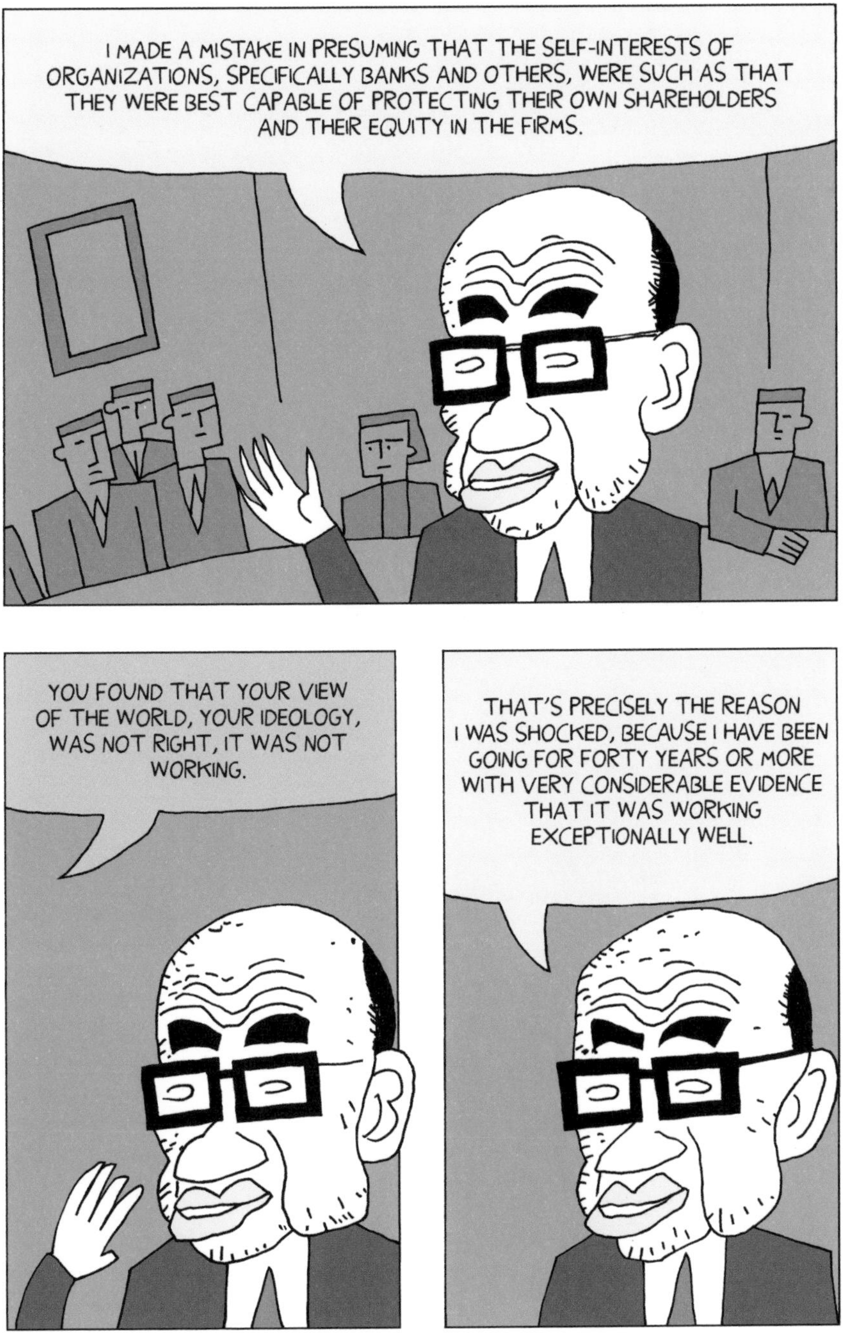
I MADE A MISTAKE IN PRESUMING THAT THE SELF-INTERESTS OF ORGANIZATIONS, SPECIFICALLY BANKS AND OTHERS, WERE SUCH AS THAT THEY WERE BEST CAPABLE OF PROTECTING THEIR OWN SHAREHOLDERS AND THEIR EQUITY IN THE FIRMS.
YOU FOUND THAT YOUR VIEW OF THE WORLD, YOUR IDEOLOGY, WAS NOT RIGHT, IT WAS NOT WORKING.
THAT'S PRECISELY THE REASON I WAS SHOCKED, BECAUSE I HAVE BEEN GOING FOR FORTY YEARS OR MORE WITH VERY CONSIDERABLE EVIDENCE THAT IT WAS WORKING EXCEPTIONALLY WELL.

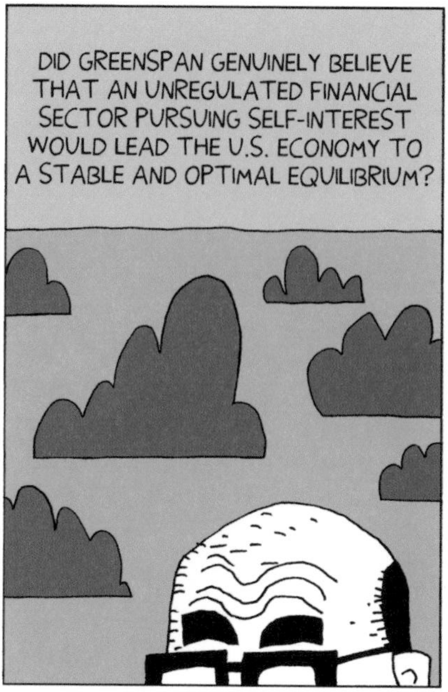
DID GREENSPAN GENUINELY BELIEVE THAT AN UNREGULATED FINANCIAL SECTOR PURSUING SELF-INTEREST WOULD LEAD THE U.S. ECONOMY TO A STABLE AND OPTIMAL EQUILIBRIUM?

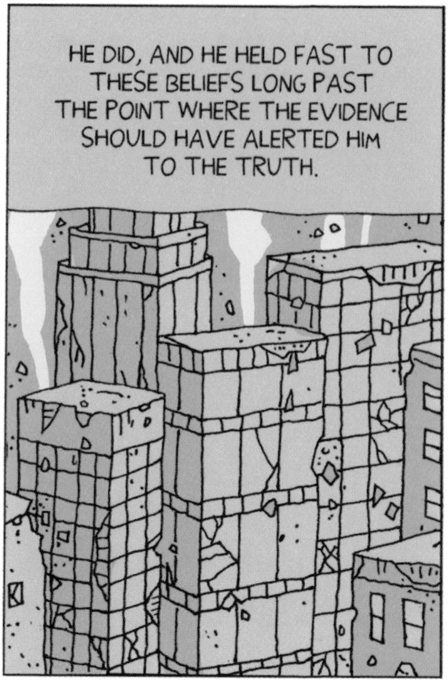
HE DID, AND HE HELD FAST TO THESE BELIEFS LONG PAST THE POINT WHERE THE EVIDENCE SHOULD HAVE ALERTED HIM TO THE TRUTH.

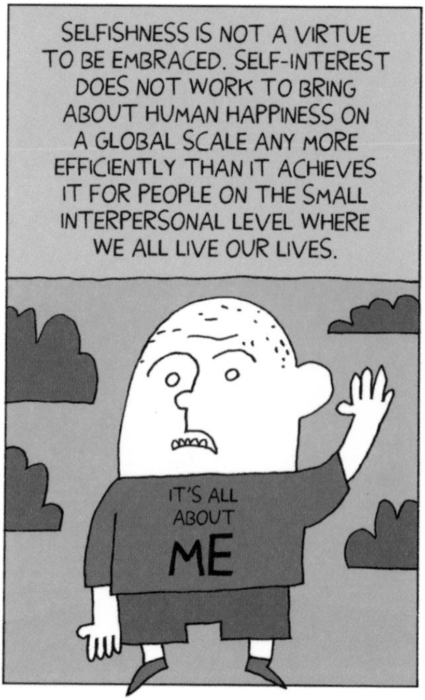
SELFISHNESS IS NOT A VIRTUE TO BE EMBRACED. SELF-INTEREST DOES NOT WORK TO BRING ABOUT HUMAN HAPPINESS ON A GLOBAL SCALE ANY MORE EFFICIENTLY THAN IT ACHIEVES IT FOR PEOPLE ON THE SMALL INTERPERSONAL LEVEL WHERE WE ALL LIVE OUR LIVES.
IT'S ALL ABOUT
ME

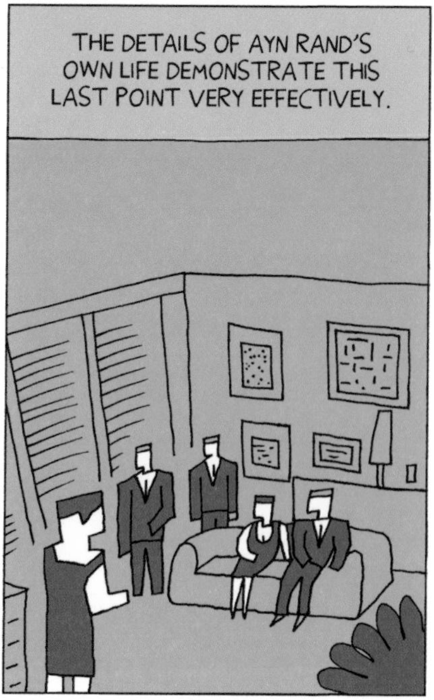
THE DETAILS OF AYN RAND'S OWN LIFE DEMONSTRATE THIS LAST POINT VERY EFFECTIVELY.

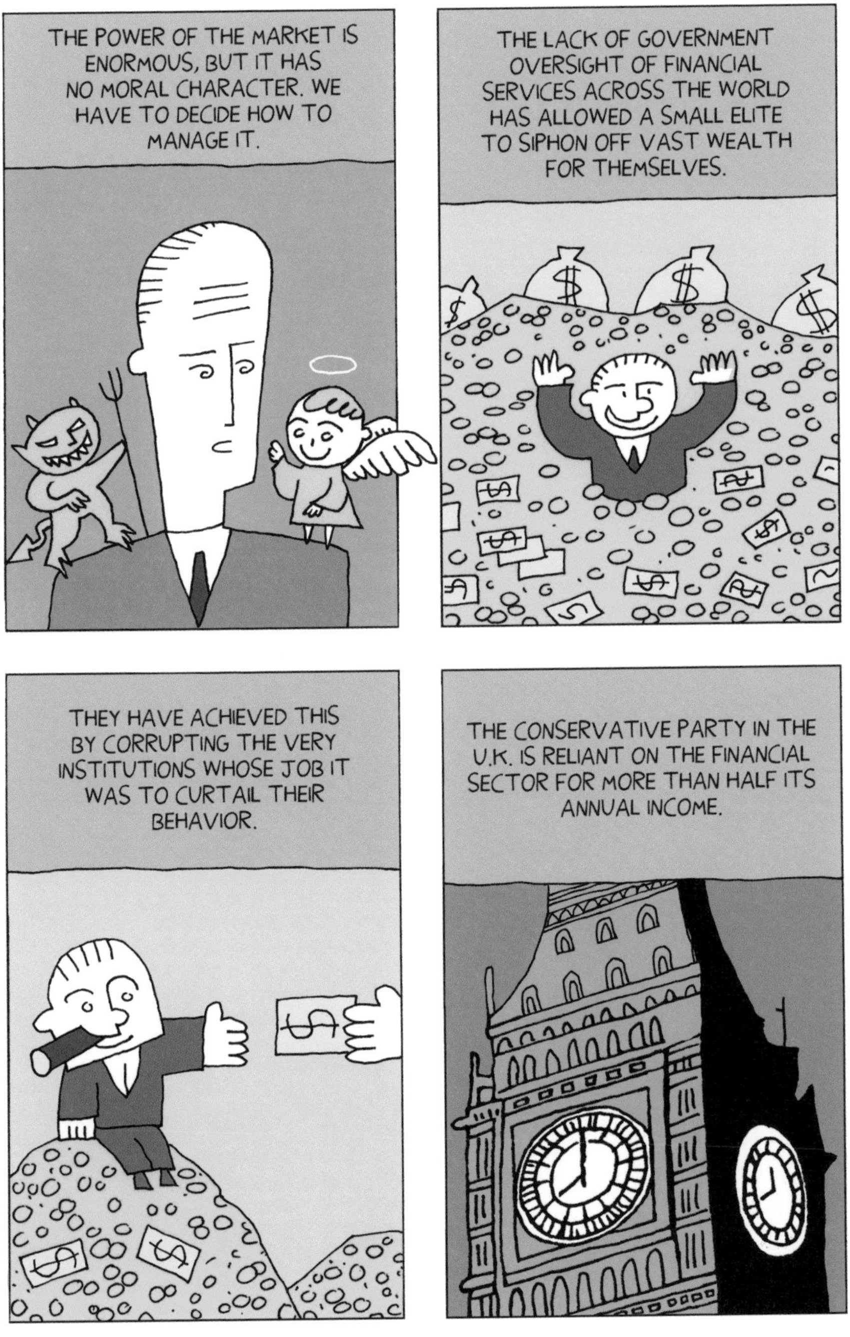
THE POWER OF THE MARKET IS ENORMOUS, BUT IT HAS NO MORAL CHARACTER. WE HAVE TO DECIDE HOW TO MANAGE IT.
THE LACK OF GOVERNMENT OVERSIGHT OF FINANCIAL SERVICES ACROSS THE WORLD HAS ALLOWED A SMALL ELITE TO SIPHON OFF VAST WEALTH FOR THEMSELVES.
THEY HAVE ACHIEVED THIS BY CORRUPTING THE VERY INSTITUTIONS WHOSE JOB IT WAS TO CURTAIL THEIR BEHAVIOR.
THE CONSERVATIVE PARTY IN THE U.K. IS RELIANT ON THE FINANCIAL SECTOR FOR MORE THAN HALF ITS ANNUAL INCOME.

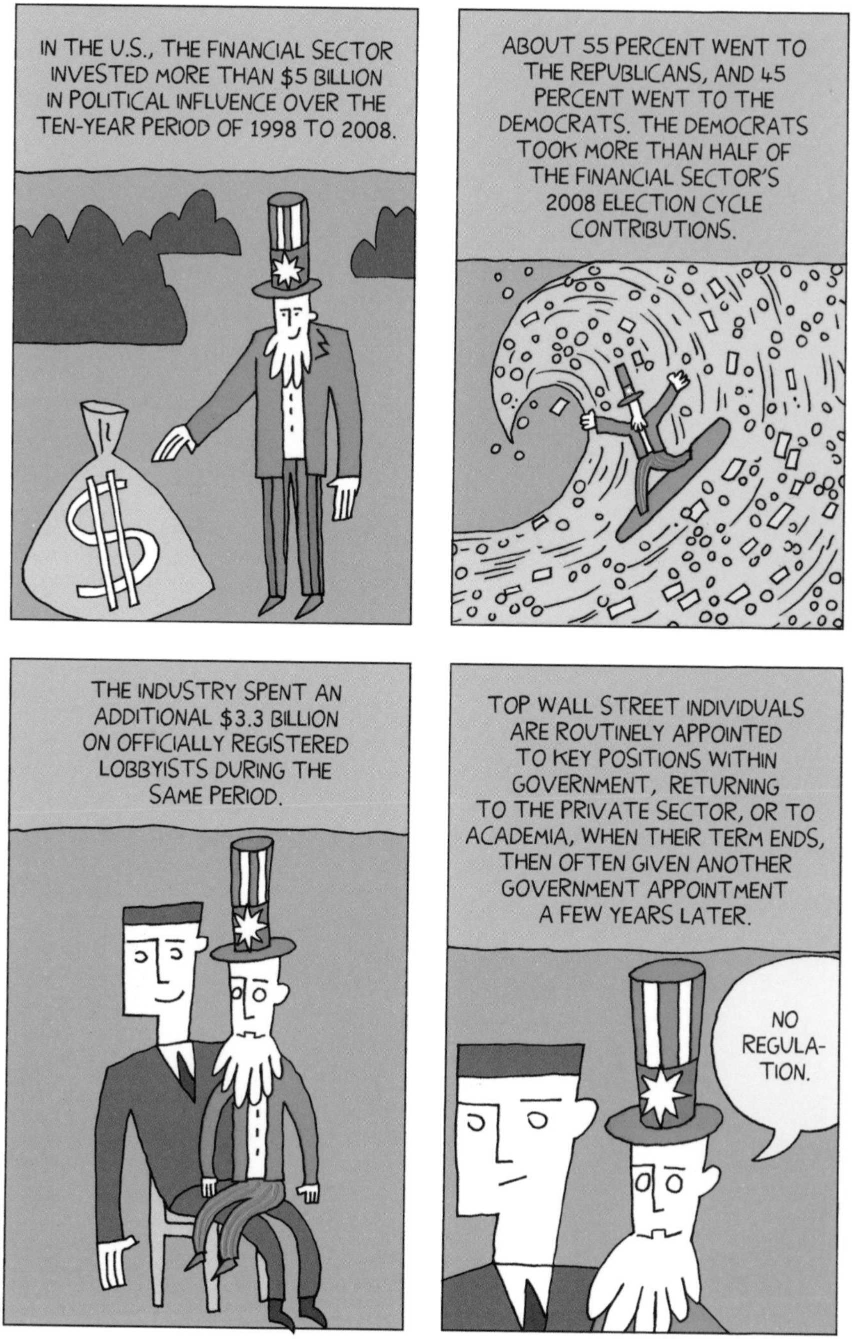
IN THE U.S., THE FINANCIAL SECTOR INVESTED MORE THAN $5 BILLION IN POLITICAL INFLUENCE OVER THE TEN-YEAR PERIOD OF 1998 TO 2008.
ABOUT 55 PERCENT WENT TO THE REPUBLICANS, AND 45 PERCENT WENT TO THE DEMOCRATS. THE DEMOCRATS TOOK MORE THAN HALF OF THE FINANCIAL SECTOR'S 2008 ELECTION CYCLE CONTRIBUTIONS.
THE INDUSTRY SPENT AN ADDITIONAL $3.3 BILLION ON OFFICIALLY REGISTERED LOBBYISTS DURING THE SAME PERIOD.
TOP WALL STREET INDIVIDUALS ARE ROUTINELY APPOINTED TO KEY POSITIONS WITHIN GOVERNMENT, RETURNING TO THE PRIVATE SECTOR, OR TO ACADEMIA, WHEN THEIR TERM ENDS, THEN OFTEN GIVEN ANOTHER GOVERNMENT APPOINTMENT A FEW YEARS LATER.
NO REGULA-TION.

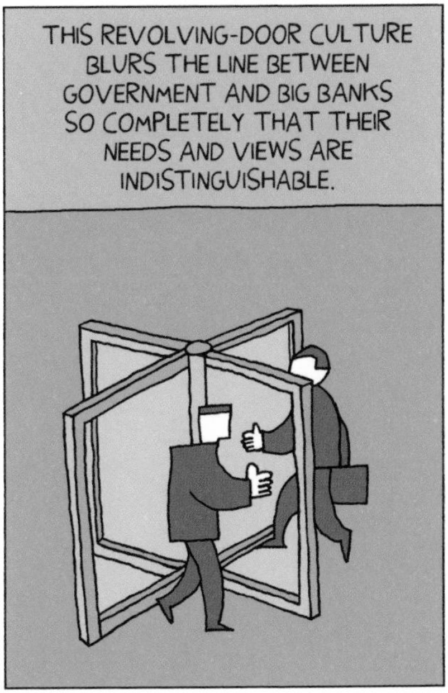
THIS REVOLVING-DOOR CULTURE BLURS THE LINE BETWEEN GOVERNMENT AND BIG BANKS SO COMPLETELY THAT THEIR NEEDS AND VIEWS ARE INDISTINGUISHABLE.

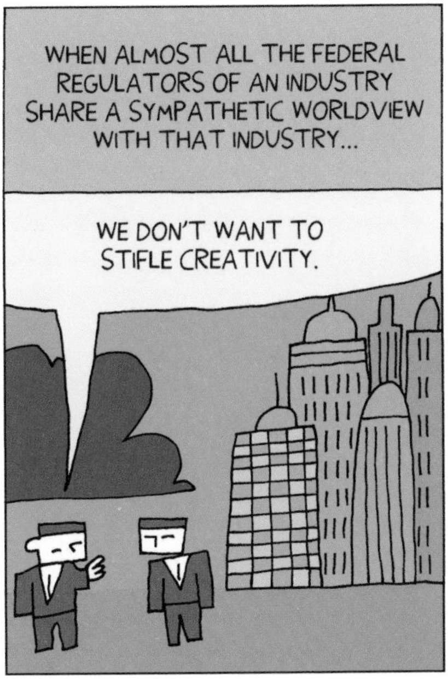
WHEN ALMOST ALL THE FEDERAL REGULATORS OF AN INDUSTRY SHARE A SYMPATHETIC WORLDVIEW WITH THAT INDUSTRY...
WE DON'T WANT TO STIFLE CREATIVITY.

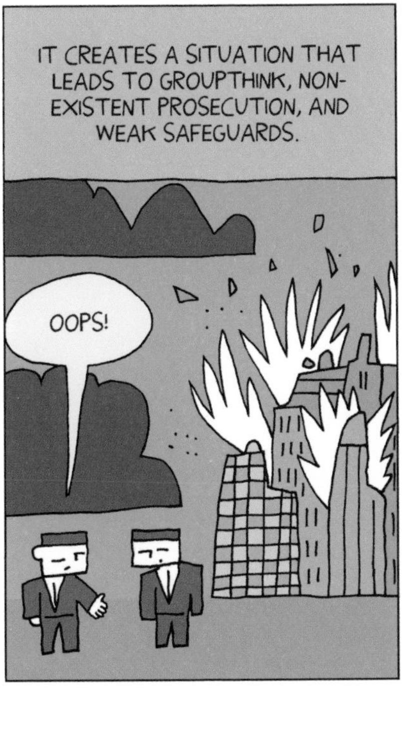
IT CREATES A SITUATION THAT LEADS TO GROUPTHINK, NON-EXISTENT PROSECUTION, AND WEAK SAFEGUARDS.
OOPS!

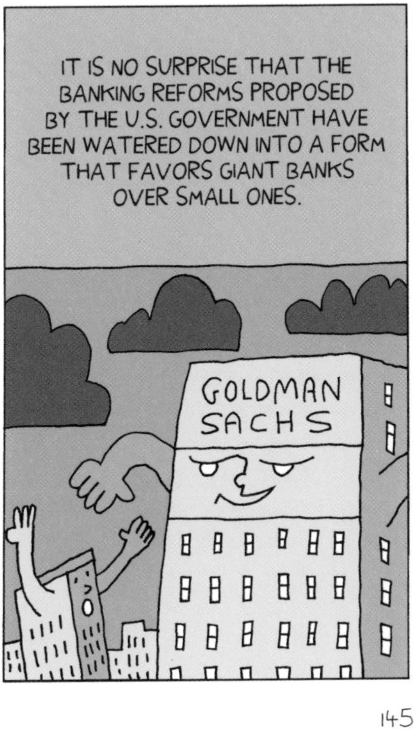
IT IS NO SURPRISE THAT THE BANKING REFORMS PROPOSED BY THE U.S. GOVERNMENT HAVE BEEN WATERED DOWN INTO A FORM THAT FAVORS GIANT BANKS OVER SMALL ONES.
GOLDMAN SACHS

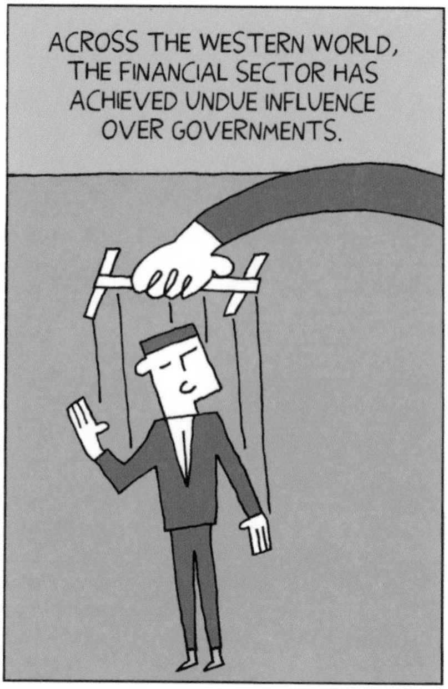
ACROSS THE WESTERN WORLD, THE FINANCIAL SECTOR HAS ACHIEVED UNDUE INFLUENCE OVER GOVERNMENTS.

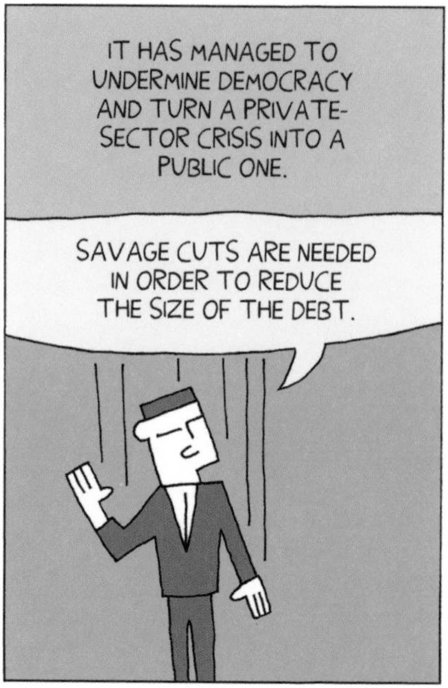
IT HAS MANAGED TO UNDERMINE DEMOCRACY AND TURN A PRIVATE-SECTOR CRISIS INTO A PUBLIC ONE.
SAVAGE CUTS ARE NEEDED IN ORDER TO REDUCE THE SIZE OF THE DEBT.

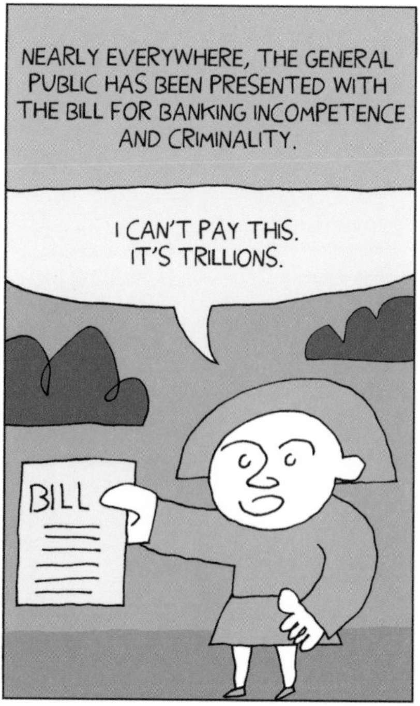
NEARLY EVERYWHERE, THE GENERAL PUBLIC HAS BEEN PRESENTED WITH THE BILL FOR BANKING INCOMPETENCE AND CRIMINALITY.
I CAN'T PAY THIS. IT'S TRILLIONS.
BILL

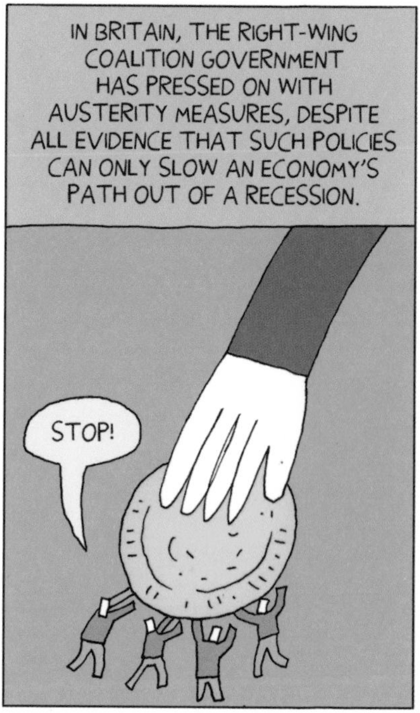
IN BRITAIN, THE RIGHT-WING COALITION GOVERNMENT HAS PRESSED ON WITH AUSTERITY MEASURES, DESPITE ALL EVIDENCE THAT SUCH POLICIES CAN ONLY SLOW AN ECONOMY'S PATH OUT OF A RECESSION.
STOP!

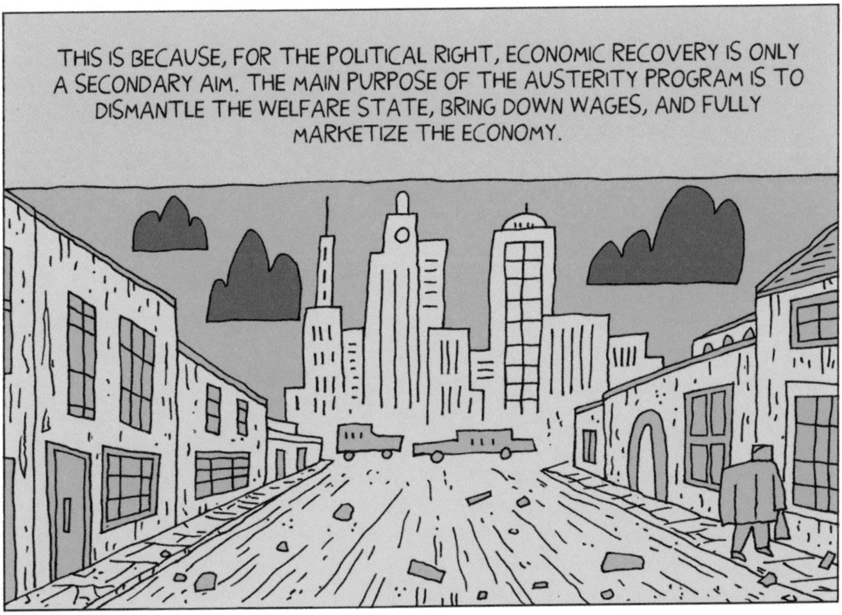
THIS IS BECAUSE, FOR THE POLITICAL RIGHT, ECONOMIC RECOVERY IS ONLY A SECONDARY AIM. THE MAIN PURPOSE OF THE AUSTERITY PROGRAM IS TO DISMANTLE THE WELFARE STATE, BRING DOWN WAGES, AND FULLY MARKETIZE THE ECONOMY.

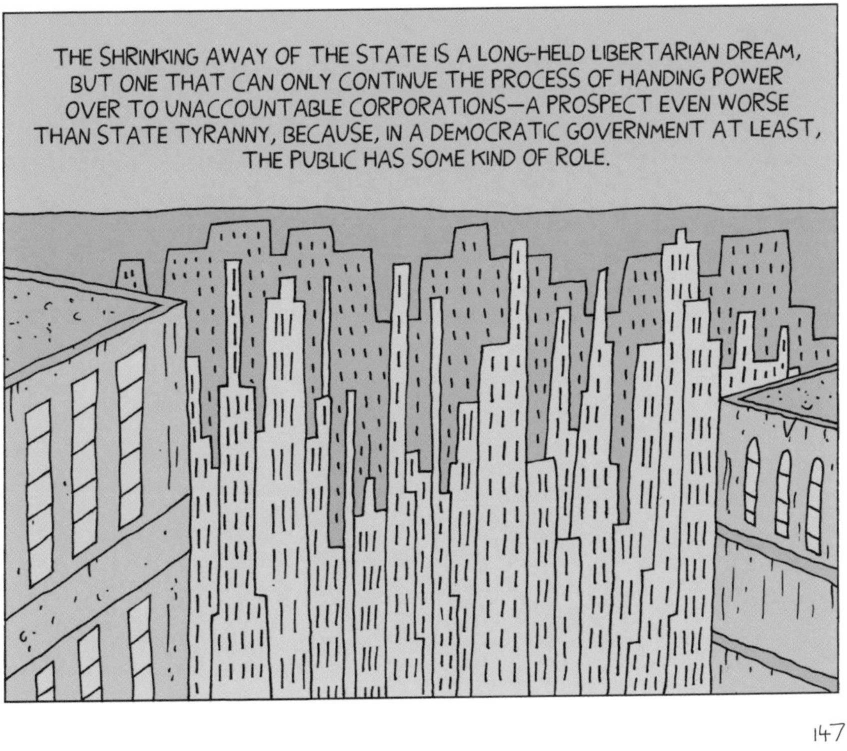
THE SHRINKING AWAY OF THE STATE IS A LONG-HELD LIBERTARIAN DREAM, BUT ONE THAT CAN ONLY CONTINUE THE PROCESS OF HANDING POWER OVER TO UNACCOUNTABLE CORPORATIONS—A PROSPECT EVEN WORSE THAN STATE TYRANNY, BECAUSE, IN A DEMOCRATIC GOVERNMENT AT LEAST, THE PUBLIC HAS SOME KIND OF ROLE.

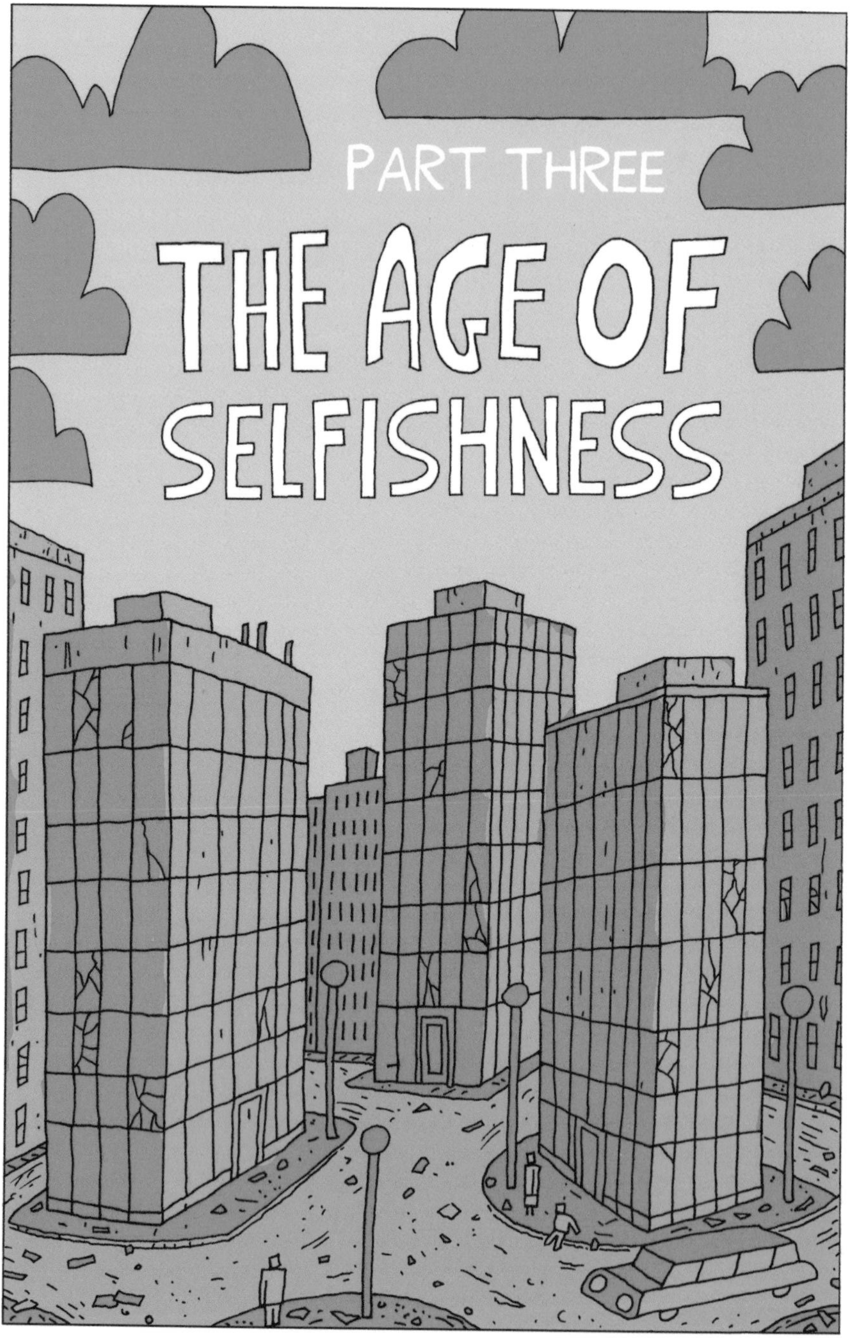
PART THREE
THE AGE OF SELFISHNESS

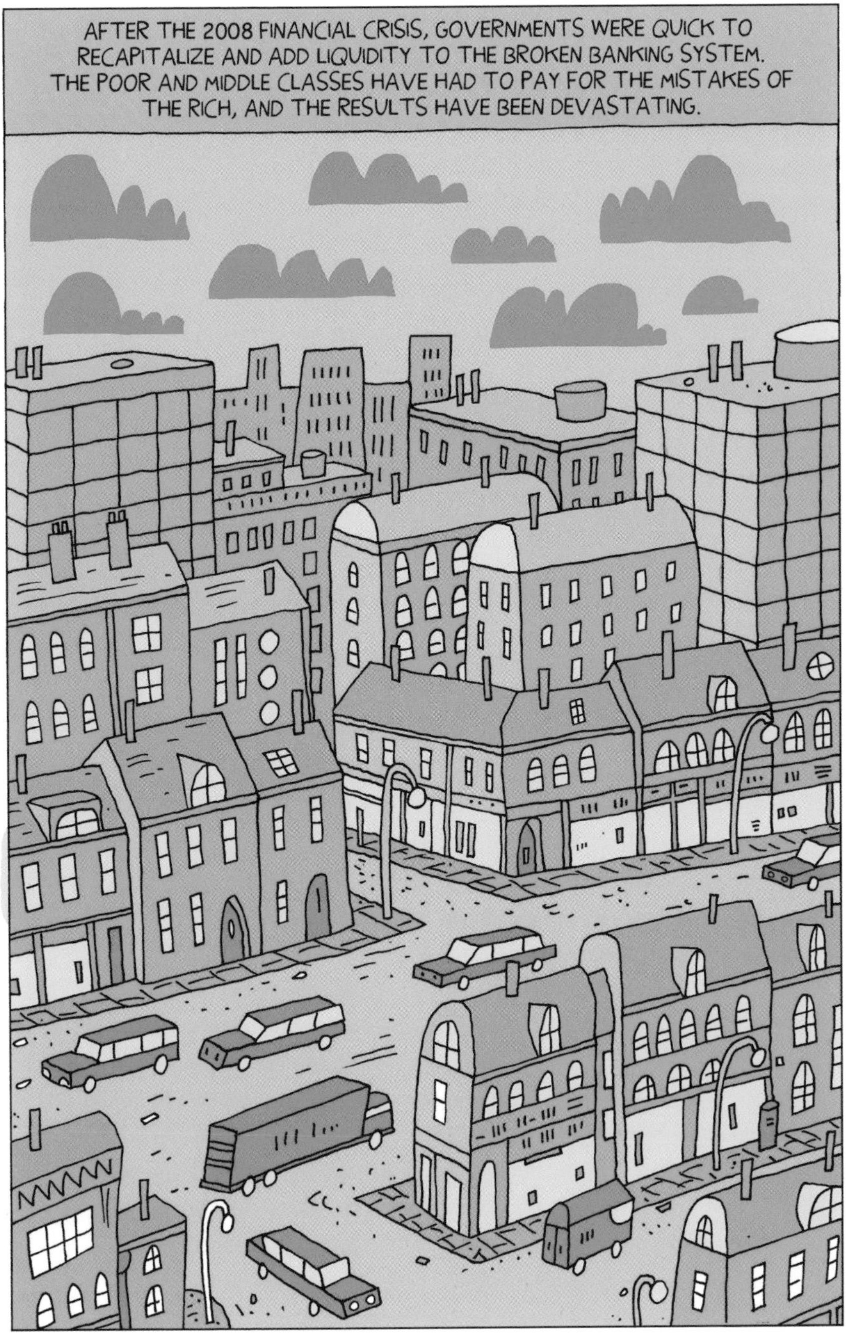
AFTER THE 2008 FINANCIAL CRISIS, GOVERNMENTS WERE QUICK TO RECAPITALIZE AND ADD LIQUIDITY TO THE BROKEN BANKING SYSTEM. THE POOR AND MIDDLE CLASSES HAVE HAD TO PAY FOR THE MISTAKES OF THE RICH, AND THE RESULTS HAVE BEEN DEVASTATING.

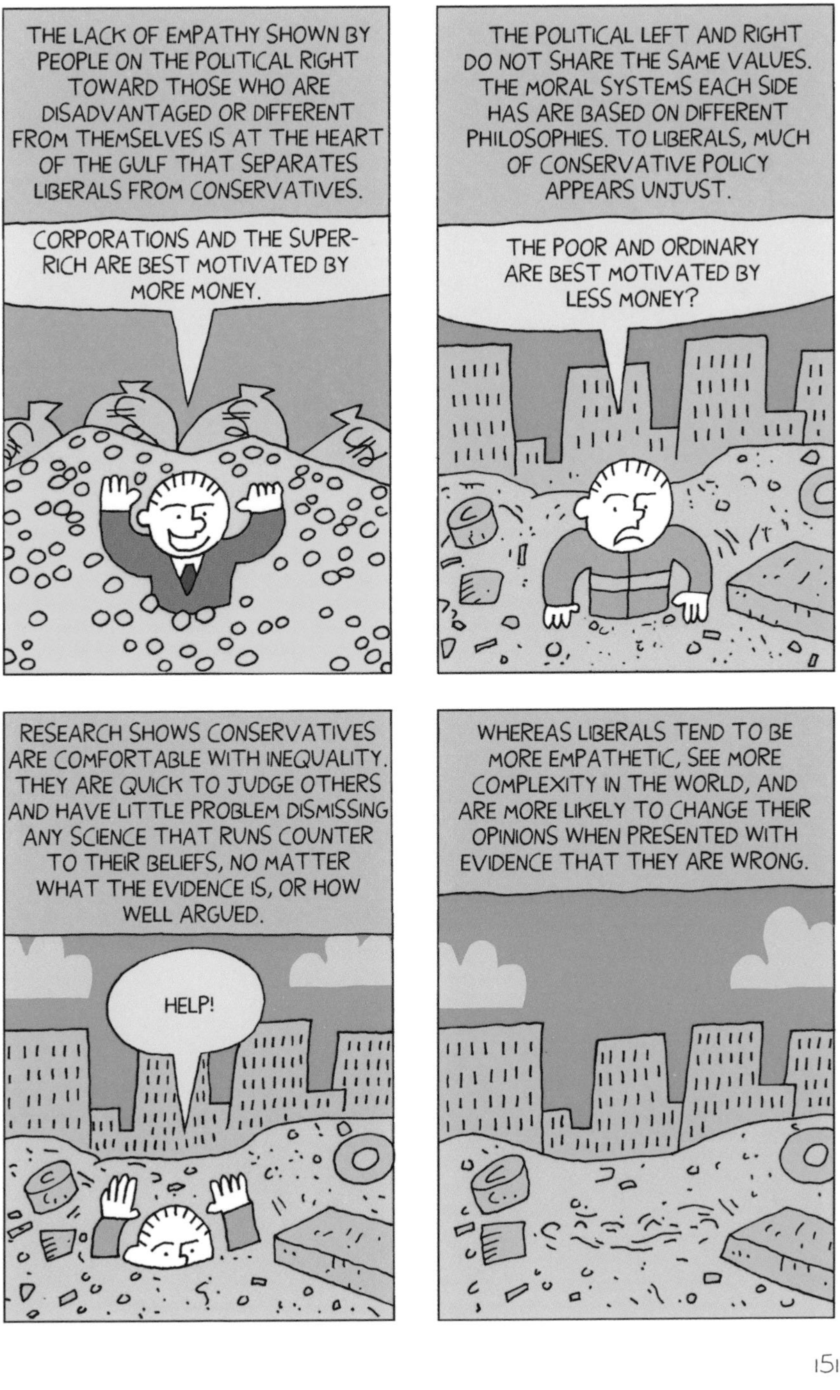
THE LACK OF EMPATHY SHOWN BY PEOPLE ON THE POLITICAL RIGHT TOWARD THOSE WHO ARE DISADVANTAGED OR DIFFERENT FROM THEMSELVES IS AT THE HEART OF THE GULF THAT SEPARATES LIBERALS FROM CONSERVATIVES.
CORPORATIONS AND THE SUPER-RICH ARE BEST MOTIVATED BY MORE MONEY.
THE POLITICAL LEFT AND RIGHT DO NOT SHARE THE SAME VALUES. THE MORAL SYSTEMS EACH SIDE HAS ARE BASED ON DIFFERENT PHILOSOPHIES. TO LIBERALS, MUCH OF CONSERVATIVE POLICY APPEARS UNJUST.
THE POOR AND ORDINARY ARE BEST MOTIVATED BY LESS MONEY?
RESEARCH SHOWS CONSERVATIVES ARE COMFORTABLE WITH INEQUALITY. THEY ARE QUICK TO JUDGE OTHERS AND HAVE LITTLE PROBLEM DISMISSING ANY SCIENCE THAT RUNS COUNTER TO THEIR BELIEFS, NO MATTER WHAT THE EVIDENCE IS, OR HOW WELL ARGUED.
HELP!
WHEREAS LIBERALS TEND TO BE MORE EMPATHETIC, SEE MORE COMPLEXITY IN THE WORLD, AND ARE MORE LIKELY TO CHANGE THEIR OPINIONS WHEN PRESENTED WITH EVIDENCE THAT THEY ARE WRONG.

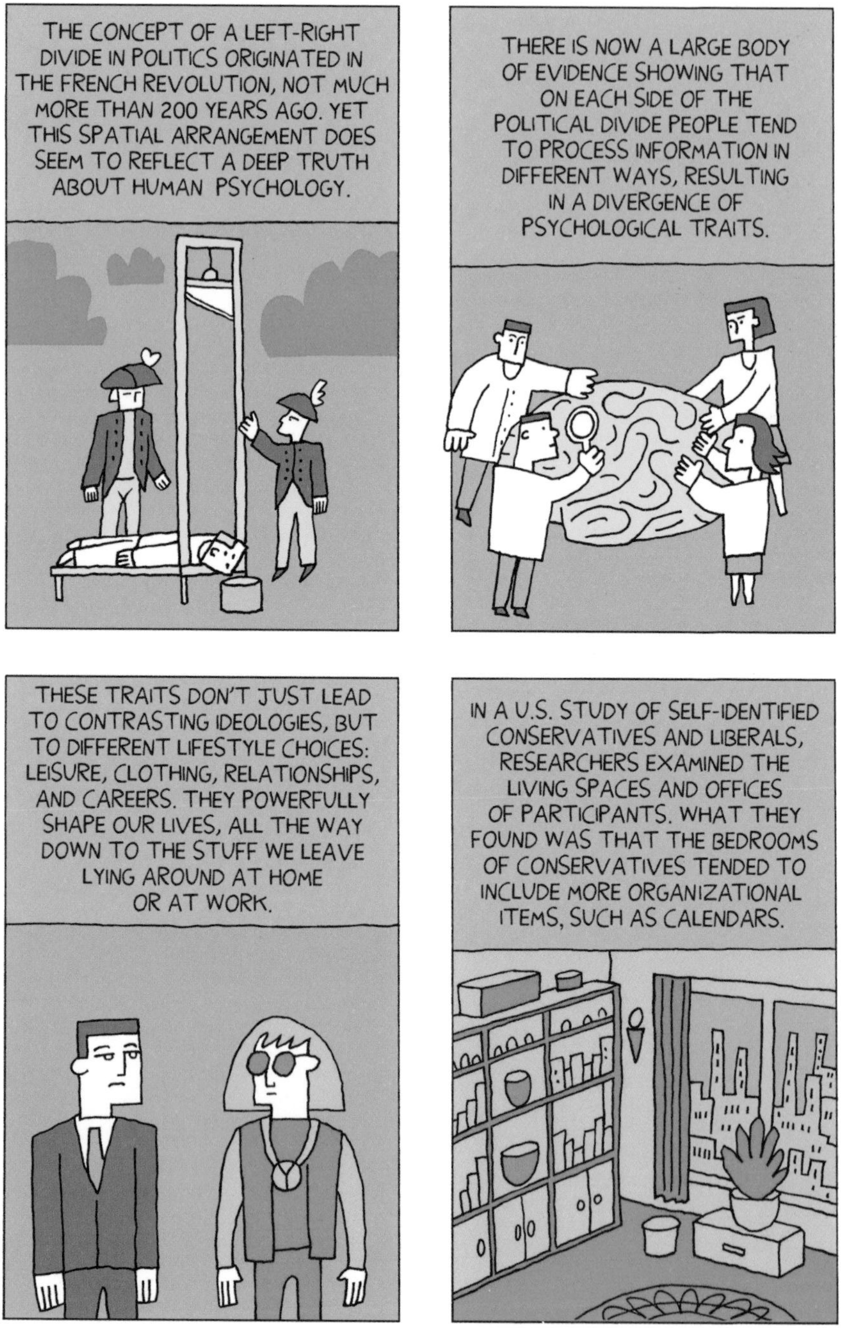
THE CONCEPT OF A LEFT-RIGHT DIVIDE IN POLITICS ORIGINATED IN THE FRENCH REVOLUTION, NOT MUCH MORE THAN 200 YEARS AGO. YET THIS SPATIAL ARRANGEMENT DOES SEEM TO REFLECT A DEEP TRUTH ABOUT HUMAN PSYCHOLOGY.
THERE IS NOW A LARGE BODY OF EVIDENCE SHOWING THAT ON EACH SIDE OF THE POLITICAL DIVIDE PEOPLE TEND TO PROCESS INFORMATION IN DIFFERENT WAYS, RESULTING IN A DIVERGENCE OF PSYCHOLOGICAL TRAITS.
THESE TRAITS DON'T JUST LEAD TO CONTRASTING IDEOLOGIES, BUT TO DIFFERENT LIFESTYLE CHOICES: LEISURE, CLOTHING, RELATIONSHIPS, AND CAREERS. THEY POWERFULLY SHAPE OUR LIVES, ALL THE WAY DOWN TO THE STUFF WE LEAVE LYING AROUND AT HOME OR AT WORK.
IN A U.S. STUDY OF SELF-IDENTIFIED CONSERVATIVES AND LIBERALS, RESEARCHERS EXAMINED THE LIVING SPACES AND OFFICES OF PARTICIPANTS. WHAT THEY FOUND WAS THAT THE BEDROOMS OF CONSERVATIVES TENDED TO INCLUDE MORE ORGANIZATIONAL ITEMS, SUCH AS CALENDARS.

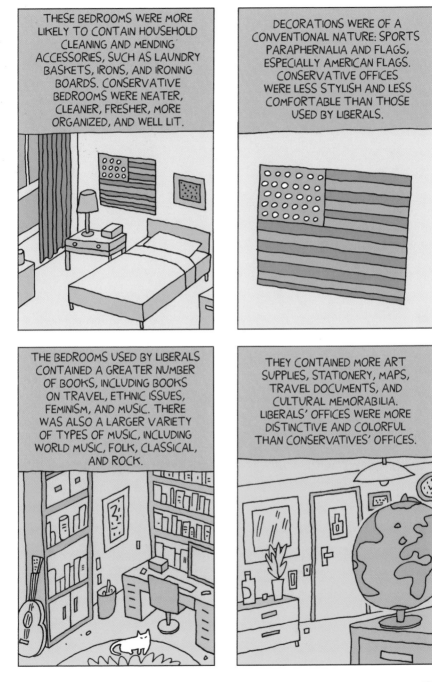

THESE BEDROOMS WERE MORE LIKELY TO CONTAIN HOUSEHOLD CLEANING AND MENDING ACCESSORIES, SUCH AS LAUNDRY BASKETS, IRONS, AND IRONING BOARDS. CONSERVATIVE BEDROOMS WERE NEATER, CLEANER, FRESHER, MORE ORGANIZED, AND WELL LIT.

DECORATIONS WERE OF A CONVENTIONAL NATURE: SPORTS PARAPHERNALIA AND FLAGS, ESPECIALLY AMERICAN FLAGS. CONSERVATIVE OFFICES WERE LESS STYLISH AND LESS COMFORTABLE THAN THOSE USED BY LIBERALS.

THE BEDROOMS USED BY LIBERALS CONTAINED A GREATER NUMBER OF BOOKS, INCLUDING BOOKS ON TRAVEL, ETHNIC ISSUES, FEMINISM, AND MUSIC. THERE WAS ALSO A LARGER VARIETY OF TYPES OF MUSIC, INCLUDING WORLD MUSIC, FOLK, CLASSICAL, AND ROCK.

THEY CONTAINED MORE ART SUPPLIES, STATIONERY, MAPS, TRAVEL DOCUMENTS, AND CULTURAL MEMORABILIA. LIBERALS' OFFICES WERE MORE DISTINCTIVE AND COLORFUL THAN CONSERVATIVES' OFFICES.

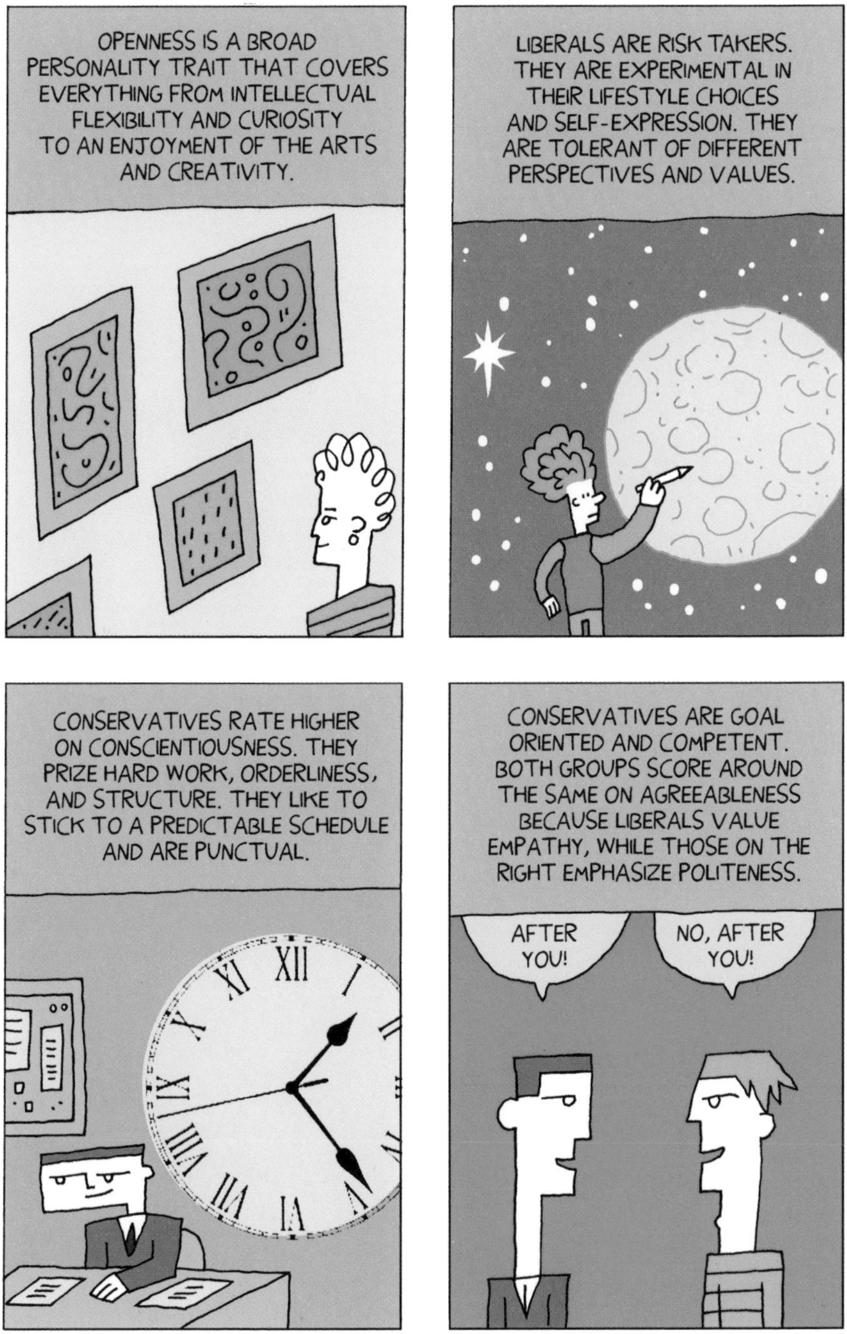
OPENNESS IS A BROAD PERSONALITY TRAIT THAT COVERS EVERYTHING FROM INTELLECTUAL FLEXIBILITY AND CURIOSITY TO AN ENJOYMENT OF THE ARTS AND CREATIVITY.
LIBERALS ARE RISK TAKERS. THEY ARE EXPERIMENTAL IN THEIR LIFESTYLE CHOICES AND SELF-EXPRESSION. THEY ARE TOLERANT OF DIFFERENT PERSPECTIVES AND VALUES.
CONSERVATIVES RATE HIGHER ON CONSCIENTIOUSNESS. THEY PRIZE HARD WORK, ORDERLINESS, AND STRUCTURE. THEY LIKE TO STICK TO A PREDICTABLE SCHEDULE AND ARE PUNCTUAL.
CONSERVATIVES ARE GOAL ORIENTED AND COMPETENT. BOTH GROUPS SCORE AROUND THE SAME ON AGREEABLENESS BECAUSE LIBERALS VALUE EMPATHY, WHILE THOSE ON THE RIGHT EMPHASIZE POLITENESS.
AFTER YOU!
NO, AFTER YOU!

LIBERALS LIKE TO THINK IN CHALLENGING WAYS. THEY ENJOY COMPLEX PROBLEMS. FOR THEM, IT IS NOT A DIFFICULTY IF THINGS ARE ILL-DEFINED OR UNRESOLVED.

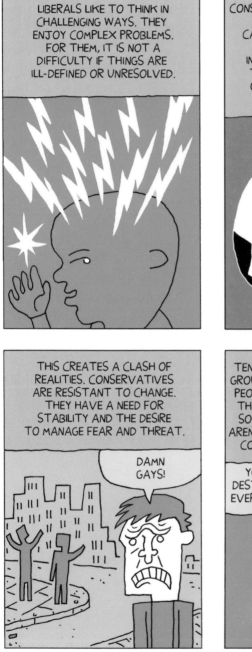

CONSERVATIVES ARE THE OPPOSITE. THEY ARE MORE LIKELY TO CATEGORIZE AND DIVIDE PEOPLE INTO EITHER GOOD OR BAD. IN THE CONSERVATIVE WORLD THERE ARE NO GRAY AREAS, ONLY THE BLACK AND WHITE OF CERTAINTY.

THIS CREATES A CLASH OF REALITIES. CONSERVATIVES ARE RESISTANT TO CHANGE. THEY HAVE A NEED FOR STABILITY AND THE DESIRE TO MANAGE FEAR AND THREAT.

DAMN GAYS!

TENSION ARISES BETWEEN THE TWO GROUPS, BECAUSE LIBERALS ARE THE PEOPLE MOST LIKELY TO GENERATE THAT DANGEROUS CHANGE IN THE SOCIAL, ARTISTIC, AND SCIENTIFIC ARENAS. AND THIS IS NOT SOMETHING CONSERVATIVES WANT TO SEE.

YOU'RE DESTROYING EVERYTHING.

I'M TRYING TO BUILD A BETTER WORLD.

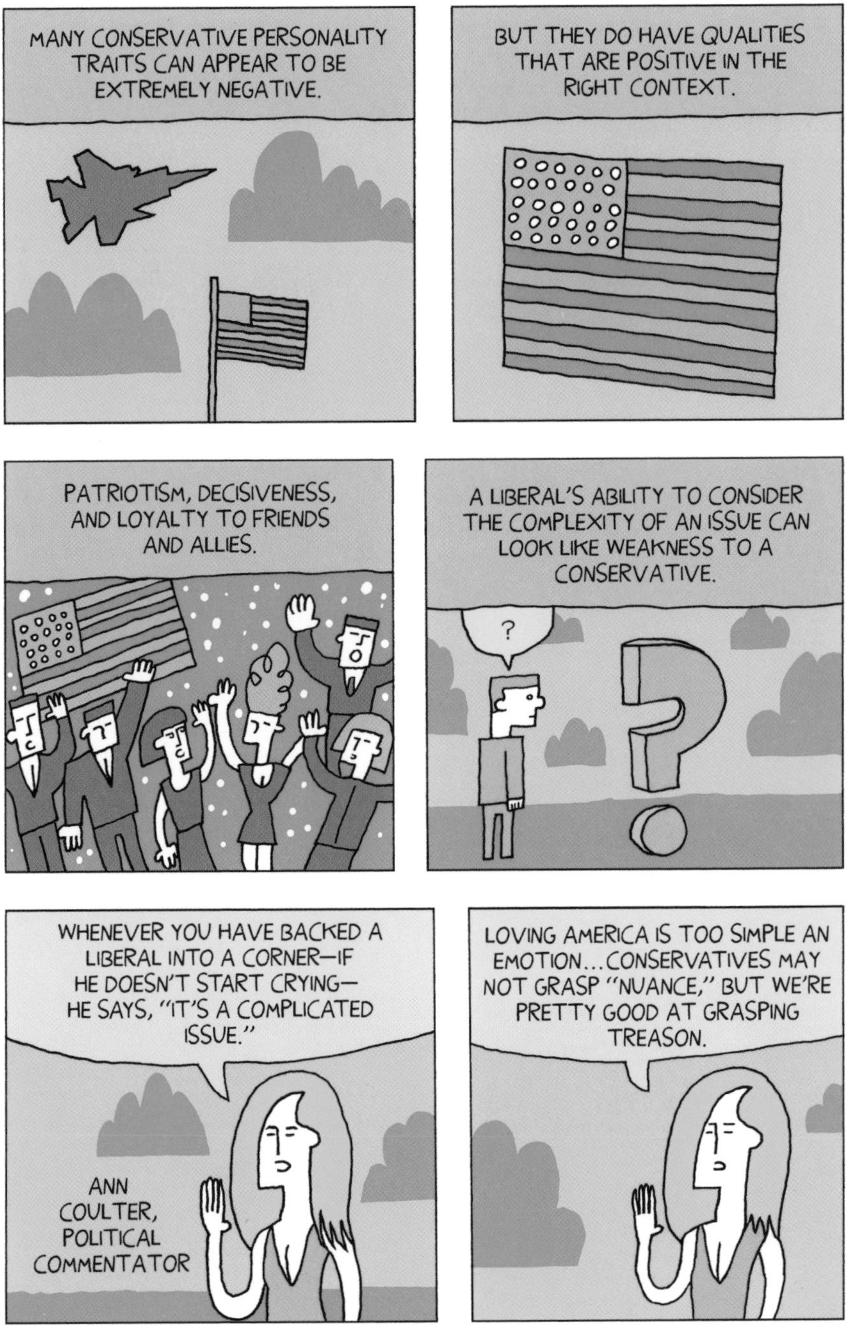
MANY CONSERVATIVE PERSONALITY TRAITS CAN APPEAR TO BE EXTREMELY NEGATIVE.
BUT THEY DO HAVE QUALITIES THAT ARE POSITIVE IN THE RIGHT CONTEXT.
PATRIOTISM, DECISIVENESS, AND LOYALTY TO FRIENDS AND ALLIES.
A LIBERAL'S ABILITY TO CONSIDER THE COMPLEXITY OF AN ISSUE CAN LOOK LIKE WEAKNESS TO A CONSERVATIVE.
?
WHENEVER YOU HAVE BACKED A LIBERAL INTO A CORNER—IF HE DOESN'T START CRYING—HE SAYS, "IT'S A COMPLICATED ISSUE."
ANN COULTER, POLITICAL COMMENTATOR
LOVING AMERICA IS TOO SIMPLE AN EMOTION...CONSERVATIVES MAY NOT GRASP "NUANCE," BUT WE'RE PRETTY GOOD AT GRASPING TREASON.

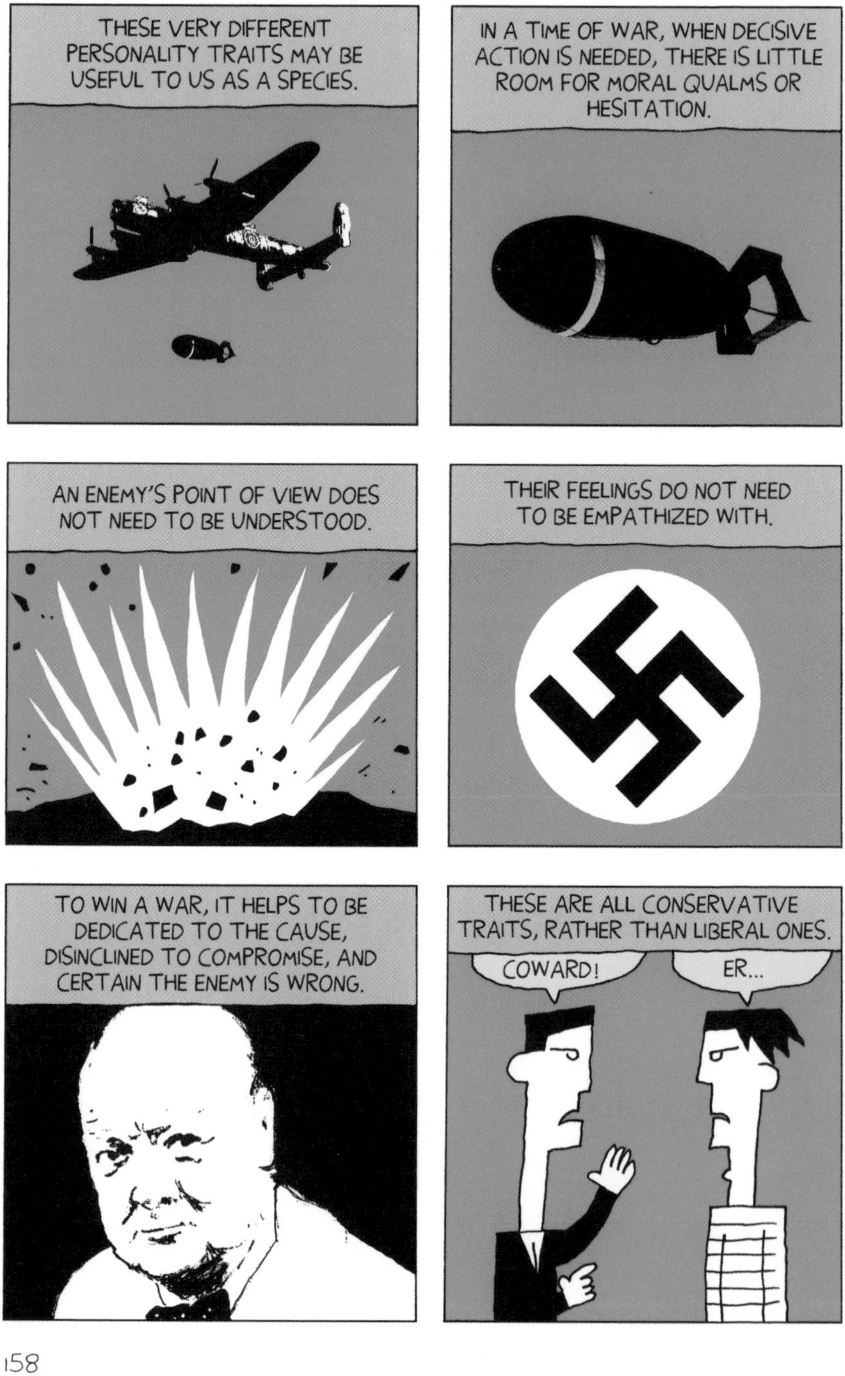
THESE VERY DIFFERENT PERSONALITY TRAITS MAY BE USEFUL TO US AS A SPECIES.
IN A TIME OF WAR, WHEN DECISIVE ACTION IS NEEDED, THERE IS LITTLE ROOM FOR MORAL QUALMS OR HESITATION.
AN ENEMY'S POINT OF VIEW DOES NOT NEED TO BE UNDERSTOOD.
THEIR FEELINGS DO NOT NEED TO BE EMPATHIZED WITH.
TO WIN A WAR, IT HELPS TO BE DEDICATED TO THE CAUSE, DISINCLINED TO COMPROMISE, AND CERTAIN THE ENEMY IS WRONG.
THESE ARE ALL CONSERVATIVE TRAITS, RATHER THAN LIBERAL ONES.
COWARD!
ER...

IS IT POSSIBLE FOR PEOPLE ON THE LEFT TO MOVE TO THE POLITICAL RIGHT? WELL, ALL THE EVIDENCE SUGGESTS THAT, UNDER CONDITIONS OF STRESS, LIBERALS BECOME MORE CONSERVATIVE IN THEIR VIEWS.

IN A STUDY AT THE UNIVERSITY OF ILLINOIS IN CHICAGO, LIBERALS AND CONSERVATIVES WERE ASKED QUESTIONS ABOUT A SCENARIO WHERE VARIOUS GROUPS HAD CONTRACTED AIDS IN DIFFERENT WAYS.

THREE OF THESE GROUPS HAD GOTTEN THE ILLNESS FROM BLOOD TRANSFUSIONS OR VIA A LONG-TERM PARTNER WHO WAS CHEATING ON THEM, OR BEFORE IT WAS WIDELY KNOWN THAT AIDS WAS SEXUALLY TRANSMITTED.

THE FOURTH GROUP WAS DIFFERENT, BECAUSE THESE INDIVIDUALS HAD CONTRACTED AIDS BY PRACTICING UNSAFE SEX WHILE BEING FULLY AWARE OF THE RISKS.

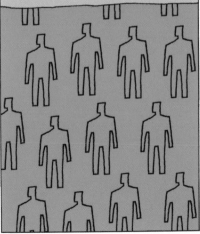

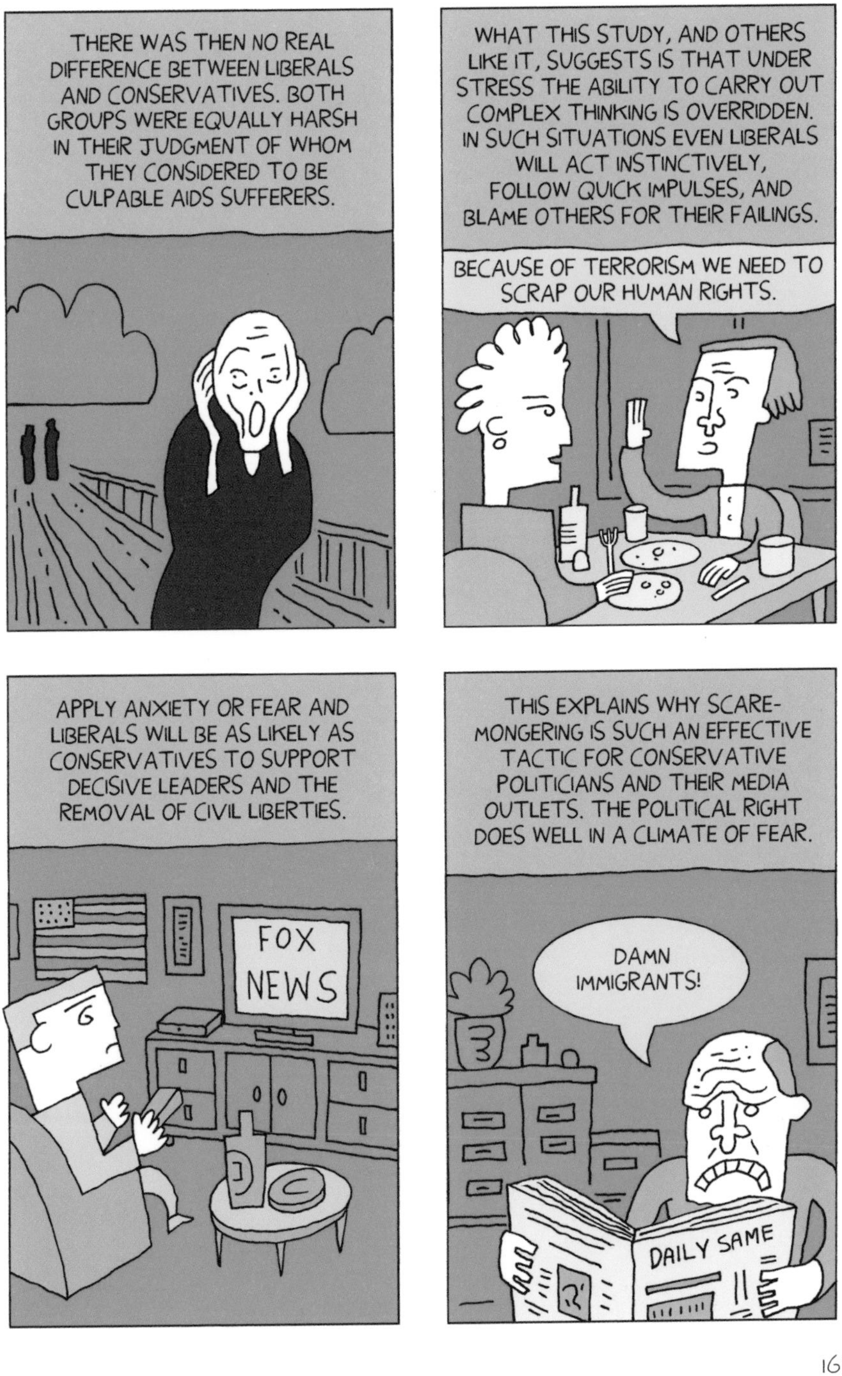
THERE WAS THEN NO REAL DIFFERENCE BETWEEN LIBERALS AND CONSERVATIVES. BOTH GROUPS WERE EQUALLY HARSH IN THEIR JUDGMENT OF WHOM THEY CONSIDERED TO BE CULPABLE AIDS SUFFERERS.
WHAT THIS STUDY, AND OTHERS LIKE IT, SUGGESTS IS THAT UNDER STRESS THE ABILITY TO CARRY OUT COMPLEX THINKING IS OVERRIDDEN. IN SUCH SITUATIONS EVEN LIBERALS WILL ACT INSTINCTIVELY, FOLLOW QUICK IMPULSES, AND BLAME OTHERS FOR THEIR FAILINGS.
BECAUSE OF TERRORISM WE NEED TO SCRAP OUR HUMAN RIGHTS.
APPLY ANXIETY OR FEAR AND LIBERALS WILL BE AS LIKELY AS CONSERVATIVES TO SUPPORT DECISIVE LEADERS AND THE REMOVAL OF CIVIL LIBERTIES.
FOX NEWS
THIS EXPLAINS WHY SCARE-MONGERING IS SUCH AN EFFECTIVE TACTIC FOR CONSERVATIVE POLITICIANS AND THEIR MEDIA OUTLETS. THE POLITICAL RIGHT DOES WELL IN A CLIMATE OF FEAR.
DAMN IMMIGRANTS!
DAILY SAME

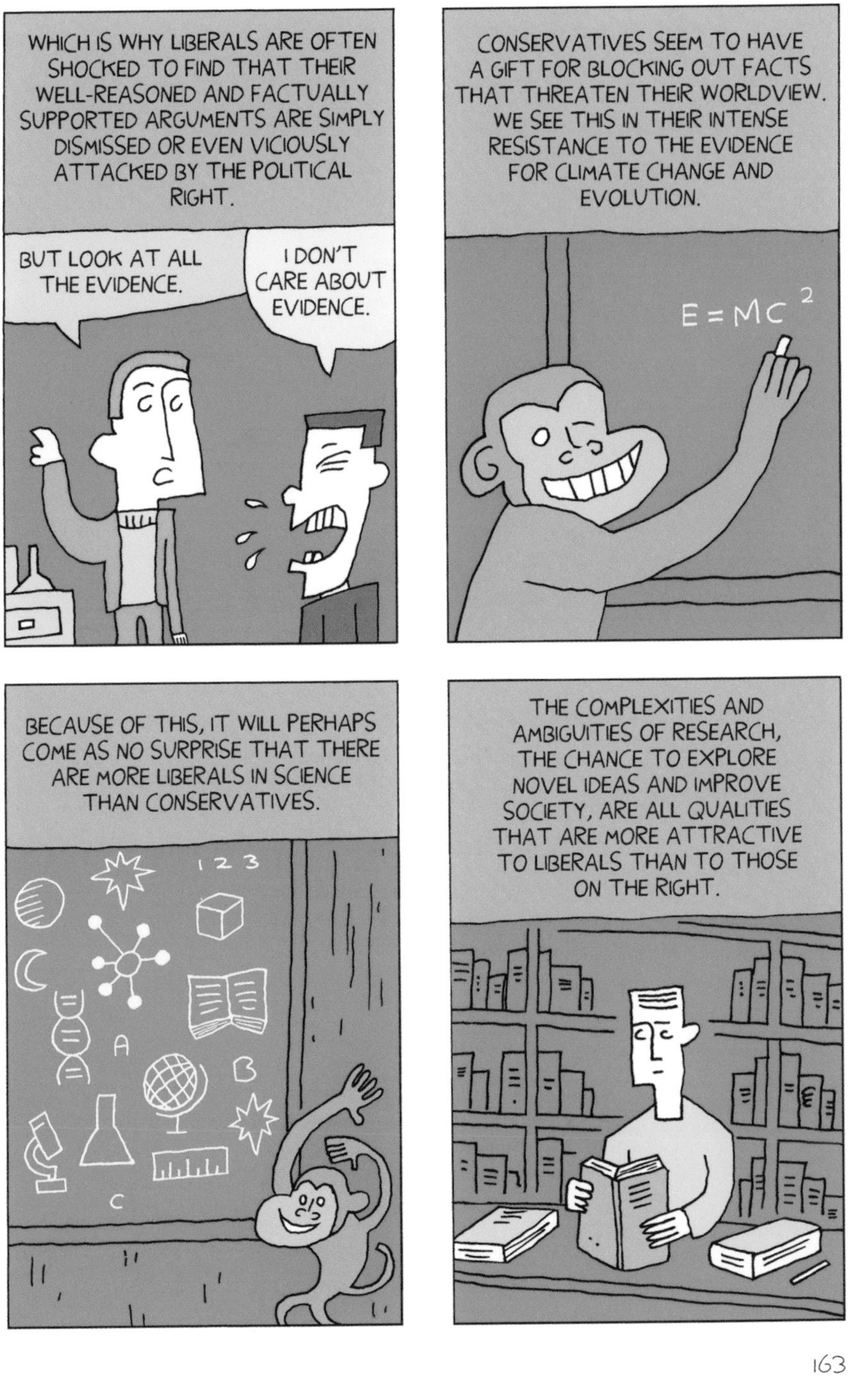
WHICH IS WHY LIBERALS ARE OFTEN SHOCKED TO FIND THAT THEIR WELL-REASONED AND FACTUALLY SUPPORTED ARGUMENTS ARE SIMPLY DISMISSED OR EVEN VICIOUSLY ATTACKED BY THE POLITICAL RIGHT.
BUT LOOK AT ALL THE EVIDENCE.
I DON'T CARE ABOUT EVIDENCE.
CONSERVATIVES SEEM TO HAVE A GIFT FOR BLOCKING OUT FACTS THAT THREATEN THEIR WORLDVIEW. WE SEE THIS IN THEIR INTENSE RESISTANCE TO THE EVIDENCE FOR CLIMATE CHANGE AND EVOLUTION.
E = MC 2
BECAUSE OF THIS, IT WILL PERHAPS COME AS NO SURPRISE THAT THERE ARE MORE LIBERALS IN SCIENCE THAN CONSERVATIVES.
1 2 3
A
B
C
THE COMPLEXITIES AND AMBIGUITIES OF RESEARCH, THE CHANCE TO EXPLORE NOVEL IDEAS AND IMPROVE SOCIETY, ARE ALL QUALITIES THAT ARE MORE ATTRACTIVE TO LIBERALS THAN TO THOSE ON THE RIGHT.

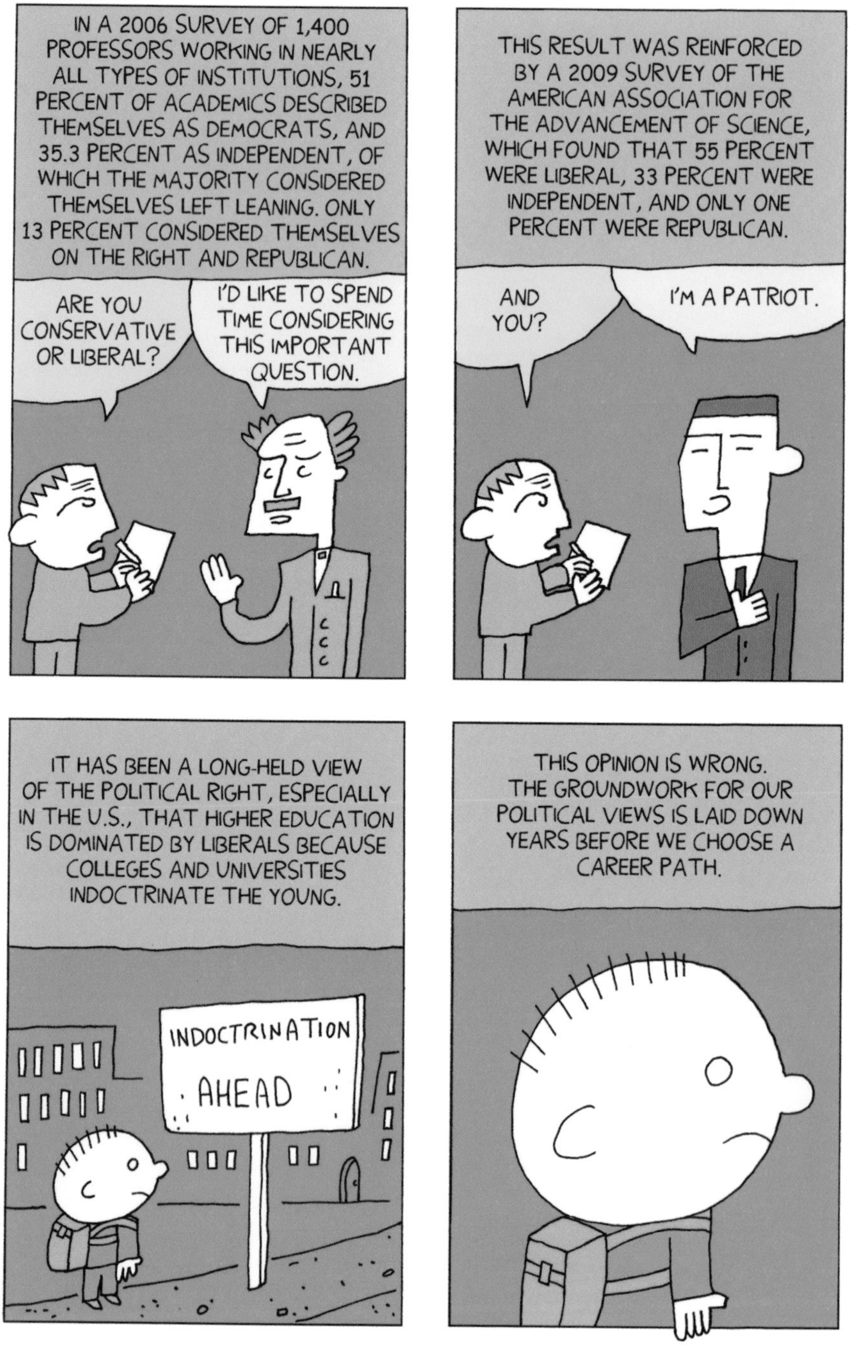
IN A 2006 SURVEY OF 1,400 PROFESSORS WORKING IN NEARLY ALL TYPES OF INSTITUTIONS, 51 PERCENT OF ACADEMICS DESCRIBED THEMSELVES AS DEMOCRATS, AND 35.3 PERCENT AS INDEPENDENT, OF WHICH THE MAJORITY CONSIDERED THEMSELVES LEFT LEANING. ONLY 13 PERCENT CONSIDERED THEMSELVES ON THE RIGHT AND REPUBLICAN.
ARE YOU CONSERVATIVE OR LIBERAL?
I'D LIKE TO SPEND TIME CONSIDERING THIS IMPORTANT QUESTION.
THIS RESULT WAS REINFORCED BY A 2009 SURVEY OF THE AMERICAN ASSOCIATION FOR THE ADVANCEMENT OF SCIENCE, WHICH FOUND THAT 55 PERCENT WERE LIBERAL, 33 PERCENT WERE INDEPENDENT, AND ONLY ONE PERCENT WERE REPUBLICAN.
AND YOU?
I'M A PATRIOT.
IT HAS BEEN A LONG-HELD VIEW OF THE POLITICAL RIGHT, ESPECIALLY IN THE U.S., THAT HIGHER EDUCATION IS DOMINATED BY LIBERALS BECAUSE COLLEGES AND UNIVERSITIES INDOCTRINATE THE YOUNG.
INDOCTRINATION AHEAD
THIS OPINION IS WRONG. THE GROUNDWORK FOR OUR POLITICAL VIEWS IS LAID DOWN YEARS BEFORE WE CHOOSE A CAREER PATH.

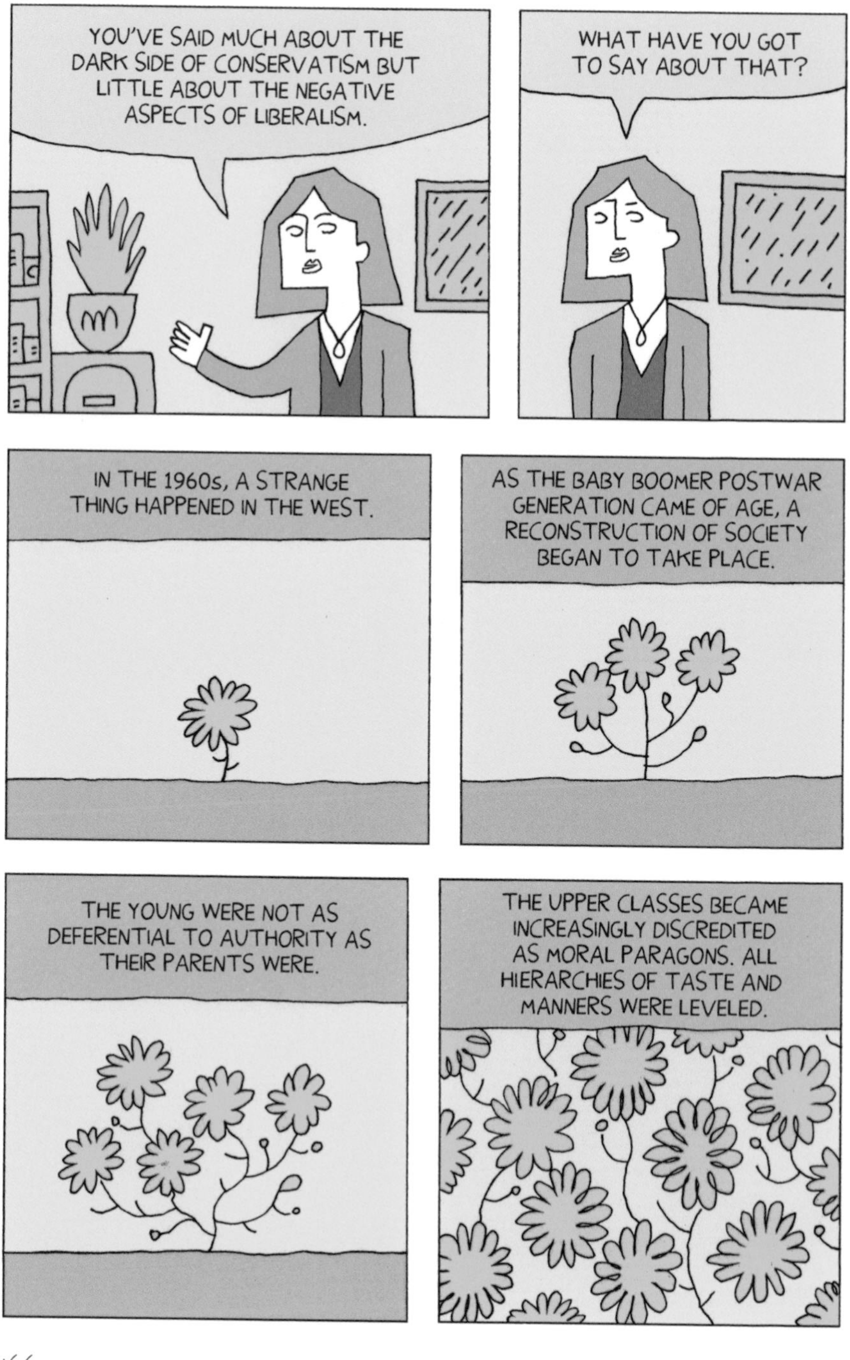
YOU'VE SAID MUCH ABOUT THE DARK SIDE OF CONSERVATISM BUT LITTLE ABOUT THE NEGATIVE ASPECTS OF LIBERALISM.
WHAT HAVE YOU GOT TO SAY ABOUT THAT?
IN THE 1960s, A STRANGE THING HAPPENED IN THE WEST.
AS THE BABY BOOMER POSTWAR GENERATION CAME OF AGE, A RECONSTRUCTION OF SOCIETY BEGAN TO TAKE PLACE.
THE YOUNG WERE NOT AS DEFERENTIAL TO AUTHORITY AS THEIR PARENTS WERE.
THE UPPER CLASSES BECAME INCREASINGLY DISCREDITED AS MORAL PARAGONS. ALL HIERARCHIES OF TASTE AND MANNERS WERE LEVELED.

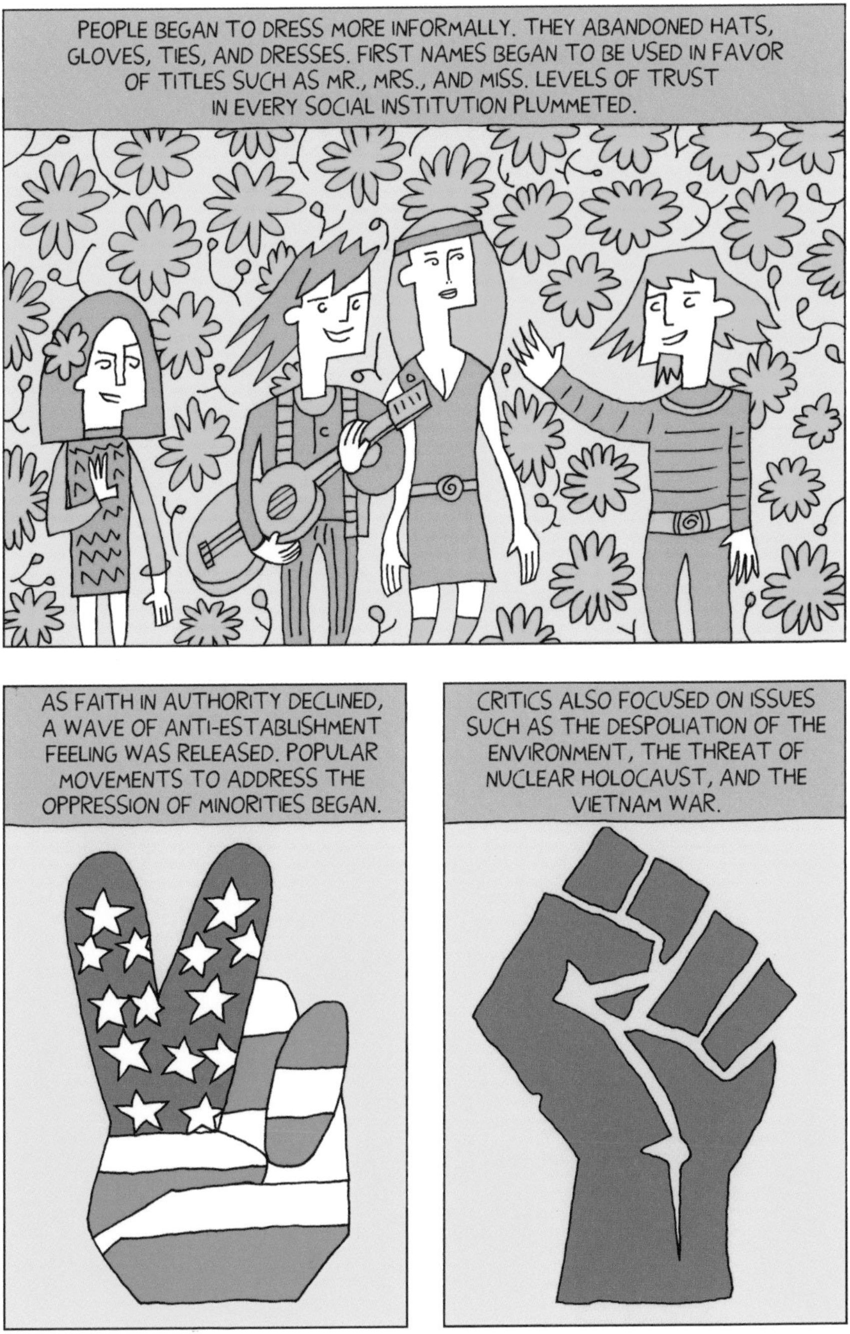
PEOPLE BEGAN TO DRESS MORE INFORMALLY. THEY ABANDONED HATS, GLOVES, TIES, AND DRESSES. FIRST NAMES BEGAN TO BE USED IN FAVOR OF TITLES SUCH AS MR., MRS., AND MISS. LEVELS OF TRUST IN EVERY SOCIAL INSTITUTION PLUMMETED.
AS FAITH IN AUTHORITY DECLINED, A WAVE OF ANTI-ESTABLISHMENT FEELING WAS RELEASED. POPULAR MOVEMENTS TO ADDRESS THE OPPRESSION OF MINORITIES BEGAN.
CRITICS ALSO FOCUSED ON ISSUES SUCH AS THE DESPOLIATION OF THE ENVIRONMENT, THE THREAT OF NUCLEAR HOLOCAUST, AND THE VIETNAM WAR.

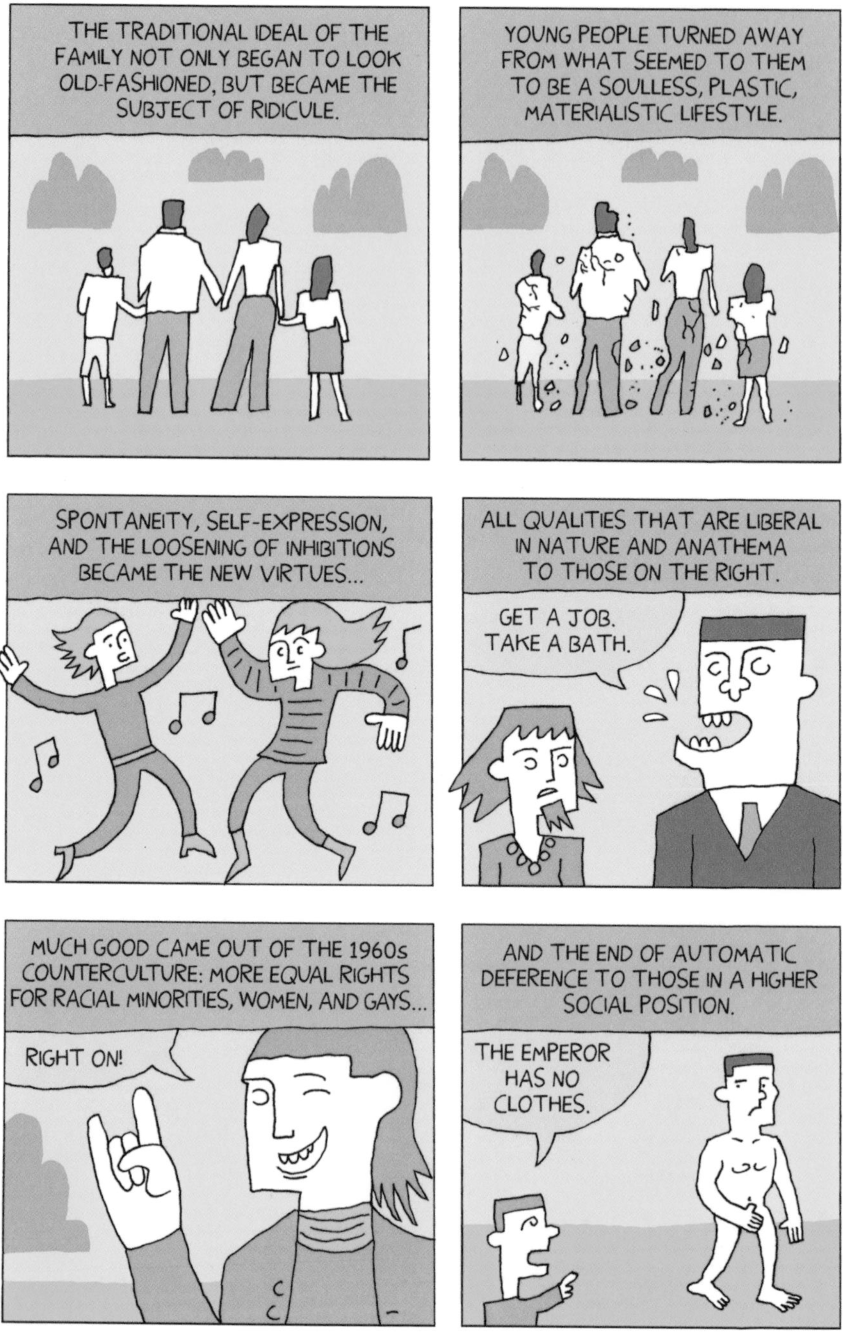
THE TRADITIONAL IDEAL OF THE FAMILY NOT ONLY BEGAN TO LOOK OLD-FASHIONED, BUT BECAME THE SUBJECT OF RIDICULE.
YOUNG PEOPLE TURNED AWAY FROM WHAT SEEMED TO THEM TO BE A SOULLESS, PLASTIC, MATERIALISTIC LIFESTYLE.
SPONTANEITY, SELF-EXPRESSION, AND THE LOOSENING OF INHIBITIONS BECAME THE NEW VIRTUES...
ALL QUALITIES THAT ARE LIBERAL IN NATURE AND ANATHEMA TO THOSE ON THE RIGHT.
GET A JOB. TAKE A BATH.
MUCH GOOD CAME OUT OF THE 1960s COUNTERCULTURE: MORE EQUAL RIGHTS FOR RACIAL MINORITIES, WOMEN, AND GAYS...
RIGHT ON!
AND THE END OF AUTOMATIC DEFERENCE TO THOSE IN A HIGHER SOCIAL POSITION.
THE EMPEROR HAS NO CLOTHES.

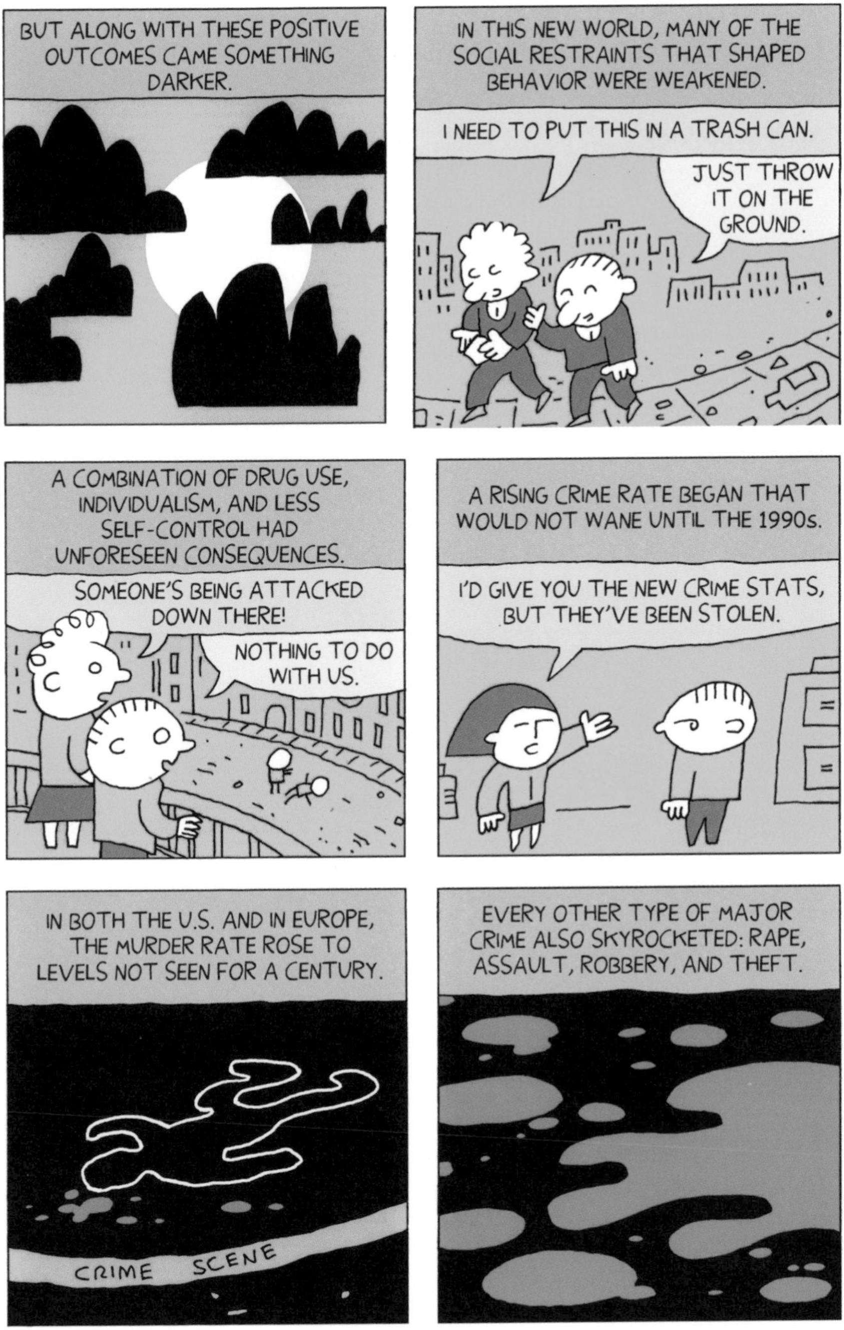
BUT ALONG WITH THESE POSITIVE OUTCOMES CAME SOMETHING DARKER.
IN THIS NEW WORLD, MANY OF THE SOCIAL RESTRAINTS THAT SHAPED BEHAVIOR WERE WEAKENED.
I NEED TO PUT THIS IN A TRASH CAN.
JUST THROW IT ON THE GROUND.
A COMBINATION OF DRUG USE, INDIVIDUALISM, AND LESS SELF-CONTROL HAD UNFORESEEN CONSEQUENCES.
SOMEONE'S BEING ATTACKED DOWN THERE!
NOTHING TO DO WITH US.
A RISING CRIME RATE BEGAN THAT WOULD NOT WANE UNTIL THE 1990s.
I'D GIVE YOU THE NEW CRIME STATS, BUT THEY'VE BEEN STOLEN.
IN BOTH THE U.S. AND IN EUROPE, THE MURDER RATE ROSE TO LEVELS NOT SEEN FOR A CENTURY.
CRIME SCENE
EVERY OTHER TYPE OF MAJOR CRIME ALSO SKYROCKETED: RAPE, ASSAULT, ROBBERY, AND THEFT.

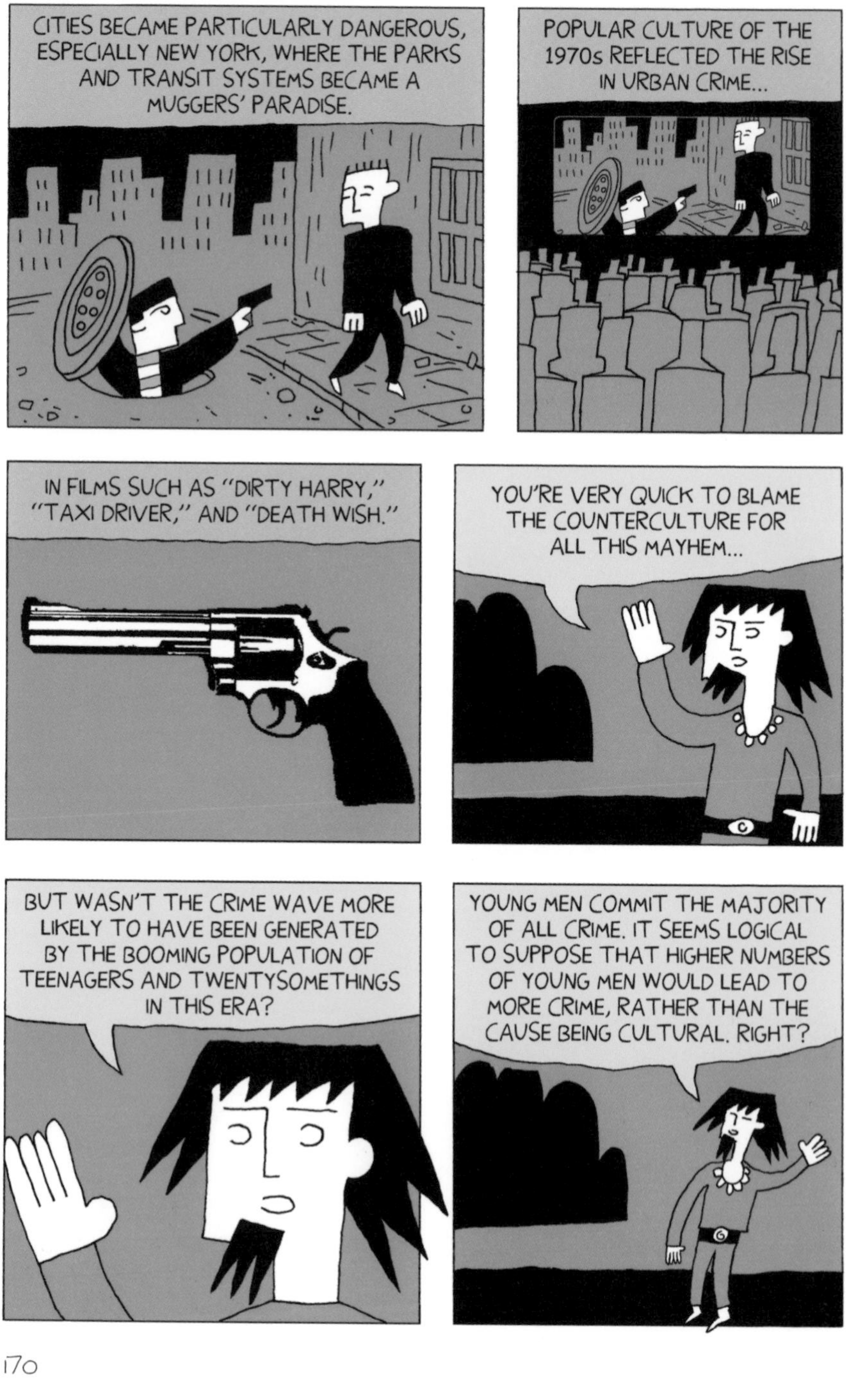
CITIES BECAME PARTICULARLY DANGEROUS, ESPECIALLY NEW YORK, WHERE THE PARKS AND TRANSIT SYSTEMS BECAME A MUGGERS' PARADISE.
POPULAR CULTURE OF THE 1970s REFLECTED THE RISE IN URBAN CRIME...
IN FILMS SUCH AS "DIRTY HARRY," "TAXI DRIVER," AND "DEATH WISH."
YOU'RE VERY QUICK TO BLAME THE COUNTERCULTURE FOR ALL THIS MAYHEM...
BUT WASN'T THE CRIME WAVE MORE LIKELY TO HAVE BEEN GENERATED BY THE BOOMING POPULATION OF TEENAGERS AND TWENTYSOMETHINGS IN THIS ERA?
YOUNG MEN COMMIT THE MAJORITY OF ALL CRIME. IT SEEMS LOGICAL TO SUPPOSE THAT HIGHER NUMBERS OF YOUNG MEN WOULD LEAD TO MORE CRIME, RATHER THAN THE CAUSE BEING CULTURAL. RIGHT?

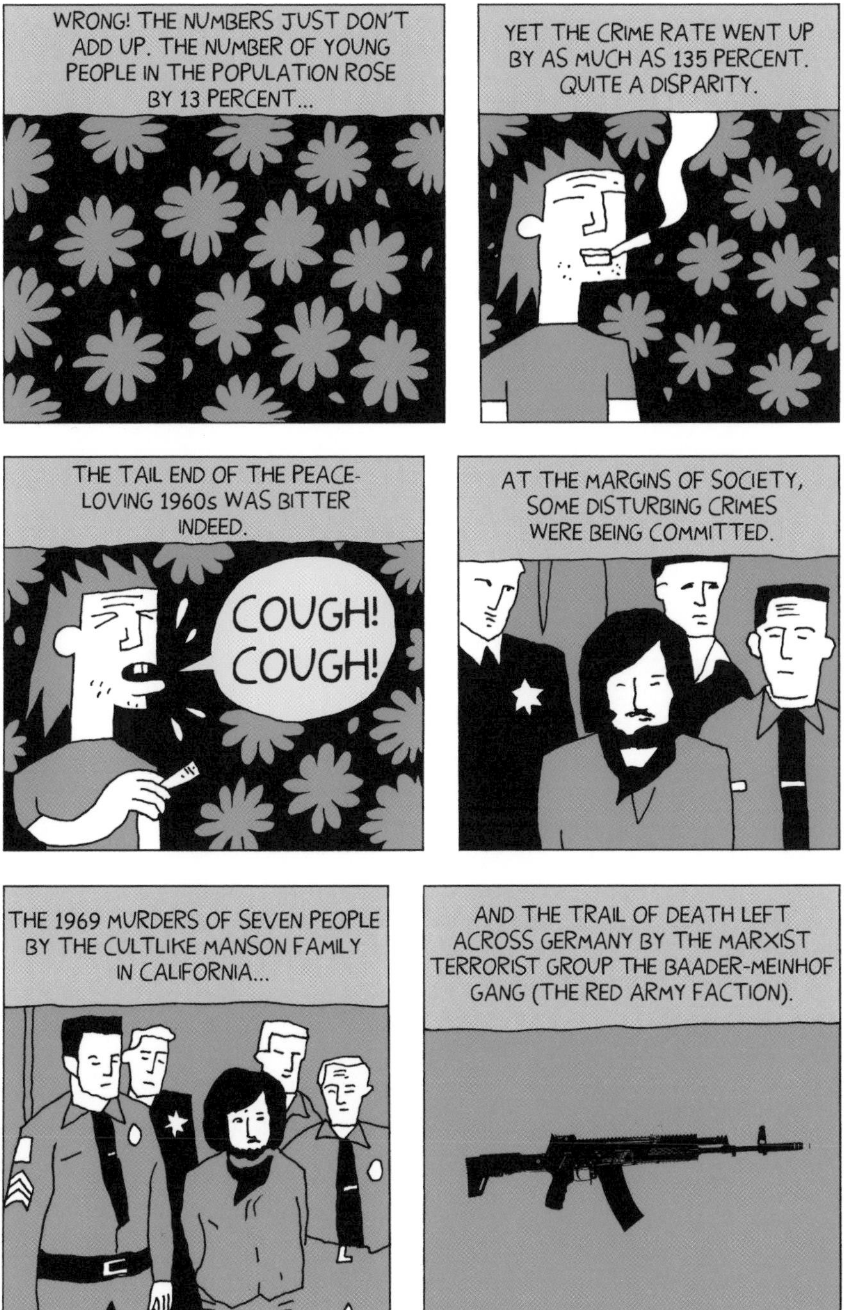
WRONG! THE NUMBERS JUST DON'T ADD UP. THE NUMBER OF YOUNG PEOPLE IN THE POPULATION ROSE BY 13 PERCENT...
YET THE CRIME RATE WENT UP BY AS MUCH AS 135 PERCENT. QUITE A DISPARITY.
THE TAIL END OF THE PEACE-LOVING 1960s WAS BITTER INDEED.
COUGH! COUGH!
AT THE MARGINS OF SOCIETY, SOME DISTURBING CRIMES WERE BEING COMMITTED.
THE 1969 MURDERS OF SEVEN PEOPLE BY THE CULTLIKE MANSON FAMILY IN CALIFORNIA...
AND THE TRAIL OF DEATH LEFT ACROSS GERMANY BY THE MARXIST TERRORIST GROUP THE BAADER-MEINHOF GANG (THE RED ARMY FACTION).

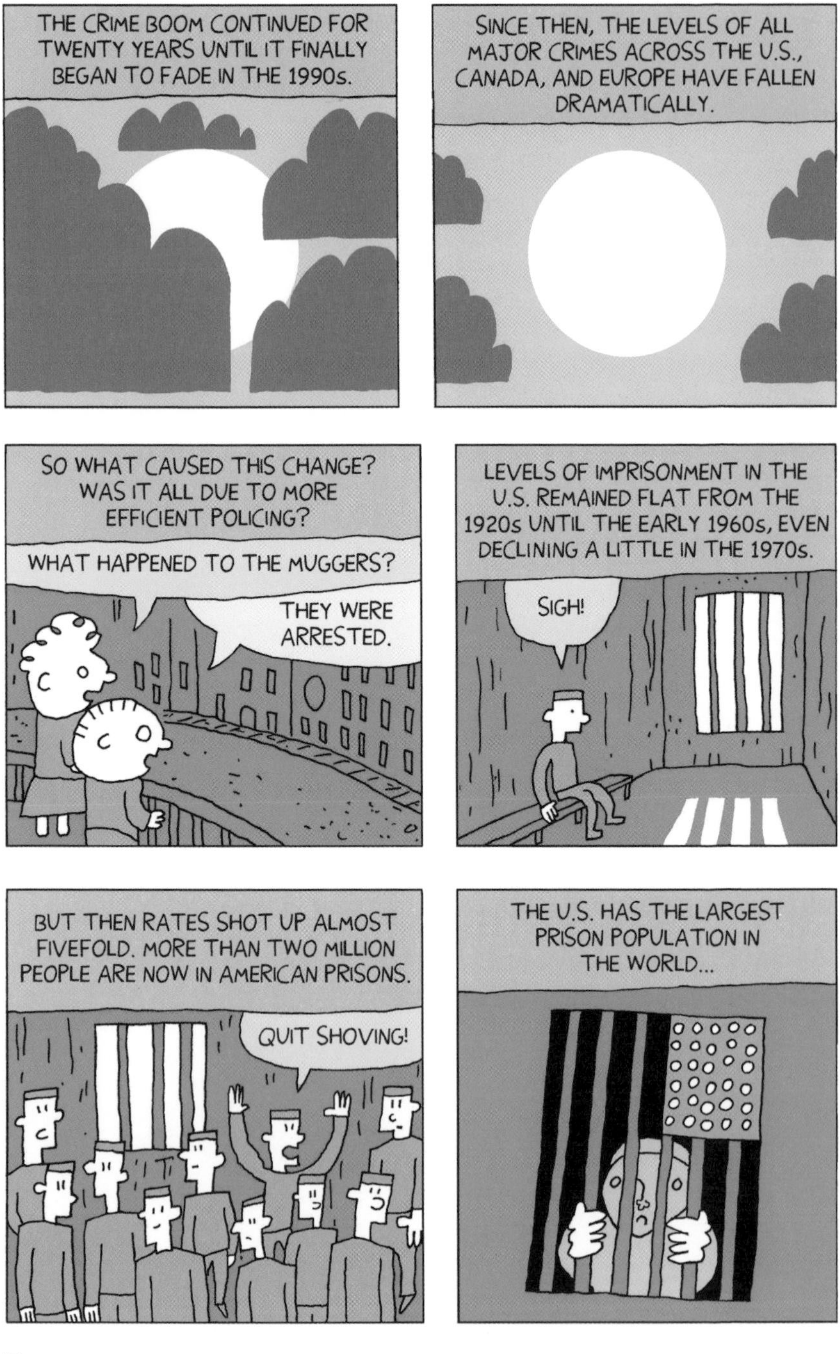
THE CRIME BOOM CONTINUED FOR TWENTY YEARS UNTIL IT FINALLY BEGAN TO FADE IN THE 1990s.
SINCE THEN, THE LEVELS OF ALL MAJOR CRIMES ACROSS THE U.S., CANADA, AND EUROPE HAVE FALLEN DRAMATICALLY.
SO WHAT CAUSED THIS CHANGE? WAS IT ALL DUE TO MORE EFFICIENT POLICING?
WHAT HAPPENED TO THE MUGGERS?
THEY WERE ARRESTED.
LEVELS OF IMPRISONMENT IN THE U.S. REMAINED FLAT FROM THE 1920s UNTIL THE EARLY 1960s, EVEN DECLINING A LITTLE IN THE 1970s.
SIGH!
BUT THEN RATES SHOT UP ALMOST FIVEFOLD. MORE THAN TWO MILLION PEOPLE ARE NOW IN AMERICAN PRISONS.
QUIT SHOVING!
THE U.S. HAS THE LARGEST PRISON POPULATION IN THE WORLD...

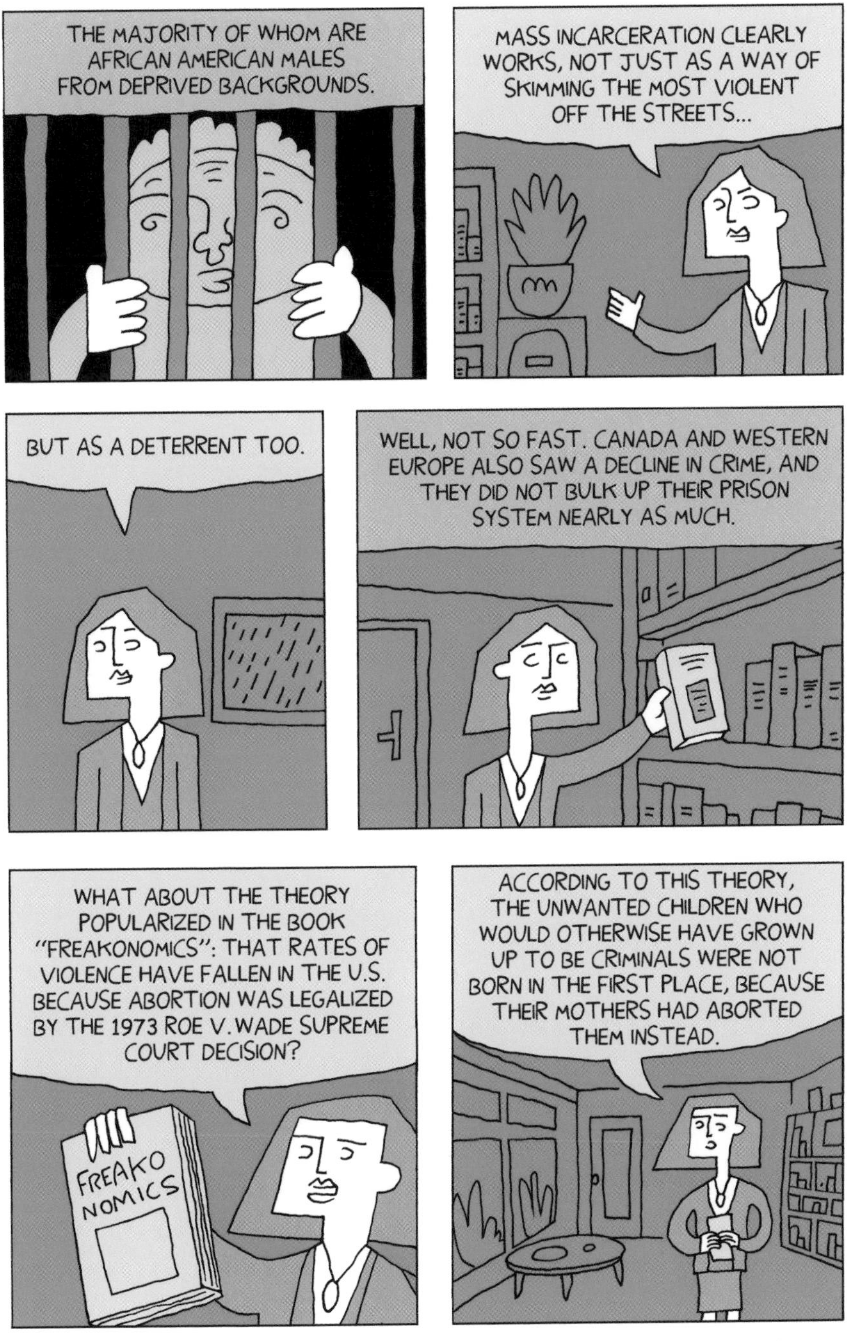
THE MAJORITY OF WHOM ARE AFRICAN AMERICAN MALES FROM DEPRIVED BACKGROUNDS.
MASS INCARCERATION CLEARLY WORKS, NOT JUST AS A WAY OF SKIMMING THE MOST VIOLENT OFF THE STREETS...
BUT AS A DETERRENT TOO.
WELL, NOT SO FAST. CANADA AND WESTERN EUROPE ALSO SAW A DECLINE IN CRIME, AND THEY DID NOT BULK UP THEIR PRISON SYSTEM NEARLY AS MUCH.
WHAT ABOUT THE THEORY POPULARIZED IN THE BOOK "FREAKONOMICS": THAT RATES OF VIOLENCE HAVE FALLEN IN THE U.S. BECAUSE ABORTION WAS LEGALIZED BY THE 1973 ROE V. WADE SUPREME COURT DECISION?
FREAKO NOMICS
ACCORDING TO THIS THEORY, THE UNWANTED CHILDREN WHO WOULD OTHERWISE HAVE GROWN UP TO BE CRIMINALS WERE NOT BORN IN THE FIRST PLACE, BECAUSE THEIR MOTHERS HAD ABORTED THEM INSTEAD.

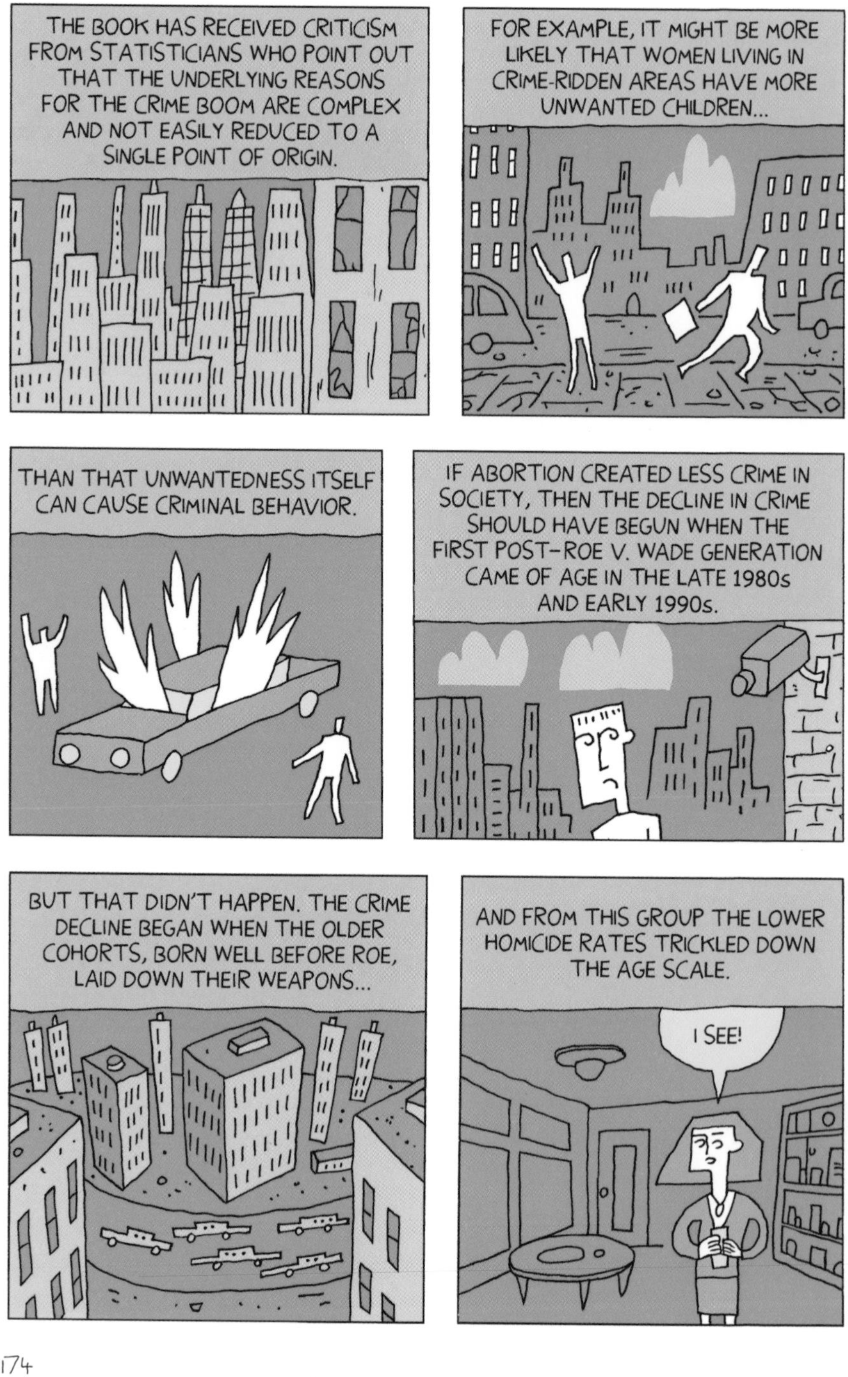
THE BOOK HAS RECEIVED CRITICISM FROM STATISTICIANS WHO POINT OUT THAT THE UNDERLYING REASONS FOR THE CRIME BOOM ARE COMPLEX AND NOT EASILY REDUCED TO A SINGLE POINT OF ORIGIN.
FOR EXAMPLE, IT MIGHT BE MORE LIKELY THAT WOMEN LIVING IN CRIME-RIDDEN AREAS HAVE MORE UNWANTED CHILDREN...
THAN THAT UNWANTEDNESS ITSELF CAN CAUSE CRIMINAL BEHAVIOR.
IF ABORTION CREATED LESS CRIME IN SOCIETY, THEN THE DECLINE IN CRIME SHOULD HAVE BEGUN WHEN THE FIRST POST–ROE V. WADE GENERATION CAME OF AGE IN THE LATE 1980s AND EARLY 1990s.
BUT THAT DIDN'T HAPPEN. THE CRIME DECLINE BEGAN WHEN THE OLDER COHORTS, BORN WELL BEFORE ROE, LAID DOWN THEIR WEAPONS...
AND FROM THIS GROUP THE LOWER HOMICIDE RATES TRICKLED DOWN THE AGE SCALE.
I SEE!

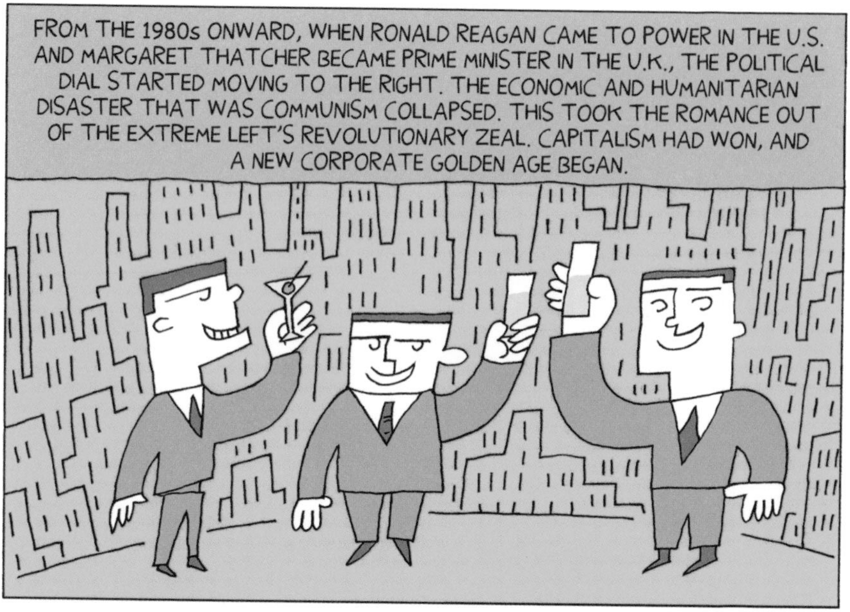
FROM THE 1980s ONWARD, WHEN RONALD REAGAN CAME TO POWER IN THE U.S. AND MARGARET THATCHER BECAME PRIME MINISTER IN THE U.K., THE POLITICAL DIAL STARTED MOVING TO THE RIGHT. THE ECONOMIC AND HUMANITARIAN DISASTER THAT WAS COMMUNISM COLLAPSED. THIS TOOK THE ROMANCE OUT OF THE EXTREME LEFT'S REVOLUTIONARY ZEAL. CAPITALISM HAD WON, AND A NEW CORPORATE GOLDEN AGE BEGAN.

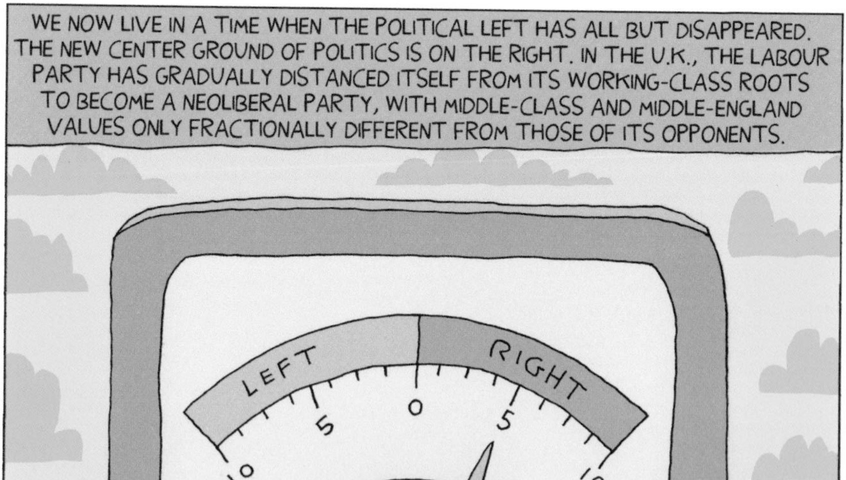
WE NOW LIVE IN A TIME WHEN THE POLITICAL LEFT HAS ALL BUT DISAPPEARED. THE NEW CENTER GROUND OF POLITICS IS ON THE RIGHT. IN THE U.K., THE LABOUR PARTY HAS GRADUALLY DISTANCED ITSELF FROM ITS WORKING-CLASS ROOTS TO BECOME A NEOLIBERAL PARTY, WITH MIDDLE-CLASS AND MIDDLE-ENGLAND VALUES ONLY FRACTIONALLY DIFFERENT FROM THOSE OF ITS OPPONENTS.
LEFT
RIGHT
10
5
0
5
10

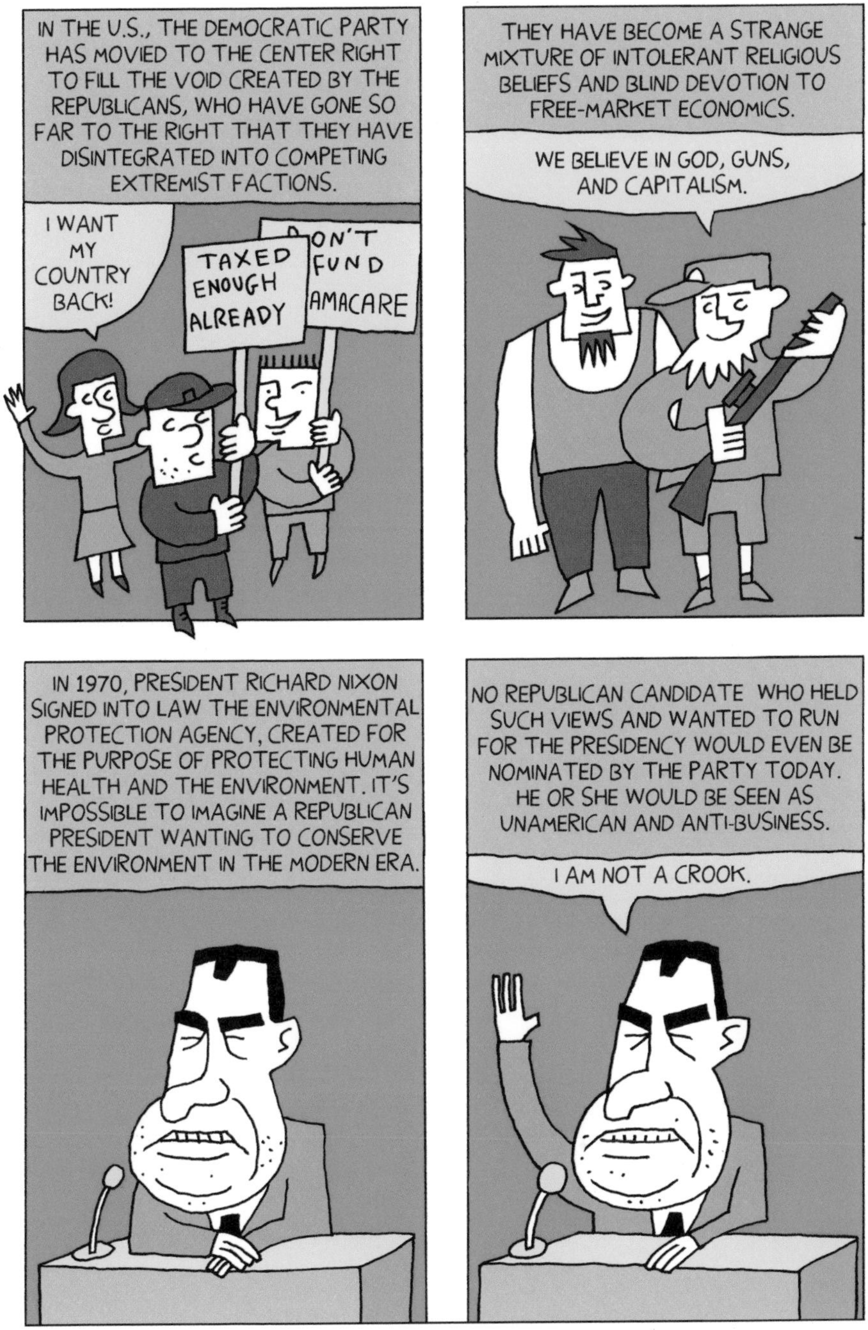

IN THE U.S., THE DEMOCRATIC PARTY HAS MOVIED TO THE CENTER RIGHT TO FILL THE VOID CREATED BY THE REPUBLICANS, WHO HAVE GONE SO FAR TO THE RIGHT THAT THEY HAVE DISINTEGRATED INTO COMPETING EXTREMIST FACTIONS.
I WANT MY COUNTRY BACK!
TAXED ENOUGH ALREADY
ON'T FUND AMACARE
THEY HAVE BECOME A STRANGE MIXTURE OF INTOLERANT RELIGIOUS BELIEFS AND BLIND DEVOTION TO FREE-MARKET ECONOMICS.
WE BELIEVE IN GOD, GUNS, AND CAPITALISM.
IN 1970, PRESIDENT RICHARD NIXON SIGNED INTO LAW THE ENVIRONMENTAL PROTECTION AGENCY, CREATED FOR THE PURPOSE OF PROTECTING HUMAN HEALTH AND THE ENVIRONMENT. IT'S IMPOSSIBLE TO IMAGINE A REPUBLICAN PRESIDENT WANTING TO CONSERVE THE ENVIRONMENT IN THE MODERN ERA.
NO REPUBLICAN CANDIDATE WHO HELD SUCH VIEWS AND WANTED TO RUN FOR THE PRESIDENCY WOULD EVEN BE NOMINATED BY THE PARTY TODAY. HE OR SHE WOULD BE SEEN AS UNAMERICAN AND ANTI-BUSINESS.
I AM NOT A CROOK.

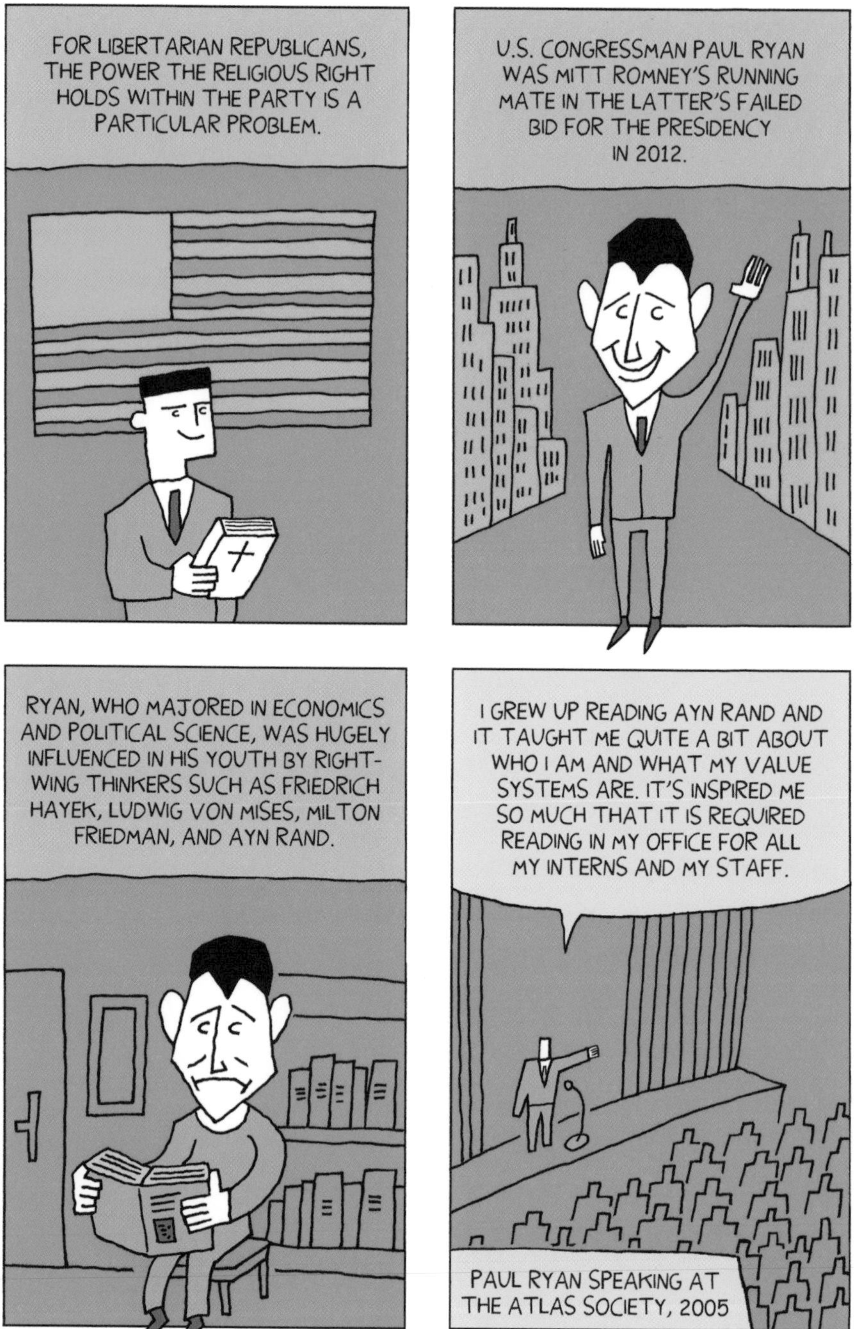
FOR LIBERTARIAN REPUBLICANS, THE POWER THE RELIGIOUS RIGHT HOLDS WITHIN THE PARTY IS A PARTICULAR PROBLEM.
U.S. CONGRESSMAN PAUL RYAN WAS MITT ROMNEY'S RUNNING MATE IN THE LATTER'S FAILED BID FOR THE PRESIDENCY IN 2012.
RYAN, WHO MAJORED IN ECONOMICS AND POLITICAL SCIENCE, WAS HUGELY INFLUENCED IN HIS YOUTH BY RIGHT-WING THINKERS SUCH AS FRIEDRICH HAYEK, LUDWIG VON MISES, MILTON FRIEDMAN, AND AYN RAND.
I GREW UP READING AYN RAND AND IT TAUGHT ME QUITE A BIT ABOUT WHO I AM AND WHAT MY VALUE SYSTEMS ARE. IT'S INSPIRED ME SO MUCH THAT IT IS REQUIRED READING IN MY OFFICE FOR ALL MY INTERNS AND MY STAFF.
PAUL RYAN SPEAKING AT THE ATLAS SOCIETY, 2005

THE FIGHT WE ARE IN HERE, MAKE NO MISTAKE ABOUT IT, IS A FIGHT FOR INDIVIDUALISM VERSUS COLLECTIVISM.

SINCE RAND'S ATHEISM IS ANATHEMA TO THE MAJORITY OF REPUBLICANS, RYAN HAS SINCE HAD TO DISTANCE HIMSELF FROM THE WRITER, CLAIMING THE CONNECTION HAD BEEN EXAGGERATED.

YOU KNOW YOU'VE ARRIVED IN POLITICS WHEN YOU HAVE AN URBAN LEGEND ABOUT YOU. THIS ONE IS MINE.

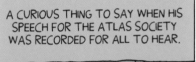

A CURIOUS THING TO SAY WHEN HIS SPEECH FOR THE ATLAS SOCIETY WAS RECORDED FOR ALL TO HEAR.

AS CHAIRMAN OF THE UNITED STATES HOUSE OF REPRESENTATIVES' BUDGET COMMITTEE SINCE 2011...

RYAN HAS PRESENTED A SERIES OF BUDGET PLANS DESIGNED TO APPEAL TO HARD-CORE REPUBLICAN VALUES.

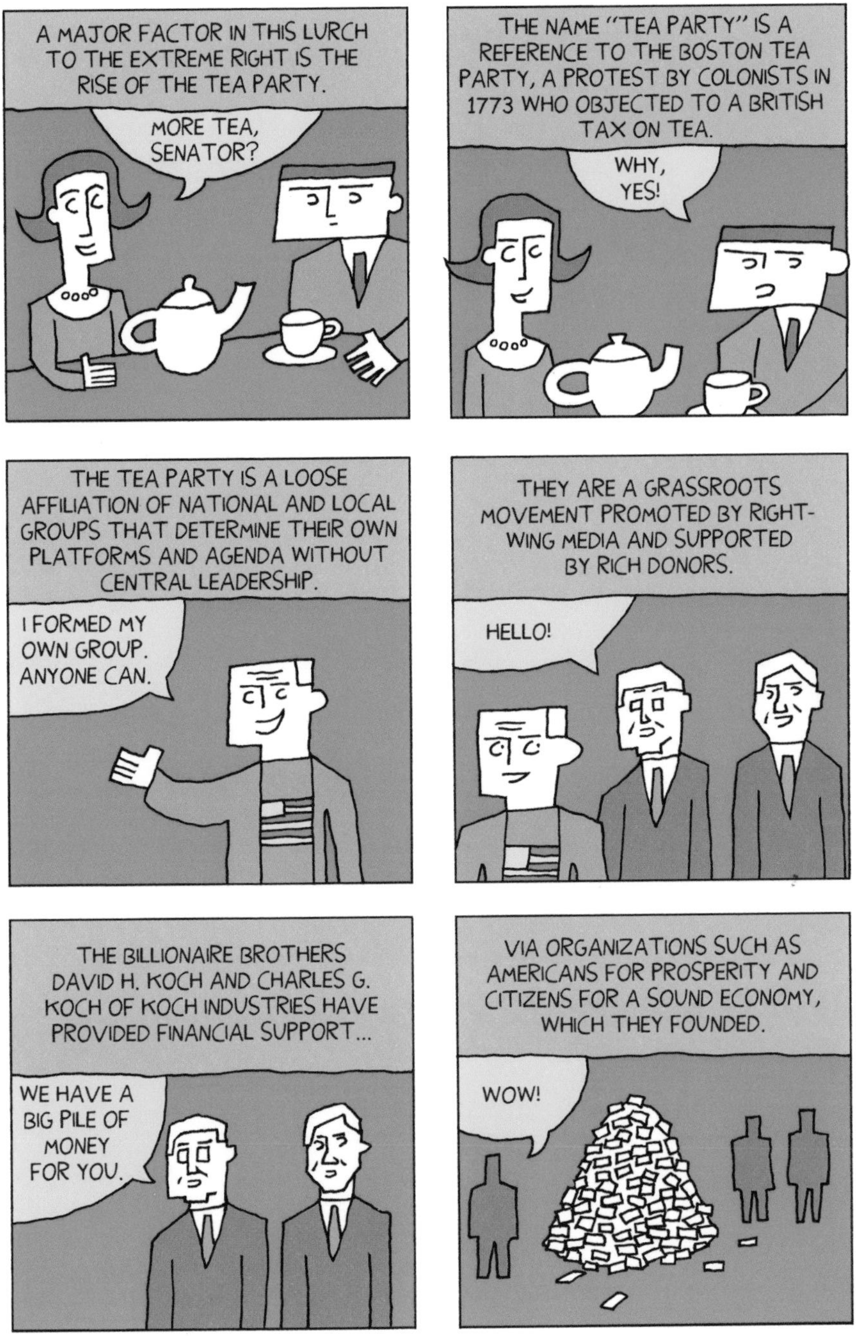
A MAJOR FACTOR IN THIS LURCH TO THE EXTREME RIGHT IS THE RISE OF THE TEA PARTY.
MORE TEA, SENATOR?
THE NAME "TEA PARTY" IS A REFERENCE TO THE BOSTON TEA PARTY, A PROTEST BY COLONISTS IN 1773 WHO OBJECTED TO A BRITISH TAX ON TEA.
WHY, YES!
THE TEA PARTY IS A LOOSE AFFILIATION OF NATIONAL AND LOCAL GROUPS THAT DETERMINE THEIR OWN PLATFORMS AND AGENDA WITHOUT CENTRAL LEADERSHIP.
I FORMED MY OWN GROUP. ANYONE CAN.
THEY ARE A GRASSROOTS MOVEMENT PROMOTED BY RIGHT-WING MEDIA AND SUPPORTED BY RICH DONORS.
HELLO!
THE BILLIONAIRE BROTHERS DAVID H. KOCH AND CHARLES G. KOCH OF KOCH INDUSTRIES HAVE PROVIDED FINANCIAL SUPPORT...
WE HAVE A BIG PILE OF MONEY FOR YOU.
VIA ORGANIZATIONS SUCH AS AMERICANS FOR PROSPERITY AND CITIZENS FOR A SOUND ECONOMY, WHICH THEY FOUNDED.
WOW!

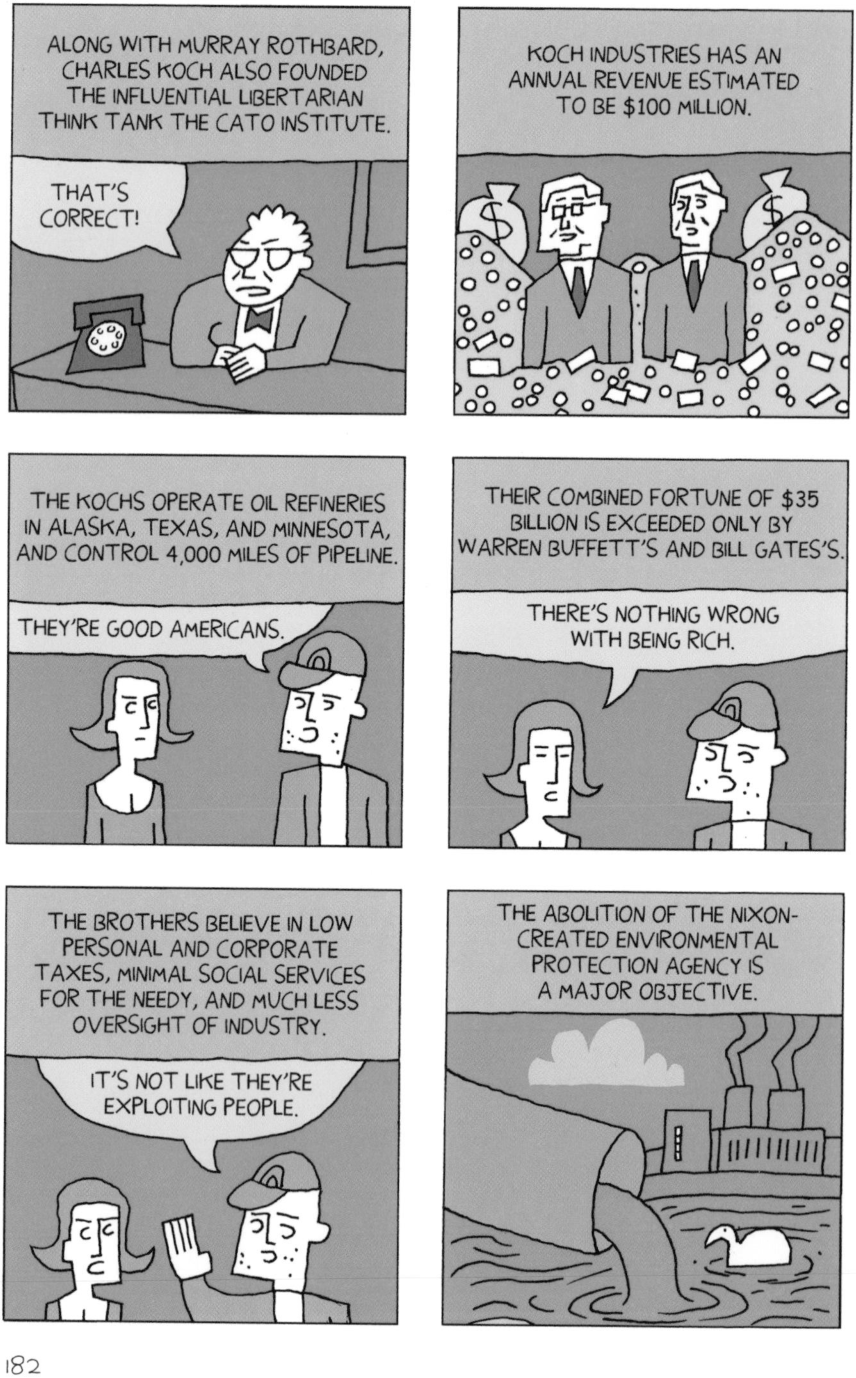
ALONG WITH MURRAY ROTHBARD, CHARLES KOCH ALSO FOUNDED THE INFLUENTIAL LIBERTARIAN THINK TANK THE CATO INSTITUTE.
THAT'S CORRECT!
KOCH INDUSTRIES HAS AN ANNUAL REVENUE ESTIMATED TO BE $100 MILLION.
THE KOCHS OPERATE OIL REFINERIES IN ALASKA, TEXAS, AND MINNESOTA, AND CONTROL 4,000 MILES OF PIPELINE.
THEY'RE GOOD AMERICANS.
THEIR COMBINED FORTUNE OF $35 BILLION IS EXCEEDED ONLY BY WARREN BUFFETT'S AND BILL GATES'S.
THERE'S NOTHING WRONG WITH BEING RICH.
THE BROTHERS BELIEVE IN LOW PERSONAL AND CORPORATE TAXES, MINIMAL SOCIAL SERVICES FOR THE NEEDY, AND MUCH LESS OVERSIGHT OF INDUSTRY.
IT'S NOT LIKE THEY'RE EXPLOITING PEOPLE.
THE ABOLITION OF THE NIXON-CREATED ENVIRONMENTAL PROTECTION AGENCY IS A MAJOR OBJECTIVE.

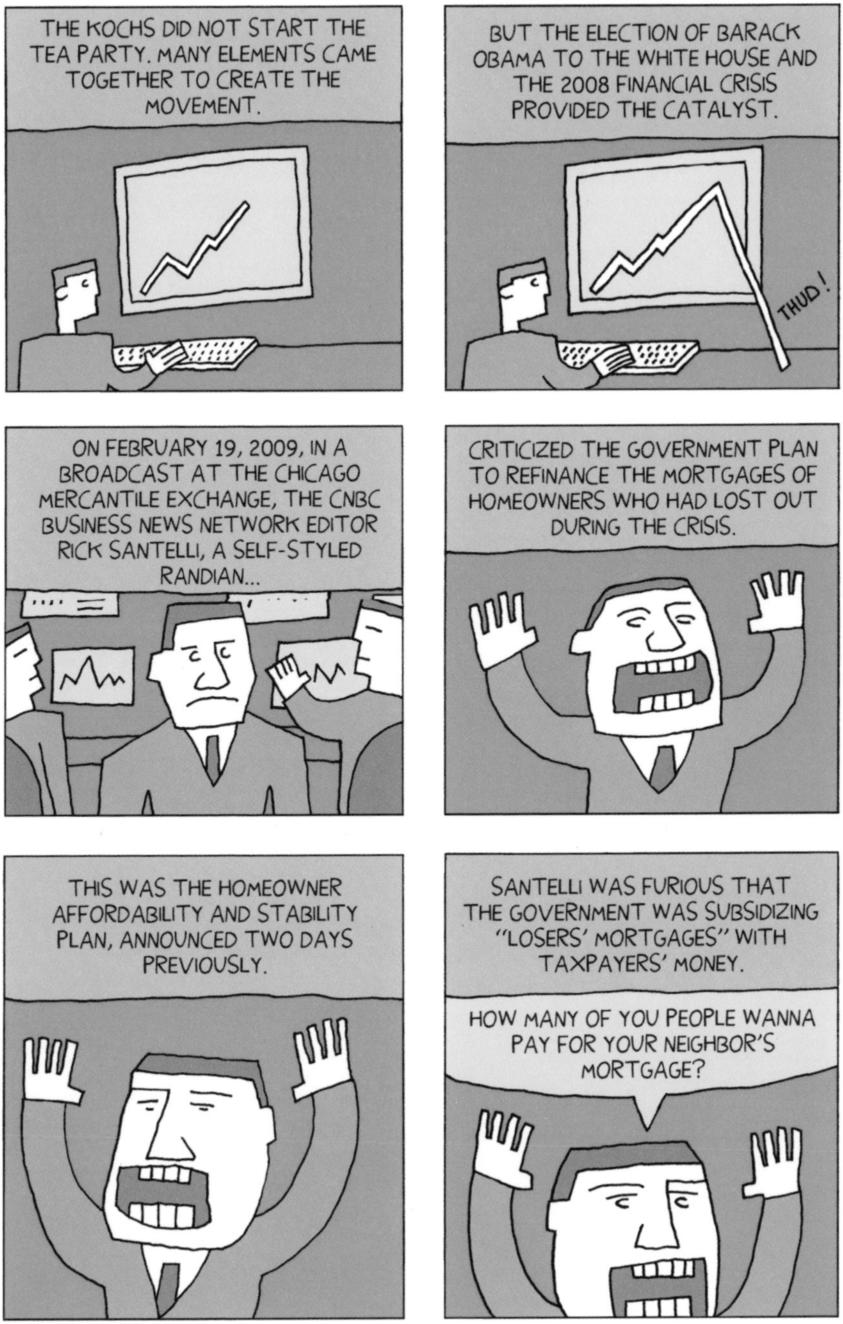
THE KOCHS DID NOT START THE TEA PARTY. MANY ELEMENTS CAME TOGETHER TO CREATE THE MOVEMENT.
BUT THE ELECTION OF BARACK OBAMA TO THE WHITE HOUSE AND THE 2008 FINANCIAL CRISIS PROVIDED THE CATALYST.
THUD!
ON FEBRUARY 19, 2009, IN A BROADCAST AT THE CHICAGO MERCANTILE EXCHANGE, THE CNBC BUSINESS NEWS NETWORK EDITOR RICK SANTELLI, A SELF-STYLED RANDIAN...
CRITICIZED THE GOVERNMENT PLAN TO REFINANCE THE MORTGAGES OF HOMEOWNERS WHO HAD LOST OUT DURING THE CRISIS.
THIS WAS THE HOMEOWNER AFFORDABILITY AND STABILITY PLAN, ANNOUNCED TWO DAYS PREVIOUSLY.
SANTELLI WAS FURIOUS THAT THE GOVERNMENT WAS SUBSIDIZING "LOSERS' MORTGAGES" WITH TAXPAYERS' MONEY.
HOW MANY OF YOU PEOPLE WANNA PAY FOR YOUR NEIGHBOR'S MORTGAGE?

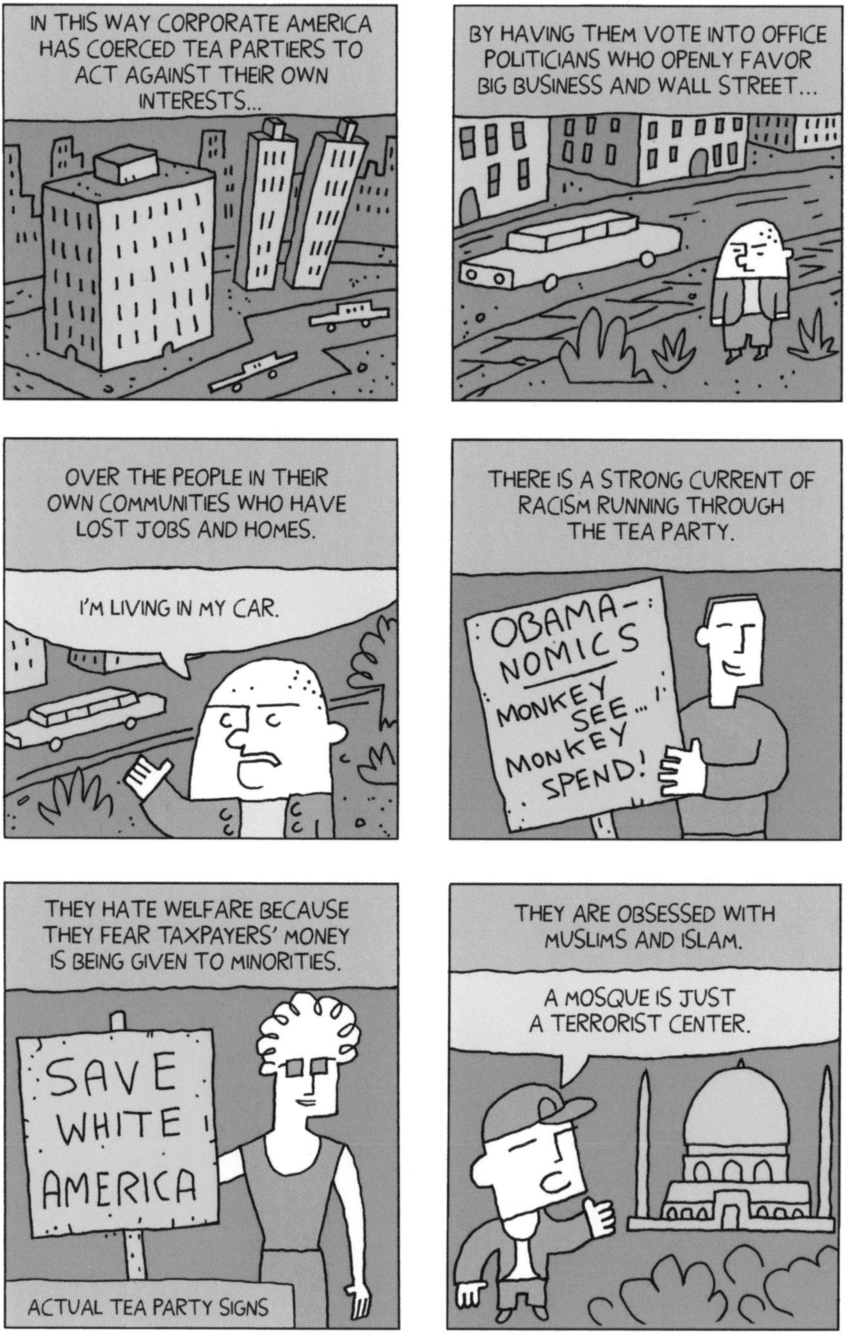
IN THIS WAY CORPORATE AMERICA HAS COERCED TEA PARTIERS TO ACT AGAINST THEIR OWN INTERESTS...
BY HAVING THEM VOTE INTO OFFICE POLITICIANS WHO OPENLY FAVOR BIG BUSINESS AND WALL STREET...
OVER THE PEOPLE IN THEIR OWN COMMUNITIES WHO HAVE LOST JOBS AND HOMES.
I'M LIVING IN MY CAR.
THERE IS A STRONG CURRENT OF RACISM RUNNING THROUGH THE TEA PARTY.
OBAMA-NOMICS
MONKEY SEE... MONKEY SPEND!
THEY HATE WELFARE BECAUSE THEY FEAR TAXPAYERS' MONEY IS BEING GIVEN TO MINORITIES.
SAVE WHITE AMERICA
ACTUAL TEA PARTY SIGNS
THEY ARE OBSESSED WITH MUSLIMS AND ISLAM.
A MOSQUE IS JUST A TERRORIST CENTER.

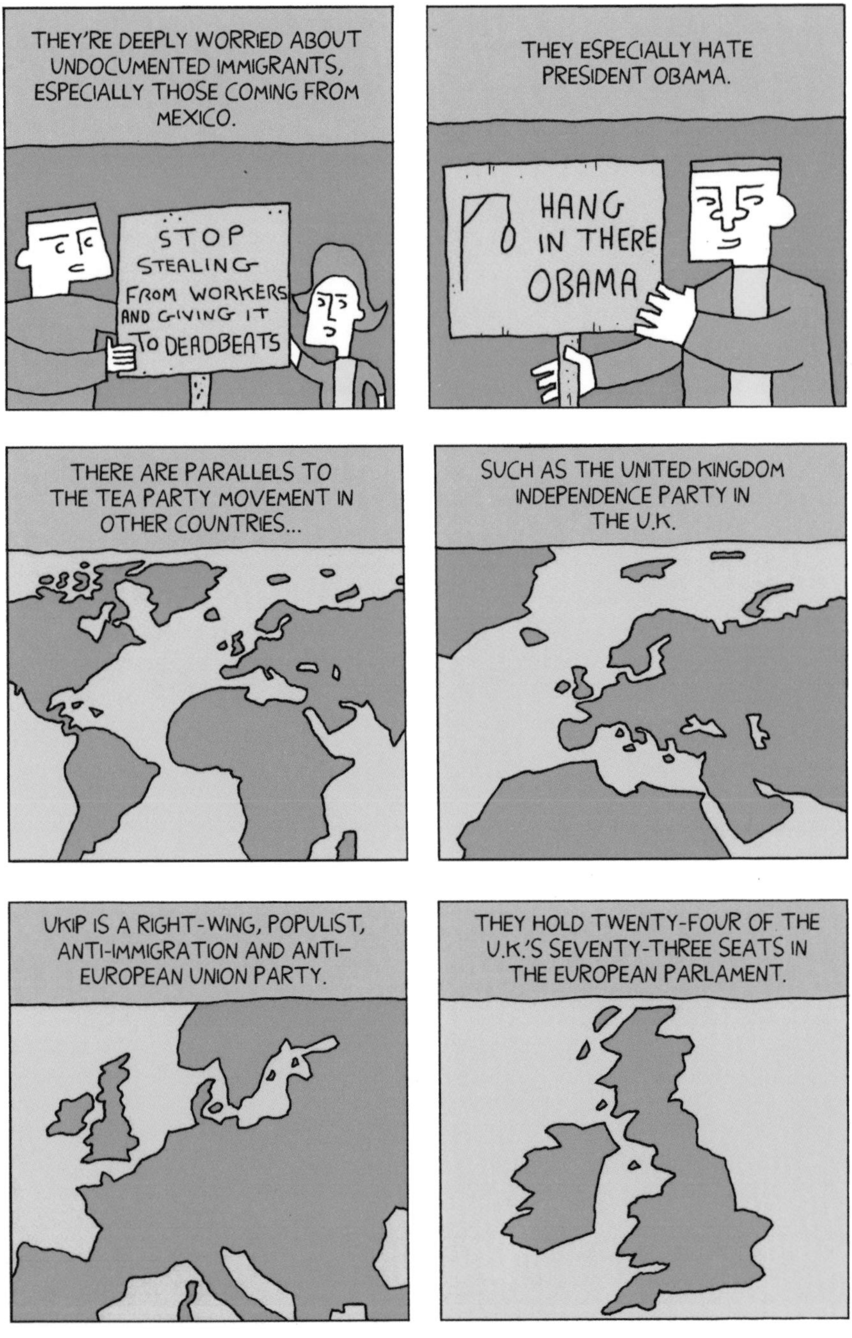
THEY'RE DEEPLY WORRIED ABOUT UNDOCUMENTED IMMIGRANTS, ESPECIALLY THOSE COMING FROM MEXICO.
STOP STEALING FROM WORKERS AND GIVING IT TO DEADBEATS
THEY ESPECIALLY HATE PRESIDENT OBAMA.
HANG IN THERE OBAMA
THERE ARE PARALLELS TO THE TEA PARTY MOVEMENT IN OTHER COUNTRIES...
SUCH AS THE UNITED KINGDOM INDEPENDENCE PARTY IN THE U.K.
UKIP IS A RIGHT-WING, POPULIST, ANTI-IMMIGRATION AND ANTI-EUROPEAN UNION PARTY.
THEY HOLD TWENTY-FOUR OF THE U.K.'S SEVENTY-THREE SEATS IN THE EUROPEAN PARLAMENT.

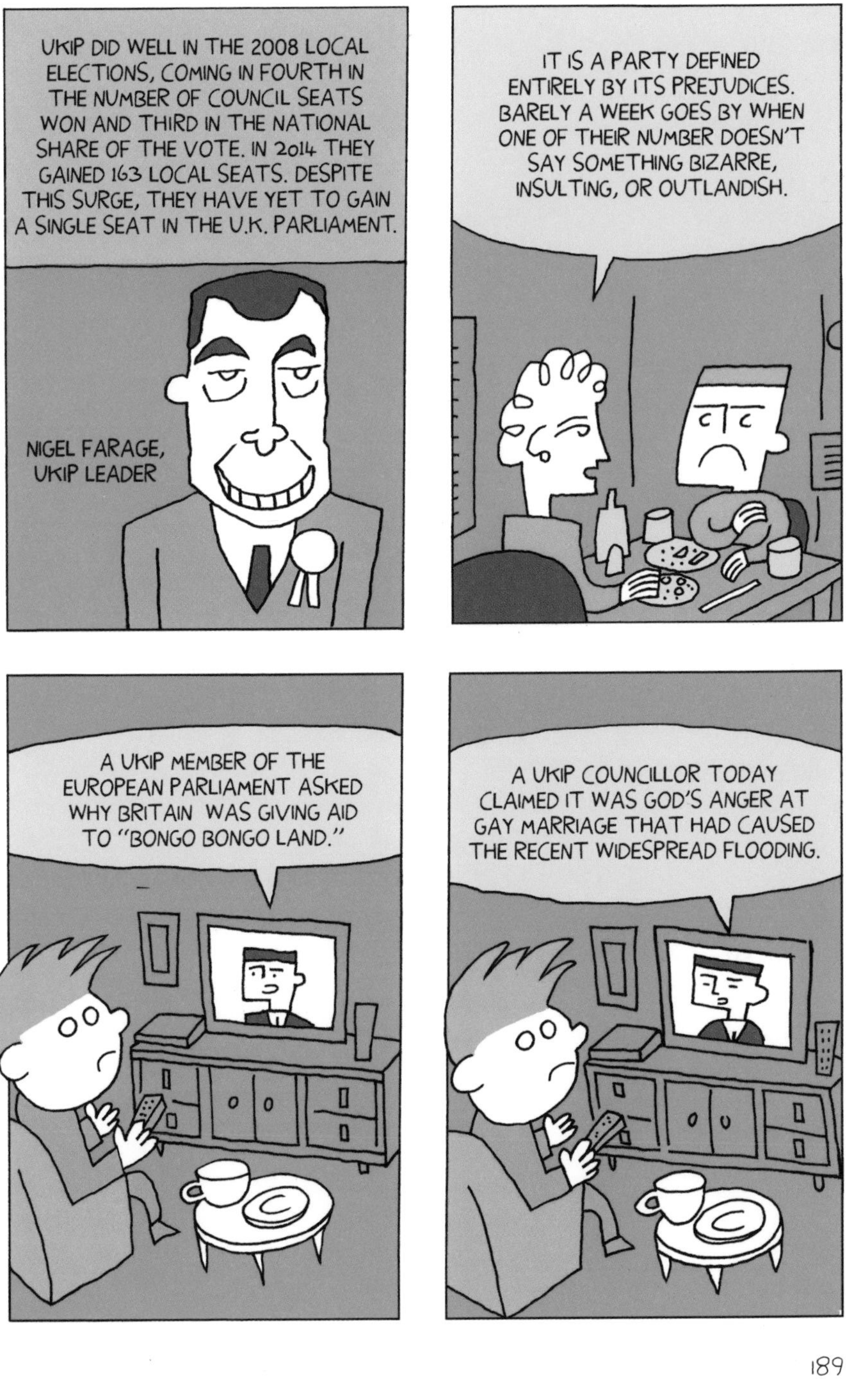
UKIP DID WELL IN THE 2008 LOCAL ELECTIONS, COMING IN FOURTH IN THE NUMBER OF COUNCIL SEATS WON AND THIRD IN THE NATIONAL SHARE OF THE VOTE. IN 2014 THEY GAINED 163 LOCAL SEATS. DESPITE THIS SURGE, THEY HAVE YET TO GAIN A SINGLE SEAT IN THE U.K. PARLIAMENT.
NIGEL FARAGE, UKIP LEADER
IT IS A PARTY DEFINED ENTIRELY BY ITS PREJUDICES. BARELY A WEEK GOES BY WHEN ONE OF THEIR NUMBER DOESN'T SAY SOMETHING BIZARRE, INSULTING, OR OUTLANDISH.
A UKIP MEMBER OF THE EUROPEAN PARLIAMENT ASKED WHY BRITAIN WAS GIVING AID TO "BONGO BONGO LAND."
A UKIP COUNCILLOR TODAY CLAIMED IT WAS GOD'S ANGER AT GAY MARRIAGE THAT HAD CAUSED THE RECENT WIDESPREAD FLOODING.

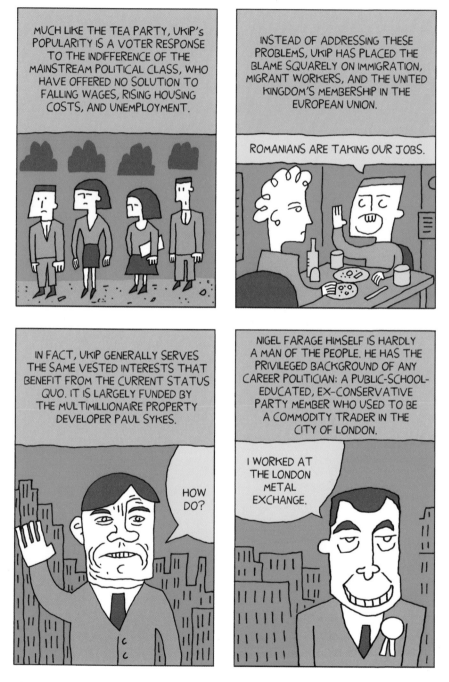

MUCH LIKE THE TEA PARTY, UKIP's POPULARITY IS A VOTER RESPONSE TO THE INDIFFERENCE OF THE MAINSTREAM POLITICAL CLASS, WHO HAVE OFFERED NO SOLUTION TO FALLING WAGES, RISING HOUSING COSTS, AND UNEMPLOYMENT.

INSTEAD OF ADDRESSING THESE PROBLEMS, UKIP HAS PLACED THE BLAME SQUARELY ON IMMIGRATION, MIGRANT WORKERS, AND THE UNITED KINGDOM'S MEMBERSHIP IN THE EUROPEAN UNION.

ROMANIANS ARE TAKING OUR JOBS.

IN FACT, UKIP GENERALLY SERVES THE SAME VESTED INTERESTS THAT BENEFIT FROM THE CURRENT STATUS QUO. IT IS LARGELY FUNDED BY THE MULTIMILLIONAIRE PROPERTY DEVELOPER PAUL SYKES.

HOW DO?

NIGEL FARAGE HIMSELF IS HARDLY A MAN OF THE PEOPLE. HE HAS THE PRIVILEGED BACKGROUND OF ANY CAREER POLITICIAN: A PUBLIC-SCHOOL-EDUCATED, EX-CONSERVATIVE PARTY MEMBER WHO USED TO BE A COMMODITY TRADER IN THE CITY OF LONDON.

I WORKED AT THE LONDON METAL EXCHANGE.

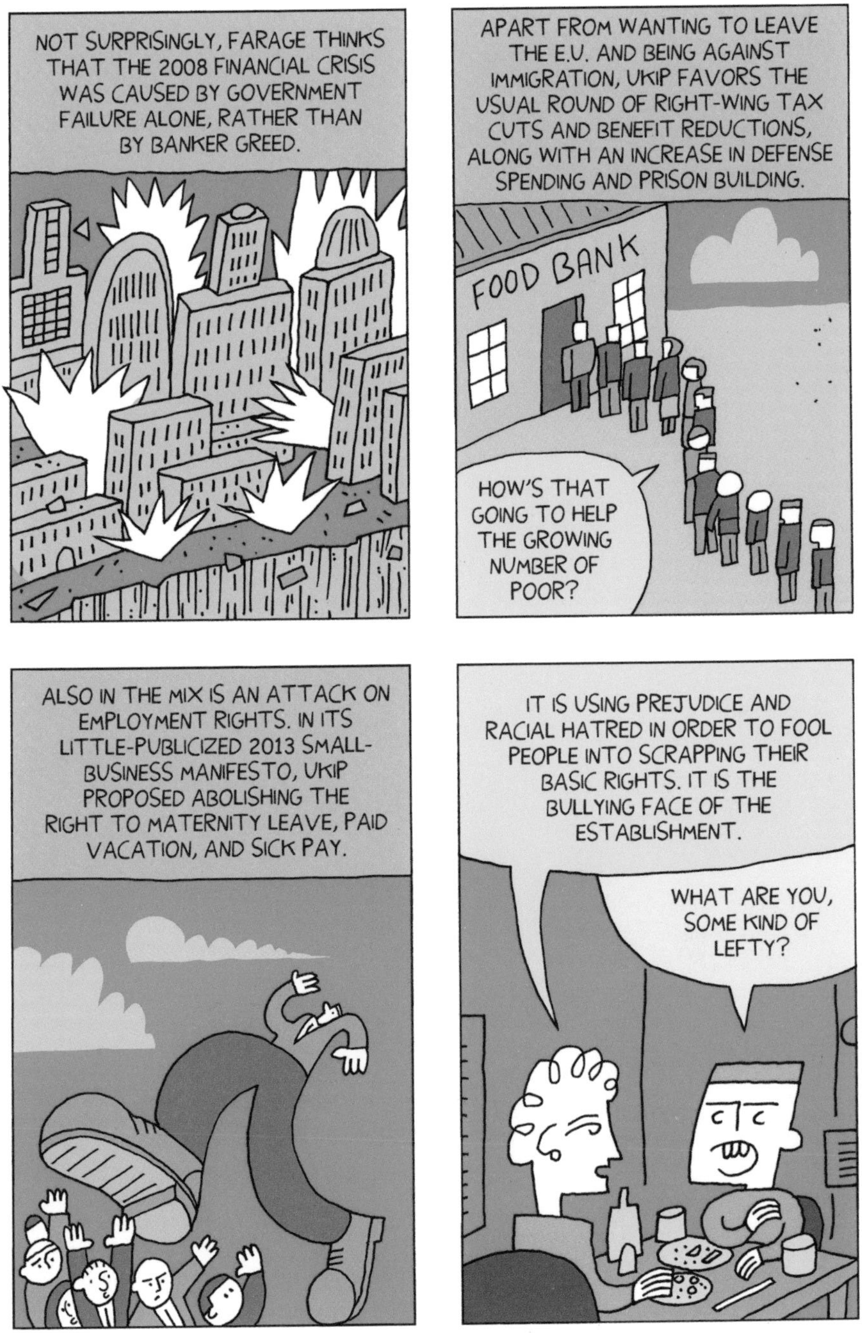
NOT SURPRISINGLY, FARAGE THINKS THAT THE 2008 FINANCIAL CRISIS WAS CAUSED BY GOVERNMENT FAILURE ALONE, RATHER THAN BY BANKER GREED.
APART FROM WANTING TO LEAVE THE E.U. AND BEING AGAINST IMMIGRATION, UKIP FAVORS THE USUAL ROUND OF RIGHT-WING TAX CUTS AND BENEFIT REDUCTIONS, ALONG WITH AN INCREASE IN DEFENSE SPENDING AND PRISON BUILDING.
FOOD BANK
HOW'S THAT GOING TO HELP THE GROWING NUMBER OF POOR?
ALSO IN THE MIX IS AN ATTACK ON EMPLOYMENT RIGHTS. IN ITS LITTLE-PUBLICIZED 2013 SMALL-BUSINESS MANIFESTO, UKIP PROPOSED ABOLISHING THE RIGHT TO MATERNITY LEAVE, PAID VACATION, AND SICK PAY.
IT IS USING PREJUDICE AND RACIAL HATRED IN ORDER TO FOOL PEOPLE INTO SCRAPPING THEIR BASIC RIGHTS. IT IS THE BULLYING FACE OF THE ESTABLISHMENT.
WHAT ARE YOU, SOME KIND OF LEFTY?

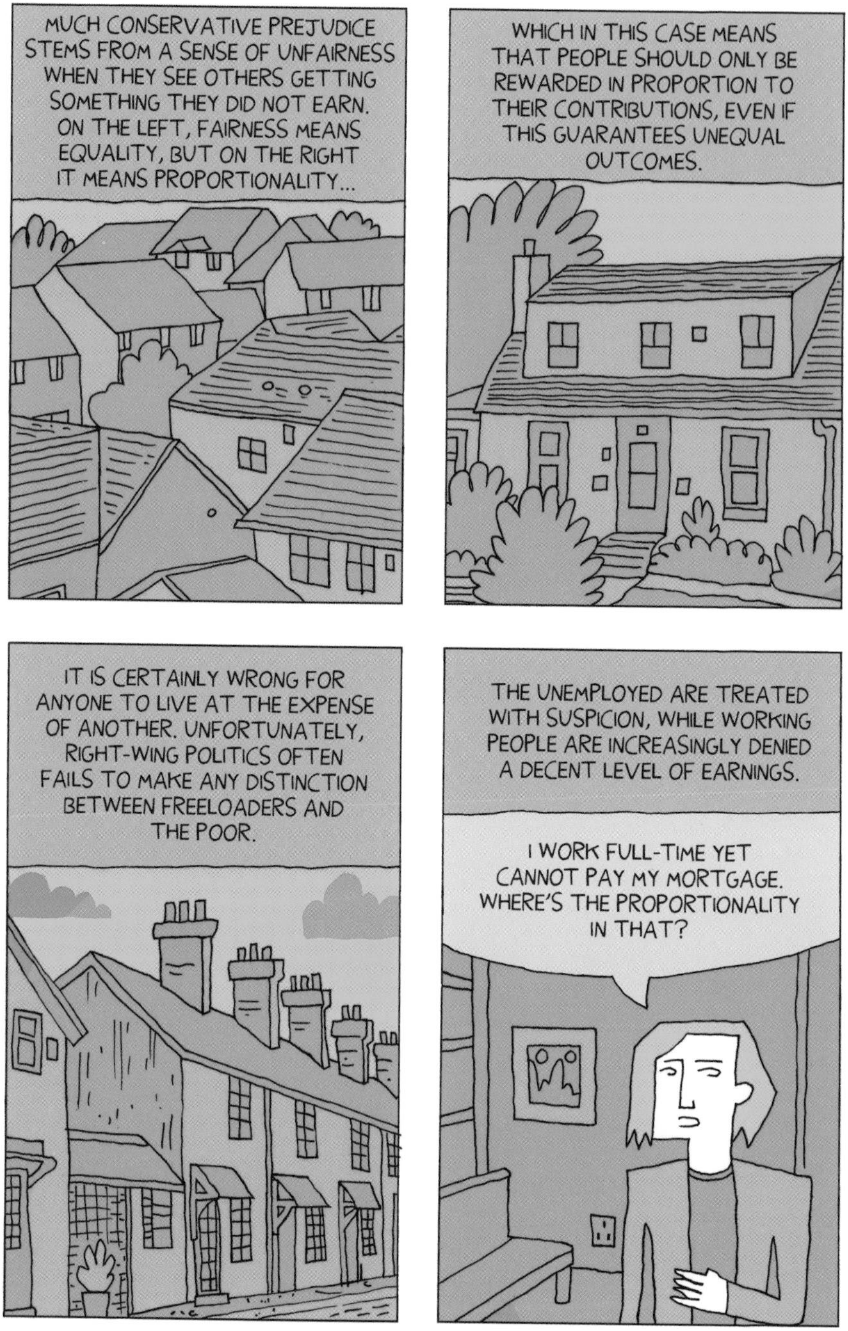
MUCH CONSERVATIVE PREJUDICE STEMS FROM A SENSE OF UNFAIRNESS WHEN THEY SEE OTHERS GETTING SOMETHING THEY DID NOT EARN. ON THE LEFT, FAIRNESS MEANS EQUALITY, BUT ON THE RIGHT IT MEANS PROPORTIONALITY...
WHICH IN THIS CASE MEANS THAT PEOPLE SHOULD ONLY BE REWARDED IN PROPORTION TO THEIR CONTRIBUTIONS, EVEN IF THIS GUARANTEES UNEQUAL OUTCOMES.
IT IS CERTAINLY WRONG FOR ANYONE TO LIVE AT THE EXPENSE OF ANOTHER. UNFORTUNATELY, RIGHT-WING POLITICS OFTEN FAILS TO MAKE ANY DISTINCTION BETWEEN FREELOADERS AND THE POOR.
THE UNEMPLOYED ARE TREATED WITH SUSPICION, WHILE WORKING PEOPLE ARE INCREASINGLY DENIED A DECENT LEVEL OF EARNINGS.
I WORK FULL-TIME YET CANNOT PAY MY MORTGAGE. WHERE'S THE PROPORTIONALITY IN THAT?

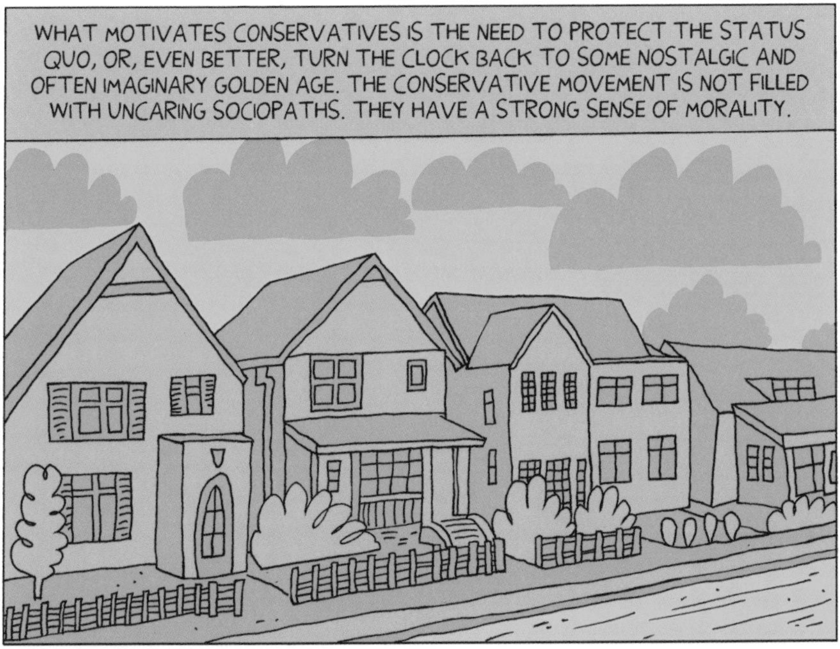
WHAT MOTIVATES CONSERVATIVES IS THE NEED TO PROTECT THE STATUS QUO, OR, EVEN BETTER, TURN THE CLOCK BACK TO SOME NOSTALGIC AND OFTEN IMAGINARY GOLDEN AGE. THE CONSERVATIVE MOVEMENT IS NOT FILLED WITH UNCARING SOCIOPATHS. THEY HAVE A STRONG SENSE OF MORALITY.

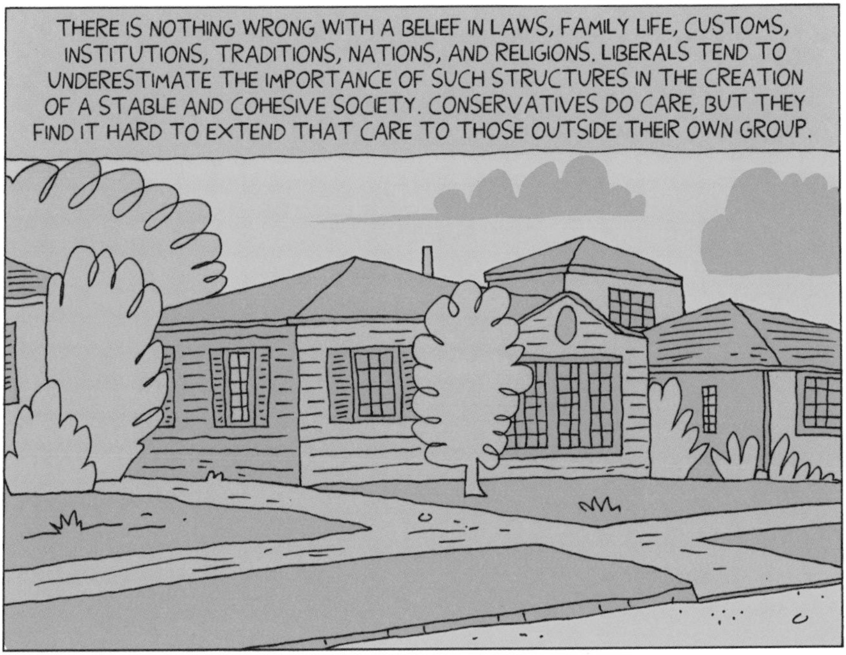
THERE IS NOTHING WRONG WITH A BELIEF IN LAWS, FAMILY LIFE, CUSTOMS, INSTITUTIONS, TRADITIONS, NATIONS, AND RELIGIONS. LIBERALS TEND TO UNDERESTIMATE THE IMPORTANCE OF SUCH STRUCTURES IN THE CREATION OF A STABLE AND COHESIVE SOCIETY. CONSERVATIVES DO CARE, BUT THEY FIND IT HARD TO EXTEND THAT CARE TO THOSE OUTSIDE THEIR OWN GROUP.

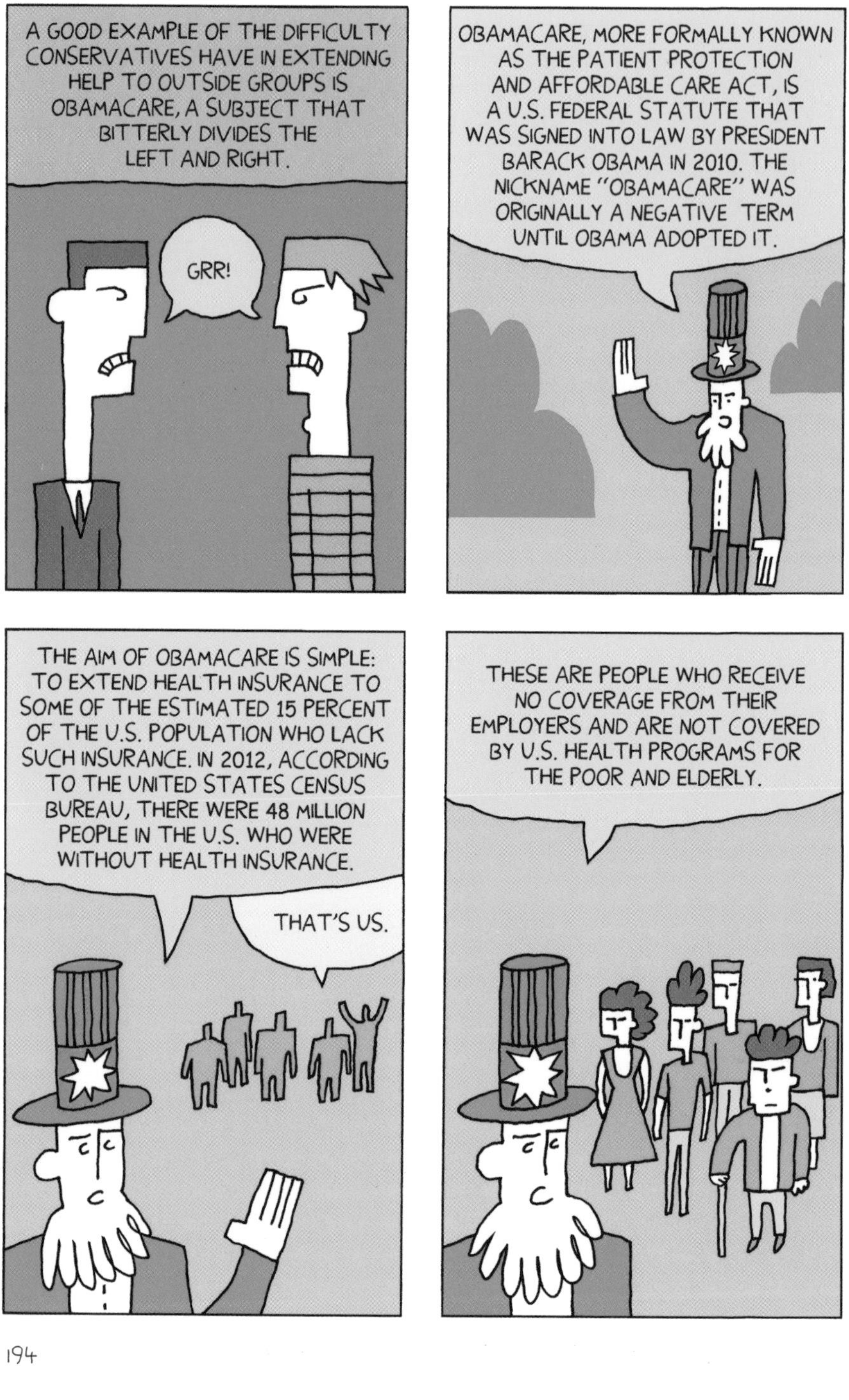
A GOOD EXAMPLE OF THE DIFFICULTY CONSERVATIVES HAVE IN EXTENDING HELP TO OUTSIDE GROUPS IS OBAMACARE, A SUBJECT THAT BITTERLY DIVIDES THE LEFT AND RIGHT.
GRR!
OBAMACARE, MORE FORMALLY KNOWN AS THE PATIENT PROTECTION AND AFFORDABLE CARE ACT, IS A U.S. FEDERAL STATUTE THAT WAS SIGNED INTO LAW BY PRESIDENT BARACK OBAMA IN 2010. THE NICKNAME "OBAMACARE" WAS ORIGINALLY A NEGATIVE TERM UNTIL OBAMA ADOPTED IT.
THE AIM OF OBAMACARE IS SIMPLE: TO EXTEND HEALTH INSURANCE TO SOME OF THE ESTIMATED 15 PERCENT OF THE U.S. POPULATION WHO LACK SUCH INSURANCE. IN 2012, ACCORDING TO THE UNITED STATES CENSUS BUREAU, THERE WERE 48 MILLION PEOPLE IN THE U.S. WHO WERE WITHOUT HEALTH INSURANCE.
THAT'S US.
THESE ARE PEOPLE WHO RECEIVE NO COVERAGE FROM THEIR EMPLOYERS AND ARE NOT COVERED BY U.S. HEALTH PROGRAMS FOR THE POOR AND ELDERLY.

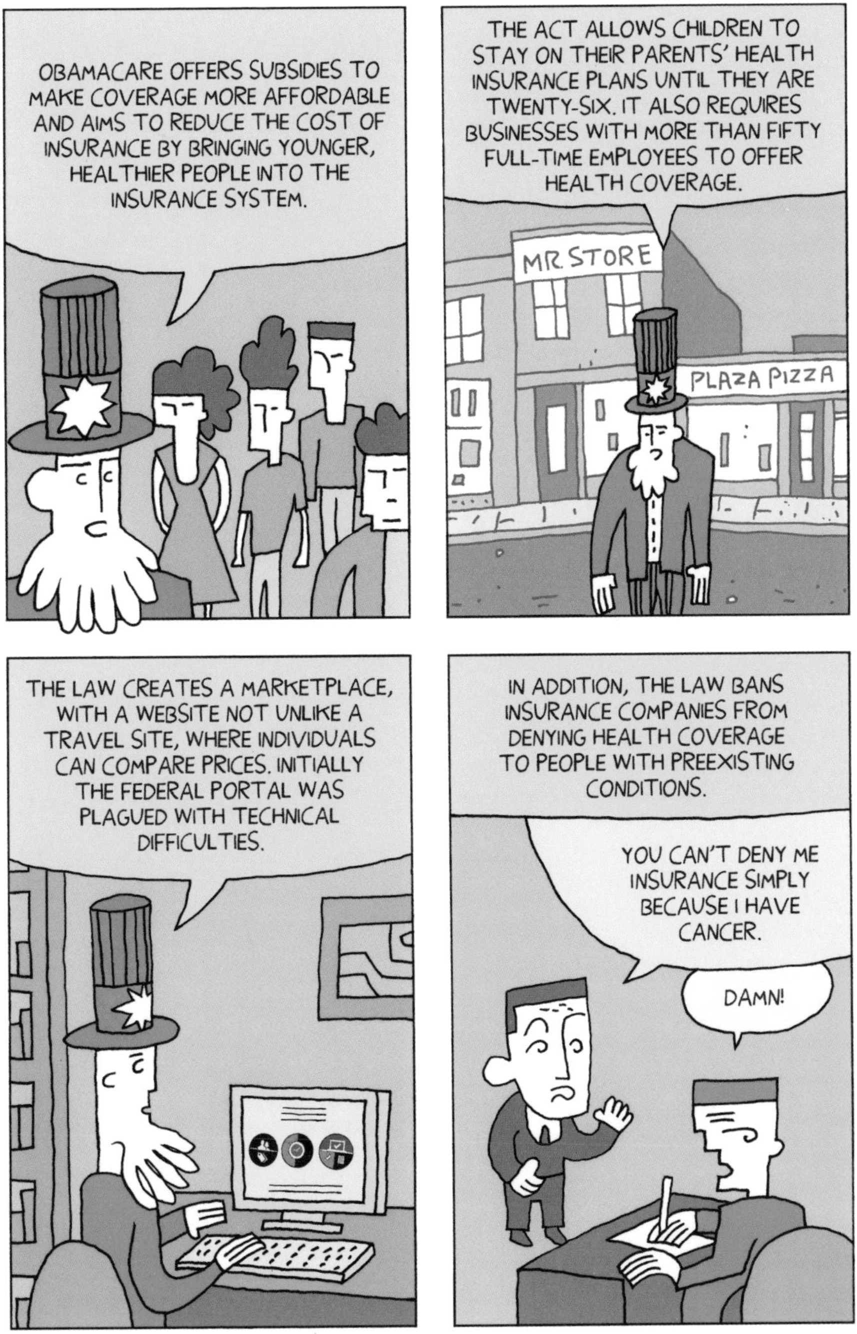
OBAMACARE OFFERS SUBSIDIES TO MAKE COVERAGE MORE AFFORDABLE AND AIMS TO REDUCE THE COST OF INSURANCE BY BRINGING YOUNGER, HEALTHIER PEOPLE INTO THE INSURANCE SYSTEM.
THE ACT ALLOWS CHILDREN TO STAY ON THEIR PARENTS' HEALTH INSURANCE PLANS UNTIL THEY ARE TWENTY-SIX. IT ALSO REQUIRES BUSINESSES WITH MORE THAN FIFTY FULL-TIME EMPLOYEES TO OFFER HEALTH COVERAGE.
MR. STORE
PLAZA PIZZA
THE LAW CREATES A MARKETPLACE, WITH A WEBSITE NOT UNLIKE A TRAVEL SITE, WHERE INDIVIDUALS CAN COMPARE PRICES. INITIALLY THE FEDERAL PORTAL WAS PLAGUED WITH TECHNICAL DIFFICULTIES.
IN ADDITION, THE LAW BANS INSURANCE COMPANIES FROM DENYING HEALTH COVERAGE TO PEOPLE WITH PREEXISTING CONDITIONS.
YOU CAN'T DENY ME INSURANCE SIMPLY BECAUSE I HAVE CANCER.
DAMN!

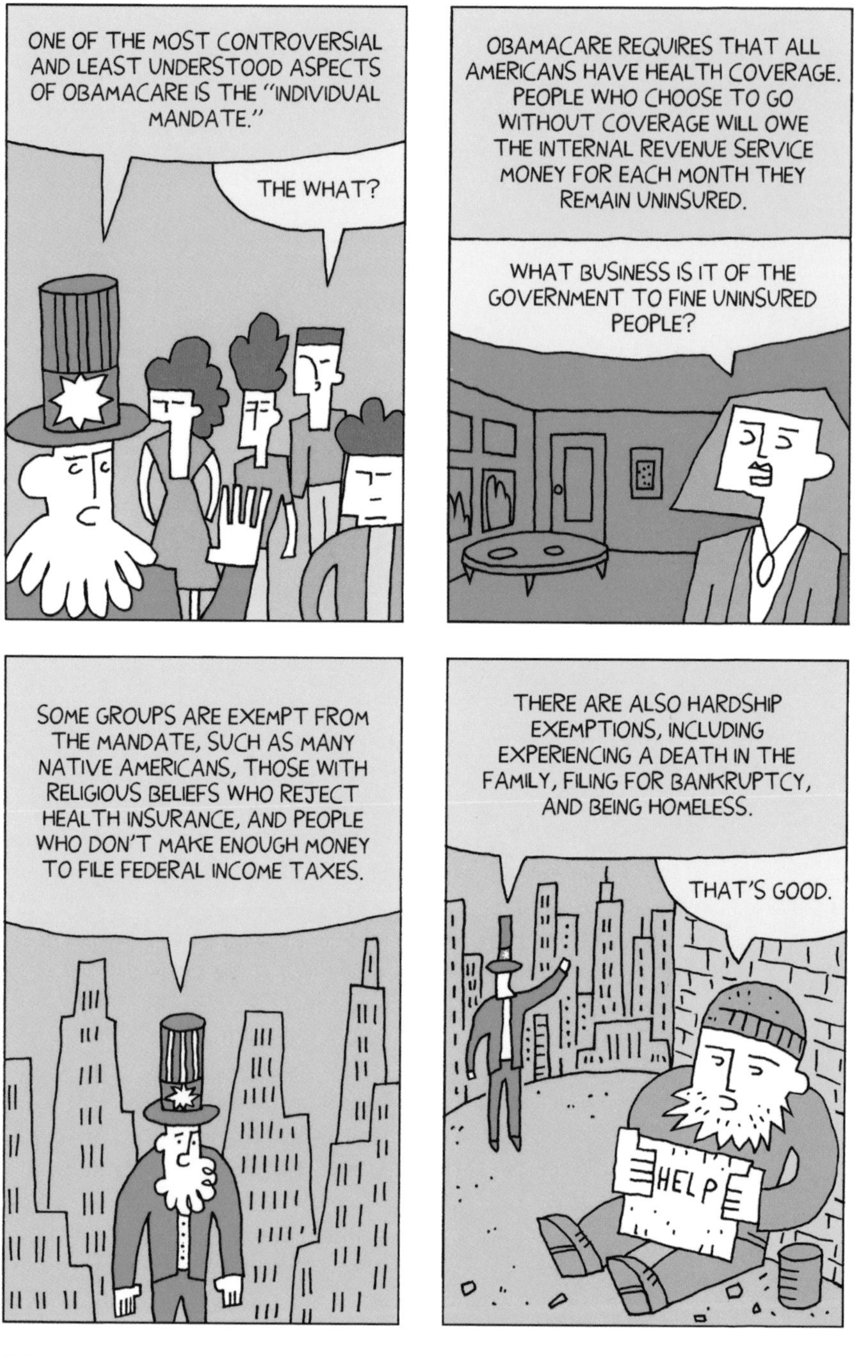
ONE OF THE MOST CONTROVERSIAL AND LEAST UNDERSTOOD ASPECTS OF OBAMACARE IS THE "INDIVIDUAL MANDATE."
THE WHAT?
OBAMACARE REQUIRES THAT ALL AMERICANS HAVE HEALTH COVERAGE. PEOPLE WHO CHOOSE TO GO WITHOUT COVERAGE WILL OWE THE INTERNAL REVENUE SERVICE MONEY FOR EACH MONTH THEY REMAIN UNINSURED.
WHAT BUSINESS IS IT OF THE GOVERNMENT TO FINE UNINSURED PEOPLE?
SOME GROUPS ARE EXEMPT FROM THE MANDATE, SUCH AS MANY NATIVE AMERICANS, THOSE WITH RELIGIOUS BELIEFS WHO REJECT HEALTH INSURANCE, AND PEOPLE WHO DON'T MAKE ENOUGH MONEY TO FILE FEDERAL INCOME TAXES.
THERE ARE ALSO HARDSHIP EXEMPTIONS, INCLUDING EXPERIENCING A DEATH IN THE FAMILY, FILING FOR BANKRUPTCY, AND BEING HOMELESS.
THAT'S GOOD.
HELP

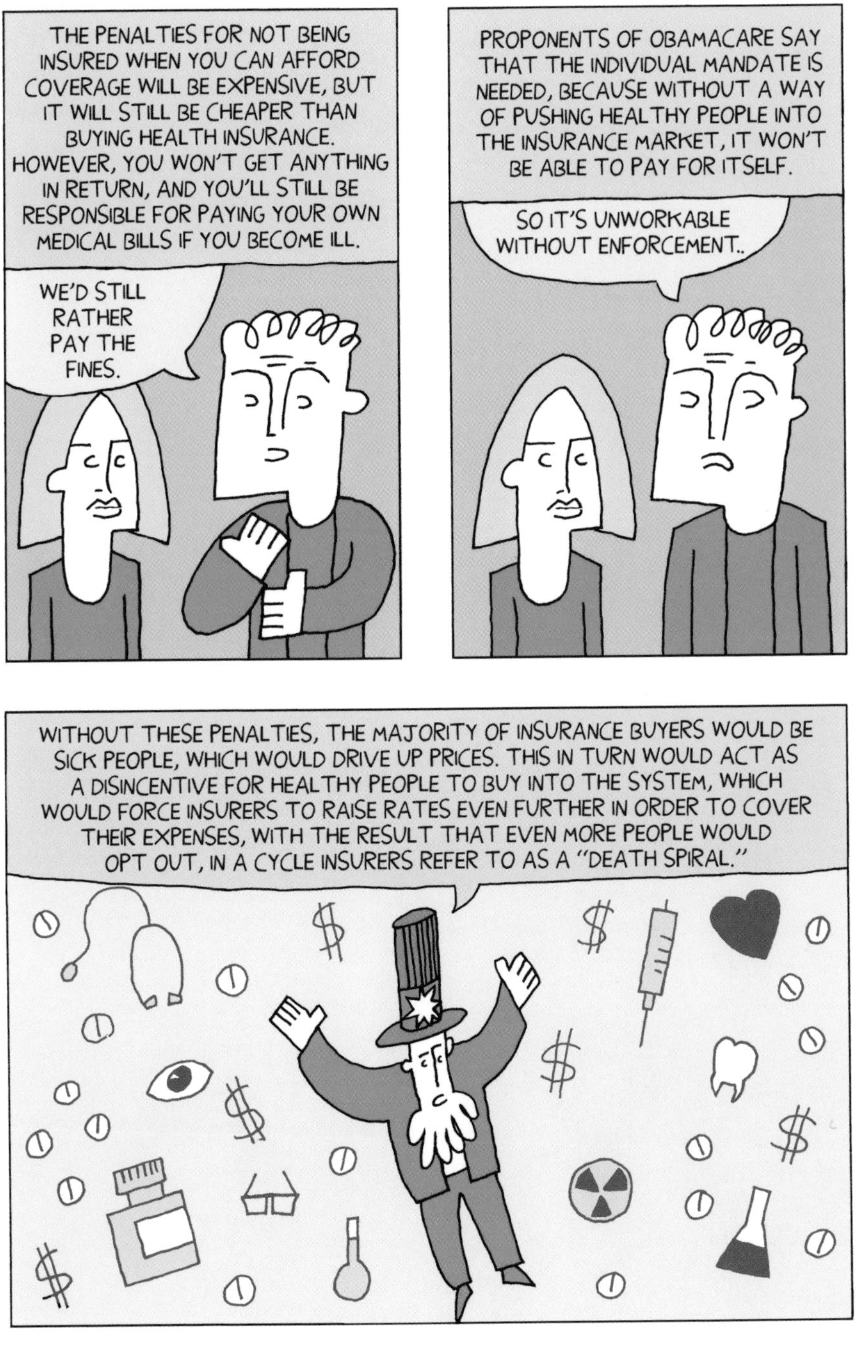
THE PENALTIES FOR NOT BEING INSURED WHEN YOU CAN AFFORD COVERAGE WILL BE EXPENSIVE, BUT IT WILL STILL BE CHEAPER THAN BUYING HEALTH INSURANCE. HOWEVER, YOU WON'T GET ANYTHING IN RETURN, AND YOU'LL STILL BE RESPONSIBLE FOR PAYING YOUR OWN MEDICAL BILLS IF YOU BECOME ILL.
WE'D STILL RATHER PAY THE FINES.
PROPONENTS OF OBAMACARE SAY THAT THE INDIVIDUAL MANDATE IS NEEDED, BECAUSE WITHOUT A WAY OF PUSHING HEALTHY PEOPLE INTO THE INSURANCE MARKET, IT WON'T BE ABLE TO PAY FOR ITSELF.
SO IT'S UNWORKABLE WITHOUT ENFORCEMENT..
WITHOUT THESE PENALTIES, THE MAJORITY OF INSURANCE BUYERS WOULD BE SICK PEOPLE, WHICH WOULD DRIVE UP PRICES. THIS IN TURN WOULD ACT AS A DISINCENTIVE FOR HEALTHY PEOPLE TO BUY INTO THE SYSTEM, WHICH WOULD FORCE INSURERS TO RAISE RATES EVEN FURTHER IN ORDER TO COVER THEIR EXPENSES, WITH THE RESULT THAT EVEN MORE PEOPLE WOULD OPT OUT, IN A CYCLE INSURERS REFER TO AS A "DEATH SPIRAL."

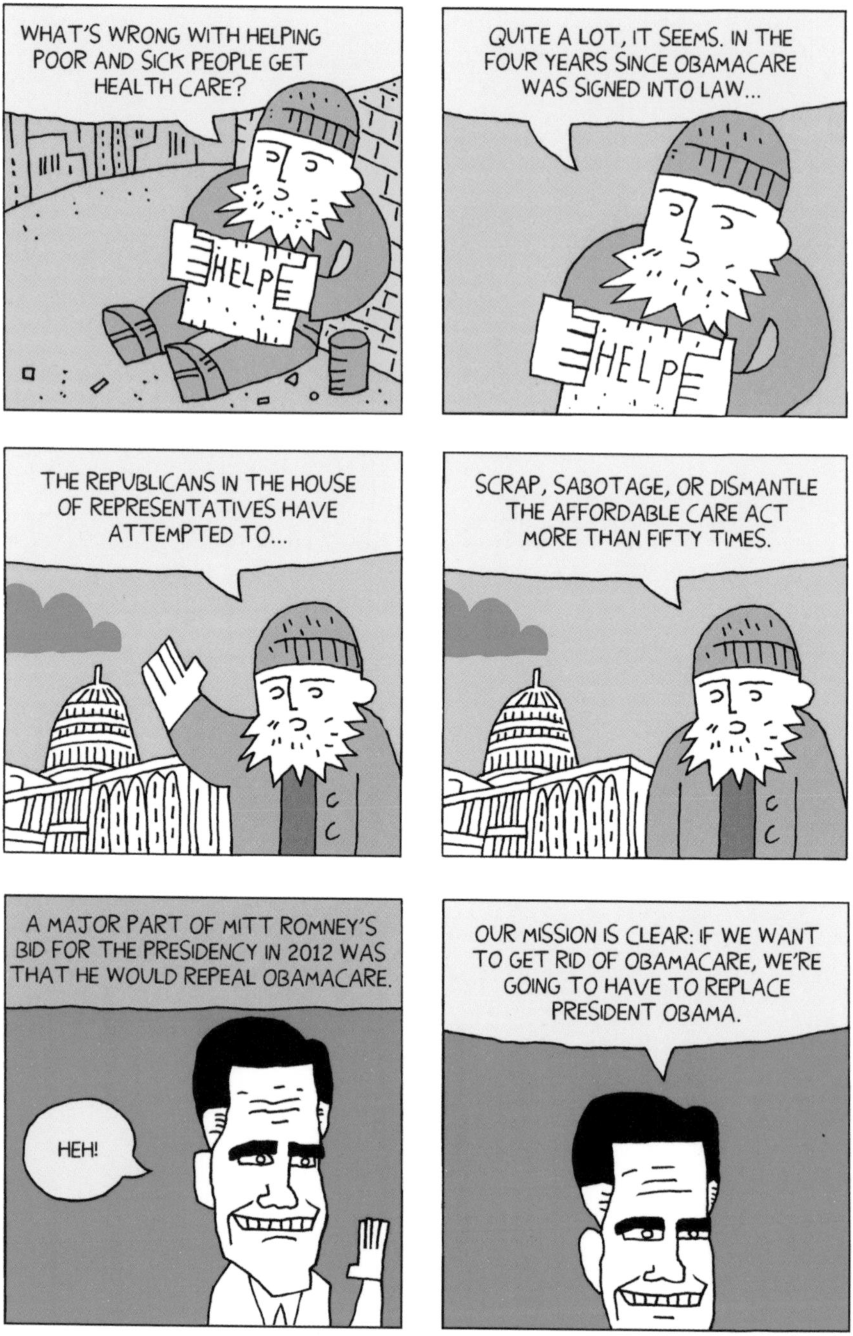
WHAT'S WRONG WITH HELPING POOR AND SICK PEOPLE GET HEALTH CARE?
HELP
QUITE A LOT, IT SEEMS. IN THE FOUR YEARS SINCE OBAMACARE WAS SIGNED INTO LAW...
HELP
THE REPUBLICANS IN THE HOUSE OF REPRESENTATIVES HAVE ATTEMPTED TO...
SCRAP, SABOTAGE, OR DISMANTLE THE AFFORDABLE CARE ACT MORE THAN FIFTY TIMES.
A MAJOR PART OF MITT ROMNEY'S BID FOR THE PRESIDENCY IN 2012 WAS THAT HE WOULD REPEAL OBAMACARE.
HEH!
OUR MISSION IS CLEAR: IF WE WANT TO GET RID OF OBAMACARE, WE'RE GOING TO HAVE TO REPLACE PRESIDENT OBAMA.

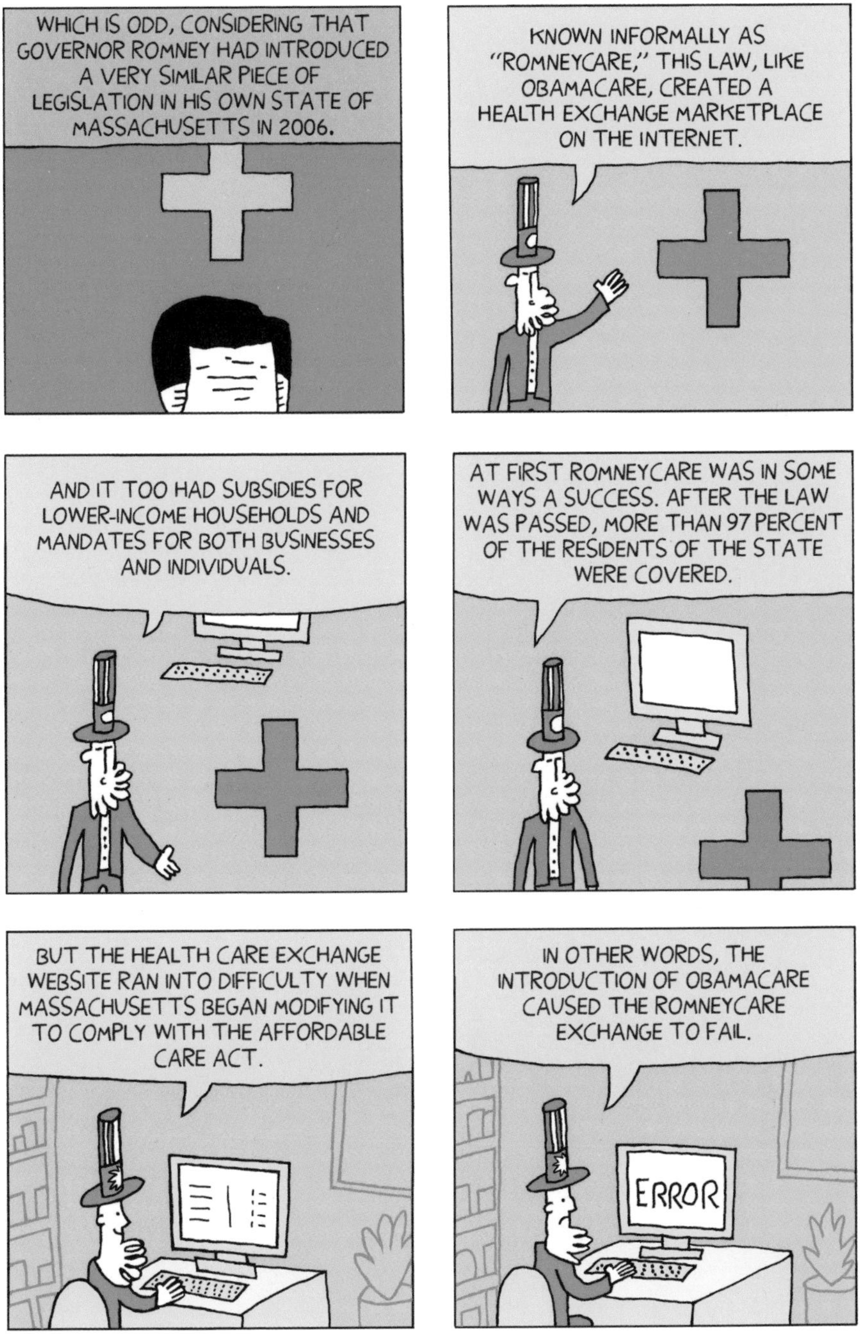
WHICH IS ODD, CONSIDERING THAT GOVERNOR ROMNEY HAD INTRODUCED A VERY SIMILAR PIECE OF LEGISLATION IN HIS OWN STATE OF MASSACHUSETTS IN 2006.
KNOWN INFORMALLY AS "ROMNEYCARE," THIS LAW, LIKE OBAMACARE, CREATED A HEALTH EXCHANGE MARKETPLACE ON THE INTERNET.
AND IT TOO HAD SUBSIDIES FOR LOWER-INCOME HOUSEHOLDS AND MANDATES FOR BOTH BUSINESSES AND INDIVIDUALS.
AT FIRST ROMNEYCARE WAS IN SOME WAYS A SUCCESS. AFTER THE LAW WAS PASSED, MORE THAN 97 PERCENT OF THE RESIDENTS OF THE STATE WERE COVERED.
BUT THE HEALTH CARE EXCHANGE WEBSITE RAN INTO DIFFICULTY WHEN MASSACHUSETTS BEGAN MODIFYING IT TO COMPLY WITH THE AFFORDABLE CARE ACT.
IN OTHER WORDS, THE INTRODUCTION OF OBAMACARE CAUSED THE ROMNEYCARE EXCHANGE TO FAIL.
ERROR

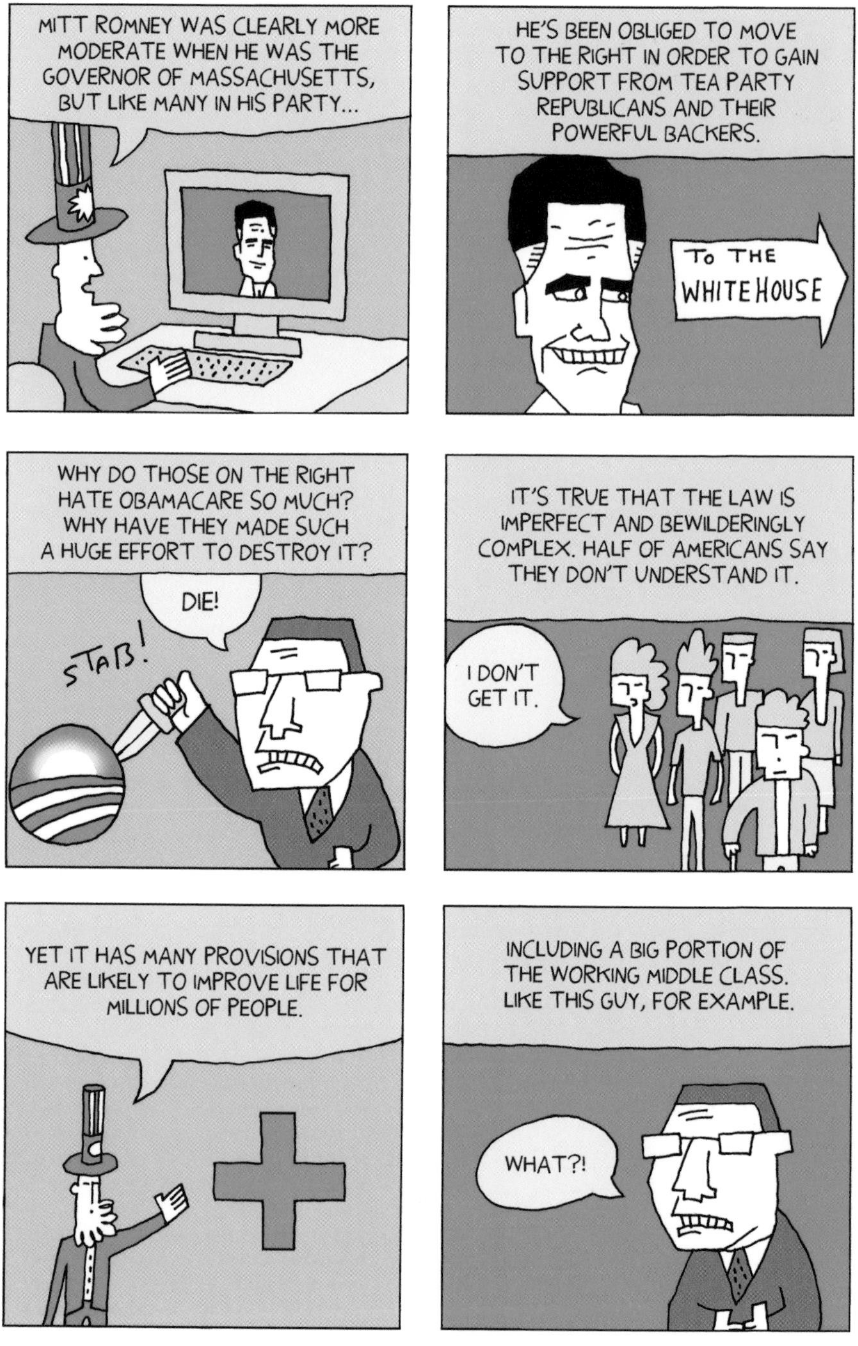
MITT ROMNEY WAS CLEARLY MORE MODERATE WHEN HE WAS THE GOVERNOR OF MASSACHUSETTS, BUT LIKE MANY IN HIS PARTY...
HE'S BEEN OBLIGED TO MOVE TO THE RIGHT IN ORDER TO GAIN SUPPORT FROM TEA PARTY REPUBLICANS AND THEIR POWERFUL BACKERS.
TO THE WHITE HOUSE
WHY DO THOSE ON THE RIGHT HATE OBAMACARE SO MUCH? WHY HAVE THEY MADE SUCH A HUGE EFFORT TO DESTROY IT?
DIE!
STAB!
IT'S TRUE THAT THE LAW IS IMPERFECT AND BEWILDERINGLY COMPLEX. HALF OF AMERICANS SAY THEY DON'T UNDERSTAND IT.
I DON'T GET IT.
YET IT HAS MANY PROVISIONS THAT ARE LIKELY TO IMPROVE LIFE FOR MILLIONS OF PEOPLE.
INCLUDING A BIG PORTION OF THE WORKING MIDDLE CLASS. LIKE THIS GUY, FOR EXAMPLE.
WHAT?!

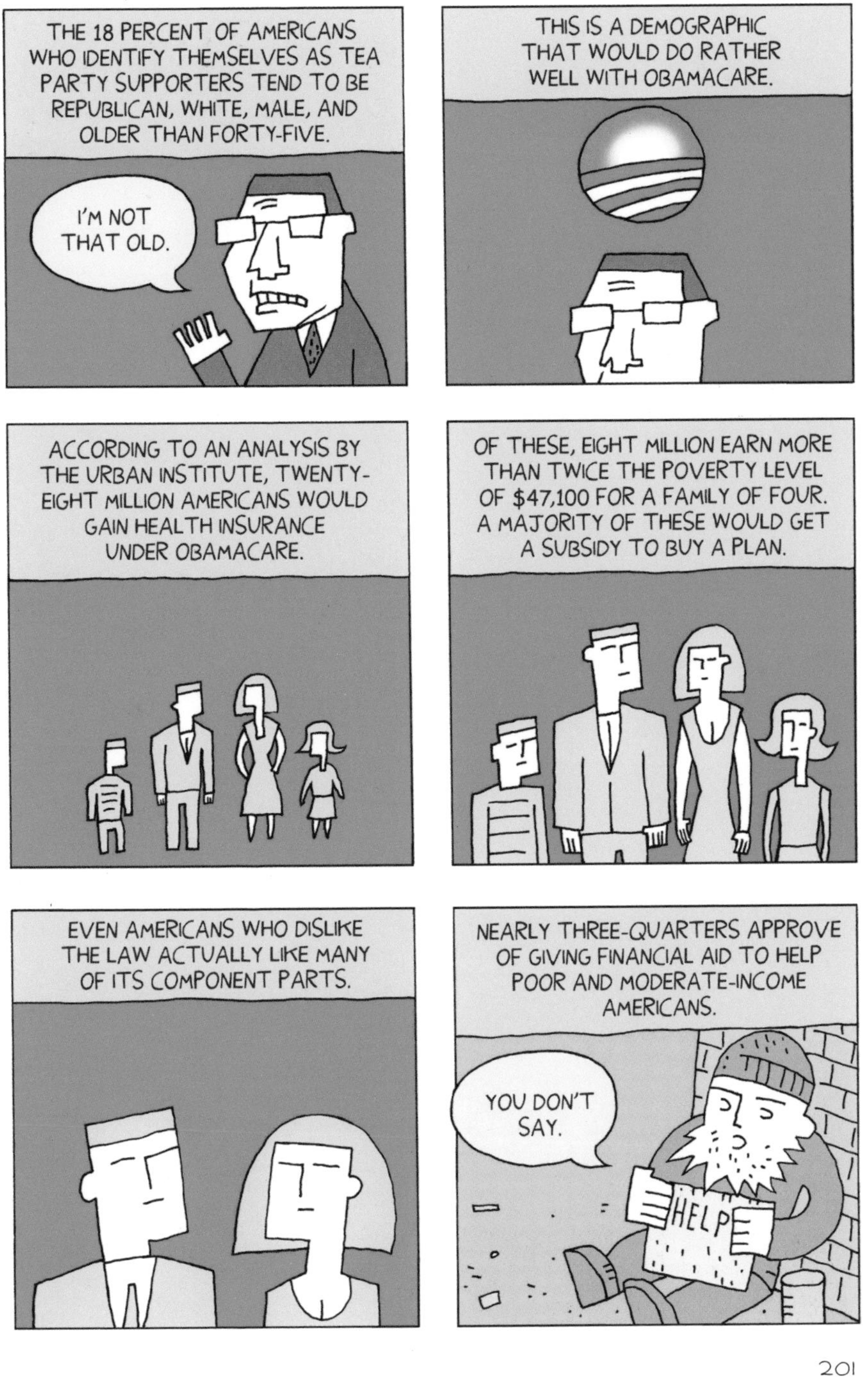
THE 18 PERCENT OF AMERICANS WHO IDENTIFY THEMSELVES AS TEA PARTY SUPPORTERS TEND TO BE REPUBLICAN, WHITE, MALE, AND OLDER THAN FORTY-FIVE.
I'M NOT THAT OLD.
THIS IS A DEMOGRAPHIC THAT WOULD DO RATHER WELL WITH OBAMACARE.
ACCORDING TO AN ANALYSIS BY THE URBAN INSTITUTE, TWENTY-EIGHT MILLION AMERICANS WOULD GAIN HEALTH INSURANCE UNDER OBAMACARE.
OF THESE, EIGHT MILLION EARN MORE THAN TWICE THE POVERTY LEVEL OF $47,100 FOR A FAMILY OF FOUR. A MAJORITY OF THESE WOULD GET A SUBSIDY TO BUY A PLAN.
EVEN AMERICANS WHO DISLIKE THE LAW ACTUALLY LIKE MANY OF ITS COMPONENT PARTS.
NEARLY THREE-QUARTERS APPROVE OF GIVING FINANCIAL AID TO HELP POOR AND MODERATE-INCOME AMERICANS.
YOU DON'T SAY.
HELP

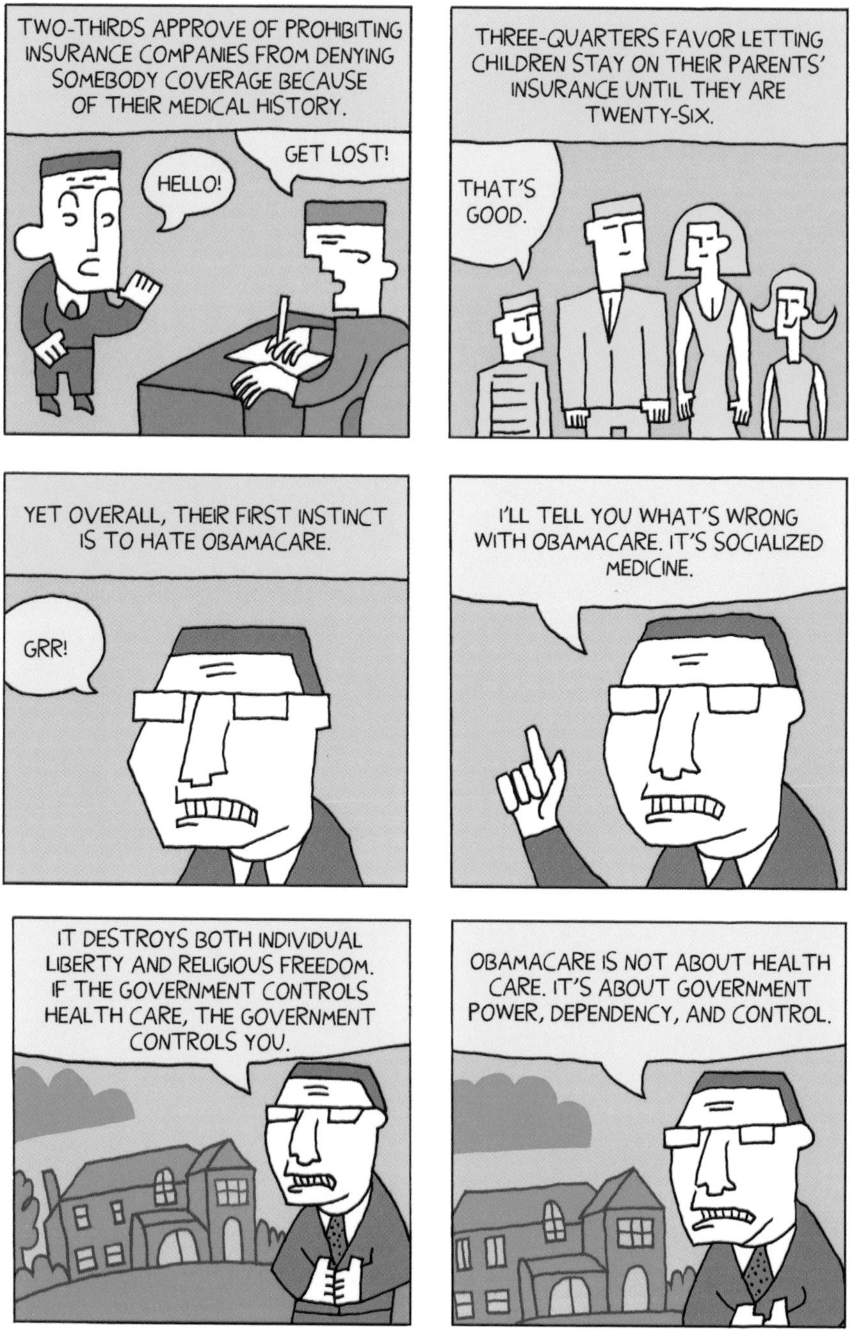
TWO-THIRDS APPROVE OF PROHIBITING INSURANCE COMPANIES FROM DENYING SOMEBODY COVERAGE BECAUSE OF THEIR MEDICAL HISTORY.
HELLO!
GET LOST!
THREE-QUARTERS FAVOR LETTING CHILDREN STAY ON THEIR PARENTS' INSURANCE UNTIL THEY ARE TWENTY-SIX.
THAT'S GOOD.
YET OVERALL, THEIR FIRST INSTINCT IS TO HATE OBAMACARE.
GRR!
I'LL TELL YOU WHAT'S WRONG WITH OBAMACARE. IT'S SOCIALIZED MEDICINE.
IT DESTROYS BOTH INDIVIDUAL LIBERTY AND RELIGIOUS FREEDOM. IF THE GOVERNMENT CONTROLS HEALTH CARE, THE GOVERNMENT CONTROLS YOU.
OBAMACARE IS NOT ABOUT HEALTH CARE. IT'S ABOUT GOVERNMENT POWER, DEPENDENCY, AND CONTROL.

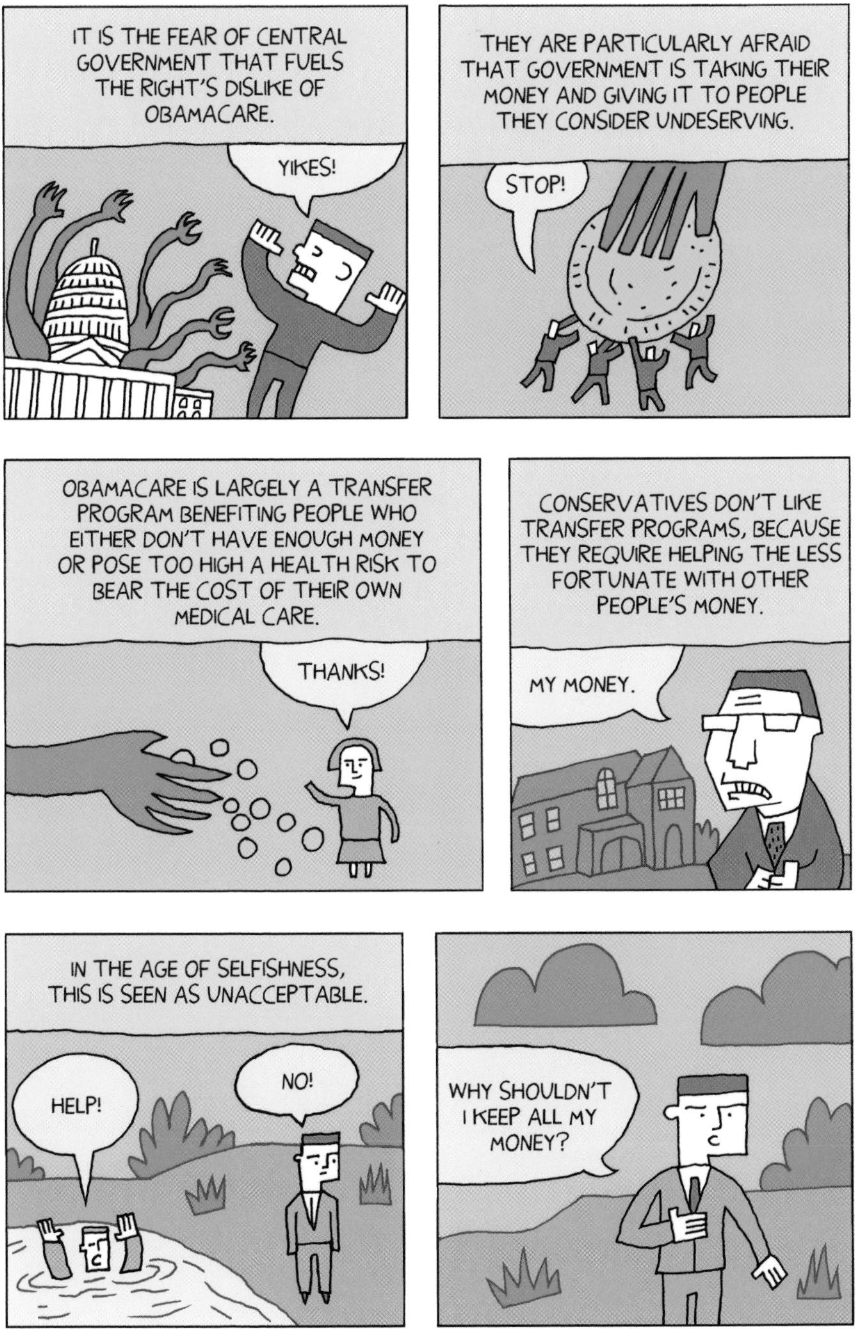
IT IS THE FEAR OF CENTRAL GOVERNMENT THAT FUELS THE RIGHT'S DISLIKE OF OBAMACARE.
YIKES!
THEY ARE PARTICULARLY AFRAID THAT GOVERNMENT IS TAKING THEIR MONEY AND GIVING IT TO PEOPLE THEY CONSIDER UNDESERVING.
STOP!
OBAMACARE IS LARGELY A TRANSFER PROGRAM BENEFITING PEOPLE WHO EITHER DON'T HAVE ENOUGH MONEY OR POSE TOO HIGH A HEALTH RISK TO BEAR THE COST OF THEIR OWN MEDICAL CARE.
THANKS!
CONSERVATIVES DON'T LIKE TRANSFER PROGRAMS, BECAUSE THEY REQUIRE HELPING THE LESS FORTUNATE WITH OTHER PEOPLE'S MONEY.
MY MONEY.
IN THE AGE OF SELFISHNESS, THIS IS SEEN AS UNACCEPTABLE.
HELP!
NO!
WHY SHOULDN'T I KEEP ALL MY MONEY?

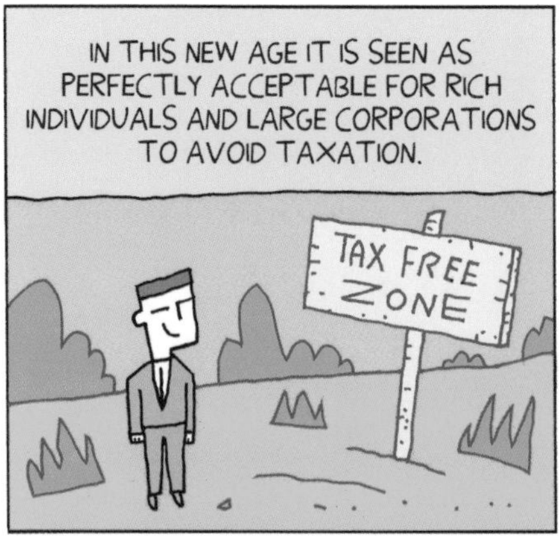
IN THIS NEW AGE IT IS SEEN AS PERFECTLY ACCEPTABLE FOR RICH INDIVIDUALS AND LARGE CORPORATIONS TO AVOID TAXATION.
TAX FREE ZONE

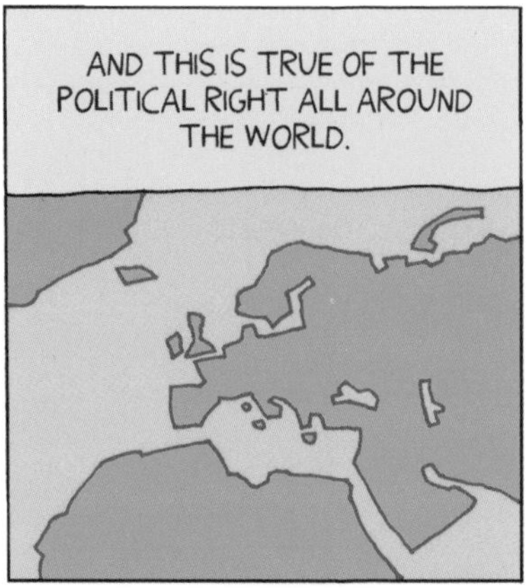
AND THIS IS TRUE OF THE POLITICAL RIGHT ALL AROUND THE WORLD.

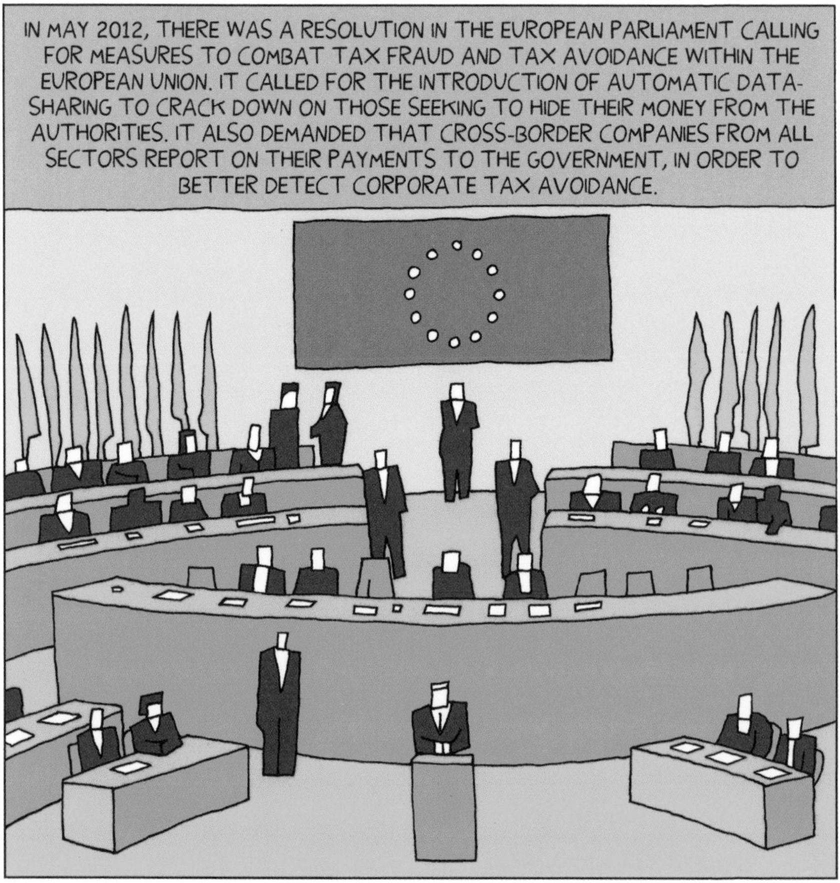
IN MAY 2012, THERE WAS A RESOLUTION IN THE EUROPEAN PARLIAMENT CALLING FOR MEASURES TO COMBAT TAX FRAUD AND TAX AVOIDANCE WITHIN THE EUROPEAN UNION. IT CALLED FOR THE INTRODUCTION OF AUTOMATIC DATA-SHARING TO CRACK DOWN ON THOSE SEEKING TO HIDE THEIR MONEY FROM THE AUTHORITIES. IT ALSO DEMANDED THAT CROSS-BORDER COMPANIES FROM ALL SECTORS REPORT ON THEIR PAYMENTS TO THE GOVERNMENT, IN ORDER TO BETTER DETECT CORPORATE TAX AVOIDANCE.

THE RESOLUTION WAS BACKED BY ALL THE MAJOR EUROPEAN GROUPS, INCLUDING THE SOCIALISTS AND DEMOCRATS, THE EUROPEAN PEOPLE'S PARTY, THE ALLIANCE OF LIBERALS AND DEMOCRATS FOR EUROPE, AND THE GREENS...

BUT NOT BY THE BRITISH CONSERVATIVES, WHO VOTED AGAINST THE MEASURES, ALONG WITH THE UNITED KINGDOM INDEPENDENCE PARTY.

FIGURES PUBLISHED BY THE CHARITY ACTIONAID IN 2013 SHOWED THAT, OF THE TOP 100 COMPANIES LISTED ON THE U.K. FINANCIAL TIMES SHARE INDEX, ONLY TWO DID NOT USE TAX HAVENS AS A TACTIC TO AVOID PAYING CORPORATION TAX.

THESE COMPANIES INCLUDED STARBUCKS, AMAZON, GOOGLE, VODAFONE, AND APPLE. ALSO ON THE LIST WERE BANKS SUCH AS BARCLAYS, HSBC, THE ROYAL BANK OF SCOTLAND, AND LLOYD'S.

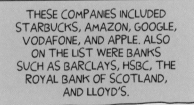

IF I BOYCOTTED ALL THESE TAX-AVOIDING FIRMS, I WOULDN'T BE ABLE TO SHOP, BANK, OR USE THE INTERNET.

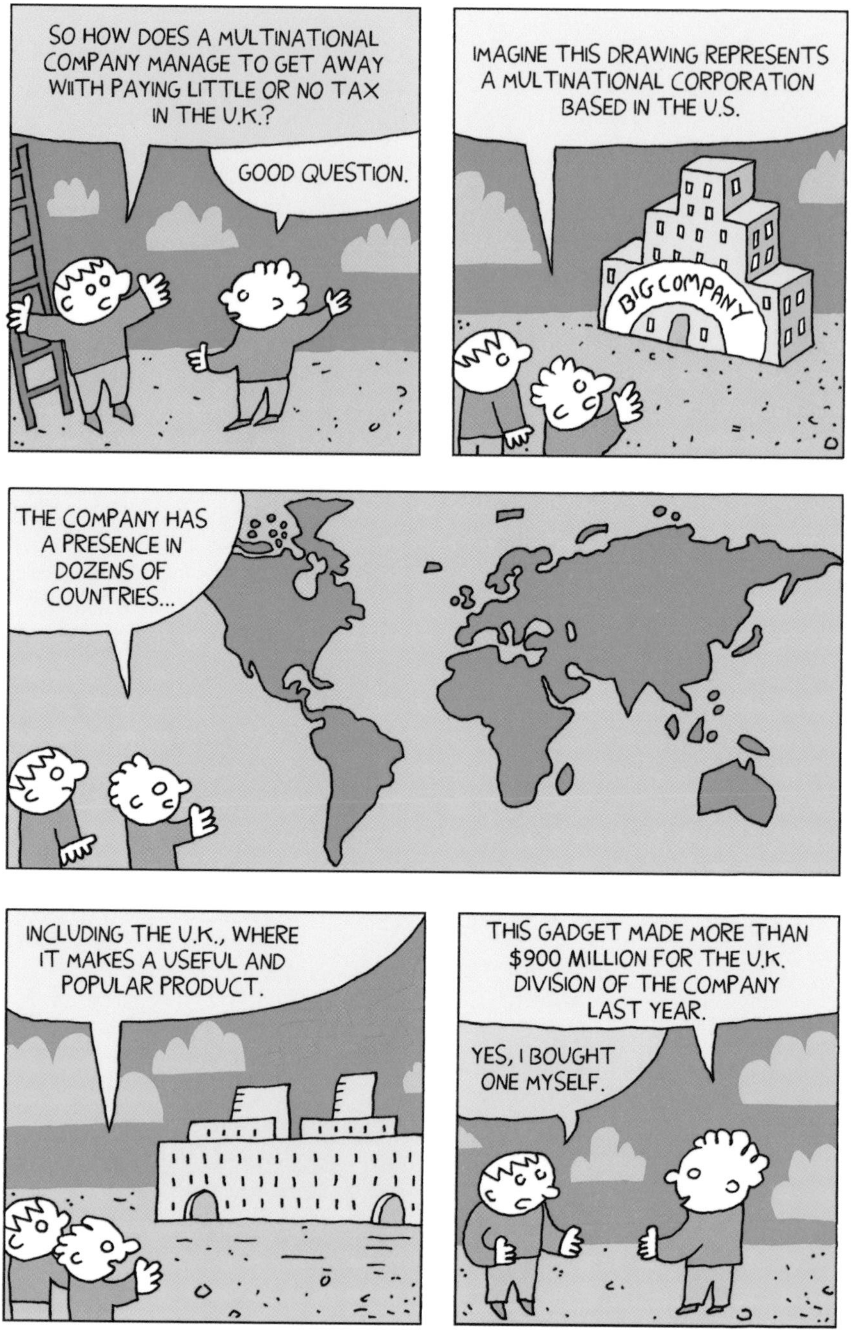
SO HOW DOES A MULTINATIONAL COMPANY MANAGE TO GET AWAY WIITH PAYING LITTLE OR NO TAX IN THE U.K.?
GOOD QUESTION.
IMAGINE THIS DRAWING REPRESENTS A MULTINATIONAL CORPORATION BASED IN THE U.S.
BIG COMPANY
THE COMPANY HAS A PRESENCE IN DOZENS OF COUNTRIES...
INCLUDING THE U.K., WHERE IT MAKES A USEFUL AND POPULAR PRODUCT.
THIS GADGET MADE MORE THAN $900 MILLION FOR THE U.K. DIVISION OF THE COMPANY LAST YEAR.
YES, I BOUGHT ONE MYSELF.

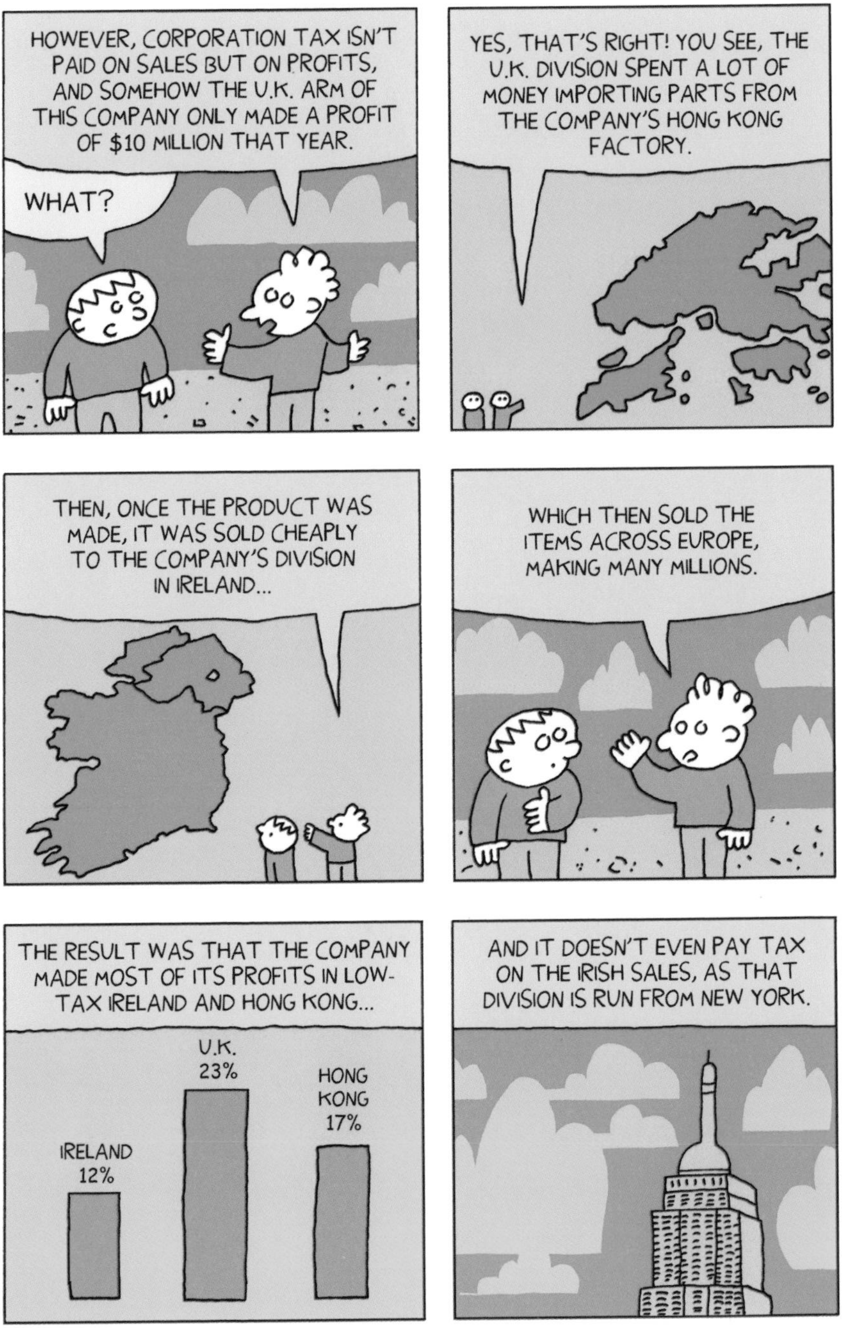
HOWEVER, CORPORATION TAX ISN'T PAID ON SALES BUT ON PROFITS, AND SOMEHOW THE U.K. ARM OF THIS COMPANY ONLY MADE A PROFIT OF $10 MILLION THAT YEAR.
WHAT?
YES, THAT'S RIGHT! YOU SEE, THE U.K. DIVISION SPENT A LOT OF MONEY IMPORTING PARTS FROM THE COMPANY'S HONG KONG FACTORY.
THEN, ONCE THE PRODUCT WAS MADE, IT WAS SOLD CHEAPLY TO THE COMPANY'S DIVISION IN IRELAND...
WHICH THEN SOLD THE ITEMS ACROSS EUROPE, MAKING MANY MILLIONS.
THE RESULT WAS THAT THE COMPANY MADE MOST OF ITS PROFITS IN LOW-TAX IRELAND AND HONG KONG...
IRELAND 12%
U.K. 23%
HONG KONG 17%
AND IT DOESN'T EVEN PAY TAX ON THE IRISH SALES, AS THAT DIVISION IS RUN FROM NEW YORK.

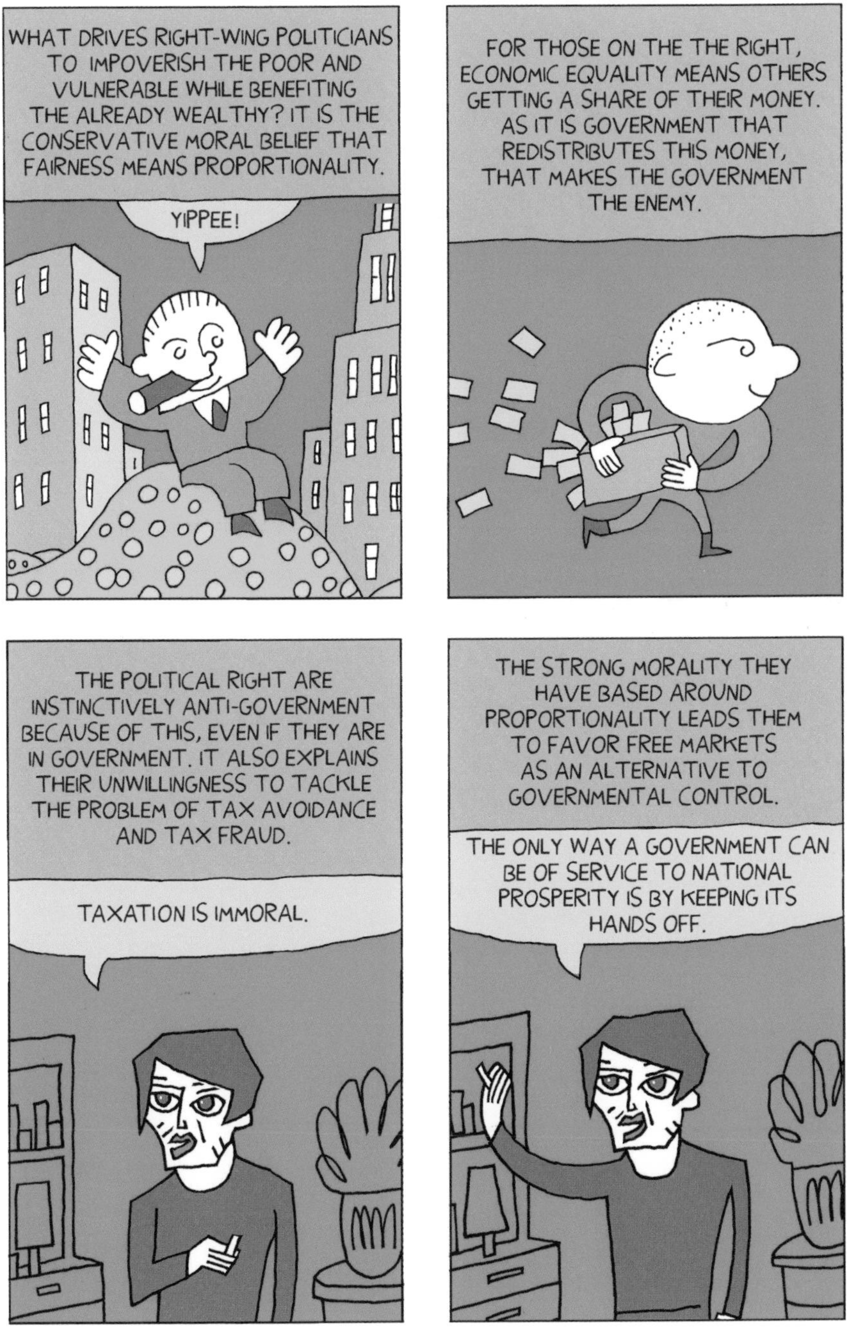
WHAT DRIVES RIGHT-WING POLITICIANS TO IMPOVERISH THE POOR AND VULNERABLE WHILE BENEFITING THE ALREADY WEALTHY? IT IS THE CONSERVATIVE MORAL BELIEF THAT FAIRNESS MEANS PROPORTIONALITY.
YIPPEE!
FOR THOSE ON THE THE RIGHT, ECONOMIC EQUALITY MEANS OTHERS GETTING A SHARE OF THEIR MONEY. AS IT IS GOVERNMENT THAT REDISTRIBUTES THIS MONEY, THAT MAKES THE GOVERNMENT THE ENEMY.
THE POLITICAL RIGHT ARE INSTINCTIVELY ANTI-GOVERNMENT BECAUSE OF THIS, EVEN IF THEY ARE IN GOVERNMENT. IT ALSO EXPLAINS THEIR UNWILLINGNESS TO TACKLE THE PROBLEM OF TAX AVOIDANCE AND TAX FRAUD.
TAXATION IS IMMORAL.
THE STRONG MORALITY THEY HAVE BASED AROUND PROPORTIONALITY LEADS THEM TO FAVOR FREE MARKETS AS AN ALTERNATIVE TO GOVERNMENTAL CONTROL.
THE ONLY WAY A GOVERNMENT CAN BE OF SERVICE TO NATIONAL PROSPERITY IS BY KEEPING ITS HANDS OFF.

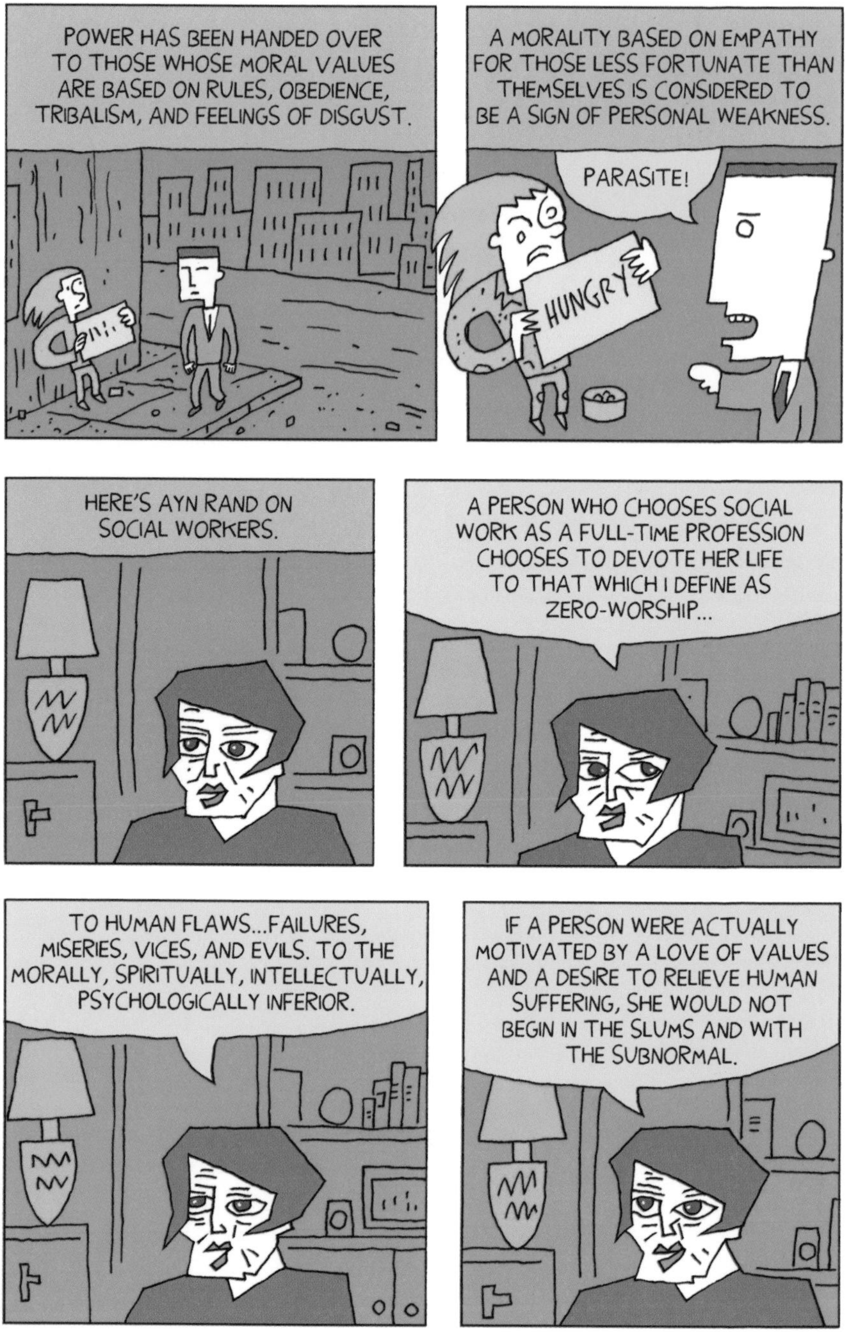
POWER HAS BEEN HANDED OVER TO THOSE WHOSE MORAL VALUES ARE BASED ON RULES, OBEDIENCE, TRIBALISM, AND FEELINGS OF DISGUST.
A MORALITY BASED ON EMPATHY FOR THOSE LESS FORTUNATE THAN THEMSELVES IS CONSIDERED TO BE A SIGN OF PERSONAL WEAKNESS.
PARASITE!
HUNGRY
HERE'S AYN RAND ON SOCIAL WORKERS.
A PERSON WHO CHOOSES SOCIAL WORK AS A FULL-TIME PROFESSION CHOOSES TO DEVOTE HER LIFE TO THAT WHICH I DEFINE AS ZERO-WORSHIP...
TO HUMAN FLAWS...FAILURES, MISERIES, VICES, AND EVILS. TO THE MORALLY, SPIRITUALLY, INTELLECTUALLY, PSYCHOLOGICALLY INFERIOR.
IF A PERSON WERE ACTUALLY MOTIVATED BY A LOVE OF VALUES AND A DESIRE TO RELIEVE HUMAN SUFFERING, SHE WOULD NOT BEGIN IN THE SLUMS AND WITH THE SUBNORMAL.

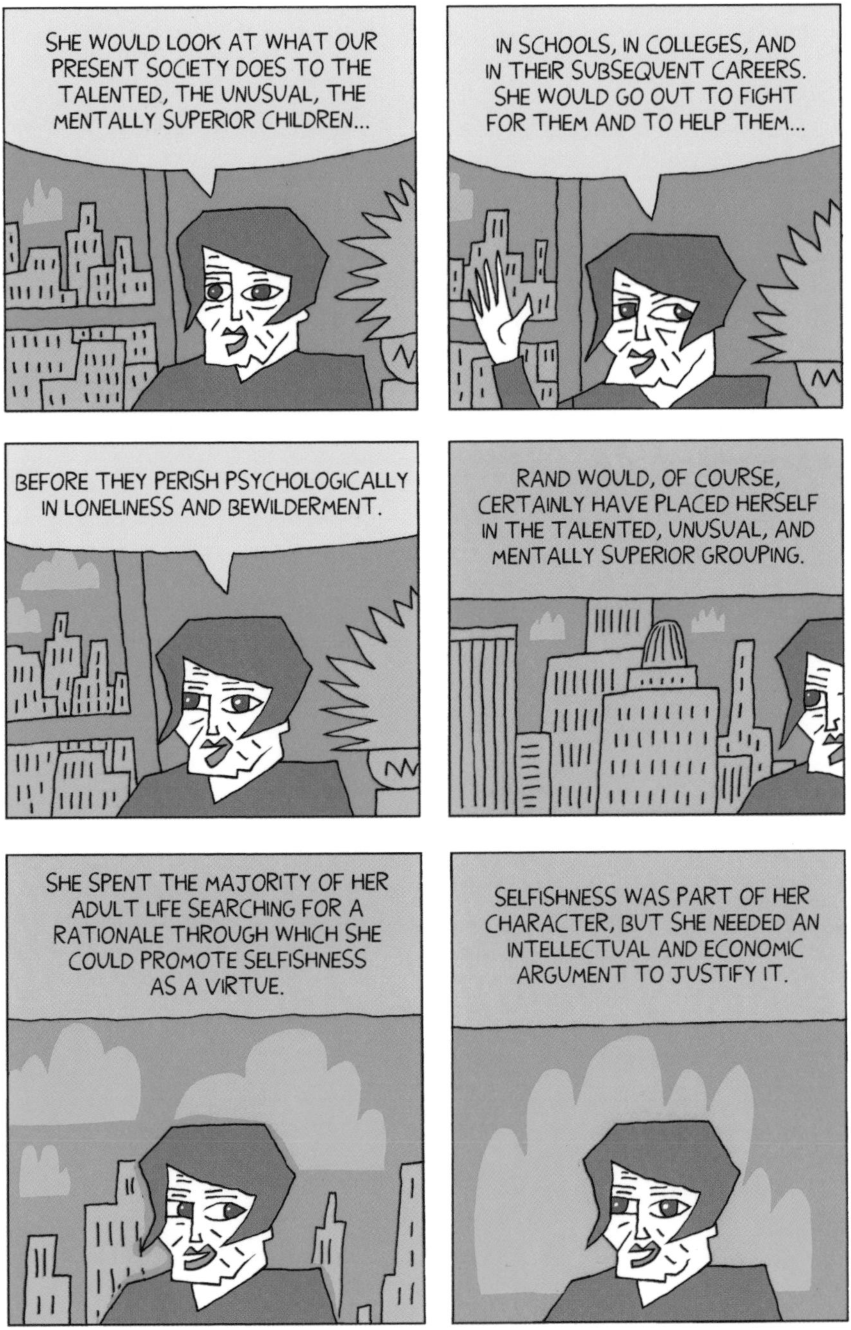
SHE WOULD LOOK AT WHAT OUR PRESENT SOCIETY DOES TO THE TALENTED, THE UNUSUAL, THE MENTALLY SUPERIOR CHILDREN...
IN SCHOOLS, IN COLLEGES, AND IN THEIR SUBSEQUENT CAREERS. SHE WOULD GO OUT TO FIGHT FOR THEM AND TO HELP THEM...
BEFORE THEY PERISH PSYCHOLOGICALLY IN LONELINESS AND BEWILDERMENT.
RAND WOULD, OF COURSE, CERTAINLY HAVE PLACED HERSELF IN THE TALENTED, UNUSUAL, AND MENTALLY SUPERIOR GROUPING.
SHE SPENT THE MAJORITY OF HER ADULT LIFE SEARCHING FOR A RATIONALE THROUGH WHICH SHE COULD PROMOTE SELFISHNESS AS A VIRTUE.
SELFISHNESS WAS PART OF HER CHARACTER, BUT SHE NEEDED AN INTELLECTUAL AND ECONOMIC ARGUMENT TO JUSTIFY IT.

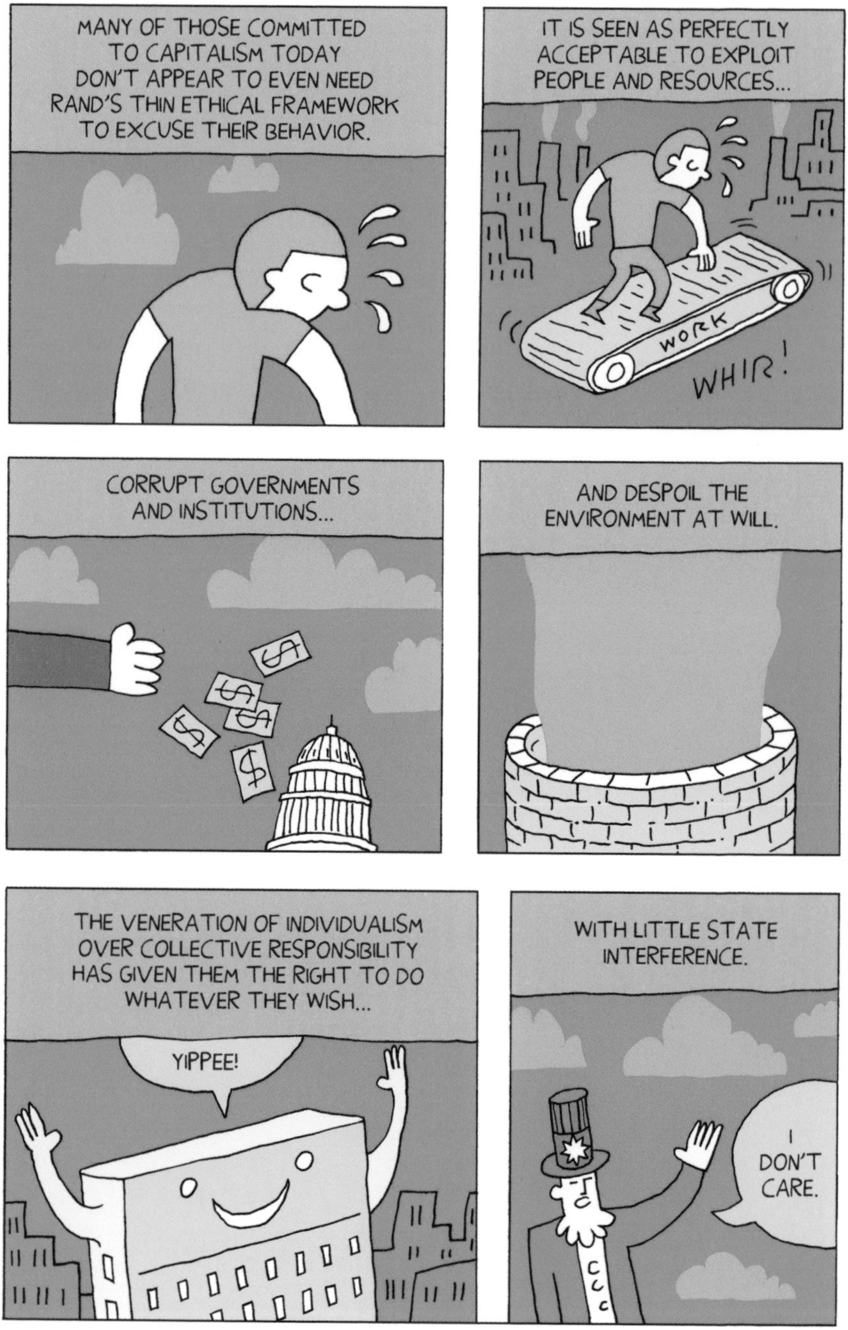
MANY OF THOSE COMMITTED TO CAPITALISM TODAY DON'T APPEAR TO EVEN NEED RAND'S THIN ETHICAL FRAMEWORK TO EXCUSE THEIR BEHAVIOR.
IT IS SEEN AS PERFECTLY ACCEPTABLE TO EXPLOIT PEOPLE AND RESOURCES...
WORK
WHIR!
CORRUPT GOVERNMENTS AND INSTITUTIONS...
AND DESPOIL THE ENVIRONMENT AT WILL.
THE VENERATION OF INDIVIDUALISM OVER COLLECTIVE RESPONSIBILITY HAS GIVEN THEM THE RIGHT TO DO WHATEVER THEY WISH...
YIPPEE!
WITH LITTLE STATE INTERFERENCE.
I DON'T CARE.

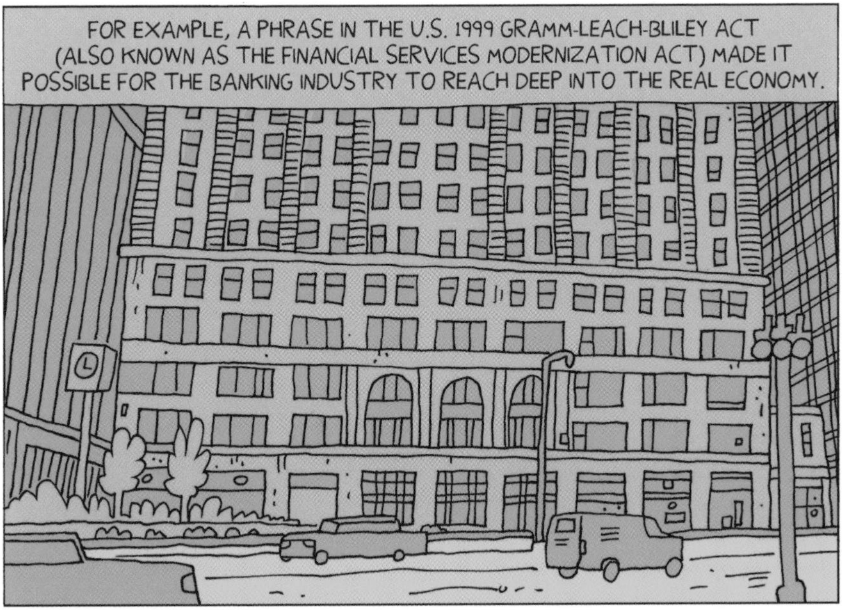
FOR EXAMPLE, A PHRASE IN THE U.S. 1999 GRAMM-LEACH-BLILEY ACT (ALSO KNOWN AS THE FINANCIAL SERVICES MODERNIZATION ACT) MADE IT POSSIBLE FOR THE BANKING INDUSTRY TO REACH DEEP INTO THE REAL ECONOMY.

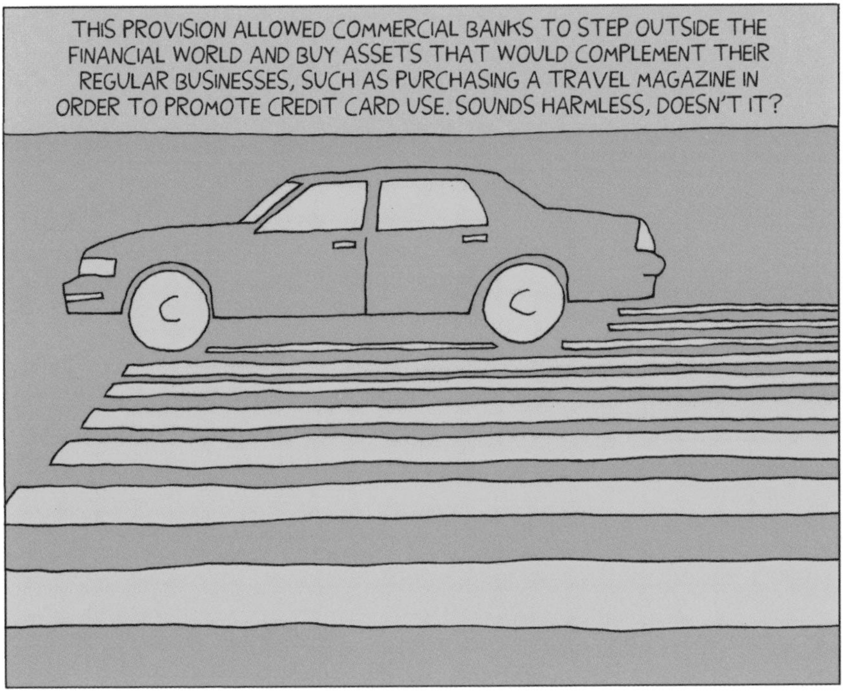
THIS PROVISION ALLOWED COMMERCIAL BANKS TO STEP OUTSIDE THE FINANCIAL WORLD AND BUY ASSETS THAT WOULD COMPLEMENT THEIR REGULAR BUSINESSES, SUCH AS PURCHASING A TRAVEL MAGAZINE IN ORDER TO PROMOTE CREDIT CARD USE. SOUNDS HARMLESS, DOESN'T IT?

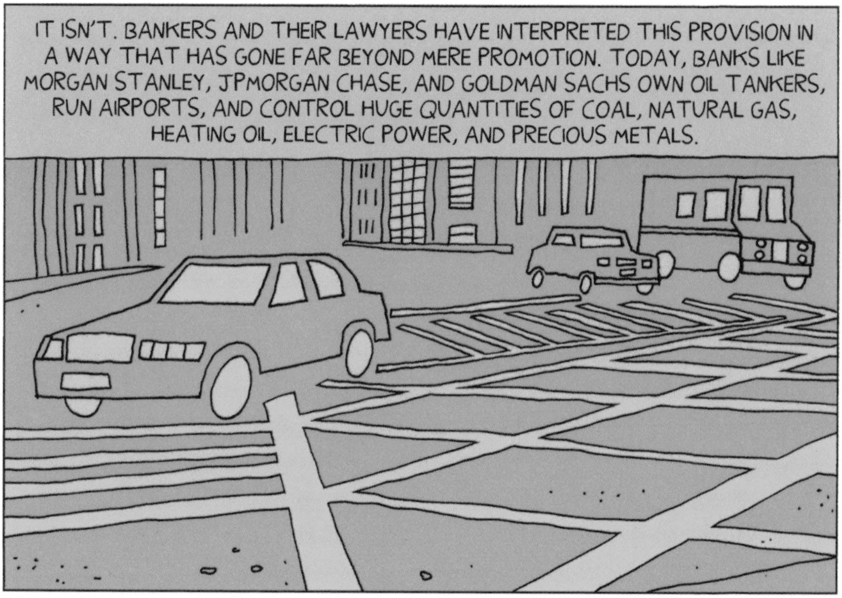
IT ISN'T. BANKERS AND THEIR LAWYERS HAVE INTERPRETED THIS PROVISION IN A WAY THAT HAS GONE FAR BEYOND MERE PROMOTION. TODAY, BANKS LIKE MORGAN STANLEY, JPMORGAN CHASE, AND GOLDMAN SACHS OWN OIL TANKERS, RUN AIRPORTS, AND CONTROL HUGE QUANTITIES OF COAL, NATURAL GAS, HEATING OIL, ELECTRIC POWER, AND PRECIOUS METALS.

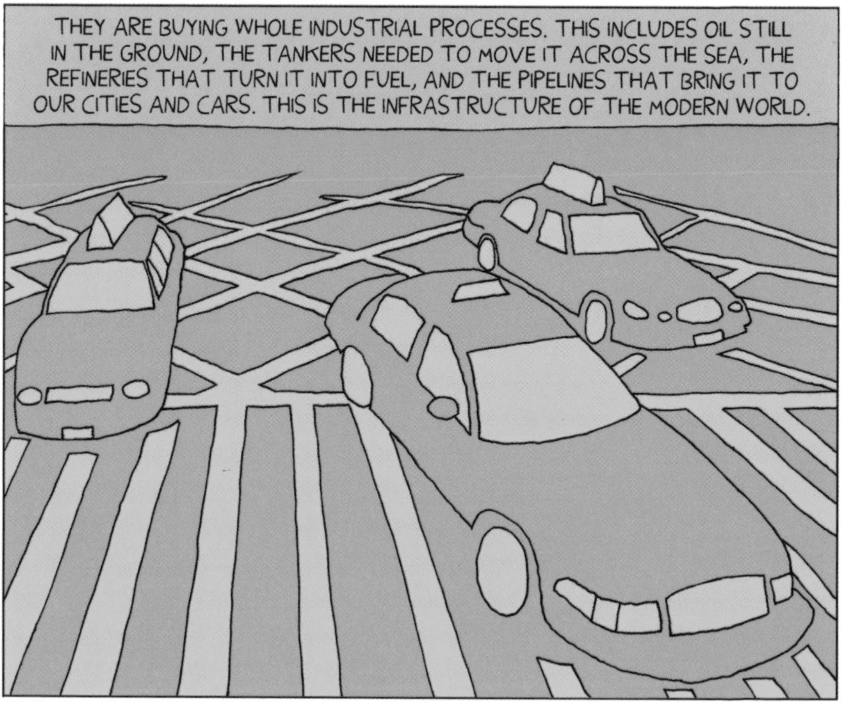
THEY ARE BUYING WHOLE INDUSTRIAL PROCESSES. THIS INCLUDES OIL STILL IN THE GROUND, THE TANKERS NEEDED TO MOVE IT ACROSS THE SEA, THE REFINERIES THAT TURN IT INTO FUEL, AND THE PIPELINES THAT BRING IT TO OUR CITIES AND CARS. THIS IS THE INFRASTRUCTURE OF THE MODERN WORLD.

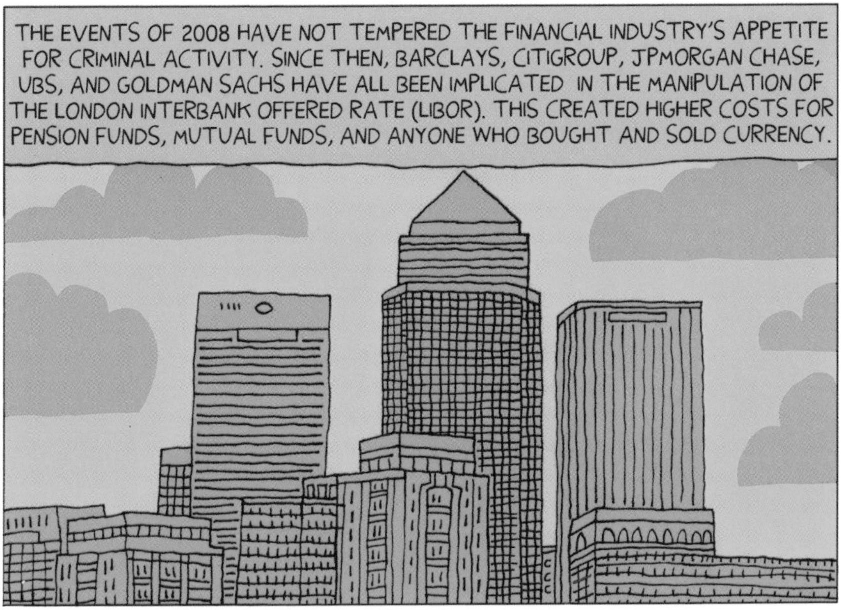
THE EVENTS OF 2008 HAVE NOT TEMPERED THE FINANCIAL INDUSTRY'S APPETITE FOR CRIMINAL ACTIVITY. SINCE THEN, BARCLAYS, CITIGROUP, JPMORGAN CHASE, UBS, AND GOLDMAN SACHS HAVE ALL BEEN IMPLICATED IN THE MANIPULATION OF THE LONDON INTERBANK OFFERED RATE (LIBOR). THIS CREATED HIGHER COSTS FOR PENSION FUNDS, MUTUAL FUNDS, AND ANYONE WHO BOUGHT AND SOLD CURRENCY.

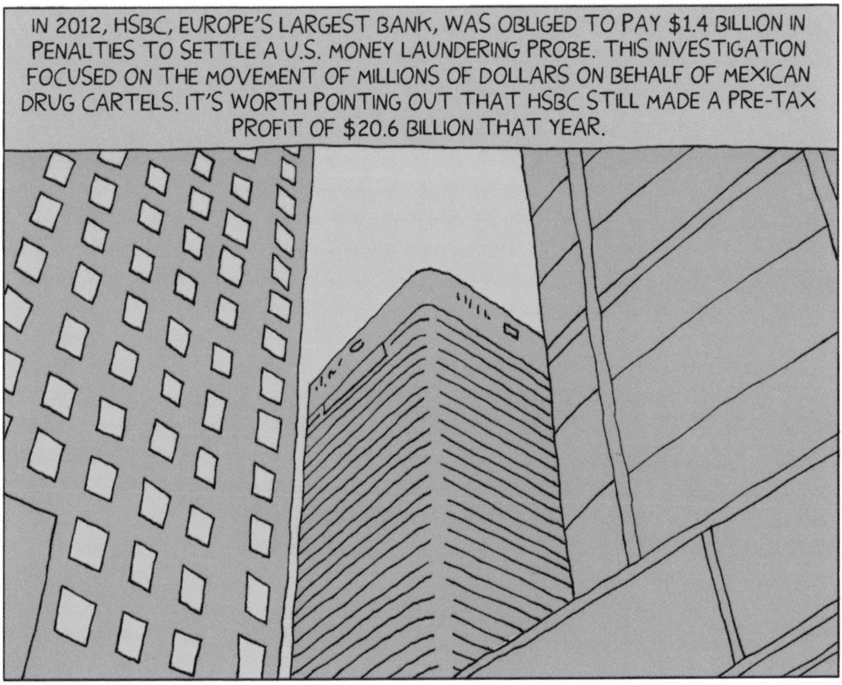
IN 2012, HSBC, EUROPE'S LARGEST BANK, WAS OBLIGED TO PAY $1.4 BILLION IN PENALTIES TO SETTLE A U.S. MONEY LAUNDERING PROBE. THIS INVESTIGATION FOCUSED ON THE MOVEMENT OF MILLIONS OF DOLLARS ON BEHALF OF MEXICAN DRUG CARTELS. IT'S WORTH POINTING OUT THAT HSBC STILL MADE A PRE-TAX PROFIT OF $20.6 BILLION THAT YEAR.

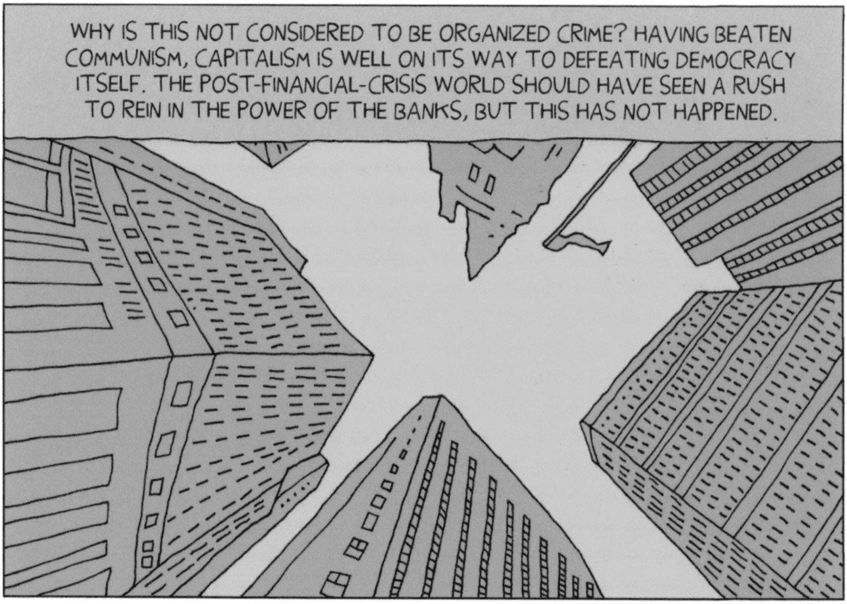
WHY IS THIS NOT CONSIDERED TO BE ORGANIZED CRIME? HAVING BEATEN COMMUNISM, CAPITALISM IS WELL ON ITS WAY TO DEFEATING DEMOCRACY ITSELF. THE POST-FINANCIAL-CRISIS WORLD SHOULD HAVE SEEN A RUSH TO REIN IN THE POWER OF THE BANKS, BUT THIS HAS NOT HAPPENED.

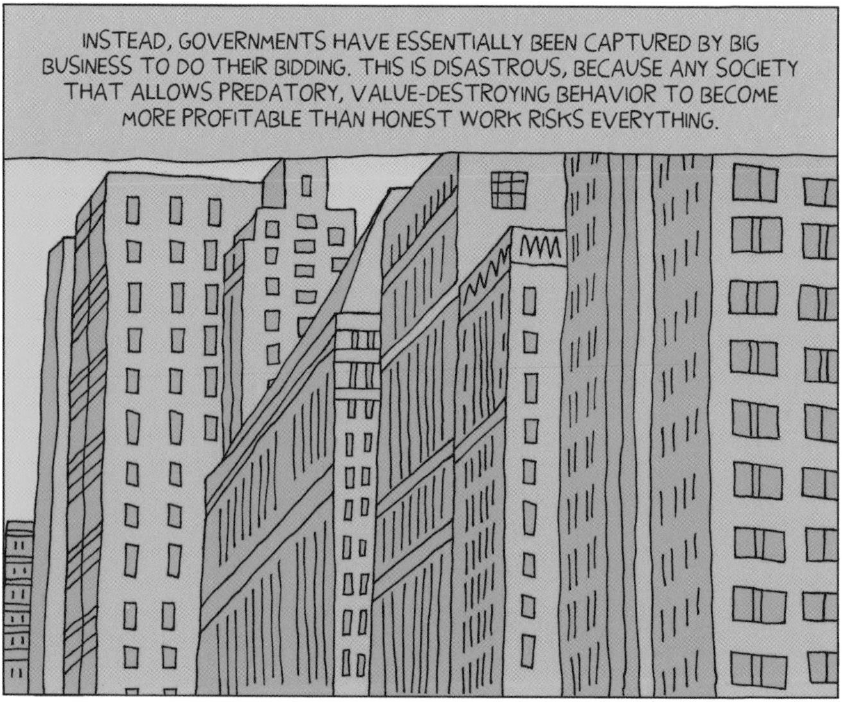
INSTEAD, GOVERNMENTS HAVE ESSENTIALLY BEEN CAPTURED BY BIG BUSINESS TO DO THEIR BIDDING. THIS IS DISASTROUS, BECAUSE ANY SOCIETY THAT ALLOWS PREDATORY, VALUE-DESTROYING BEHAVIOR TO BECOME MORE PROFITABLE THAN HONEST WORK RISKS EVERYTHING.

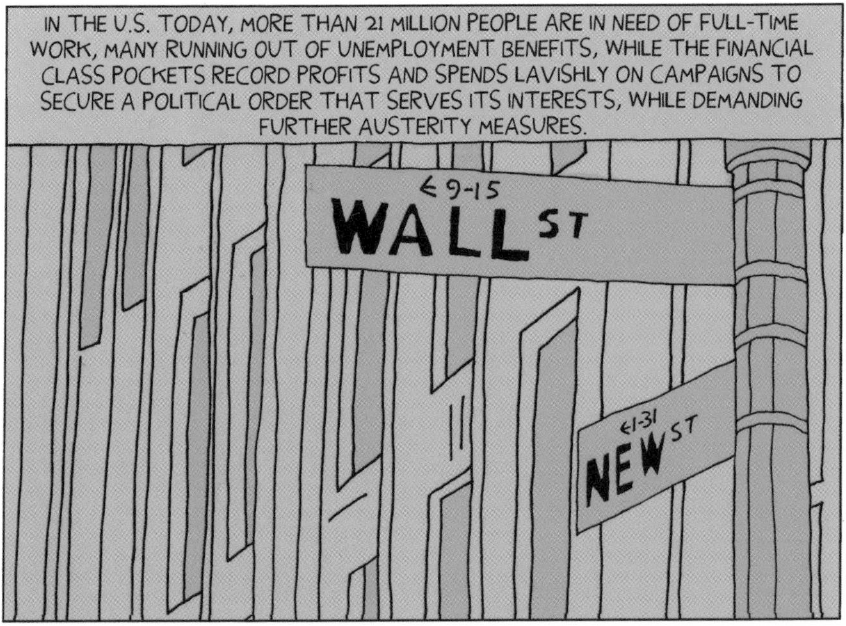
IN THE U.S. TODAY, MORE THAN 21 MILLION PEOPLE ARE IN NEED OF FULL-TIME WORK, MANY RUNNING OUT OF UNEMPLOYMENT BENEFITS, WHILE THE FINANCIAL CLASS POCKETS RECORD PROFITS AND SPENDS LAVISHLY ON CAMPAIGNS TO SECURE A POLITICAL ORDER THAT SERVES ITS INTERESTS, WHILE DEMANDING FURTHER AUSTERITY MEASURES.
← 9-15
WALL ST
←1-31
NEW ST

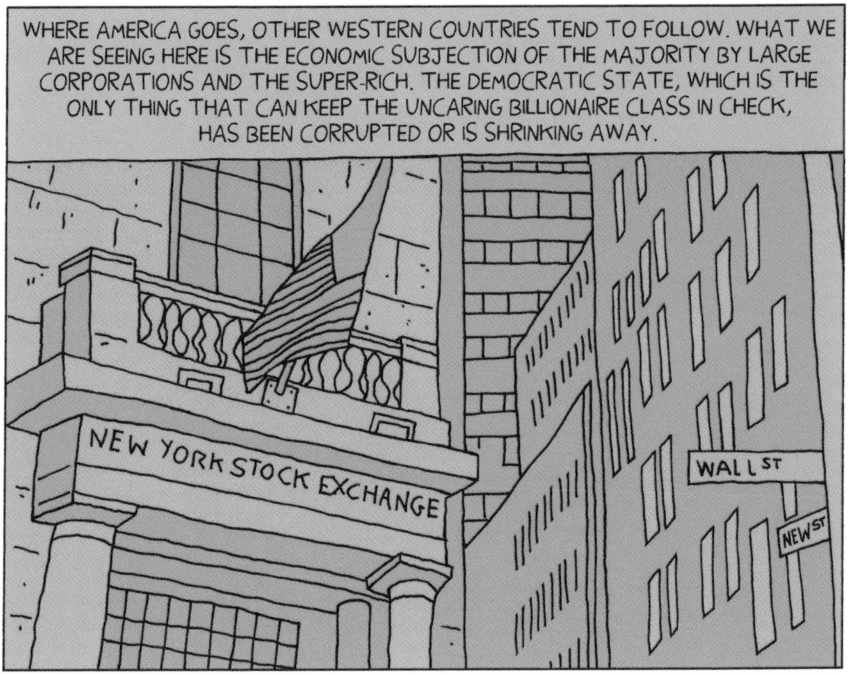
WHERE AMERICA GOES, OTHER WESTERN COUNTRIES TEND TO FOLLOW. WHAT WE ARE SEEING HERE IS THE ECONOMIC SUBJECTION OF THE MAJORITY BY LARGE CORPORATIONS AND THE SUPER-RICH. THE DEMOCRATIC STATE, WHICH IS THE ONLY THING THAT CAN KEEP THE UNCARING BILLIONAIRE CLASS IN CHECK, HAS BEEN CORRUPTED OR IS SHRINKING AWAY.
NEW YORK STOCK EXCHANGE
WALL ST
NEW ST

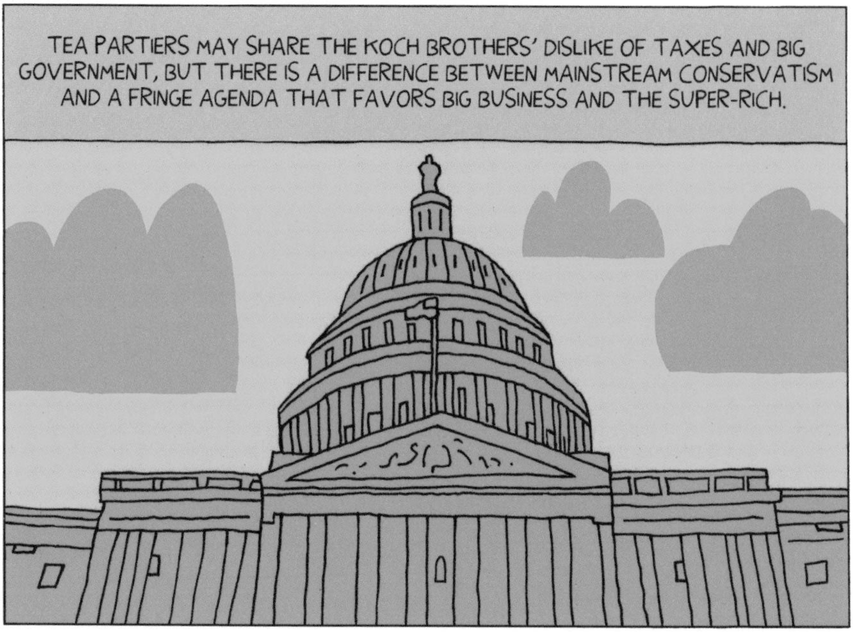
TEA PARTIERS MAY SHARE THE KOCH BROTHERS' DISLIKE OF TAXES AND BIG GOVERNMENT, BUT THERE IS A DIFFERENCE BETWEEN MAINSTREAM CONSERVATISM AND A FRINGE AGENDA THAT FAVORS BIG BUSINESS AND THE SUPER-RICH.

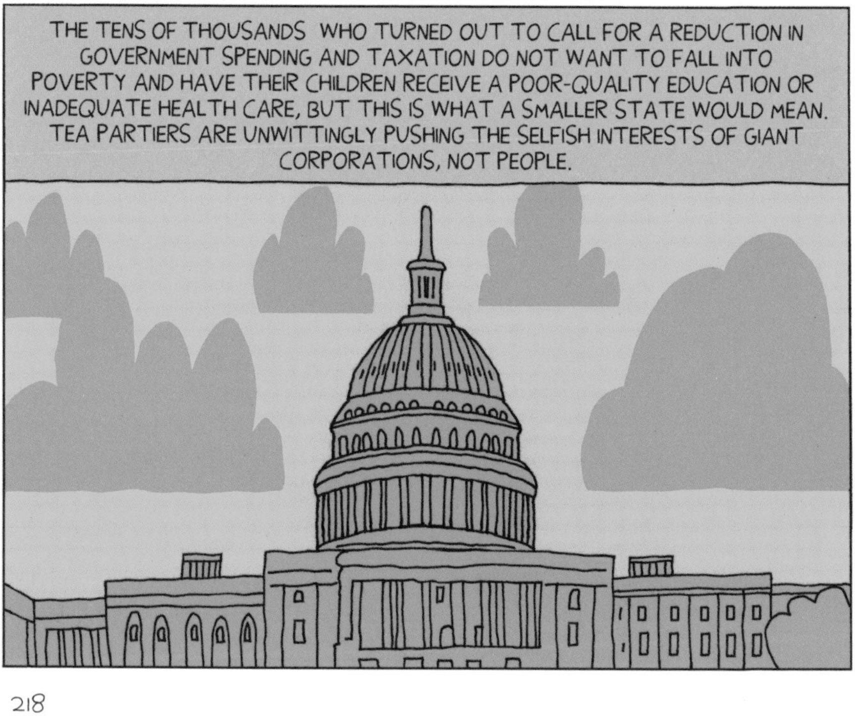
THE TENS OF THOUSANDS WHO TURNED OUT TO CALL FOR A REDUCTION IN GOVERNMENT SPENDING AND TAXATION DO NOT WANT TO FALL INTO POVERTY AND HAVE THEIR CHILDREN RECEIVE A POOR-QUALITY EDUCATION OR INADEQUATE HEALTH CARE, BUT THIS IS WHAT A SMALLER STATE WOULD MEAN. TEA PARTIERS ARE UNWITTINGLY PUSHING THE SELFISH INTERESTS OF GIANT CORPORATIONS, NOT PEOPLE.

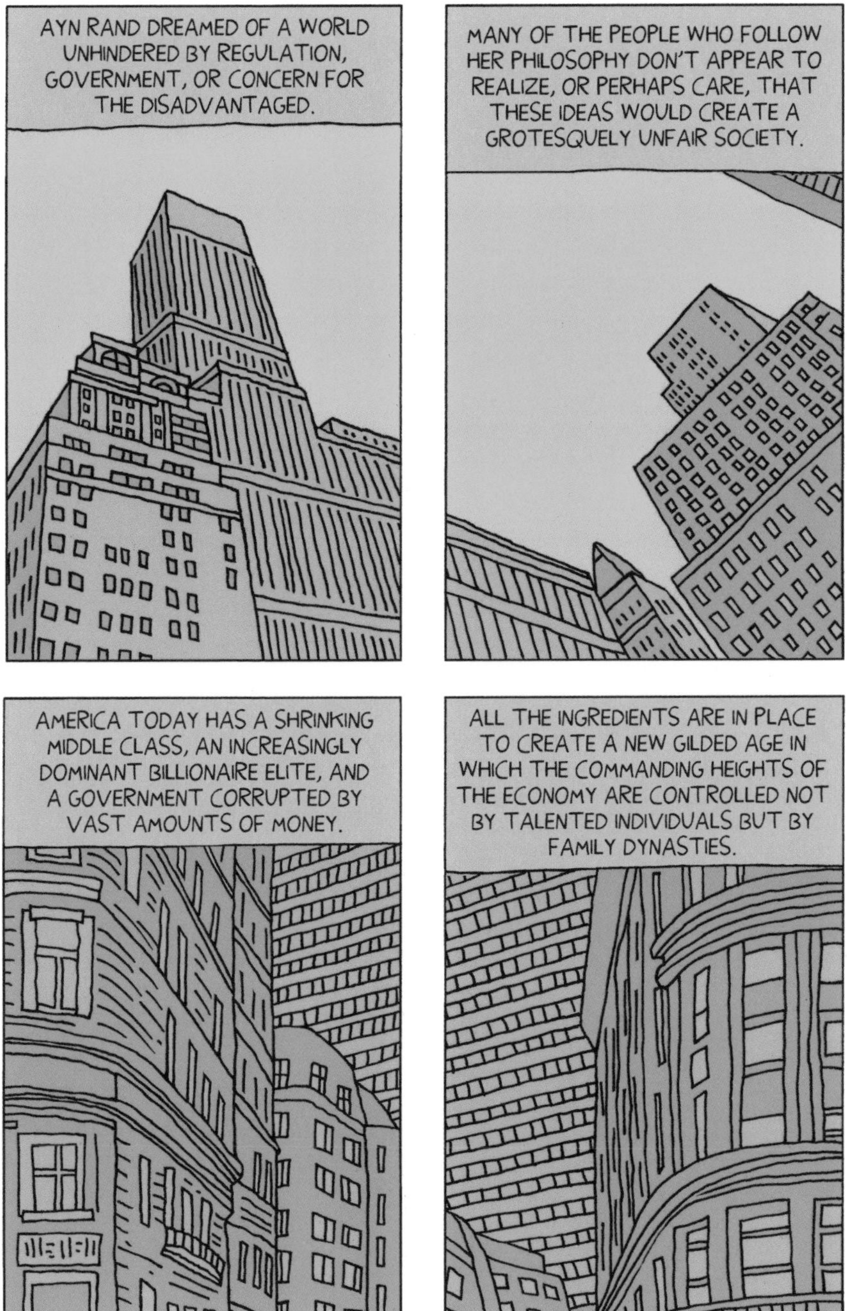
AYN RAND DREAMED OF A WORLD UNHINDERED BY REGULATION, GOVERNMENT, OR CONCERN FOR THE DISADVANTAGED.
MANY OF THE PEOPLE WHO FOLLOW HER PHILOSOPHY DON'T APPEAR TO REALIZE, OR PERHAPS CARE, THAT THESE IDEAS WOULD CREATE A GROTESQUELY UNFAIR SOCIETY.
AMERICA TODAY HAS A SHRINKING MIDDLE CLASS, AN INCREASINGLY DOMINANT BILLIONAIRE ELITE, AND A GOVERNMENT CORRUPTED BY VAST AMOUNTS OF MONEY.
ALL THE INGREDIENTS ARE IN PLACE TO CREATE A NEW GILDED AGE IN WHICH THE COMMANDING HEIGHTS OF THE ECONOMY ARE CONTROLLED NOT BY TALENTED INDIVIDUALS BUT BY FAMILY DYNASTIES.

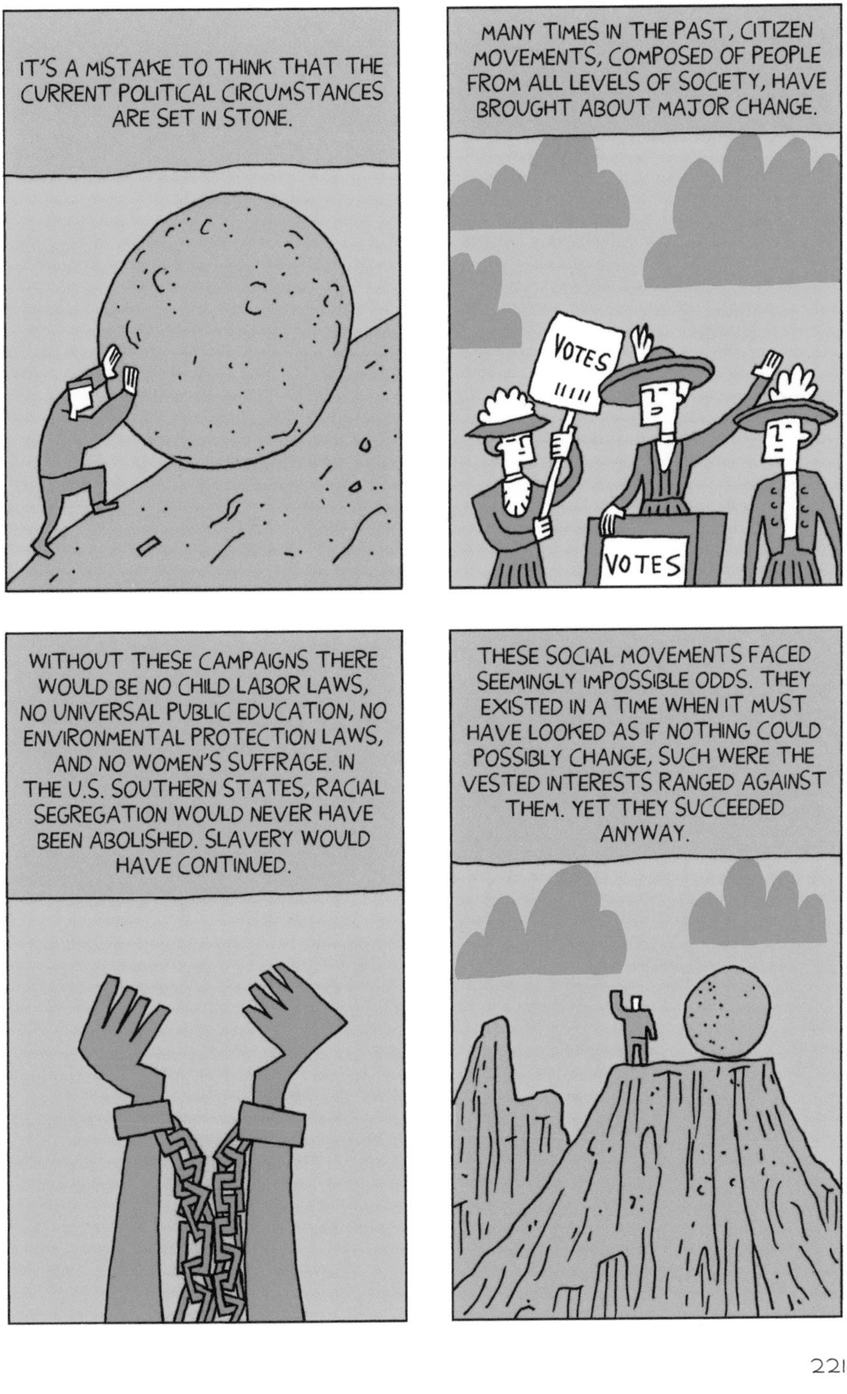
IT'S A MISTAKE TO THINK THAT THE CURRENT POLITICAL CIRCUMSTANCES ARE SET IN STONE.
MANY TIMES IN THE PAST, CITIZEN MOVEMENTS, COMPOSED OF PEOPLE FROM ALL LEVELS OF SOCIETY, HAVE BROUGHT ABOUT MAJOR CHANGE.
VOTES
VOTES
WITHOUT THESE CAMPAIGNS THERE WOULD BE NO CHILD LABOR LAWS, NO UNIVERSAL PUBLIC EDUCATION, NO ENVIRONMENTAL PROTECTION LAWS, AND NO WOMEN'S SUFFRAGE. IN THE U.S. SOUTHERN STATES, RACIAL SEGREGATION WOULD NEVER HAVE BEEN ABOLISHED. SLAVERY WOULD HAVE CONTINUED.
THESE SOCIAL MOVEMENTS FACED SEEMINGLY IMPOSSIBLE ODDS. THEY EXISTED IN A TIME WHEN IT MUST HAVE LOOKED AS IF NOTHING COULD POSSIBLY CHANGE, SUCH WERE THE VESTED INTERESTS RANGED AGAINST THEM. YET THEY SUCCEEDED ANYWAY.

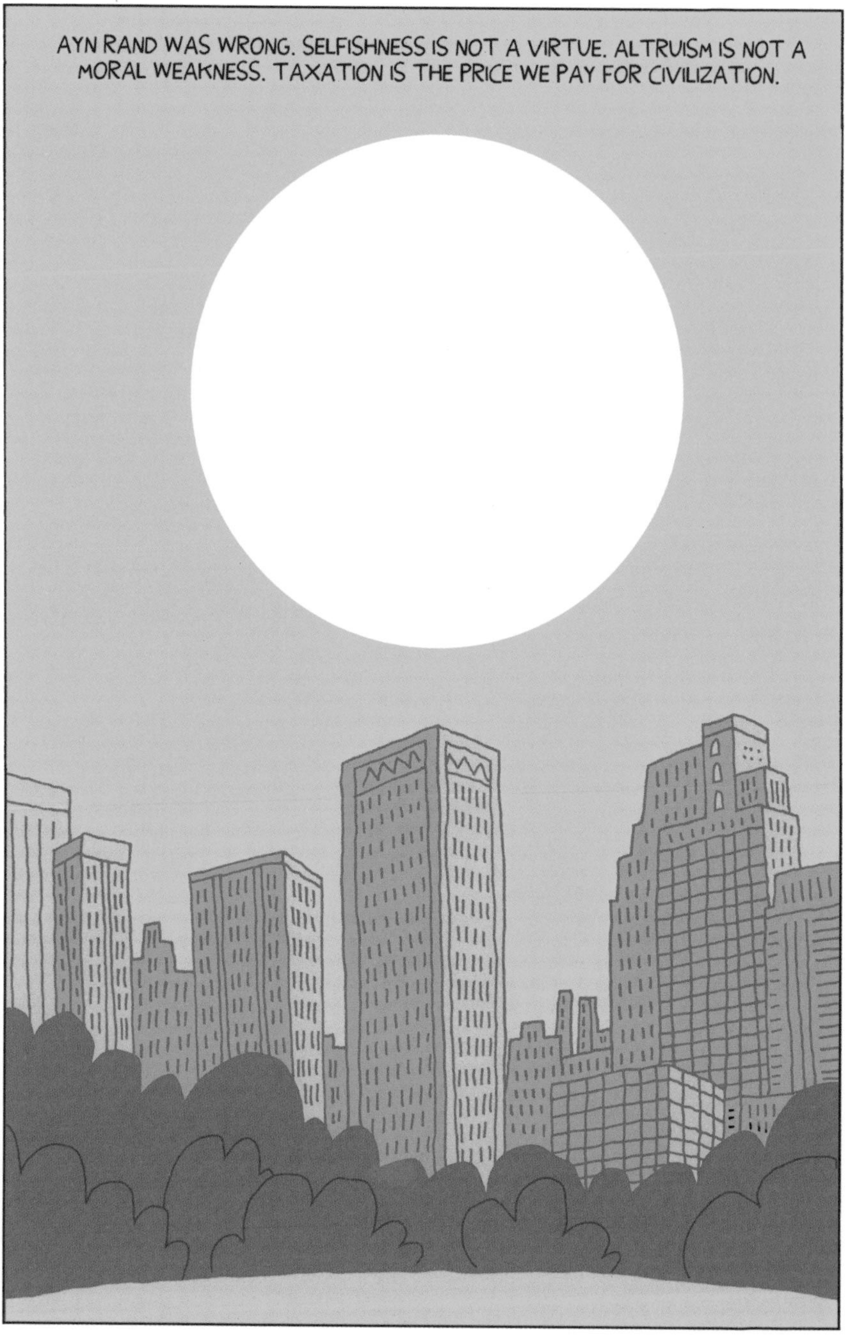
AYN RAND WAS WRONG. SELFISHNESS IS NOT A VIRTUE. ALTRUISM IS NOT A MORAL WEAKNESS. TAXATION IS THE PRICE WE PAY FOR CIVILIZATION.

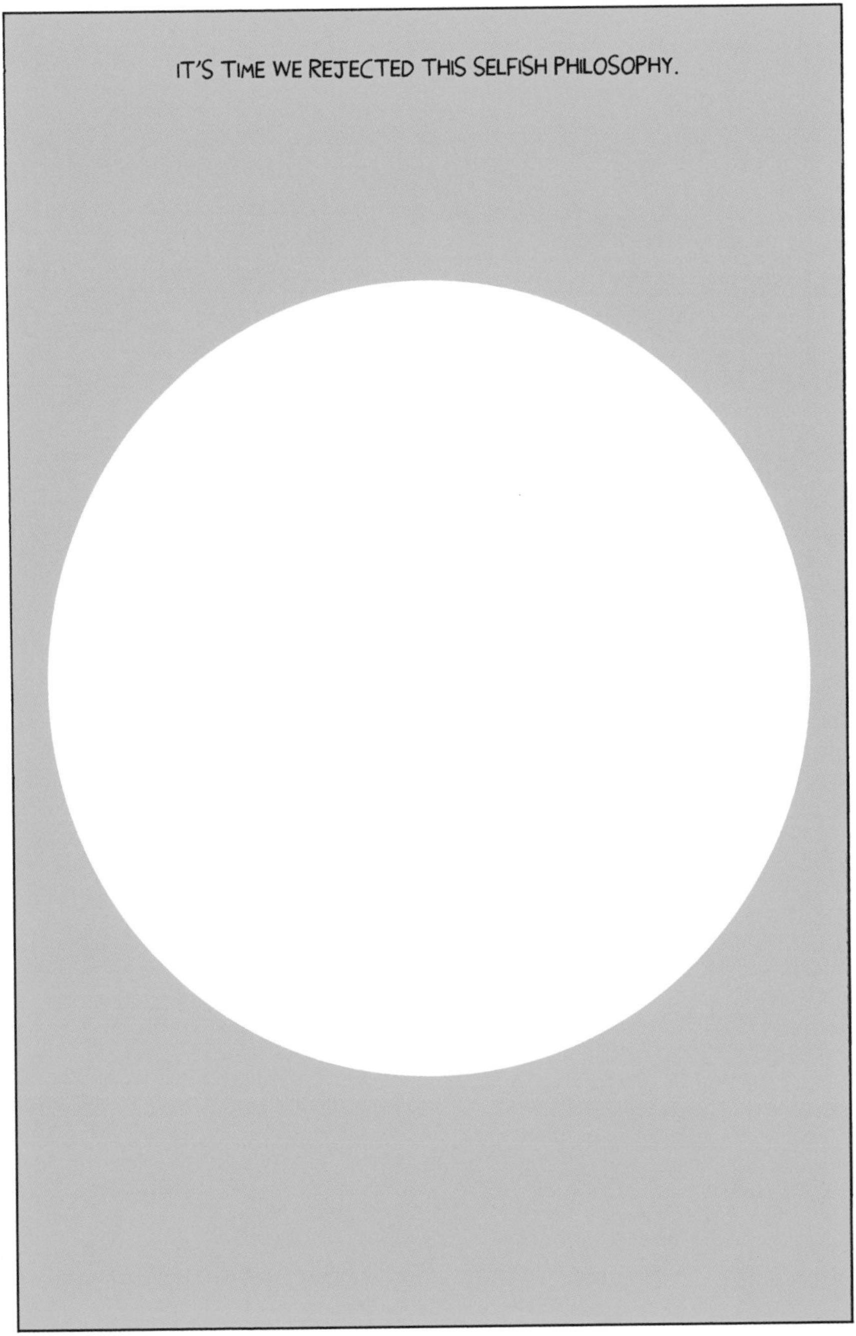
IT'S TIME WE REJECTED THIS SELFISH PHILOSOPHY.

SOURCES

Part One: Ayn Rand

Branden, Barbara. *The Passion of Ayn Rand*. New York: Doubleday, 1998.

Burns, Jennifer. *Goddess of the Market: Ayn Rand and the American Right*. New York: Oxford University Press, 2009.

Greenspan, Alan. *The Age of Turbulence: Adventures in a New World*. New York: Penguin, 2007.

Heller, Anne C. *Ayn Rand and the World She Made*. New York: Anchor Books, 2009.

Mallon, Thomas. "Possessed: Did Ayn Rand's Cult Outstrip Her Canon?" *New Yorker*, November 9, 2009. www.newyorker.com/reporting/2009/11/09/091109fa_fact _mallon (accessed September 13, 2013).

Rand, Ayn. *Atlas Shrugged*. New York: Random House, 1957.

——. *The Fountainhead*. Indianapolis, Indiana: Bobbs Merrill, 1943.

——. *We the Living*. New York: Macmillan, 1936.

Weiss, Gary. *Ayn Rand Nation: The Hidden Struggle for America's Soul*. New York: St. Martin's Griffin, 2013.

Part Two: The Crash

Balzli, Beat. "Greek Debt Crisis: How Goldman Sachs Helped Greece to Mask Its True Debt." *Spiegel Online International*, February 8, 2010. www.spiegel.de/international /europe/greek-debt-crisis-how-goldman-sachs-helped-greece-to-mask-its-true- debt-a-676634.html (accessed September 25, 2013).

Born, Brooksey, interview. *Frontline*, PBS, October 20, 2009. www.pbs.org/wgbh/pages/ frontline/warning/interviews/born.html (accessed September 23, 2013).

Cahoon, Scott. "Wall Street Revolving Door." *Too Big Has Failed*, May 30, 2013. www .toobighasfailed.org/wall-street-revolving-door (accessed September 25, 2013).

Cohan, William D. "How Goldman Killed A.I.G." *New York Times*, February 16, 2011. opinionator.blogs.nytimes.com/2011/02/16/how-goldman-killed-a-i-g-and-other -stories (accessed September 23, 2013).

Ensor, Josie. "How the City Bankrolls the Conservatives." *Telegraph*, October 1, 2010. www.telegraph.co.uk/news/politics/8800457/How-the-City-bankrolls-the -Conservatives.html (accessed December 18, 2013).

Ferguson, Charles. *Inside Job: The Financiers Who Pulled Off the Heist of the Century*. Oxford, England: Oneworld, 2012.

Goodwin, Michael. *Economix: How Our Economy Works (and Doesn't Work), in Words and Pictures*. New York: Abrams ComicArts, 2012.

Greenspan, Alan. Letter to the editor. *New York Times*, November 3, 1957. graphics8. nytimes.com/packages/pdf/business/20070915RAND_nyt_greenspanletter.pdf.

Lanchester, John. *Whoops! Why Everyone Owes Everyone and No One Can Pay*. London: Penguin, 2010.

Lewis, Michael. *The Big Short: Inside the Doomsday Machine*. London: Penguin, 2011.

Madrick, Jeff. "How Alan Greenspan Helped Wreck the Economy." *Rolling Stone*,

June 16, 2011. www.rollingstone.com/politics/blogs/national-affairs/how-alan
-greenspan-helped-wreck-the-economy-20110616 (accessed June 12, 2013).

McLean, Bethany, and Joe Nocera. *All the Devils Are Here: Unmasking the Men Who Bankrupted the World.* London: Portfolio Penguin, 2010.

"Prosecuting Wall Street." *60 Minutes*, December 5, 2011. www.cbsnews.com/news
/prosecuting-wall-street (accessed September 20, 2013).

Smith, Greg. "Why I Am Leaving Goldman Sachs." *New York Times*, March 14, 2012.
www.nytimes.com/2012/03/14/opinion/why-i-am-leaving-goldman-sachs.html
(accessed September 18, 2013).

Stiglitz, Joseph E. *Freefall: Free Markets and the Sinking of the Global Economy.*
London: Penguin, 2010.

Taibbi, Matt. "The People vs. Goldman Sachs." *Rolling Stone*, May 11, 2011. www
.rollingstone.com/politics/news/the-people-vs-goldman-sachs-20110511 (accessed
September 23, 2013).

Tett, Gillian. *Fool's Gold: How Unrestrained Greed Corrupted a Dream, Shattered Global Markets and Unleashed a Catastrophe.* London: Abacus, 2010.

Thompson, Don. "Christopher Warren, Fraud Suspect, Caught at Border with $70,000
in Cowboy Boots, $1M in Swiss Bank Certificates." *Huffington Post*, November 2,
2009. www.huffingtonpost.com/2009/02/12/christopher-warren-fraud
-_n_166340.html (accessed September 16, 2013).

Part Three: The Age of Selfishness

"Atos Disability Benefits Row: Epileptic Colin Traynor's Death Blamed on Stress of Being
Found Fit for Work." *Huffington Post*, September 26, 2012. www.huffingtonpost.
co.uk/2012/09/26/atos-disability-benefits-colin-traynor-epilepsy-_n_1917042
.html (accessed September 14, 2013).

Bloodworth, James. "Coalition Presides Over Shocking Increase in Number of People
Using Food Banks." *Left Foot Forward*, April 23, 2013. www.leftfootforward.org
/2013/04/coalition-presides-over-1000-increase-in-number-of-people-using
-food-banks (accessed June 14, 2013).

Glaze, Ben. "Linda Wootton: Double Heart and Lung Transplant Dies Nine Days After
She Has Benefits Stopped." *Mirror*, May 26, 2013. www.mirror.co.uk/news/uk
-news/linda-wootton-double-heart-lung-1912498 (accessed September 14, 2013).

Jones, Ashley. "Tea Party: Palin's Pet, or Is There More to It Underneath?" *U.S. Money
Talk*, October 5, 2010. www.usmoneytalk.com/finance/tea-party-palins-pet-or-is
-there-more-to-it-underneath-910 (accessed May 1, 2014).

McDonald, Craig. "Heartbroken Dad Blames Benefits Axemen for Driving His Ill Son to
Commit Suicide." *Daily Record*, September 13, 2013. www.dailyrecord.co.uk
/news/scottish-news/heartbroken-dad-blames-benefits-axemen-2292176
(accessed September 14, 2013).

Mooney, Chris. *The Republican Brain: The Science of Why They Deny Science—and Reality.* Hoboken, New Jersey: John Wiley & Sons, 2012.

Paramaguru, Kharunya. "Britain's Breadline: Austerity Leads to Growing Ranks of the
Hungry." *Time*, November 22, 2013. world.time.com/2013/11/22/britains-breadline
-austerity-leads-to-growing-ranks-of-the-hungry (accessed November 22, 2013).

"Paul Sykes: The Man Spending Millions to Make UKIP's Posters Visible from Space."
    Guardian, April 23, 2014. www.theguardian.com/politics/shortcuts/2014/apr/23
    /paul-sykes-ukip-britain-out-of-europe (accessed May 1, 2014).

Pinker, Steven. *The Better Angels of Our Nature: A History of Violence and Humanity.*
    London: Allen Lane, 2011.

Ramesh, Randeep. "Atos Apologises to Long-Term Sick Wrongly Assessed as Fit for Work."
    Guardian, April 17, 2013. www.theguardian.com/society/2013/apr/17/atos
    -apologises-long-term-sick (accessed September 14, 2013).

Rich, Frank. "The Billionaires Bankrolling the Tea Party." *New York Times*, August 28,
    2010. www.nytimes.com/2010/08/29/opinion/29rich.html (accessed May 1, 2014).

"Rick Santelli: Tea Party." *Freedom Eden*, February 19, 2009. www.freedomeden.blogspot
    .co.uk/2009/02/rick-santelli-tea-party.html (accessed May 1, 2014).

Rogers, Simon. "UK Welfare Spending: How Much Does Each Benefit Really Cost?"
    Guardian, January 8, 2013. www.theguardian.com/news/datablog/2013/jan/08/uk
    -benefit-welfare-spending (accessed June 14, 2013).

Ryan, Frances. "Rod Liddle's Attack on Disability Cannot Be Ignored." *Guardian*, January
    30, 2012. www.theguardian.com/commentisfree/2012/jan/30/rod-liddle-attack
    -disability (accessed September 14, 2013).

Taibbi, Matt. "The Vampire Squid Strikes Again: The Mega Banks' Most Devious Scam Yet."
    Rolling Stone, February 12, 2014. www.rollingstone.com/politics/news/the-vampire
    -squid-strikes-again-the-mega-banks-most-devious-scam-yet-20140212 (accessed
    February 12, 2014).

Taylor, Byron. "UKIP Threat to Workers' Rights Exposed." *GMB*, May 2, 2014. www.gmb
    .org.uk/newsroom/ukip-threat-to-workers-rights-exposed (accessed May 5, 2014).

Taylor, Keith. "UKIP's Stance on the City Undermines Its Anti-Establishment Rhetoric."
    Huffington Post, April 30, 2014. www.huffingtonpost.co.uk/keith-taylor/ukips-stance
    -onthe-city-_b_5239470.html (accessed May 1, 2014).

Walker, Peter. "Benefit Cuts Are Fuelling Abuse of Disabled People, Say Charities."
    Guardian, February 5, 2012. www.theguardian.com/society/2012/feb/05/benefit
    -cuts-fuelling-abuse-disabled-people (accessed November 24, 2013).

GLOSSARY

asset
Something that provides income or other value to its owner.

bailout
The financial rescue of a struggling borrower, which may be a company or bank.

base rate
The key interest rate set by a country's central bank. The overnight interest rate it charges banks for lending to them.

bond
A loan or IOU, in which the authorized issuer owes the holders a debt and is obliged to pay interest at regular dates and repay the whole sum at a later date. They can be issued by companies, banks, or governments to raise money. Banks and investors buy and trade bonds.

capital
For investors, "capital" refers to their stock of wealth, which can be put to work in order to earn income. For companies, it typically refers to sources of financing such as newly issued shares. For banks, it refers to their ability to absorb losses in their accounts. If a bank writes off a loss on one of its assets—for example, if it makes a loan that is not repaid—then the bank must also write off a corresponding amount of its capital. If a bank runs out of capital, then it is insolvent, meaning it does not have enough assets to repay its debts.

central bank
A country's central bank has responsibility for setting the base interest rate, controlling the money supply, and acting as banker to other banks. The U.S. central bank is the Federal Reserve.

collateralized debt obligation (CDO)
A financial structure that groups individual loans, bonds, or other assets in a portfolio or bundle, which can then be traded. In theory, CDOs attract a higher credit rating than individual assets, owing to the risk being more diversified. But as the performance of many assets fell during the financial crisis, the value of many CDOs was also reduced.

commodity
Commodities are raw products that have a common market price and can be traded on a stock exchange in fixed quantities. The commodities markets range from wheat,

cotton, sugar, and cocoa to industrial metals such as iron ore and copper, and energy products such as oil and natural gas.

credit default swap (CDS)

A financial contract that provides insurance-like protection against the risk of a borrower defaulting on its debts.

credit rating

The assessment given to debts and borrowers by a ratings agency according to their safety from an investment standpoint—based on their "creditworthiness," or the ability of the company or government that is borrowing to repay. Ratings range from AAA, the safest, down to D. Ratings of BBB– or higher are considered "investment grade."

default

A default occurs when a borrower has broken the terms of a loan or other debt, e.g., missing a payment. The term is also used to mean any situation that makes it clear that a borrower can no longer repay debts in full, such as bankruptcy.

derivative

A financial contract that provides a way of investing in a particular product without having to own it directly. The value of a derivative can depend on anything from the price of coffee to interest rates. Derivatives allow investors and banks to hedge their risks or to speculate on markets.

float

Flotation on a stock market is the process of changing a private company into a public company by issuing shares and inviting the public to purchase them. Flotation allows companies to obtain financing from outside the company to fund a new project or expansion. The term is commonly used in the U.K.; the term "going public" in an IPO (initial public offering) is more widely used in the U.S.

foreclosure

A situation in which a homeowner is unable to make full principal and interest payments on his or her mortgage, which allows the lender to seize the property and sell the home.

future

A futures contract is an agreement to buy or sell a commodity at a predetermined future date and price. It could be used to hedge or to speculate on the price of the commodity. Futures contracts are traded on a stock exchange.

gross domestic product (GDP)

A measure of economic activity in a country, namely of all the services and goods produced in a year. There are different ways of calculating GDP: through output, through income, and through expenditure.

hedge

To hedge is to make an investment specifically in order to reduce the risk of price fluctuations in the value of an asset. Airlines might, for example, hedge against rising oil prices by agreeing in advance to buy their fuel at a set price. In this case, a rise in price would not harm them—nor would they benefit from any drop.

hedge fund

A private investment fund that uses a range of sophisticated strategies to maximize returns, including hedging, leveraging, and derivatives trading.

leverage

Leveraging means borrowing money to add to your own in order to make a larger investment. The more you borrow in proportion to the funds you already have, the more this can increase both gains and losses; therefore, leveraging increases risk as well as reward.

liquidity

How easy something is to convert into cash. A bank account, for example, is more liquid than a house. If you needed to sell your house quickly to pay bills, you would have to drop the price to get a sale, so it is not a liquid asset.

liquidity crisis

A situation in which it suddenly becomes much more difficult for banks to obtain cash due to a general loss of confidence in the financial system. Investors (and, in the case of a bank run, even ordinary depositors) may withdraw their cash from banks, while banks may stop lending to each other. Because most of a bank's money is tied up in loans, even a healthy bank can run out of cash and collapse. Central banks usually respond to a liquidity crisis by providing emergency bailout cash loans to the struggling bank.

mutual fund

An investment vehicle that is made up of a pool of money collected from multiple small investors for the purpose of investing in securities such as shares, bonds, and other assets. One of the main advantages of mutual funds is that they give small investors access to professionally managed, diversified portfolios of securities, which would be difficult to create with a small amount of capital. Each shareholder participates in the gain or loss of the whole fund.

negative equity

A situation in which the value of a house is less than the amount of the mortgage that still has to be paid off.

security

An asset or contract that can be assigned a value and then traded. It could be a stock or share, a bond, or a CDO. The term is usually seen in the plural, i.e., "securities." Separately, the term "security" is also used to mean something that is pledged by a borrower when taking out a loan. For example, mortgages are usually secured on the borrower's home. This means that if the borrower cannot repay, the lender can seize the security—the home—and sell it in order to help repay the outstanding debt. This meaning is also called "collateral."

securitization

Turning something into a security. For example, taking the debts from a number of mortgages and combining them to make a financial product, which can then be traded. Investors who buy these securities receive income when the original home buyers make their mortgage payments.

stock

A type of security that signifies a unit of ownership in a company and represents a claim on part of its assets and earnings. Being a shareholder entitles the holder to a share in any profits, if they are declared in the form of dividends. While shares are often used to refer to the stock of a corporation, they can also represent ownership of other classes of financial assets, such as mutual funds.

toxic debts/loans

Debts or loans that are very unlikely to be recovered from borrowers. Most lenders expect that some customers will not be able to repay; the term "toxic debt" describes a whole package of loans that are unlikely to be repaid.

GLOSSARY SOURCES

BBC News. www.bbc.co.uk/news/business-15060411

Investopedia. www.investopedia.com/dictionary

ACKNOWLEDGMENTS

I HAD A LOT OF HELP WRITING *THE AGE OF SELFISHNESS*. I owe a huge debt of gratitude to the many writers whose work I read during the long process of research. Without them, this book would be very light on information. So thanks to Anne C. Heller, Jennifer Burns, Charles Ferguson, John Lanchester, Gillian Tett, Bethany McLean, Joe Nocera, Michael Lewis, Chris Mooney, Joseph Stiglitz, Gary Weiss, and, of course, Ayn Rand herself. It's well worth reading all of the books I've used as source material for *The Age of Selfishness*.

Others who gave me help and support in various ways include Paul Gravett, Nick Abadzis, Ian Williams, Simon Fraser, Lizz Lunney, Sarah McIntyre, Graham Johnstone, Tom Spurgeon, Eric Orchard, Julie Crack, Michael Goodwin, Jon Ronson, Nye Wright, Vivekanand Sridhar, Jonathan Edwards, and my parents.

Thanks to Candida Lacey, Adrian Weston, Linda McQueen, Corinne Pearlman, and everyone at Myriad Editions.

And lastly, a big thanks to Charles Kochman, Nicole Sclama, Pamela Notarantonio, Jen Graham, and all at Abrams ComicArts for their enthusiasm, hard work, and faith in this book.

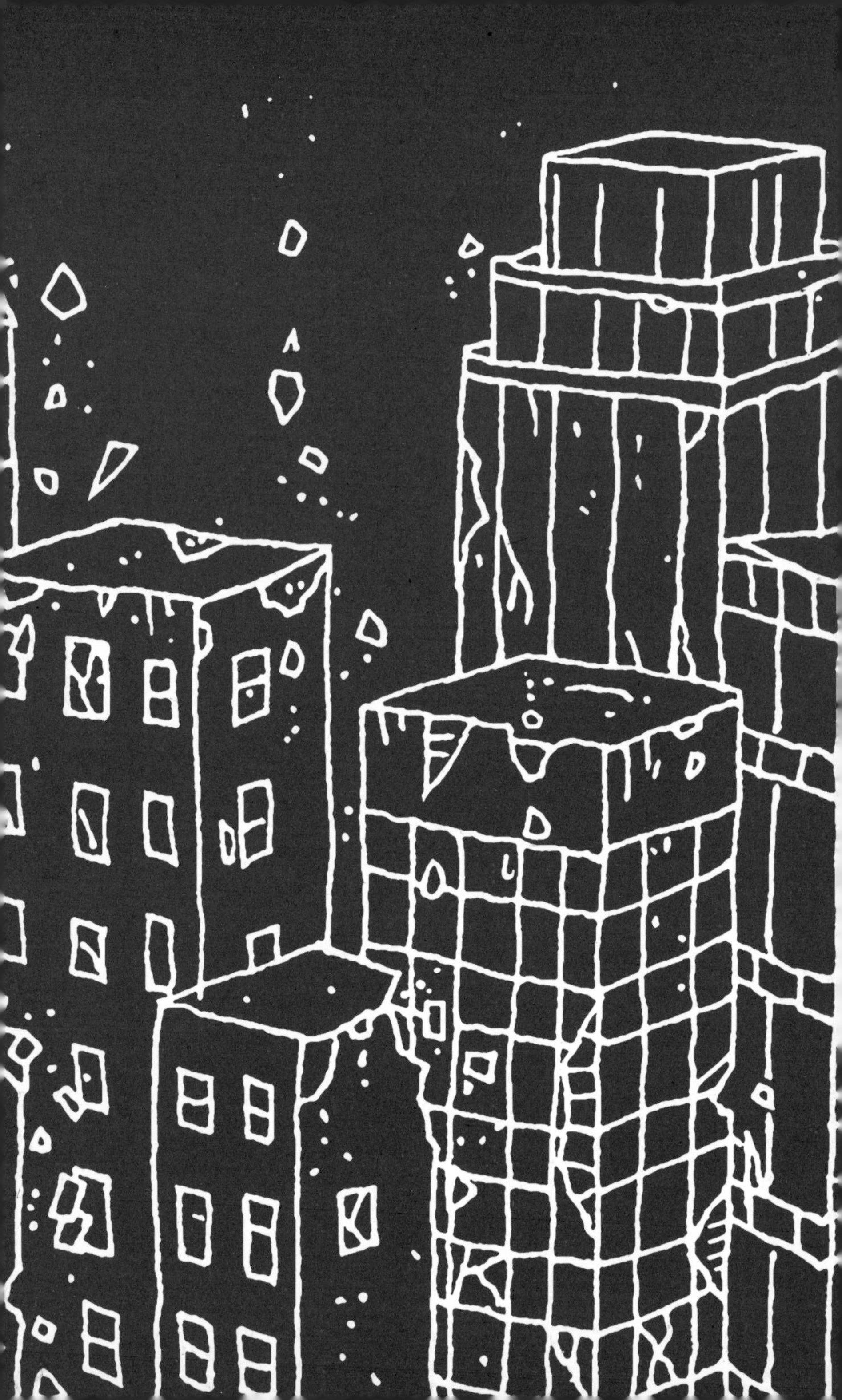